Propert
Economic Context

Monographs in Economic Anthropology, No. 14

Edited by

Robert C. Hunt
Antonio Gilman

University Press of America,® Inc.
Lanham • New York • Oxford

University Press of America,® Inc.
4720 Boston Way
Lanham, Maryland 20706

12 Hid's Copse Rd.
Cummor Hill, Oxford OX2 9JJ

Printed in the United States of America
British Library Cataloging in Publication Information Available

Copublished by arrangement with the Society for Economic Anthropology

Library of Congress Cataloging-in-Publication Data

Property in economic context / edited by Robert C. Hunt, Antonio Gilman.
p. cm. —(Monographs in economic anthropology ; no 14)
l. Property. 2. Primitive property. 3. Economic Anthropology. I. Hunt, Rjobert C. II. Gilman, Antonio. III. Series.
431-404 B.C. I. Title.
GM449.P74 1998 306.3'2 —dc21 98-10501 CIP

ISBN 0-7618-1063-3 (cloth: alk. ppr.)
ISBN 0-7618-1064-1 (pbk: alk. ppr.)

™ The paper used in this publication meets the minimum requirements of American National Standard for information Sciences—Permanence of Paper for Printed Library Materials, ANSI Z39.48—1984

Contents

Part III
Modern Colonial Encounters

Preface

Robert C. Hunt and Antonio Gilman

We sent out the following call for papers for the 1994 Spring Meeting of the Society for Economic Anthropology. This forms the context in which the papers that follow should be read.

Economic anthropology has put much of its recent effort into the analysis of exchange, and somewhat less of an effort into the understanding of production. It can also be said that property is a significant part of the economy, and that understanding property and how it relates to other social and cultural phenomena ought to be a central concern of economic anthropology.

There appear to be several general questions we might ask about property in the economic context: (1) how it evolved, (2) how it relates to other social and cultural phenomena, (3) conflicts involving different sets of property rules, and (4) how best to describe it.

It is clearly the case that property must have evolved in human history. It is perhaps not so clear how it evolved, although there has been some work on the matter (Leacock 1954; Murphy & Steward 1960; Fried 1967; Demsetz 1967; Pryor 1973; North & Thomas 1977). What kinds of objects became the property of what kinds of social units, with what rights and duties, in what sequence, and with what consequences, has not been a subject of comprehensive analysis.

Property is, in some theory and in some folk cultures, strongly linked with several other phenomena, including stratification, conflict between groups, distribution of wealth, efficiency and effectiveness of production regimes, ability to exercise effective demand, the rule of law, democracy, and distributive social justice. These effects are on occasion perceived or alleged to work in both directions—usually property causes or affects other phenomena, and occasionally these other phenomena affect property. We now live in a world awash in the belief that "private property" is a solution to problems of production and distribution. There has been insufficient attention paid to the (perhaps spurious) generalizations which have so handily become a major policy push for advanced nations.

It is not rare to find situations where there are different sets of property rules. When states colonize or penetrate a hinterland new sets of property rules are often imposed. There may well ensue conditions whereby people can contest over which rules apply.

In addition to the relationship of property to other social and cultural phenomena, there is also the question/problem/issue of how best to describe and analyze property. At the most general level Bromley and Cernea (1989) have argued that there are four general property regimes.

(1) *Res nullius*: open access, resources and objects owned by no-one prior to appropriation. Access open to all.
(2) *Res comunes*: common property, resources and objects owned by a corporate group. Access limited to group members.
(3) *"Private" property*: resources and valuables owned by jural persons, usually individuals, but can be corporations. Access controlled by the owner, and usually limited to the owner.
(4) *State property*: resources and valuables owned by the state. Access controlled by the state. Varies from highly restricted access (CIA files) to virtually open access (some national parks).

Each of these property regimes involves social units, rights, duties, and objects that are "owned" (Hallowell 1943; Appell 1983). It is possible to be very clear about these matters, although our modern ethnographies are not as clear as they might be. To take an issue from my own special field, irrigation, there is much loose writing about "water rights", and virtually no detailed ethnography which makes it clear what is owned, by what social units, with what rights and duties.

Preface

In the field of economic anthropology little attention has been paid to the **concept** of property in recent years (although land as property has received considerable attention.) In the past it was different. Lowie has a chapter on property in *Primitive Society* (1920), and Herskovits devoted 1 section (of 6), a total of 4 chapters and 82 pages to property in *The Economic Life of Primitive Peoples* (1940).

Property has not been a major focus of economic anthropology in the recent past. Yet it is important for understanding evolution, production, consumption, and exchange. Furthermore, there may be little agreement on what property is, and how to describe it.

We call for papers on:

(1) The analysis of property itself, in terms of social units, rights, duties, and "objects" owned.
(2) The evolution of property, particularly in archaeological time.
(3) The analysis of the relationship between a property regime and economic phenomena, such as levels of production and effects of distribution.
(4) The contested and negotiated aspects of property, including legal pluralism, state-local differences, overlapping claims, ambiguities, and strategies for capture and use of property.

We hope to have papers which are ethnographic, comparative, historical or archaeological, singly or in any combination. Ethnographic and theoretical analyses are both welcome. Papers on Common Property are most appropriate. Papers which unpack "private" property, or which examine rights in persons (labor, reproduction, etc.) would be especially stimulating.

References Cited

Appell, G.
1983 Methodological problems with the concepts of corporation, corporate social grouping, and cognatic descent group. *American Ethnologist* 10:302-11.

Bromley, D., & M. Cernea
1989 *The Management of Common Property Natural Resources: Some Conceptual and Operational Fallacies* (World Bank Discussion Papers, 57). Washington, D.C.: The World Bank.

Demsetz, H
1967 Toward a theory of property rights. *American Economic Review* 62(2):347-59.

Fried, M.H.
1967 *The Evolution of Political Society*. New York: Random House.

Hallowell, A.I.
1943 The nature and function of property as a social institution. *Journal of Legal and Political Sociology* 1:115-38.

Herskovits, M.J.
1940 *The Economic Life of Primitive Peoples*. New York: Alfred A. Knopf.

Leacock, E.
1954 *The Montagnais "Hunting Territory" and the Fur Trade* (American Anthropological Association, Memoir 78). Menasha: American Anthropological Association.

Lowie, R.H.
1920 *Primitive Society*. New York: Liveright.

Murphy, R., & J. Steward
1960 Tappers and trappers. *Economic Development and Cultural Change* 4:335-53.

North, D.C., & R.P. Thomas
1977 The first economic revolution. *The Economic History Review* 30:229- 41.

Pryor, F.L.
1973 *Property and Industrial Organization in Communist and Capitalist Nations*. Bloomington: Indiana University Press.

Part I

Concepts of Property

Chapter One

ꕥ

Concepts of Property: Introduction

Robert C. Hunt

This section of the volume consists of three papers, by Robert Hunt, Walter Neale, and Duran Bell. The papers by Neale and Bell were given at the Annual Meeting. Hunt's was written later.

Robert Hunt's paper is an exploration of the concept of property. Theories are about phenomena and the relationships between those phenomena. Theories are not possible unless those phenomena are represented by concepts that are reasonably clearly stated and reasonably unambiguous. Concepts are necessary (but not sufficient) for effective theory.

Hunt finds that some properties of property are clearly conceptualized. For example, property is a social relationship between social units, involves rights and duties, and also involves "objects" that are owned. Most scholars assign property relations to the jural realm, and therefore transactions about objects that involve violence are usually outside the realm of property. Other properties of property, Hunt finds, are not so clear. The boundary between property and nonproperty is particularly turbulent. Few of the papers in this volume agree on what is, and what is not, a property relationship. The meaning of "jural," central to the concept of property, seems to be unexamined in the literature.

Hunt discusses several nomothetic propositions about the relationship of property rules to other phenomena, such as economic efficiency, social inequality, and distributive justice. Property (or private property) is good or bad. It is necessary for economic efficiency. It produces social inequality. It promotes social welfare, or it promotes distributive injustice. He notes that all of these depend upon a clear definition of what is property. Without clear definitions of the phenomena there can be no effective theory. He suggests that because there is so much nonagreement on the concept of property, there is little reason to believe in the nomothetic propositions. He also finds little comparative empirical scholarship to test these nomothetic propositions.

Duran Bell's paper wrestles with the distinction between property and nonproperty. Bell contrasts rights in persons with rights in things. Rights in person are part of social membership. Rights in things are between persons, and about things. Many instances of access to resources come about due to rights in person, not rights in things. Property rights, for Bell, are limited to rights in things which can be alienated in a market. Bell disagrees with the economistic notion that social benefit will come about when all rights are freely exchanged. Rights in person, he argues, are not exchangeable, and rights in persons are essential to every society.

Walter Neale's paper argues that property must be understood in terms of the local cultural system. If our own concepts of property are applied to other societies the results are almost certain to be misunderstandings. (One implication might be that there is no universal analytic concept of property.)

Anthropology has at least two missions, the ethnographic—a clear and detailed understanding of a local reality—and the comparative—exploring relationships among phenomena. Neale is here focusing on the need to achieve and present a detailed understanding of some particular local system. The comparative mission, however, demands concepts which have cross-cultural analytic validity. There is therefore tension between the ethnographic mission, with its emphasis on (perhaps unique) local phenomena, and the comparative mission, with its needs for concepts which apply across systems. Neale privileges the ethnographic mission, and has little to offer the comparative mission.

One lesson to be drawn from these papers is that there are several definitions of property on the table. It follows that there should be a serious attempt to arrange a confrontation of these definitions, involving both ethnography and comparison.

Chapter Two

ꟹ

Properties of Property: Conceptual Issues

Robert C. Hunt

This essay is designed to probe an important concept[1] in economic anthropology—property. It extends the thinking that was presented in the call to the Conference. The comparative study of phenomena demands reasonably clear concepts, and theory building also demands clear concepts. Theory and its testing with empirical data are therefore dependent upon concept development.

The subject of property ought to be of vital interest to the economic anthropologist, and it has not been. It is hard to think of production without the concept of property. The natural resources, the tools, on occasion the labor, and the products can all be subject to property rules, and at least the products themselves are very widely subject to property rules. It is difficult to think of legitimate exchange without property being involved. How else does party A have the right to exchange away (to party B) that which is being exchanged? Our ethnographic descriptions of economies performing should always contain statements on property.

Shifting to the implications or consequences of property (and types of property regimes), our social environment is rife with propositions which allegedly have the status of laws of the universe. "Under capitalism private property produces exploitation and immiseration of the poor." "The most efficient use of resources is under private property, and the most effective public policy is to privatize everything everywhere." "The most effective way to achieve sustainable use of renewable natural resources is either by State control, by Private control, or by Common Property Management" (depending upon which faction you belong to).

These supposed consequences are all important issues, some of them bearing in immediate ways upon public policy decisions of the most powerful institutions in our contemporary world. Ideally these propositions would be based on clearly worked out hypotheses carefully tested by systematic comparison using a large number of detailed cases studies.

I suggest that these nomothetic propositions are ideology masquerading as findings. I suggest that the detailed case studies do not exist, largely because there has been (1) little interest in describing property in the case studies, and (2) what little description we have is usually expressed in western folk terms, rather than in the analytic terms we have developed in the discipline. I suggest further that no substantial progress on the theoretical and substantive issues can be made until there is fairly widespread use of fairly precise concepts. Until the discipline constructs and systematically uses the analytic concepts there will be little theoretical progress made.

The major goal of this essay is to examine the conceptual framework available in the field and to push it forward by a small increment. I will argue that such authors as Hallowell, Hoebel, and Appell have made major contributions to the analytic concepts of property, that all anthropologists should be aware of these contributions, and that these analytic concepts should be a part of our conceptual apparatus, along with descent, agriculture, and stratification.

The Analysis of Property

There is a long history of dealing with property in anthropology. Most monographs before World War II had chapters on material culture and on inheritance, and much information on some forms of property was included. Herskovits's text in 1940 contains a massive section on property, where he considers the various "objects" that are made into property in different cultures. The primary emphasis in this early stage was on the object. Since that time two "objects" have received the lion's share of attention, land and transfers at marriage.

Around the time of World War I the legal scholar Hohfeld (1919) published two articles presenting the argument that, in addition to the object (land, etc.), jural matters involve social relationships. If property is a jural relationship, then property is productively seen as a social relationship between owner and nonowners with respect to that object. Hallowell (1943) brought Hohfeld's insights into the anthropological analysis of property and set forth the basic components of the property relationship.

Hallowell wrote that a property relationship was a social relationship involving the owner (party A) who had rights and duties with respect to nonowners (party/ies B), in regard to whatever the "object" was that was owned by A. He thereby brought about two shifts in focus for the anthropologist, from the object to the relationships between parties, and from ordinary language to jural language.

The Hallowell position presents three components for possible analysis: social statuses, rights and duties, and the objects. Hallowell shifted his own attention from the objects to the social statuses.

Hoebel's (1954: 55-63) summary of primitive law included a section on property.[2] Hoebel accepts Hallowell's position and pays particular attention to rights and duties. Hoebel has a clear and brief introduction to the basic analysis of rights and duties by Hohfeld (Hoebel 1954: 46-50). The Hohfeld position on rights and duties is complex—Hohfeld should be read, but Hoebel should be read first—and precise. It is also almost entirely ignored in the anthropological investigations of social structure and social relationships. It is thereby also ignored in analyses of property.

Hoebel's summary of the rights and duties is as follows:

Person A		**Person B**
I. Demand-right	<——>	Duty
II. Privilege-right	<——>	No-demand-right
III. Power	<——>	Liability
IV. Immunity	<——>	No-power

Demand right means that A expects B to do what A wants; the matched duty means that B is expected to do what A wants. Privilege right means that A is free to do a number of things; the no-demand-right of B is that he not interfere with A's action. Power means that A may voluntarily create a new legal relation (for instance, a debt) affecting B; liability means that B is subject to that new legal relation once A creates it. Immunity means that A need not respond to B's attempt to create a new legal relation with A; no power means that B can not voluntarily create that new relationship with A.

Stated so briefly, these concepts are not easy to grasp. Shortage of space prohibits an extensive explication here. For a clear demonstration of the usefulness of this framework I strongly encourage everybody to re-read Hoebel's book. The chapter on the Trobriands for example has much to say about property, and it is greatly illuminated by Hoebel's application of the Hohfeld categories to Malinowski's ethnography.

The nature of A and B as social units in this analysis have been illuminated by Ward Goodenough. In his book on kin and property in Truk, Goodenough (1951) performs a clear and illuminating analysis of various levels of kin groups and persons and how they relate to property.

A recent contribution to the social part of the concept of property comes from George Appell in his analysis of jural and social entities, especially in the context of groups. Appell is interested in property analysis and is particularly concerned to be clear about what sorts of social entities hold these rights and duties. Appell distinguishes between jural entities and social entities. Jural entities are those that may enter into jural relations. Social entities are those that are recognized in the local folk system of social relations. A jural entity may not have a social counterpart (corporations that have no members, for example, but the corporation may enter into contracts, sue, and so on). A corporate group is a bounded set of members who can be represented by one or more of the members, and the act of a member is binding on the set. Usually there is an office which represents the group to others. Corporate groups are social entities, and they are often jural entities. As jural entities they sometimes "own" property and are in an owner-other relationship with individuals, other corporate groups, and perhaps with jural entities that are not social entities (Appell 1983, 1984, 1995).

To the rights and duties part of the analysis it seems useful to add some propositions on use and transfer. There are a number of ways that one can use an owned "object," including transit (of land), extracting wild products from (hunting, fowling, fishing, gathering), planting in or on, building in or on, etc. The implicit meaning of the verb "use" here is that there is some benefit, perhaps including a benefit stream, that is the result of the use.

There are also a number of ways that rights in an owned "object" can be transferred. They can be given away, traded, bartered, sold, mortgaged, or loaned.

There has long been a desire to talk about property in terms of major forms—private and state were in focus for a long time. State property is probably fairly clear: the state, qua state, is the jural entity that holds a bundle of rights to some of the "objects" that are owned in that society. The State as jural entity will relate to various kinds of jural entities within that state, including individuals. There are two moral positions on state property, that it is just and that it is unjust.

Private property is not quite so clear. The owner (as a jural entity) is *not* the state and is often thought to be an individual. The owner holds all, or most, of the rights, including the rights to transform (i.e., develop), destroy, and alienate. There are two moral positions on private property, that it is just and that it is unjust.

With the publication of Hardin's (1968) Tragedy of the Commons article interest in another form, common property, was restimulated. It had long been said that objects owned by everyone were cared for by no-one. Sometimes this is used to describe state property. But Hardin's made-up examples suggested another category, neither state nor private. There has been a revival of interest in the form and consequences of common property, in part as a strategy to manage natural resources.

Bromley and Cernea (1989) present a discussion of analytic categories that are neither state nor private, common property and *res nullius*. Under common property a corporate group owns some rights in (usually) a common pool resource, so the jural entity is that corporate group (there are many irrigation systems in the USA that manage common property). The other jural entities include the state, neighboring corporate groups, individuals who are not members of the corporate group, and those individuals who are members of the corporate group. The corporate group has both internal and external jurality (it is a jural entity both for its members and for nonmembers). The corporate group can exclude nonmembers from receiving any access to the resource owned and can regulate the rate of use of the resource by its own members (Hunt 1988; Bromley & Cernea 1989; Ostrom 1990).

Res nullius is often included in these discussions: it refers to "objects" which are not owned by any social unit. Open access is the term often used for resources such as trees in a forest, fish in the open sea, wild game on land, etc. In fact, *res nullius* is not a form of property at all and does not belong in a typology of types of property (see Wang [1996] for a discussion).

Into the classical western folk dichotomy of state and private property, then, Hardin attempted to drive the wedge of the "commons." "Commons" needs to be split into two concepts, common property and *res nullius*, which have very different properties.

The classification of types of property, including state, private, common, and open access, has some serious problems. There is confusion between private and individual. The "state" is ambiguous. Common property may be a form of private property. This schema is a western folk concept and is not systematic in the way it uses a number of different dimensions. The dimensions involved are (1) the kind of social unit, here state, corporate group, and whatever "private" means; (2) the rights and duties, including especially alienation in a market; and (3) the "objects" owned (common pool resources in the case of common property).

The most written about form of property is "private" property. The properties of "private" property are contested, and exactly what is meant by it is rarely clear. It seems generally agreed that the "private" owners are not the state and that alienation is one of the central rights.

"Private" property is a remarkably vague concept. It is an incomplete and confusing mixture of social unit ("individual") and of the rights and duties. We can gain a better understanding of what is meant by disaggregating the three dimensions and discussing them separately.

These three forms of property (state, private, common) distinguish some kinds of rights-holders. State property has the state as the jural unit. Common property is owned by a corporate group (and not by the state). Private property refers to individuals, partnerships, or corporations as jural units and not to the state. Private property is a residual category and may simply be opposed to state. If this is the case, then the opposition could well be between private and public. The state would be a public entity. Some corporate groups owning common property could be public entities (see Wang 1996).

Under "private" property there are several kinds of jural unit that may own property rights. An individual is one. Another kind is a marital pair. Another kind is the Iban bilek household, a corporate unit which owns rights to an apartment in the long-house and rights to agricultural land (Freeman 1955). Other kinds include partnerships and corporations. All have to be jural units to hold these rights to property. The corporate groups (what some of us have called common property managers) own water rights, or irrigation canals. This jural unit "owns" rights to water, or use of canals, or a dam, etc. With private property, then, the individual is only one of the potential owners: there can be groups of various sorts (and even person-less corporations) that are "private" owners of property.

Some jural units that own property are public entities, such as the state, provinces of the state, parastatal agencies, and lower-level administrative units of government. Named administrative units (*municipios*) in Mexico are said to "own" communal land. What this meant in northern Oaxaca in the 1960s was that from the point of view of the community there is land inside the village boundary which is not owned by individuals or families. The land is used for swidden agriculture, and one's access to the land is a function of (a) residence in the village and (b) permission of the community authorities to cultivate the plot.

The Mexican nation was locally thought to have declared that these "unowned" lands are *terrenos baldios*: they were untitled, no-one paid taxes on them, and in consequence from the state's point of view they belonged to the state (a jural unit). A major thrust of the modernization of the second half of the 19th century was to "privatize" these lands. Individual title to some of this land could be acquired by a "private" jural entity by surveying the plot, acquiring a title, and eventually paying taxes on it. It was still happening in 1963. Communal lands of a village could be converted into private land in this fashion. The best agricultural lands in San Andres Teotilalpam were, in 1963, under "private" ownership. Titles existed, and the specific plot could be sold or devolved to heirs.

The social structure of the holders of rights needs careful specification. Some of the irrigation systems in California are Irrigation Districts, which have been set up as Public rights holders. Others are Mutual Companies, which are set up as Private rights holders. The first is territorial and is voted into existence by an election held among the residents of that territory (often a county, but not necessarily). The second is not territorial, but a function of location or holding rights to some resource (such as land or water). California law permits, and indeed encourages, both kinds (Maass & Anderson 1978; Wang 1996).

The use of "private" for one kind of jural entity holding property rights would seem to imply that the opposite would be "public," not "state" and "common." The state is one form of "public," and there are many others. Provinces, counties, and towns and villages might be other forms of public. Private could mean any *non*-public rights-holders and would include some common property managers.

On the dimension of the social unit that owns the property, then, common property is not opposed to private and state forms of property. Rather, corporate groups managing common property can be found in both the public and private domains. (Of course, we also need clear definitions of public and private. The utility and universality of this distinction has been challenged by Naomi Quinn [1977].)

The second dimension is rights and duties. It is clear that in some cases rights to an "object" can be held by two or more jural units simultaneously. We understand how to think about bundles of rights. If there are three or more rights in an object, the rights may belong to different "owners". In one case rights 1 and 2 may belong to jural unit A, and right 3 belongs to B. In another case, right 1 may belong to A, and rights 2 and 3 belong to B. There are multiple rights to an object, and how they are combined may not be predictable. A clear example is "privately owned" real estate in the USA, where the "owner" has many rights, but some are held by the mortgage bank and some by the local community (zoning regulations, right of eminent domain).

There are some "objects" of property in all societies where all the rights to it are held by a single jural entity, and on some occasions that jural entity may actually be an individual. One "meaning" of private property is the individual as jural unit owning all the rights to an object, including the rights to exclude others, destroy, transform, lend, and alienate. The "virtue" of private property probably derives from the owner having the largest possible set of rights and other jural entities having the smallest possible set of rights.

The actual distribution of rights to owned objects is rarely clearly stated. Residual rights may be very hard to detect, short of a breach of the jural rules.

The third dimension is the "objects" owned. There are large literatures on land tenure, and much is known about rights in the products of labor, in personal effects, and in a wide variety of intangibles (songs, spells, dances, and so on). With respect to common property, the only distinction in play here would seem to be common pool resources (Ostrom 1990). Common property management regimes are never talked about as owning other kinds of objects. In fact, when they operate irrigation systems these corporate groups do own other kinds of objects, including buildings, vehicles, and bank accounts. We have concentrated on the common pool resources to the neglect of other objects.

The distribution of use rights and transfer rights and their correlations with other features of society have been the major concern of property analysis in anthropology (and in economics as well). Less attention has been paid to the jural entities, or to the content of the rights and duties.

It is thus likely that the usual distinction between "private" property and "state" property is a folk distinction, not an analytic one, and that it masks more than it reveals. The folk notion of private property is focused on a concentration of the use rights and the transfer rights on a private and (preferably) a unitary social unit. In Hohfeld's terms the "owner" has a maximum of privilege rights and immunity rights. Presumably this confers the greatest freedom of action on the owner.

Assertions about the effects of different forms of property, and thus of their moral position, are currently based on the portmanteau terms "state" and "private." Evaluations of the validity of these assertions will not be possible unless and until the concepts have been formulated in an analytic way.

Conceptual Problems with Property

Folk and Analytic Concepts

Once our attention has been shifted from the objects owned to the social relationships that constitute their owned-ness, we also have to shift our attention from (usually) material manifestations to other phenomena, such as social units, jural units, and rights and duties. These latter have a strong representation in the local, natural language, and their analysis has to have a strong component of language.

The ethnographic analysis of property must be anchored in the local culture, and local folk concepts are crucial to the enterprise. Our own language for thinking about property has come straight from an elaborate specialized folk system, that of Anglo-British jurisprudence.[3] In order to capture local distinctions we will have to have a near-mastery of the local jural thought. In order to understand the local reality with respect to property we need to learn the folk concepts they use to discuss and decide on such matters.

At the same time, we also have two other missions, the building of theory and the comparison of many empirical cases. A plethora of local folk concepts will not serve the comparative or theorizing missions. Instead we must work out analytic concepts, ones that are relatively free of the ethnocentric bias from any particular folk system. Such analytic systems evolve, sometimes very slowly (see Service [1985] for an overview of kinship studies during a century). It takes something like 200 years of effort before clarity, precision, and consensus occur (see Hunt [1996] for a discussion). Some progress in constructing the analytic system for property has been made, although the diffusion of the concepts into the discipline has been very meager.

Violence

Virtually every human social system we know contains the possibility of violence and particularly the likelihood of using violence in gaining possession of objects. Some societies make the violent acquisition of objects a major goal for the ambitious man (as in raiding for horses on the Plains [Nugent 1993]). The victors in a war can usually keep whatever goods can be picked up from the vanquished and the objects may include land, villages, and people. These become property in every sense of the word.

Our folk system for thinking about property is anchored in the peace of the jural system: the jural system is about peaceful resolution of disputes.[4] Violence is defined as disorder.[5] In consequence we are not usually attuned to thinking about property in the context of violence. Theft is usually condemned when committed by A against B if both are members of a group that forbids theft. But theft by A against B if they are members of two hostile groups is a different matter. The spatial maneuvering of groups with segmented patrilineal kinship is usually not thought to be theft, or trespass, but it is the use of greater numbers to persuade the neighbors to move their fields or cattle because one's own needs are expanding and more land is needed (see Bohannan & Bohannan 1968).

In a word, we have a bias towards the jural, that is the peaceful, ways of dealing with what we usually call property. I suggest that it is a bias, and that more systematic attention paid to violence would pay handsome rewards.

Jural Issues

Appell puts "jural" entities in the center of the analysis of property. "Jural" appears in a very large number of monographs. It is the foundation stone of comparative legal analysis. Yet one searches in vain for a clear definition of "jural," and one searches in vain for a clear presentation of a semantic field in which jural is one of two or more sub-fields.

There has long been an argument over whether the simpler societies have "law" and "government." In the absence of law can there be jural relations? Our analysis of property, embedded as it is in the jural realm, needs a clarification of that realm and some notion of where its boundaries are.

Property vs. Nonproperty

There are many discussions of property in anthropology, and especially outside it. We generally say, now, that property involves two jural entities, A and B, with rights and duties to each other with respect to some "object" that is "owned." So we at least think we have a fairly clear idea of what the properties of property are.

Some of the properties of property are that the owner (A) has rights of exclusion (demand rights) with respect to B, that A has (demand) rights to the income stream with respect to B, and that A has (privilege) right to transfer some use rights in the object to another party (by gift, sale, trade) with respect to B.

This much is at least on the table for discussion.

But there are other properties of property that very much need discussion, clarification, and empirical work. One of them is that there are some properties of property that are not unique to property. This raises the question of the boundary between property and everything else.

For all property, the use of possessive pronouns is appropriate. But not all uses of possessive pronouns signal the existence of property. "My" bicycle, "your" car, "her" computer signal property, but "his" hand, "your" soul, do not (in America).

For all property relations there are rights and duties. But not all social rights and duties involve property. The right to harvest all the apples from my tree on my land is a property right, but the right to demand sexual fidelity from a spouse is not (in America).

If this analysis is accepted, then we have an unclear boundary between property rights and other properties of social relationships. I do not see how this can be solved. But it is clearly a problem, and it clearly needs solution.

Commons

There is a substantial ambiguity that perpetually entangles analysts of property. Garret Hardin's landmark 1968 article "The Tragedy of the Commons" set just about everybody off on a false scent. His basic point—that in some situations actions that are rational from the point of view of the actor have deleterious effects for the group in the long run (the externality problem)—is quite correct and very important.

Unfortunately, he labelled the situation as one of a Commons.[6] A long line of us have objected to this confusion of Common Property with an unregulated and unowned resource.[7] I propose that it be called a Commons, different from Common Property. As so many have pointed out, what Hardin called a Commons is *not* owned and is not a form of property management. It is usually referred to with the Roman term *res nullius*. On the other hand, as so many of us have pointed out, common property *is* owned (National Academy of Sciences 1986; Bromley & Cernea 1989; Ostrom 1990). A corporate group owns rights in some resource in common, excludes nonmembers, realizes a benefit stream from use of the resource, and manages the rate of use by the members of the corporate group. Clearly property relations are involved.

Substantive Problems with Properties of Property

Human Universal?

Some analysts of the human condition have claimed that property is a universal attribute of human society (Murdock 1949; Hockett 1973; Brown 1992). This is a question in part of the distribution of a social phenomenon among human societies. In that respect it is a question with an empirical answer. I simply note that the empirical work will depend utterly on the definition of property and of not-property. Where that dividing line is drawn will almost certainly have an enormous effect upon the answer.

Nonhuman Property?

Is property a human invention, or are there property relationships in the societies of other species? We as anthropologists have a strong disposition (a) to find some institutions universally distributed among humans (e.g., religion, marriage, property, incest taboo) and (b) to find them *only* among the human species. There are complicated motives for both of these desires.[8] The empirical answer to this question is not at all clear.

A social analysis of property proceeding from Hohfeld though Hallowell to Goodenough, Hoebel, and Appell has anchored property in jurality. The jural entity, and the rights and duties, are dominant. What then do we make of social relationships among baboons, wolves, elephants, red deer, etc.? Do they have jural phenomena? If not, can they have property relations? Hockett (1973) says they do have property, but he does not anchor his analysis of property in the jural realm. Hallowell seems to think that nonhumans do not have property. This is an interesting question for the comparative social scientist. The answer to this question is not evident.

The Evolution of Property Relations

Whether or not chimpanzees and Homo erectus had property relations, there are striking differences in property relations among the human societies we know. The range of units that have rights and duties, the range of rights and duties, and the range of objects that are the object of these rights and duties are enormous. The products of human labor are very widely owned. Incorporeal property seems to be found among all varieties of human society, suggesting that it may have a different basis than land for property relations. Clearly market systems are not widely distributed (although trade is universal), and so the market components of property have evolved and deserve close attention in an evolutionary framework.

It is repetitive to say so, but the entirety of the effort to untangle the evolution of property relations depends upon the definition of property.

The Implications/Consequences of Property

There are a number of popular positions based on some set of propositions about property that are stated as generalizations of universal scope. Economic efficiency is supposed to be promoted by private, as opposed to public forms of property management. The argument usually runs that individuals know their own interests better than do some larger groups (kin groups, communities, states), that locating decision making about resources and expenditures at those individuals promotes their welfare better than any other locus for decisions, and that allocating as many rights as possible to those individuals promotes efficiency. Thus private property (and the assumed free markets as well) is associated with economic efficiency. (When combined with the invisible hand, such a system is also assumed to promote social welfare.)

Anthropologists have long claimed that social stratification is associated with unequal access to productive resources (Fried 1967). How this unequal access is structured is not always clear, but such authors as Sahlins (1972) and Johnson and Earle (1987) associate it with property. So stratification, for some, is dependent upon property and unequal access to property within some social group.

Distributive justice has been a prominent concern of social thinkers in the West for millennia. (Distributive justice in a state, where there is by definition stratification, which by definition is associated with unequal access to resources, is often contrasted with the ways things are.) Early Christians, Marx and Engels, and vast numbers of others have argued for institutionalizing processes which would reduce the inequality implied by the existence of pure private property.

That same private property which is supposed to promote economic efficiency is also supposed to promote economic inequality. These two fundamental social goals, economic efficiency and the amelioration of economic inequality, are both said to be based on property rights.

A narrower focus for the study of some of the implications of property is to be found in studies of the economy and inheritance. Levinson and Malone (1980: 135) point out that Murdock's *Social Structure* (1949) called attention to the lack of comparative study of property. They observe that by 1980 only the work of Goody (1976) and his colleagues had been published. Goody's work concentrated on the relationship between forms of inheritance and forms of society and posited cause and effect sequences. By the time of Ember and Levinson's (1991) review, one more publication had been added to the list (Schlegel & Eloul 1988). As important as property and its management and transfer are supposed to be, there is remarkably little systematic testing of its role.

Two points should be made. First, all these positions depend utterly on the concepts of property which are at their base. It is an unusual analyst who is clear about the property concepts they are using. Second, all these positions make clear and simple declarations about the effects of property as if it was known, simply and clearly, what those effects are. In the absence of detailed comparative studies, the conclusion that all these positions are based on ideology and/or assumption, rather than upon knowledge, is inescapable.

The knowledge we need to support, or correct, any of these positions is not in our hands. It could be acquired by means of careful comparative testing of hypotheses so formulated that they could be rejected. But they have not been. Those of us who are scientists are duty-bound to be deeply skeptical of these positions and of the policies based on them that are being used to manage so much of the institutional world we live in.

Conclusions

Property would seem to be a fundamental concept for the analysis of economy and of society. It is supposed to have profound consequences for stratification, for resource use, for economic efficiency, and for justice. Before these proposition are accepted and used to justify policy, they would ideally be subjected to rigorous empirical testing.

There are some very precise, clear, and productive distinctions available in the anthropological literature. Property is usefully regarded as a relationship between jural entities, each of which has a bundle of rights or duties, with respect to a vast range of "objects" (which need not be material). It is useful to distinguish between use rights and transfer rights.

For all that we have some clear and precise concepts, our distinctions between state and private, between jural and nonjural, and between property and nonproperty are vague. In the long run the growth of our knowledge will be dependent upon making progress in dealing with these distinctions.

The clear distinctions that we have are very rarely used by ethnographers, or by theoreticians. There is a general tendency to use the term "property" loosely and in western folk senses. Two consequences are that our ethnographic base of property studies is far less rich than it could or should be and that the general propositions about the function of property forms are far closer to prejudice than they are to knowledge.

Tis a pity, for the questions being asked here go to the heart of provisioning and justice for the human species.

Acknowledgments

Jean-Philippe Colin gave this essay a close and creative reading. I have not taken all of his advice, and that responsibility is of course mine. Sally Falk Moore also made an important suggestion early on.

I presented the normal State, Private, and Common scheme to the students in the Brandeis University Sustainable International Development program (Ruth Morgenthau's Politics 280 in the Fall of 1995). The students were most vigorous in challenging the meanings of the term common property. On reflection I discovered that they had indeed found a problem with the schema. I have attempted to revise so as to provide more clarity. I am particularly indebted to Rabson Dhlodhlo, D.M.U.L.A. Dissanayake, and Hopewell Peterson.

Notes

1. There are a number of important concepts in economic anthropology that yield nicely to a sustained examination of the concepts themselves: property, surplus, gift, commodity, exchange, are among them. See Appadurai (1986) for a good example with respect to commodity.
2. The jural cast of property analysis was thereby set for anthropology. I will have something to say on the consequences of this position later on in this essay.
3. Although western jurisprudence is a set of folk systems (we Anglo-Americans are embedded in a Common Law tradition, but there are others, particularly the Napoleonic Code, in Europe), most folk do not control it, or understand it. In fact, there is a common folk mistrust of the specialists (lawyers) of those folk systems.
4. Sahlins's (1972) negative reciprocity is jarring in its shift from jural to nonjural relations. It is a case of violence, unlike the other two.
5. A major intellectual shift in the second half of the 20th century has been to take a fresh look at the "violence" directed by a social system towards its insider members. In the usual case, this was defined locally not as violence, but as proper and jural constraint or retribution.
6. This mistake has been repeated so many times it is tedious to even try to collect all the references. For a striking one see North and Brown (1977).
7. See Ciriacy-Wantrup and Bishop (1975) and Bromley and Cernea (1989) for trenchant, clear, and precise analyses of the differences between the two.
8. The desire to find important and central institutions among all humans is part of an agenda to fight racism and other forms of ethnocentrism. Ethnocentric bias often denigrates other groups because they lack some important feature, such as a proper sense of honor, or proper marriages. Part of the struggle has been to convince western governments and policy makers that small scale societies are fully human, and in order to do this we have to show that all them have the core human institutions. It is a laudable struggle, one that anthropologists have led for many decades. It has at least one damaging result, which is a tendency to define institutions in such a way that they are found among all humans. See Spiro (1966: 188-91) on the definition of religion and the desire to find religion in all human societies. While a moral goal, it has not always had positive effects upon the development of our scientific discipline. I am less sure about the motive to declare humans to share very little with other species. As a student of Earl Count (a truly comparative social scientist) I am predisposed to find continua across species boundaries, rather than to deny them.

References Cited

Appadurai, A.

1986 Introduction: commodities and the politics of value. In A. Appadurai (ed.), *The Social Life of Things*, pp. 3-63. Cambridge: Cambridge University Press

Appell, G.N.

1983 Methodological problems with the concepts of corporation, corporate social grouping, and cognatic descent group. *American Ethnologist* 10:302-11.

1984 Methodological issues in the corporation redux. *American Ethnologist* 11:815-17.

1995 Community resources in Borneo: failure of the concept of common property and its implications for the conservation of forest resources and the protection of indigenous land rights. In G. Dicum (ed.), *Local Heritage in the Changing Tropics: Innovative Strategies for Natural Resource Management and Control*. Yale School of Forestry and Environmental Studies, Bulletin 98:32-56. New Haven: Yale School of Forestry and Environmental Studies.

Bohannan, P., & L. Bohannan

1968 *Tiv Economy*. Evanston: Northwestern University Press.

Bromley, D., & M. Cernea

1989 *The Management of Common Property Natural Resources: Some Conceptual and Operational Fallacies* (World Bank Discussion Papers, 57). Washington, D.C.: The World Bank.

Ciriacy-Wantrup, S.V., & R.C. Bishop

1975 "Common Property" as a concept in natural resource policy. *Natural Resources Journal* 15:713-27.

Ember, C.R., & D. Levinson

1991 The substantive contributions of worldwide cross-cultural studies using secondary data. *Behavior Science Research* 25:79-140.

Freeman, D.

1955 *Iban Agriculture*. London: Her Majesty's Stationery Office.

Fried, M.H.

1967 *The Evolution of Political Society*. New York: Random House.

Goodenough, W.H.

1951 *Property, Kin, and Community on Truk* (Yale University Publications in Anthropology, 46). New Haven: Yale University Press.

Goody, J.
1976 *Production and Reproduction: A Comparative Study of the Domestic Domain*. Cambridge: Cambridge University Press.

Hallowell, A.I.
1943 The nature and function of property as a social institution. *Journal of Legal and Political Sociology* 1:115-38.

Hardin, G.
1968 The tragedy of the commons. *Science* 162:1243-48.

Herskovits, M.H.
1940 *The Economic Life of Primitive Peoples*. New York: Alfred A. Knopf.

Hockett, C.F.
1963 *Man's Place in Nature*. New York: McGraw Hill.

Hoebel, E.A.
1954 *The Law of Primitive Man*. Cambridge, MA: Harvard University Press.

Hohfeld, W.N.
1919 *Fundamental Legal Conceptions as Applied in Judicial Reasoning*. New Haven: Yale University Press.

Hunt, R.C.
1988 Social organization of irrigation: the irrigation community. Paper presented at the World Congress of Rural Sociology, Bologna, Italy.
1996 Apples and Oranges. Unpublished manuscript.

Johnson, A., & T. Earle
1987 *The Evolution of Human Society*. Stanford: Stanford University Press.

Levinson, D., & M.J. Malone
1980 *Toward Explaining Human Culture: A Critical Review of Worldwide Cross-Cultural Research*. New Haven: HRAF Press.

Maass, A., & J. Anderson
1978 *And the Desert Shall Rejoice*. Cambridge, MA: MIT Press.

Murdock, G.P.
1949 *Social Structure*. New York: Macmillan.

National Academy of Sciences
1986 *Proceedings of the Conference on Common Property Resource Management, April 21-26, 1985*. Washington, D.C.: National Academy Press.

North, D.C., & R.P. Thomas
1977 The first economic revolution. *The Economic History Review* 30:229- 41.

Nugent, D.

1993 Property relations, production relations, and inequality: anthropology, political economy, and the Blackfeet. *American Ethnologist* 20:336-62.

Ostrom, E.
1990 *Governing the Commons: The Evolution of Institutions for Collective Action.* Cambridge: Cambridge University Press.

Quinn, N.
1977 Anthropological studies of women's status. *Annual Review of Anthropology* 6:181-225.

Sahlins, M.
1972 *Stone Age Economics.* Chicago: Aldine.

Schlegel, A., & R. Eloul
1988 Marriage transactions: labor, property, and status. *American Anthropologist* 90:291-309.

Service, E.
1985 *A Century of Controversy.* Orlando: Academic Press.

Spiro, M.
1966 Religion: problems of definition and explanation. In M. Banton (ed.), *Anthropological Approaches to the Study of Religion*, pp. 45-72. London: Tavistock.

Wang, C.-R.
1996 Canal Irrigation Systems Governed by Common Property Management Principles. Unpublished Ph.D. dissertation, Department of Anthropology, Brandeis University.

Chapter Three

ꟹ

The Social Relations of Property and Efficiency

Duran Bell

There can hardly be any word more freighted with meaning than "property." The linguistic history of this term indicates that its current connotation developed rather recently, during the period of an ascendant mercantile and industrial capitalism. Its basic and original meaning had been in reference to a *characteristic* of a person; so that when first applied to land during the 1700s, it was understood that property in land was indicative of the social position of the individual who owned it. On this basis, it was quite natural for "property" to be ascribed later to productive capital and industrial plant as those possessions became the more essential indicators of social position.

According to Macpherson (1985: 81-82) the meaning of property narrowed over time to emphasize exclusive use rights to material things and "then, with the rise of the capitalist market economy, the bulk of actual property shifted from often nontransferable rights to a revenue from land, charters, monopolies, and offices, to transferable rights in freehold land, saleable leases, physical plant, and money. Property became predominantly a right to things."

It is difficult in this day to recognize the revolutionary and culturally peculiar nature of the right of alienation in relation to land ("real property"). As Peters (in this volume) indicates so powerfully, the customary view of land was as a place to which individuals and groups belonged; people were of a place. And it was only with the gradual domination of commercial and capitalist interests during the 18th and 19th centuries that full supremacy could be gained for the notion that place was a thing that belonged to some individual.

The "people of a place" had been those who by virtue of birth and social station share with others rights to the use and revenue of some set of resources. Hence, "place" was more than geography; it included quintessentially the corporate group that had use rights to the resources therein. Hence, people and place were, each of them, both people and place; neither being definable without the other. The concept, "place of a person," divests the place of its people to become a thing, a thing to be transferred among persons, together with its use rights and revenue rights: it becomes property. Clearly, the people of the place must be ousted as a precondition for this transformation; only then can land devolve from its use as a commons to become an alienable thing of its owner. Hudson (in this volume) points out that Bronze Age Babylonian society possessed nothing that resembles the modern concept of property, so that the term should not be used in reference to land and other resources in that system.

While it is true that there are alienable things in almost every society, those things do not deserve the term property unless social position is determined by reference to things. However, in traditional systems things are not, themselves, the basis for the determination of social position; rather, social position tends to be the basis for making claims against things. For example, in Imperial China a wealthy peasant could realize prestige from his skill, hard work and intelligence, but he was still a peasant. Transforming that wealth into social position involved using it for the education of a son and the passing of competitive examinations by that son. Chinese merchants were particularly subjected to condemnation *no matter how great their wealth in things*, unless their resources became the basis for entry into the "gentry."

Some readers may feel that by stripping other societies of property we are engaged in the creation of "otherness:" "We have property; they do not." However, once we develop a more accurate picture of rights of person and rights in resources, we may conclude with Ciriacy-Wantrup and Bishop (1975: 720-21) that "the substitution of private ownership for common ownership is not in itself a socially desirable change," with the implication that differences associated with otherness need not be negatively valued.

Forms of Right

The Declaration of Independence makes reference to "inalienable rights." These inalienable rights are often thought to be rights that are not subject to alienation by the force of political authority, the actual behavior of governments notwithstanding. However, there is a meaning of inalienable that is verifiably a distinguishing characteristic of certain rights: some rights cannot be alienated voluntarily by means of sale. Most notable among these rights are those of citizenship (the right to vote, to receive a passport, and a number of unspectacular entitlements, such as eligibility to apply for Fulbright Scholarships). These rights are inalienably attached to the person on the basis of some intrinsic characteristics of that person; and they can be called *rights of person*. An individual may be stripped of some or all of his rights of person by the state in the event that he is found to have committed a serious transgression against the prevailing rules of behavior. However, those rights cannot be alienated voluntarily by the individual to whom they adhere.

On the other hand, there are rights for which alienation is fully expected and socially facilitated. In capitalistic economies wherein social position is derived primarily from the exchange of things and labor power, rights of alienation have been called *property rights*. We will say that if some *characteristic* of a resource is subject to legitimate and legally protected voluntary alienation, then there is a property right in that characteristic. For example, a person may have the right to reside in a hotel with an annual lease; this is a *use right* in relation to a resource. But if this person has the right to sell this lease, then there is a property right in the lease (characteristic) of the hotel (resource).[1] Furthermore, when one alienates some characteristic of a resource, one sells the property rights that adhere to the characteristic. So, when the right to use a thing or to receive revenue from it is sold, the right to sell it is also sold. For this reason we may say that property rights generate *rights in property*.

It is common speech to claim that a person owns "the property" in reference to a resource. However, this assertion is unambiguous only if the full spectrum of resource-characteristics is owned by this person. For example, a hotel is a resource with a multiplicity of characteristics, each of which may bear use and revenue rights and each being subject to a de-coupling from the set of other characteristics. Hence, its occupants may have alienable use rights to their apartments, some business firm may have *alienable rights* to manage it; while someone else may hold *alienable rights* to receive revenue. Finally, the right to destroy or alter the hotel may be controlled by the state in terms of Historical Preservation. In this event various characteristics of the hotel are the bases for a number of property rights; but we should not use the term property in reference to the hotel, itself. The hotel can be referred to as property only if all of its relevant characteristics are bundled together in a single right of alienation. Few will claim that use rights constitute property rights when the holder of rights of alienation and rights to revenue is known to be a different person. But it is common to make reference to property in cases where there are no rights of alienation in resource-characteristics.

For example, Demsetz (1967) tells the story of how "property" rights developed among the Montagnais in the regions around Quebec during the 17th and 18th centuries. This Native American group became involved in the fur trade and sought to protect from others the exploitation of fur resources in its immediate domain. It did so by securing privileged use rights for each agnatic group to specific blocks of land. In the absence of these rights, there might have been a tendency for some people to exploit aggressively those common resources for personal gain to the disadvantage of all, a "tragedy of the commons."

However, Demsetz is wrong to say that this a story about rights in property. We are informed by Leacock (1954: 1-2) that these groups could not alienate their holdings in land to other agnatic groups or to persons in other tribes: "Nor is there any prestige attached to holding a sizable territory or any emphasis on building up and preserving the paternal inheritance. Neither can land be bought or sold. In other words, land has no value as "real estate" apart from its products. What is involved is more properly a form of usufruct than "true" ownership."

The story of the Montagnais is one about the conversion of an *open access resource* (to which no one holds any rights whatsoever) into a *commons* (to which only members of the agnatic group have rights of use). The confusion manifested by Demsetz has been strongly attacked by Bromley (1989), McCay and Acheson (1987), and others. It is a common error among economists to attribute to the commons the potential weakness of open access; and having conflated the commons with open access, there is a failure to recognize that the benefits of restricted use can be realized with the commons.

A similar point can be made about land on the feudal manor. Peasants held inheritable use rights to their land and the lord held an inheritable right to receive a share of revenue from the estate as a fief from the king to whom he owed military service. But it would have been de-stabilizing for the manor to be subject to rights of alienation. The granting of property rights in land (and serfs) would have enabled an ambitious noble to begin a process of land aggregation and consolidation that could eventually challenge royal power itself. Hence, the feudal manor was not real estate, or property. Ownership rights in those estates were not established until the revolutionary change in laws associated with the enclosure acts.

There is much confusion on this point, partly because the ideologists of capitalism prefer a muddled conception of the matter. They seek to conflate capitalism with buying and selling, and property with use-rights. Once this muddle is accepted, capitalism can be said to have deep roots in human history, beginning with "truck and barter;" and it is possible to disguise the truly revolutionary nature of private property relative to traditional rights to resources and relative to traditional allocations of the fruits of collective effort. The same objective is achieved by conflating open access resources with the commons. It has the implication that there is no feasible alternative to private property as a basis for the social organization of scarce resources, an argument sharply discredited by Ciriacy-Wantrup and Bishop (1975).

There is a growing literature, especially outside of economics, that recognizes the essential distinction between open access resources and the commons. However, that literature typically refers to the commons (with exclusive use rights) as "common property." Bromley (1989), for example, while greatly advancing our understanding of the commons, is fairly explicit in defining property by reference to exclusive use, without apparent concern for the fact that the holder of use rights may differ from the holder of the rights to revenue and alienation. McCay and Acheson (1987) use the term common property even more broadly to include open access resources. Bromley and McCay-Acheson elaborate on the alternatives to private property in the effective management of scarce resources (an issue on which I am in emphatic agreement). However, my concern here is to differentiate between rights in property and various rights in nonproperty, especially rights of person.

Rights of Person

There are many rights that cannot be alienated by the person who holds them; they can be only transmitted to heirs. Furthermore, these heirs qualify for ownership by virtue of age, sex, and parentage; that is, by birth not by achievement. In the context of contemporary capitalism we find that a person's right to vote, or to be free from slavery, or to have freedom of speech, cannot be sold.[2] Nor can one sell the responsibility-cum-liability to serve in the military. These are rights and liabilities that reside with the person by some principle of *entitlement*, rather than in the resources to which a person is entitled. They are *rights of person*.

However, contemporary ideology is quite uncomfortable with *categories of person* as factors in the structuring of a social system. The good (bourgeois) society is thought to be constructed, at least metaphorically, through a social contract among socially equivalent individuals. People may differ in their wealth accumulations, but not in their right to accumulate; they may differ in their innate capacities, but not in the right to express and develop fully those capacities. We have here the idea of society as a collection of individuals who lack intrinsic differentiation. Categories of person, on the other hand, recall the too-slowly weakening legacy of a feudal past, where one's ultimate social placement and achievements were largely a function of sex and parentage.

It was against such feudal ideologies that the bourgeoisie required a philosophical alternative on the dawn of its ascendancy. And the adopted alternative—rights in property—was revolutionary in form and consequence. However, the displacement of rights of person by rights in property has always been quite selective. Most prominently, citizenship has been preserved as the basis of person-categories with rights being sharply curtailed for the noncitizen. Age, too, remains an unchallenged basis for formal differentiation; so that legal differentiations apply for those under the age of 18 or 21 and to those over the age of 55, 62 or 65. Gender and racial classifications have also been traditional bases of person-category, but often under conditions of questionable legitimacy. The purposes for which rights of person are derived and ideologically justified vary widely. The social history of a group, its current and past forms of social organization and technology, and its class structure and power relations all conspire to give specific form to its system of rights.

Although Harold Demsetz (1967) does not argue explicitly against all rights of person, his use of the exchange paradigm in attacking selected rights and responsibilities could be applied quite broadly. Demsetz (1967) argues for the displacement of rights of person by rights in property. For example, he suggests that military service should be induced by means of higher wages, instead of the draft. And if the draft must continue, he favors allowing those who are subject to the draft to offer a cash payment for exemption. That is, he opposes this basic responsibility of citizenship unless it can be converted into a property that is subject to purchase by the state.

One way of accommodating the concern of Demsetz would be to confer full rights of alienation upon draft status, allowing it to be sold to the highest bidder in an *international* market for military personnel.[3] The person who seeks military exemption must be replaced; and if a military obligation were converted into a lien-encumbered property, its replacement could become the responsibility of the original owner.

The fundamental premise of the argument in favor of granting rights in a military obligation is that the we can maximize the aggregate social product by permitting the execution of mutually beneficial exchanges. Since the sellers and purchasers of a right or obligation are all better off, the society must be better off (given a conception of society as a simple collection of such individuals).

An inefficiency associated with the lack of property rights arises in another of the situations posed by Demsetz. Demsetz implicitly insists that "freedom" should be property, so that its optimal allocation among persons can be achieved: "A law which gives the firm or the taxpayer clear title to slave labor would necessitate that the slave owners take into account the sums that slaves are willing to pay for their freedom. . . . It is the prohibition of a property right adjustment, the prohibition of the establishment of an ownership title that can thenceforth be exchanged, that precludes the internalization of external costs and benefits" (Demsetz 1967: 349).

While this argument may represent a fine example of hard-headed economic reasoning, it reflects an unawareness of rights that rest on principles other than the logic of property. The price theoretic form of that logic assures us that no right can be optimally allocated among persons unless it is placed on the open market. For example, by converting the right to vote into property, the state would allow those rights to accumulate in the hands of those for whom they can be more instrumental and allow the previous owners of those rights to receive preferred alternatives, making both parties better off. Even the right to free speech may find a limited market. Presumably, the purchaser, while enjoying no greater freedom, would benefit from the silencing of specific others (as in legal proceedings).

However, we understand from history that the nature of a society—the structure of social classes, the central dynamic forces shaping the growth in population, technology, and wealth—depend on how rights are allocated among groups and individuals. For example, we prefer that the economically powerful not be able to purchase votes. The general social consequences are thought to overwhelm the benefits of isolated dyadic exchanges in property rights. Similarly, the decision to abolish slavery did not rest on some arcane observation on the benefits of mutual and voluntary exchange processes. It was a choice between two fundamentally incompatible ruling elites, such that the social infrastructure and public policies of one group could not coexist with those of the other. It was a choice between rural slavery and its associated mercantile underpinnings versus an urban industrial capitalism based on free labor. These are meta-societal matters that cannot be addressed by the algebra of indifference curves.

Right of Prior Possession

There has perhaps never been any right more fundamental to the development of social relations and social systems than the right of prior possession. Yet, few of us are aware of it. It is not part of the set of rights enshrined in the Constitution or in the noble speech of the politicians of recent times. Yet, no right can be more fundamental. It is on the basis of this traditional right that a person can claim indefinite use to land that he clears for cultivation, so long as he continues to make effective use of it. It is the basis of the transmissible use rights of serfs and peasants to their share of the arable in the absence of formal, or state, codification. The right of prior possession has been essential to the social order.

The right of prior possession suggests that the initial occupant of a resource should be allowed to use it without undue compromise from the actions of others. The continued operation of the right of prior possession can be seen, daily, in the form of "No Trespassing" signs along roadways. Without the presence of such signs a person could covertly make a "conventional use" of the unoccupied resource, either for a walking path or as a place of permanent residence. It then becomes feasible that these conventional uses take precedence, by right of prior possession, over alternative uses subsequently sought by the owner of property rights.

If a residential community exists prior to the planned construction of a polluting factory, the liability for that pollution (in health losses or housing values) must be incident entirely upon the factory. By the right of prior possession, the community should not be faulted for having located itself in the lovely valley that subsequently and unpredictably became the site of a belching factory. Yet, the analytical edifice constructed by Ronald Coase (1960) rests critically on a casual denial of the right of prior possession. He has reference to this right as the *doctrine of lost grant*. This doctrine states "that if a legal right is proved to have existed and been exercised for a number of years the law ought to presume that it had a legal origin" (p. 14). In reference to this doctrine Coase says that "[t]he reasoning employed by the courts in determining legal rights will often seem strange to an economist . . ." for whom, he believes, maximal economic production is the only relevant criterion (p. 15). The inscrutability of judges on these matters arises from that fact that the doctrine of lost grant is a right that cannot readily be converted into a property right, since it adheres necessarily to *the person* whose situation was prior. (A person who purchases a house from an original owner and after the construction of the factory has no claim for damages.)

Coase presents the case of a physician who builds an examination room whose walls adjoin that of the neighborhood baker, only to find that the noise of the baker's machines is disturbing to his business; and he files suit against the baker. The court decided in favor of the physician! Coase supports this judgement on the grounds that the baker and the physician are *equally at fault*, arguing that the noise of the baker's machinery caused no nuisance until the building of the room by the physician. He is indifferent between two circumstances: (a) the baker has the option of paying for the right to continue operations, or (b) the physician has the option of paying for him to stop, because they differ only in the consequences for the distribution of income, not the level of total production.

But the right of prior possession is not designed to determine the optimal distribution of income. It is related, instead, to the maintenance of orderly social processes, much the same way that the rules of "rights of way" are useful in various modes of transportation. A person who possesses rights of way, or who holds rights of prior possession, may be willing to compromise those rights when provided adequate compensation. A person hurrying to the hospital could (in the absence of transaction costs) purchase rights of way from their "natural owners" (say, those with green lights). But when a violation of rights of way leads to an accident, the two parties are not equally at fault, even though both cars are necessary to the accident.[4] Hence, a more balanced solution to the baker-physician problem would be to allow the alienation of rights of prior possession, when appropriate. In this case the physician could pay the baker for any compromise of his rights of prior possession. This option is technically superior to that chosen by Coase. A judicial destruction of the assets inherent in the right of prior possession and the creation of stronger rights in property, as an asset for the gentry, do not constitute a Pareto-optimal change: we have no basis for claiming that society is better off.

The abrogation of the baker's rights of prior possession in favor of the property interests of the politically dominant gentry, in the case discussed by Coase, was part of a more general process by which the traditional rights of the peasantry gave way to the demands of mercantile and industrial interests. Coase is certainly free to support the special interests of the gentry; however, he is not plausibly indifferent to the distribution of income when he denies the baker's right of prior possession in favor of rights in property.

Private Property

If it is true that property rights reside in the alienability of a set of resource-characteristics, then *private* property rights are rights of a particular form. As a technical concept, private property rights are embodied in a specific rule for the allocation of rights to revenue from a production process involving human and nonhuman resources. This rule specifies that *all* of the revenue generated by a process of cooperative production belongs to the owner of capital (and/or natural resources); and the capital goods used in the production process are called "private property." In other words, private property is the characteristic of a resource whose use in production is associated with the particular rule of revenue.

In contrast the "traditional" methods of allocation involved a sharing of revenue or the sharing of work-time. Both of these methods have been observed in "feudalistic" systems of production. These traditional methods are corporate in the sense that there are socially accepted, or rightful, shares of the product of an estate or a field that belongs to the direct producer and another share the belongs to the landlord. Or in other cases workers may be expected to allocate a share of their work-time to the fields of the lord and reserve the remainder for their own product. Notwithstanding the gross differentials in real income, these are systems of sharing, wherein workers and their lords belong to a single group within which revenue is divided.

With systems of private property, however, workers no longer have rights to shares of group output. As the owners of human resources, workers receive *wages* in exchange for the alienation their *labor* under conditions where the exchange value of that labor is determined by a labor market. It is conventional to claim that the wages of labor are provided by the sale of product, thus implying that workers receive a share of that product. However, this is not the case, except at the level of the economy as a whole.[5] Even if the market value of a product suddenly fell to zero, the earned reward to labor would be unaffected; and it is the capitalist who would suffer a loss. Private property, then, rests on the ideology that the exchange value of productive effort (wages) should be independent of the market value of the product.[6] Hence, the benefits that accrue to the owners of capital are maximized when the benefits to labor are minimized, given the appropriate level of output.

Economic efficiency is achieved when it is not possible to produce a particular combination of goods at a lower cost of inputs, where "inputs" includes the providers of labor services. It is clear, then, that economic efficiency addresses not only the level of output, but deals directly with the distribution of that output among individuals. And as such, it is a revolutionary principle. Rather than specify appropriate benefits on the basis of inalienable characteristics of individuals relative to other individuals, as we find in "traditional" systems, the principles of private property and efficiency require the allocation of benefits on the basis of the relationship of individuals to capital. Efficiency, then, is an ideology for the rationalization of a particular form of distribution.

A number of societies have made the transition from systems of nonproperty resource management to systems of private property. These transitions have been associated both with demographic pressures that induce pressure for a larger share of resources to the common people at the expense of the elite and with pressures from members of the elite to gain a larger share of social resources, often as a result of having observed the higher standards of living enjoyed by dominant classes elsewhere. The pressures are resolved by the elite with its adoption of the principles of private property and efficiency.

In contrast to traditional criteria of allocation, the doctrine of efficiency thrives on a redundancy of hands; and the immediate consequence of abandoning traditional forms has been to reduce the share of the social product allocated to the direct producer. There is found in the system of private property a means of increasing economic efficiency—increasing the share of the social product to the upper classes—by means of a rule that grants all rights to revenue to the owners of land and abolishing the traditional use rights (rights to revenue) of the common people. Private property in land in the face of an excessive rural population provided the conditions for the subjugation of the peasantry and working classes to the standards of economic efficiency.

The effects of demographic growth have been prominent in discussions of the process by which systems of open access are abandoned in favor of the commons, or in favor of private property. Libecap (1989) discusses a number of instances where a crowded resource terrain leads to increasing "common pool losses" in the context of *open access* and induce negotiation toward an allocation of rights. McCay (1987) points to inadequacies of the open access mode in fisheries and the development of rights in a commons. For open access to retain feasibility, the relevant resource must not be scarce. Either the commons or private property appears to be an essential mechanism for resource allocation among rival claimants.

But since the commons requires a formula by which a members of a collectivity share a resource, demographically stimulated increases in resource demands will eventually threaten the viability of the commons. Even though the commons was a necessary solution to the crowding of open access, continued population growth renders that solution inadequate. The problem is resolved by an abrogation of the rights of the commons and the imposition of the norms of private property.

However, private property does not present us with a simple end-game; even private property rights are vulnerable to obsolescence in the face of demographic pressure. Capitalism has, in fact, only accelerated rates of demographic growth, rapidly crowding the planet to such an extent that it becomes difficult for individuals to exploit resources without affecting the resources and/or well-being of adjacent others (Sax 1983). This is a problem of "externalities;" and it constitutes a *contradiction* to the fuller development of private capitalism. That is, it becomes less and less plausible that the granting of "full property rights" to resources will be in the public interest, or in the interest of the owners of property. Sax argues that the social benefits of nonexclusive use are increasing relative to those of private property. The evolving solution to this problem is the reconstitution of the commons on a new, post-industrial, basis in order to assure that public interests are advanced by private initiative.

Sax (1983) discusses the case of Penn Central Transportation Co. v. City of New York (438 U.S. 104, 1978) where the owners of the Penn Central building were not allowed to replace it with a high-rise building on the grounds that doing so would destroy a socially valued scenic amenity. As Sax emphasizes, this was not a case of a polluting nuisance: the property owners adjacent to Penn Central had already exercised their option to build high-rises.

> We have endowed individuals and enterprises with property because we assume that the private ownership system will allocate and reallocate the property resource to socially desirable uses. Any such system of allocation will, of course, fail from time to time. But when the system regularly fails to allocate property to "correct" uses, we begin to lose faith in the system itself. Just as older systems of property, like feudal tenures, declined as the became nonfunctional, so our own system is declining to the extent it is perceived as a functional failure. (Sax 1983: 481)

We should now understand the court's position as one that recognizes the *rights of prior possession* of those have been allowed to enjoy a customary amenity. The Coasian inscrutability of the judges in this case is readily resolved once we accept the implications of congestion upon the general social desirability of independent judgements by property owners, and recognize as well the fundamental importance of the right of prior possession to the maintenance of social order.

Conclusion

Within any society there is a system of rights by which individuals may gain legitimate access to resources. In some societies it is rights of person that dominates this allocation process; and individuals may belong on the basis of age, sex and parentage to several corporate groups within which these rights are realized. For example, a man within a patrilineal tribal society may belong to a domestic group, to a lineage and to a tribe. From each of these groups he may make rightful claims against a share of the resources as a function of the social position implied by his age and parentage. Additionally, individuals may be able to gain additional benefits through the alienation of rights in certain things.

Private property defines a particular method for the allocation of benefits. However, we find no society in which those rules are deemed to be sufficient. Since property is an attribute of characteristics of resources, the manner in which those attributes are combined and separated in relation to rights of alienation is subject to decision in the political and judicial process. And there is widespread regulation of the manner in which individuals are allowed to pursue rights of private property in relation to various resources, depending on the kind of industry or market in which those rights reside. The specification of rights and the determination of the set of individuals who have access to those rights is the root of the political process in most societies; and the ideologies of property and efficiency have been central to determining the claims of dominants within industrial economies. However, rights of person remain essential as a context for the expression of property rights.

Notes

1. Of course, a right must be held with some degree of security in order for an expenditure to be justified in exchange for it. Rights that are at risk of abrogation suffer steep discounts in the open market. But to the degree that rights are secure, they may be sought by those lacking in them.
2. Actually, I have recently become aware of "confidentiality clauses" in legal agreements, whereby individuals accept payments on the condition that they not disclose publicly certain information. These agreements appear not to be binding before a court of law.
3. We cannot restrict the market for draft status to any subset of those who are physically capable (such as "citizens" or males only) without creating yet another right of person.
4. Rights of way are clearly rights of person because the law refuses to recognize the validity of their alienation. The police will be unimpressed by the claim that you have paid other drivers for the right to drive through the red light, since that right is not transferrable. Nor can one offer to pay the police directly for this privilege, since doing so would be an attempt to bribe a public official. Rights of way are not allowed to become property.
5. A given firm is more profitable, other things equal, the less it pays to its workers. However, the set of all firms in an economy must depend on the purchasing power of consumers, many of whom may be workers. For this reason the stability and growth of the economy will depend on the adequacy of the share of national income that accrues to workers, given other parameters of the system.
6. The estate of a slave holder is also a form of private property, so long as land is alienable, because the owner claims full rights to revenue. In this case, however, the providers of human resources do not own those resources, and hence, can have no right to wages (or to anything whatsoever).

References Cited

Bromley, D.W.
1989 Property relations and economic development: the other land reform. *World Development* 17(6):867-77.

Ciriacy-Wantrup, S.V., & R.C. Bishop
1975 "Common property" as a concept in natural resources policy. *Natural Resources Journal* 15(4):713-27.

Coase, R.H.
1960 The problem of social cost. *The Journal of Law and Economics* 3(1):1- 69.

Demsetz, H.
1967 Toward a theory of property rights. *American Economic Review* 57(2):347-59.

Leacock, E.
1954 *The Montagnais "Hunting Territory" and the Fur Trade* (American Anthropological Association Memoir, 78). Menasha: American Anthropological Association.

Libecap, G.D.
1989 *Contracting for Property Rights*. Cambridge: Cambridge University Press.

Macpherson, C.B.
1985 *The Rise and Fall of Economic Justice and Other Papers*. Oxford: Oxford University Press.

McCay, B.J.
1987 The culture of the commoners. In B.J. McCay & J.M. Acheson (eds.), *The Question of the Commons: The Culture and Ecology of Communal Resources*, pp. 195-216. Tucson: University of Arizona Press.

McCay, B.J., & J.M. Acheson
1987 Human ecology of the commons. In B.J. McCay & J.M. Acheson (eds.), *The Question of the Commons: The Culture and Ecology of Communal Resources*, pp. 1-34. Tucson: University of Arizona Press.

Sax, J.L.
1983 Some thoughts on the decline of private property. *Washington Law Review Jurisprudential Lecture Series* 58:481-496.

Chapter Four

Property: Law, Cotton-pickin' Hands, and Implicit Cultural Imperialism

Walter C. Neale

The New Economic History—an approach that has enjoyed here considerable vogue for two decades now—treats *property* as an idea of general applicability, one that can be used in analyses of efficiency and social change in virtually any society (North & Thomas 1977; North 1990; Williamson 1985; Fenoaltea 1975; McCloskey 1976; Coase 1937, 1960; Demsetz 1967—see Notes on Sources at the end of this paper). The idea of property used is a rather narrowly modern and western concept of rights and powers. In nonwestern and comparative studies we are typically careful not to impose our own models of religion or kinship or other aspects of social structure upon other societies, but with our own ideas of property we are apt to be careless.

It is the thesis of this paper that *property* is a fine rubric for a wide range of interests and social phenomena, but that it would be a gross error to think that the term has such clear meaning that it can be used as a general or pan-cultural term beyond the simple assertion that every culture probably has had and has some equivalent to the command, "Keep your cotton-pickin' hands off my [whatever]."

Discussions of property should *not be phrased*—as they often are—*as a question about* whether there are peoples who have no ideas about who gets to use what; all societies must have some set of rules about the matter. Actually the discussion usually proceeds along these lines: "Property rights [which always appear implicitly as those rights typically associated with fee simple ownership in the United States] are found everywhere." "No, that is not true." "Oh yes it is—please name the time and place where people have not had the concept 'mine.'" The issue should be how access and use are organized by each society. If by the evidence it turns out that one can assert general propositions with more specific content than "cotton-pickin' hands," then fine. But, meanwhile, evidence seems to support a contrary proposition. What is needed is a focus on the issues of *who* does (and who does not) get to use *what*, in *what ways*, and when (that is, in what circumstances). *Property* is an appropriate rubric for this focus, but a rubric without specific content, certainly not as a Platonic universal. We can have definitions and classifications for properties in specific societies, often for similar rights and responsibilities in a number of related societies; but that is all.[1]

If there can be no universal characterization of property or kinds of property, then it follows that there can be no theory of the origins of "property," nor can there be a universal pattern in the way or ways in which the rules of property change. We cannot know how specific ideas of "property" first began because we enter history *in medias res*, and we cannot have a general theory of changes in the rules of property because processes of change vary from society to society—they are historically path-dependent.

In what follows I have drawn heavily from old sources: partly because I think that they are the best, but also to show that what should be said about the New Economic History was said long ago. Also, the examples that I use are mostly about property (and not-property) in land. There are many sorts of property in many things, and today property in land is much less important than other sorts of properties. However, an important part of the newer literature deals with property in land, and such expertise as I have is in land tenures.

Sir Henry Maine and How to Do History Right

Maine's *Ancient Law* (1917) may be understood as (among other things) an exemplar of the Historical Method and the Comparative Method (Maine's capitalizations). The primary trait of the Historical Method is that one can say nothing about events, conditions, or systems unless one has evidence from the place and time. Thus *Ancient Law* begins with the Homeric Epics and Rome's Decemviral Tables. About what went before, Maine says nothing because he had no evidence from an earlier time for these places (we now have Linear B; Maine did not). His point is that we cannot use logic to derive what happened before: that would be guesswork, what Maine calls Speculative History (about which more shortly).

We can, however, use his Comparative Method to suggest details for which a context exists but about which no evidence remains. In Maine's use, the Comparative Method does not allow of just any comparisons. If Society #1 has Traits A, B, D, E, and F, and Society #2 has Traits A, B, C, D, and F; then one may take it as reasonably probable that, were our records more complete, they would show that Society #1 once had Trait C and Society #2, Trait E. This not only makes it possible to "fill in" aspects of a society; it permits one to compare paths of change. Thus, for instance, if law in Society #2 was dominated by sacred tradition and Trait C were closely related to that tradition, then one could plausibly account for the absence of C in Society #1 by the known demise of its sacred tradition. In filling out his accounts of Roman and Hindu societies, Maine first pointed out that these—and the Slavic and Celtic societies (see also Maine, 1885)—shared Indo-European languages, their early religions had much in common, and their societies shared other traits such as the patriarchal family (to which we might prefer to give the names oikos, familia, or joint family). He carefully eschewed comparisons with east Asian and Semitic societies because they did not share common linguistic or cultural roots with Indo-European societies. In short, the Comparative Method does not allow one to argue that people are territorial because wolves and some tropical fish are.

Speculative History, or, How to Do History Wrong

According to Maine (1917: 149-50),

> What mankind did in the primitive state may not be a hopeless subject of inquiry, but of their motives for doing it, it is impossible to know anything. . . . Sketches of the plight of human beings in the first ages of the world are effected by first supposing mankind to be divested of a greater part of the circumstances by which they are now surrounded, and by then assuming that, in the condition thus imagined, they would preserve the same sentiments and prejudices by which they are now actuated,—although, in fact, these sentiments may have been created by those very circumstances of which, by hypothesis, they are to be stripped.

This passage summarizes what Maine called Speculative History. One need only add that, in strip-searches for the essence, what is left as the essence depends entirely upon the order in which the strip is conducted.

North and Thomas's argument (1977) exemplifies Speculative History. They postulate that an increasing population led to the development of agriculture.[2] Agriculture in turn required the invention of property to protect the cultivator's right to the produce of his labor. This argument is remarkably close to that of Blackstone ("who is always," said Maine [1917: 148], "a faithful index of the average opinions of his day . . ."). Blackstone argued (Maine 1917: 148-49, quoting Blackstone) that "*when mankind increased in number*, it became necessary to entertain conceptions of more permanent dominion, and to appropriate to *individuals* not the immediate use only, but the very substance of the thing to be used" (emphasis added).

The Blackstone/North/Thomas proposition that property in land stems from the need to protect the efforts and livelihoods of people seems reasonable—which is *not* the same as historically accurate. But why should the desire be fulfilled by property in *land*? P.J. Bohannan (1963) has pointed out that some African systems provided no rights over specific portions of the earth's surface but, rather, a "right to farm." Is this a property? Or is it a right of a members of a society, as some other societies provide the right to vote? Typically Indian villages, highly inegalitarian as they were, used to provide a guarantee of participation in the harvest to all villagers (except merchants and moneylenders). Was this a property? A right to farm did mean a right to exclude others from the land under one's wife's or daughter's hoe that season. But rights to farm or to participate in the division of the harvest do not constitute a property in land (rights and duties, yes, properties, no). It is indisputable that the practice of agriculture requires some sort of organization (as it is indisputable that the practice of anything requires some sort of organization), but we are not justified in assuming that it requires the same sort of organization everywhere. Why, for instance, was individual property in land the outcome of the practice of agriculture in Mesopotamia (if it was[3]) but not in the Nile valley or in much of sub-Saharan Africa?

More than 130 years ago Maine had the answer to the rationalist, utilitarian arguments with which the New Economic Historians answer such questions. Bentham proposed that—I am quoting Maine (1917: 70)—:

> societies modify, and have always modified, their laws according to their views of general expediency. It is difficult to say that this proposition is false, but it certainly appears to be unfruitful. For that which seems expedient to a society, or rather to the governing part of it, when it alters a rule of law is surely the same thing as the object, whatever it may be, which it has in view when it makes the change. Expediency and the greatest good are nothing more than different names for the impulse which prompts the modification; and when we lay down expediency as the rule of change in law and opinion, all we get by the proposition is the substitution of an express term for a term which is necessarily implied when we say that a change takes place.

All that the new economic historians have added appears to be an express term of almost exclusive emphasis upon the material (or financial) wellbeing of individuals.

Private Property, Public Space, and Natural Law

Any kind of property has meaning only in contrast to other kinds of property, and property itself has meaning only in contrast to other kinds of rights and powers. As John R. Commons (1968: 214-15) said of early Norman England:

> William the Conqueror and his lawyers did not distinguish his property from his sovereignty. Both were possessions rather than property. He was both landlord and King. The soil belonged to him by right of conquest, and the people were his subjects. Property and sovereignty

> were one, since both were but dominion over things and persons. Similar notions of ownership and lordship prevailed throughout the descending ranks of freemen. . . . Property was lordship by virtue of possession. It was a personal relation of command and obedience.

In such circumstances, *dominion* would be a better term than property. Our system of property took shape only when sovereignty and property became clearly differentiated—the crown (and then, more generally, the government) getting most of the sovereignty, individuals getting much of the property.

Similarly, for *private* to have meaning, it must contrast with activities, rights, duties, and roles that belong in a *public* space.

Maine began his account of the evolution of Roman ideas of property with a state of affairs in which only the *oikos* or *familia*, never the individual, had a social role. All important things—land, cattle, arms, slaves, i.e., the *res mancipi* under the hand (dominion) of the patriarch, who represented the *familia*—could not be alienated because they were an integral part of these primary social units.[4] There could be no personal property. The Romans slowly altered this state of affairs. They changed the ways in which succession to the whole estate (familia) could occur, first by using legal fictions and then, increasingly, by praetorian edict, and finally by allowing testators to bequeath. Then they extended the application of the new rules to merge transfers of *res mancipi* (the important things) into the rules for transfers of *res nec mancipi*—and also by allowing women to come out from under the dominion of the *patria potestas* and thus to own their own property. Crucial to this change was the creation of a public space: to wit, the Roman army. It was a bit silly, really impossible, to have soldiers, to say nothing of generals and the administrators of distant provinces, under the absolute power of their fathers.[5]

With the spread of empire it was also necessary to formulate rules governing interactions between Romans and members of the subject Italian societies. For this purpose the Romans evolved the idea of the common-to-all-peoples "law of nations" that later, under the intellectual influence of the Greeks, merged into a *natural law* of human societies.[6]

I have told this story to make the point that private contrasts with public. I have also told it to make the point that our ideas of property derive from a history—sometimes more, sometimes less knowable—a *western* history that we can trace back for some time indeed, but still for only a small portion of that minimum estimate of 80,000 years during which Both-Genders-Sapiens have been using their heads and their genes.

Roots of Our Ideas about Individual Private Property

Our ideas about property derive rather narrowly from western law: Roman, British, Napoleonic. Central to our ideas of property is the individual. The individual as the centerpiece or archetype for property has several roots. First, the development of Roman law, culminating in Justinian's code, endowed individuals with property rights. These ideas became built into the development of western law as the Church incorporated major elements of the Justinian Code into its canon law. (And it should be noted, as Maine did, that this was equally true of the common law of England, continually being "discovered" by justices who were educated in the only place that they could be educated, in the Church.) Entwined with the development of Roman law and then with the development of thought during the Renaissance were Greek ideas of natural law; and both Greek and Roman thought built upon the idea of citizenship—***a*** citizen. Add to this a peculiar aspect of the Reformation, the insistence that people only related to God as individuals. Next, the rights of individuals and decisions by individuals became central to the development of social and political philosophy during the 17th and 18th centuries. Although the Greek-washed mind constantly strives for consistency, there is little reason to believe that ideologies or religions require internal consistency, let alone that their applications should be consistent—for instance, after the Romans, none of these emphases on the individual did women much good.

From the Individual to the Multiglomerate

Early in the 17th century the king's courts, and especially Justice Coke, began to give Anglo-American property its specifically English form (see Commons 1968: ch. 6). Its formulation as peculiarly individual came at the cusp of the 17th and 18th centuries.

After the Puritan Commonwealth and the Revolution of 1688 the British were confronted with a problem. In the older Christian view power over land and the people thereon descended from God through his Son to Peter and the bishops or Rome, to kings and from kings to nobles and lesser people. But the British had cut off the head of one king and driven another out. The line of justification from Peter to the merchants of London and the squirearchy of the countryside was a bit flimsy. Fortunately for the British establishment, John Locke came up with the labor theory of property (a bit of an irony when Marx extended the logic to all value). Although it need not have done so, this labor theory of property did tie power over things directly to individuals. And it ensconced private property as a characteristic of universal natural law. The French Revolution and the Napoleonic Code owed a similar but more Rousseauvian debt in resolving a similar need for a secular justification. However much these ideas have spread across the world, they originated in the evolution of western ideas, problems, and solutions, not in a universal rationality or in Eve's mitochondrial DNA. What we had, then, were not further, inevitable steps on the road to individual property (or other individual rights) but contexts of ideas and circumstances in which people sought to sort out their problems.

Having separated individual private property from sovereignty, we have gone on to create some strange private properties. Using the granting of charters—a social device that gave pieces of sovereignty to towns and guilds, and then to great trading companies—we have created private individuals with perpetual life, corporations. To these creatures we have given not only the right to use things and to exclude others from their use; we have also given them the right to realize the value of their expected future income streams from the property (Commons 1968: 17).[7] The idea that some of the most famous corporations are called *societies anonymes* may cause a smile. A visiting Martian ethnographer is likely to break into raucous laughter when told that the property of transnational multiglomerates is private.

Processes of Change

One important element that is missing from analyses founded upon the individual—as the analyses of the New Economic Historians are—is social process, how new perceptions of expediency (or salvation) are worked into the unarticulated as well as the explicit rules affecting the way people may, must, or may not act. Economists and economic historians of the new persuasion fail to build into their analyses the truth that, while social processes are always acted out by individuals striving to achieve whatever they are trying to achieve, they are always acting within a set of rules and perceptions that are given them by the accident of birth and the processes of acculturation. They are not pin-balls, bounced about automatically by the springs of culture, independently of or without desires, wills, and cunning; quite the opposite. But what they want and how they perceive the opportunities and means to go about getting what they want depends in very large part upon the society in which they live. Thus it may be true—or it may not be true—that early Mesopotamian cultivators evolved a system of private property; but if they did, it would have been in response to changing circumstances *as they perceived* the changing circumstances and *as they perceived* the rewards, possibilities, and opportunities. When Douglass North (1990) explains change by attributing it to a drive for efficiency, he is but substituting another express term for Bentham's expediency. Neither phrase tells us about process.

To illustrate process I return to John R. Commons's (1968) account of how the Anglo-American world arrived at its rules for modern property. In the Anglo-American system, when one party to a dyad of conflicting interests wishes to stop the other party from a course of action, or to force the other party to act in a different way, it takes the other party to court, claiming that the other party is violating the rules. In reaching a decision—we say, "in interpreting the law"—the court (here read, "judge or judges") may change the rules, and what the court says about the rules is *authoritative*. It is the authoritative character of court decisions that makes the new rules binding. As governors of Arkansas and Alabama have said, "The decision was wrong, but what the Supreme Court says is the law of the land is the law of the land and must be obeyed."

In "Toward a Theory of Property Rights" Demsetz (1967: 354) says that his purpose "is to discern some broad principles governing the development of property rights *in communities oriented to private property*" (emphasis added). In his account of the Montagnais trappers who responded to the opportunities presented by the fur trade by dividing "fur-bearing land" among agnatic groups, Demsetz presents no account of *how* they reached this solution to the danger that some overly eager trappers would wreck the opportunities of others, nor does he present evidence that the Montagnais were "oriented to private property."[8] He has illustrated his "principles," but he has not established their range, nor explained how they were put into effect.[9]

Evidence That Other Systems Are Truly Other

Africa: Rights You Got, Property You Don't

Bohannan (1963) contrasts the European view of land as divided into pieces permanently fixed on a grid of the earth's surface with the view of place as where-we-are among other groups. The more closely related we are to another group, the shorter the distance between us, no matter what the odometer says. Conversely, when moving across the earth's surface as we shift our farming, we move toward the most distant people (odometer to the contrary notwithstanding). There is no way one can talk in the European sense about "exclusive possession" because it is not clear what such an African possesses; nor what another, nearby African possesses. What is clear is that "we move our farming thataway" because land thataway is more available to us because it is more distant.

India: Property Rights are Only Sun-baked

In Hindi *pukka* means pure, boiled, baked, proper, and generally contrasts with *kuccha*. Pukka bricks are kiln-baked; kuccha bricks are sun-baked. Daniel Thorner (1973: 13) characterized all Indian tenures, present as well as past, with the remark, "to this date [1956] there has not emerged in India a fully developed or pukka private property in land."

Kuccha Rights, Example #1

W.C. Bennett (1878: 49-50) reports the use, in grants to *talukdars* (people with effective local authority), of words from old Persian deeds that specified the sale of all proprietary right. But in fact "any interference [with the former proprietor's rights in trees] would have been considered as an unpardonable usurpation," and the sellers' rights in land were never disturbed. We are not told why the Persian wording was used. Perhaps the prestige of a Persian (Moghul) deed lent dignity to the grant. Whatever the truth of this guess, any guess based on modern western (or Persian) ideas about property would almost certainly be worse. In any case, this peculiar use of the Persian deed must have had its own history.

Kuccha Rights, Example #2

Andre Wink's (1986) study of agrarian society and politics in 18th-century Maharashtra makes a point of the great difficulty in finding English words to express the system he was examining and, perforce, he made *fitna* central to his analysis. Fitna translates as rebellion and sedition (if one loses), but as "drawing" to a new king/emperor/leader if the shift of loyalty succeeds. In form the grant of land (and of aspects of what we would call sovereignty) is from king to rural gentry (Wink's term). In substance the title and power are granted to the new suzerain by local gentries; the sovereign's grant merely "regularizes" the fitna that gave him the overlordship.

Private? Public? Government? Individual? Communal? Corporate? I would prefer something like "divided dominion."

Conclusion

The implicit cultural imperialism of my title is the effort to apply modern western ideas about property—ideas that are ideologically and historically specific—to all sorts of rules about whose cotton pickin' hands have access for what purposes to what things. It is astounding—although not surprising, given the continuing ethnocentrism of economic theory—that the new economic history should incorporate western ideas about property in a manner so soundly criticized Maine one and a third centuries ago. Seen in this context, the New Economic History represents a recurring tendency to use a central organizing idea of the western cultural heritage to interpret other cultures. Anthropological studies are the antidote.

My conclusion—indeed, my plea—is that we be rank empiricists and discover and report rules of access before, not after, we invent universal concepts of property.

Notes on Sources

The New Economic History interprets the past with the assumptions and arguments of economic micro-theory of prices. It is not the same as Cliometrics (the muse with measurement), but the two are closely allied.

Cliometrics dates from the early 1950s when a group of economic historians from the economics side argued that economic historians should make much more use of numbers and statistical analyses. (Oral tradition has it that the idea was first bruited during a late night drinking session at a meeting of the Economic History Association. I believe the tradition.) The idea was admirable and there has been some fine Cliometric work, but sometimes the history is overwhelmed by the numbers. More importantly, Cliometrics often adopts economic theory *a priori* to shape and solve problems. If Cliometrics was conceived in the early 1950s, its actual birth was Conrad and Meyer's (1958) "The Economics of Slavery in the Ante-Bellum South." Conrad and Meyer used numerical records to establish that slavery was profitable in the ante-bellum South. The question was a quite proper historical question—was slavery profitable?—and their answer, "Yes," convincing.[10] However, the economic theory became increasingly marked over time. McCloskey (1978: 15) approvingly characterized Cliometrics thus: "Not counting but economic theory, especially the theory of price, is the defining skill of Cliometricians. . . . A cliometrician is an economist applying economic theory . . . to historical facts (not always quantitative) in the interest of history (not economics)." (The last phrase may be a bit self-serving.)

The New Economic History sometimes uses Cliometrics' quantitative facts, but the use of and faith in the universality of a micro-theory developed to describe nineteenth-century firms is its dominant characteristic (hence Anne Mayhew [frequent oral communications] has characterized it as history with time held constant). Of the works by New Economic Historians that I list among the sources I refer only to North and Thomas (1977), North (1990), and Demsetz (1967) in the text. (Properly speaking, Demsetz should not be classified as a New (or any sort of) Economic Historian, but his piece cited not only draws on both history and a nonliterate society; it deals with the issue at hand and illustrates in short compass the traits of the genre.) The other citations are to items mentioned in this Note on Sources.

McCloskey (1976) illustrates the problems associated with the fine line between the best of Cliometrics and the replacing of history with economic theory. Using manorial records, McCloskey showed that changes in the acreages under individual peasant tenure and under seigneurial tenure were consistent with the proposition that the kind of tenure was chosen to avert risk (a proposition common to the literature on third world countries since the 1950s). But, quite possibly, the changes were equally or more consistent with other hypotheses that could be derived from other events occurring on the manors whose records McCloskey examined. McCloskey's statistical testing could not engage such questions. In an important sense, history was left out of the analysis. In statisticians' terms, history consists of samples of one drawn from universes of one. This does not allow for significant improbabilities because there are no degrees of freedom; and here lies the fine line between opening up new interpretations of what happened and choosing the economistic interpretation because it is consistent with economic theory. Fenoaltea's (1975) well-argued analysis of changes in the commons (in an argument not dissimilar to Demsetz's) crosses that fine line; his article is an excellent example of the New Economic History. The numbers and the statistical tests have disappeared; what remains is economic theory and citations of accounts by historians that are consistent with Fenolatea's argument (which is not the same as an attempt at proof that all, most, or the best historians support his position).

North (1990) is an intriguing effort at criticism of the New Economic History, especially for its failure to take account of institutions. Each chapter begins with a fine statement of a problem with the New Economic History, but then each chapter attempts to solve it with ideas drawn from economics. A search for economic efficiency—often delayed by existing institutions—becomes the long-run cause of institutional change. To add plausibility to his argument, North frequently calls upon the idea of "transactions costs" to explain why economic efficiency is delayed. The idea of transactions costs originated in an effort to explain why, in an economy believed to be essentially competitive, there should be large scale organizations and imperfections in markets (Coase 1937, 1960). The idea makes some sense when one thinks of costs of writing and enforcing contracts; but it has been extended (North would have had to extend it if it had not already been extended) to include any consideration that could bear on a decision to act or not to act.[11] One is tempted to remark that Oedipus would have not had the problems that he did if only someone had told him that there were very high transactions costs around Thebes.

Acknowledgments

The author is deeply indebted to Caroline Chanock of La Trobe University (Australia) for making sense of his ideas.

Notes

1. Readers will note that my argument has much in common with that of Peters (this volume).
2. Anne Mayhew (1982) provides a thorough and, I think, devastating criticism of North and Thomas's article. Here I deal only with their implicit assumption that property is a natural outcome of agriculture. Note here that the assumptions about hunter-gatherers-herders forced (or induced) into agriculture by limits on exploitable resources runs entirely counter to Marshall Sahlins' (1972: ch. 1) account of "primitive affluence."
3. Hudson (this volume) says that it was *not* individual property in land.
4. In more recent years the work of Moses Finley (1959) and Walter Donlan (1994) on Homeric society supports Maine's interpretation.
5. In "Delict and Crime," the last chapter of *Ancient Law*, Maine points out that the idea of publicly recognized wrong-doing derives from the creation and extension of public space and the associated increasing limitations on the powers of the father. If *pater-et-familia* could no longer be considered the effectively responsible unit for all of its members, then the Republic had to step in to control the actions of individuals.
6. These pieces of Maine's argument are the context for his famous dictum about progressive societies moving from status to contract (as also are the seldom quoted paragraphs preceding the dictum). Taken out of context, the dictum sounds terribly 19th century European, arrogant, and wrong. But he has already made it clear that the societies about which he speaks are Indo-European, and that progressive means having moved toward a system in which the law is constantly (if only slowly) adapted to constantly changing actual rules of common behavior by consciously legislating, free of (or freer of) the restraints of sacred tradition.
7. Commons first makes the point on page 17. His account of the development of the right runs through the whole book, especially the first 213 pages.
8. Although Demsetz never made it part of his property argument, it may be relevant that the Montagnais were in close contact with a much more powerful society that did have ideas about and rules of property rather close to ours.
9. Bell (this volume) points out that Demsetz's argument is in error even when one adopts our modern terminology.
10. A closely related question—would slavery therefore end shortly?—shows a definite economistic bias. Twenty years later, at a meeting of the Economic History Association, John Meyer said that he and Conrad had thought that, were slavery unprofitable, they would be showing that it was doomed to a short life expectancy; but that now, after twenty years of mature reflection, he had decided that, no matter what the economics, one person would enslave another whenever he could.

11. See Neale (1993) for a more extended and less kindly commentary on North (1990).

References Cited

Bennett, W.C.
1878 *The Final Settlement Report on the Gonda District*. Allahabad: North-West Provinces and Oudh Government Press.

Bohannan, P.J.
1963 "Land," "tenure," and land tenure. In D.P. Biebuyck 1963 (ed.), *African Agrarian Systems*, pp. 101-15. London: Oxford University Press.

Coase, R.H.
1937 The nature of the firm. *Economica* 4:386-405.
1960 The problem of social cost. *Journal of Law and Economics* 17:53-71.

Commons, J.R.
1968 *Legal Foundations of Capitalism*. Madison: University of Wisconsin Press. First published 1924.

Conrad, A., & J. Meyer
1958 The economics of slavery in the ante-bellum South. *Journal of Political Economy* 66(2):95-130.

Demsetz, H.
1967 Toward a theory of property rights. *American Economic Review* 57(2):347-59.

Donlan, W
1994 Chief and followers in pre-state Greece. In C.A.M. Duncan & D.W. Tandy (eds.), *From Political Economy to Anthropology: Situating Economic Life in Past Societies*, pp. 34-51. Montreal: Black Rose Books.

Fenoaltea, S.
1975 Authority, efficiency, and agricultural organization in medieval England and beyond: a hypothesis. *The Journal of Economic History* 35(4):693- 718.

Finley, M.
1959 *The World of Odysseus*. Cleveland: World Publishing. First published 1954.

Maine, H.S.
1885 *Lectures on the Early History of Institutions*. London: John Murray.
1917 *Ancient Law*. New York: E.P. Dutton (Everyman's). First published 1861.

Mayhew, A.
1982 The first economic revolution as fiction. *The Economic History Review* 35(4):568-71.

McCloskey, D.N.
1976 English open fields as behavior towards risk. *Research in Economic History* 1:124-70.
1978 The achievements of the cliometric school. *The Journal of Economic History* 38(1):13-28.

Neale, W.C.
1993 Review of D.C. North, *Institutions, Institutional Change, and Economic Performance* (Cambridge: Cambridge University Press, 1990), in *Economic Development and Cultural Change* 41(2):422-25.

North, D.C.
1990 *Institutions, Institutional Change, and Economic Performance*. Cambridge: Cambridge University Press.

North, D.C., & R.P. Thomas
1977 The first economic revolution. *The Economic History Review* 30:229- 41.

Sahlins, M.
1972 *Stone Age Economics*. Chicago: Aldine-Atherton.

Thorner, D.
1973 *The Agrarian Prospect for India*. 2nd edition. Columbia, MO: South Asia Books. First published 1956.

Williamson, O.E.
1985 *The Economic Institutions of Capitalism: Firms, Markets, Relational Contracting*. New York: The Free Press.

Wink, A.
1986 *Land and Sovereignty in India: Agrarian Society and Politics under the Eighteenth-Century Svarajya*. Cambridge: Cambridge University Press.

Part II

Property in Precapitalist Societies

Chapter Five

ꟸ❧

Property in Precapitalist Societies: Introduction

Antonio Gilman

This section of the volume presents papers that illustrate the nature and development of property regimes in chiefdoms and early states, on the one hand, and address some of the methodological difficulties involved in such studies, on the other. Costin, Durrenberger, Earle, Fleming, Hudson, and McAnany presented initial versions of their papers at the 1994 Conference; Gilman's was written later. Although these papers (Gilman's apart) seek to elucidate the particular characteristics of unique historical trajectories and pay close attention to the cultural particularities of the cases they examine, all are firmly committed to a comparative, processual perspective. Partly this may be because (apart from Fleming's Swaledale case) the societies they examine developed outside the pressure of capitalist encroachment and need not be defended against forces that use universalizing economic principles to justify their depredations. Partly this is because the evidence on which they rely—archaeological, historical, and even literary—is too sparse or biased to be interpreted without positing that the actors who made the histories they examine were in some broad sense rational. The contributors to this section would agree with Cowgill (1975: 514) that:

> one's notions about what is in the best interests of oneself, one's close kin, or associations, institutions, or social categories or classes with which one closely identifies are major determinants of politically and economically relevant aspects of behavior. . . . If we understand the situational and institutional contexts in which individuals find themselves, their notions about their own self-interest become quite understandable, and perhaps even predictable.

In the end, the particularities elucidated by anthropology's ethnographic project can only be evaluated against the generalizing, nomothetic perspective of anthropology's comparative project.

Patricia McAnany's paper develops archaeological evidence in the light of ethnohistoric information about traditional Maya agricultural methods and land tenure. The ethnohistoric evidence indicates that traditional Maya cultivation was not, as often has been argued, based on swiddening, but rather involved fixed-plot agriculture. These fields were inherited, and possession of them was validated by appeal to one's ancestors. Turning to the archaeological evidence, McAnany demonstrates that forest clearance in the vicinity of Formative period K'axob was followed by the conversion of certain residential platforms into status-linked ceremonial structures, structures which were subsequently converted into burial shrines. These structures are interpreted as "creating a genealogy of place . . . linked to the transmission of resources between generations." They materialize, in the sense of De Marrais et al. (1996), an elite's claim to preferential access to improved land.

Timothy Earle's discussion of the development of land tenure in Hawaii is explicitly set within an evolutionist framework defined by Lockeian notions of property: as the exploitation of land is intensified, claims to that land become more exclusive. Ethnohistoric evidence is clear that in the late 18th century Hawaiian chiefs claimed ownership of all the land, had overseers that managed improved land (irrigation systems and terraced dryland fields), and extracted tribute from commoners permitted to cultivate it. Earle argues that this system developed as follows: The initial settlement of the islands would have relied mainly on extensive dry farming for subsistence, but as population expanded deforestation and erosion led to increased competition over land between communities and at the same time increased the areas of valley-bottom alluvium suitable for irrigation. Chiefs, who had achieved their preeminence in warfare over land, consolidated their power by organizing the construction of irrigation systems and dryland terraces, resource spaces whose productivity would attach primary producers to them over the long term.

In the face of problematic ethnohistoric evidence on the property system of the Inka empire, Cathy Costin's paper deploys archaeological evidence to show that rural communities, the state, and elites and their institutions they belonged to each held independent usufruct rights to resources, such as clay, metal, and building-stone. Clearly, even in a setting in which there was no market in real property and in which the state could override the claims of local communities or other institutions, there was a differentiated access to resources sufficiently stable to show clear distinctions in the archaeological record. Costin's reasonable view that usufruct rights constitute a proxy for privilege-rights opens useful methodological avenues for other archaeologists.

Michael Hudson's contribution shows the importance of debt foreclosure as a means of developing private landholdings in Bronze Age Mesopotamia and in the Byzantine Empire. Hudson envisages a property regime with two main sectors, public (temple and palace) and collective (the mass of the population). Through their kin groups, commoners gained access to the land needed to support themselves and to meet their corvée and military service obligations to the state. Wealthy families could loan money to commoners in difficulties in exchange for usufruct rights to the land, the commoners becoming in effect sharecroppers on their own land. Hudson does not discuss the origins of the wealth that permitted some families to make loans to others—presumably temple and palace officials could divert some of the income they managed for their own benefit, and warfare also would have provided opportunities for differential enrichment. He concentrates, rather, on the long-term damage of such indebtedness to the citizens directly and to the state, which could not count on the indebted for military and other service. Rulers issued Clean Slate proclamations cancelling debts and returning land usufruct rights to commoners so as to restore the capacity of commoners to contribute their public service, but their repeated issuance demonstrates the importance of the debt mechanism for the expansion of private property holdings in the ancient world.

Paul Durrenberger's paper uses the "Free State" of Medieval Iceland as an illustration of Fried's (1967) argument that private property requires state institutions. Iceland was settled in the 9th century by Norwegian chiefs fleeing the imposition of a feudal state in their homeland. Upon arrival these leaders claimed the best land for themselves and allocated other land to their followers. By the early 10th century the settlement of the island was complete, and leaders could only expand their holdings at the expense of others. In the absence of state institutions that could settle disputes between them (institutions that would cost them the independence they had emigrated from Norway to maintain), the chiefs fought one another until only one controlled the entire island. This case presents interesting parallels to the Hawaiian case discussed by Earle, with the difference that thuggery was unaccompanied by investment as a strategy to raise chiefly income.

The focus of Andrew Fleming's paper is not on how elites aggrandize their private holdings, but on how commoners organize their collective ones. He posits a range of institutional settings for the exploitation of communal property: commons may be collective, managed, or competitive. Analysis of toponyms and of surviving field systems permits Fleming to reconstruct the early Medieval commons system in Swaledale as closer to the collective end of the cooperative/competitive range. At the same time, he can discern significant differences in property regimes between Norse-occupied western and English-occupied eastern Swaledale, with a greater emphasis on individual holdings (cf. Durrenberger, this volume) in the former area. Fleming shows how one can contextualize the rationality of individuals beyond the simplicities of game theoretical models.

Antonio Gilman's paper tries to draw together the methodological approaches developed by various of the contributors to this volume so as to suggest that even in completely prehistoric contexts one can suggest differences in property regimes. Paralleling Earle's approach, he suggests that comparative ethnology is consonant with a Lockeian view of property development: as production systems are intensified, property holdings become more exclusive. The predictions which such a model makes for particular prehistoric cases based on the nature of production (an area of human activity relatively susceptible to archaeological reconstruction) can be tested by examining patterns of the consumption and expenditure of elites and non-elites (the approaches respectively adopted by McAnany, Costin, and Earle and by Fleming in this volume).

References Cited

Cowgill, G.L.
1975 On causes and consequences of ancient and modern population changes. *American Anthropologist* 77:505-25.

De Marrais, E., L.J. Castillo, & T. Earle
1996 Ideology, materialization, and power strategies. *Current Anthropology* 37(1):15-31.

Fried, M.H.
1967 *The Evolution of Political Society: An Essay in Political Anthropology*. New York: Random House.

Chapter Six

ཙ྇ཡ

Obscured by the Forest: Property and Ancestors in Lowland Maya Society

Patricia A. McAnany

An Archaeological Perspective on Property

Property is something that is claimed—by individuals, by families, by kin groups, by lords, and ultimately by sovereign political units. As Robert Hunt discusses (this volume), complex webs of duties, rights, and privileges link individuals, and their labor, to that which is claimed: that being a host of material things ranging from land to personal ornamentation. As an archaeologist, my approach to property is overtly evolutionary or transformational. That is, I am interested in the general trend toward increasingly restrictive property rights as it relates to the emergence of institutionalized inequality.

Unlike researchers who deal with living systems in which behavior can be directly observed (although generally not totally understood), archaeologists infer property relations from corollary material remains. We often construct models, ethnographically or ethnohistorically derived, against which archaeological data can be examined. In this respect, archaeological research on the subject of property is a first-order derivative, for "property" per se is never directly excavated archaeologically, but rather, property relations are inferred from the analysis of material remains.

For these reasons, this chapter deals primarily with the detection of changing relationships between people and the material things they claim, whether those claims were lodged by virtue of labor invested or through societal principles of inheritance. I focus specifically on land resources and changing patterns of land tenure. As the definition proffered in the opening sentence of this chapter intimates, a liberal definition of the term property is employed here. To my mind the term need not be restricted to a capitalist mode of production within which material things are bought and sold or otherwise alienable. In other words, I use the term property as a concept which refers not only to things which are claimed but also to the social, economic, and ritual context within which such claims exist.

I ask the reader to take a long and broad view of property by considering forms of land tenure among ancient and contemporary Maya of Mesoamerica. Employing a *longue durée* perspective (Braudel 1980), I examine the tempo and trajectory of changing property relations in Formative Maya society (800 B.C.-A.D. 250). I suggest that one of the most sensitive and diagnostic indicators of more restrictive forms of resource access is the institution of ancestor veneration. This effectively locks access to parcels of land within individual families and kin segments. Ethnographic and ethnohistoric materials from the Maya region attest to the focal importance of ancestor veneration in matters of land. Due to the complete and erroneous acceptance of expansive milpa agriculture (analogous to swidden or slash-and-burn farming) as the dominant form of lowland, tropical farming, however, more restrictive forms of property relations have often been overlooked, first by ethnohistorians and then by archaeologists, in order to build a simplified, monolithic model of ancient and contemporary Maya land tenure—one that would contrast nicely with the intricacies of Classic Maya hieroglyphic writing and sculptural tradition. Property relations, furthermore, can be perceived as a type of palimpsest in which more inclusive forms are partially but never totally overwritten by less inclusive arrangements. This process can reverse itself in times of societal collapse—sixteenth-century Yucatán being a case in point. The Formative Maya site of K'axob, Belize, provides a case study in which less inclusive arrangements, the *sine qua non* of emergent inequality, are inferred by reference to corollary changes in house form, burial patterns, and macrobotanical remains.

Property in the Maya Region

Is a forest a tract of communal-use land or is it an inherited fallow field? Traditionally inhabitants of temperate environments have answered this simple question in favor of the former assertion. As we shall see below, however, there is much reason to believe that tenth-century dwellers of the tropical Yucatán would have answered in favor of the latter definition. This discrimination lies at the heart of our studies of Maya property relations as the following example illustrates. In a Yucatec document of 1561 and another on the reverse of the "same sheet . . . is recorded an individual title to a tract of land and its conveyance 'to the principal men of the town here at Ebtun.' The vendor states that it is the 'title of the forest of my ancestors'" (Roys 1943: 37). From the many litigious land documents of the town of Ebtun, ethnohistorian Ralph Roys transcribed the following Maya testimony: "*ti yet . . . u [mah]antic kax u manab tu than lae yume hex talbal kax*," which he translated simply as "This, lord, is an inherited forest" (Roys 1939: 265).

Upon closer inspection of these statements and others, however, it becomes evident that the Yucatec Maya of the Colonial period perceived their land-tenure system to be one in which rights were inherited through an ancestral line and in which boundaries of lands were carefully noted. The translation cited above is from the Titles of Ebtun, a collection of Colonial-period documents recorded between 1600 and 1823 and maintained by people of the eastern Yucatec town of Ebtun. These records chronicle a series of land agreements and surveys defining (1) the contested provincial boundaries between Cupul towns and those of Sotuta and Cochuah; (2) the boundaries separating town or lineage lands of Ebtun and Kaua from those of Cuncunul, Tekom, and Tixcacalcupul; and (3) the 182-year legal battle for the recovery of the Tontzimin tract, which had been sold to an "outsider" (Roys 1939: 51). The testimony was given by Lorenzo Tus who, in 1713, spoke of his right to two tracts of inherited land despite his lack of supporting legal documentation. The term "inherited" as used by the Colonial Maya seems meant to convey a precedent of prior rights to certain agricultural fields, going back several generations and possibly to pre-Hispanic times. Yet, the phrase is translated simply as "This, lord, is an inherited forest," with the Yucatec Maya word *kax* being translated simply as "forest." The same translation (*kax* as "forest") is employed hundreds of times throughout the translation of this and other documents. In using the word "forest," Roys evokes an image of unspoiled wilderness, a great place to go deer hunting, for instance, but not a place of agricultural lands that may be in various stages of fallow. In terms of property issues, Roys's choice of words evokes a notion of communal resources rather than more restricted kin-based property. Is this an accurate translation of what Lorenzo Tus meant when he used the word *kax*? Or is it a translation that obscures the restrictive characteristics of Maya land use, tenure, and inheritance? The Yucatec Maya Cordemex dictionary (Barrera Vásquez 1980: 387) suggests multiple meanings for the term *kax* including "*bosque*" (forest or woods), "*arboleda*" (grove), "*montaña o monte*" (mountain forest or thicket regrowth), "*campo donde hay monte*" (an agricultural field in which there is thicketlike regrowth), and "*selva*" (rain forest). The variety of definitions suggests that the word *kax* has many meanings, only some of which are what we in English call a "forest." A compound expression, *u k'axil kab*, appears in the earlier Motul dictionary. This expression is defined as "*monte para colmenas, bueno para colmenas*" (Martínez Hernández 1929: 241), or a fallow field in whose regrowth makesit a good place for beehives. My main point here is that *kax* has several meanings, and most of the instances of *kax* in documents should be translated as fallow field, not forest.

In the lowland Maya region, consequently, fields exist in the "forest," or *kax*. As the term *kax* has no satisfactory equivalent expression in Spanish or English, there is a cognitive dissonance to the thought and translation process—a dissonance which, I suggest, has contributed to a gross oversimplification of our conceptualization of the structure of lowland agriculture and of Maya principles of property. Earlier scholars, in fact, often delighted in contrasting the sophistication of Maya hieroglyphic script with the purported simplicity of contemporary and past farming techniques (e.g., Roys 1943: 38; cf. Turner 1978). Often not factored into the "timeless model" of Maya milpa farming was the fact that five hundred years of slavery, servitude, debt peonage, and massive population reduction and relocation had altered patterns of land use and tenure and stripped them down to all but the essential human : land relationship. In the tropics, the most basic form of farming is some variant of slash-and-burn agriculture, which became a prevalent practice during late Colonial and ethnographic times. A relatively recent revision within Maya archaeology has entailed the amplification of Classic Maya agricultural techniques to include wetland reclamation, terracing, and orchard cultivation—all of which require long-term labor investment (Fedick 1994; Gómez-Pompa et al. 1990; Harrison & Turner 1978; Pohl 1990; and Turner 1983, among others). In the wake of this revision, however, no re-evaluation of the organization of land tenure or of property relations has been attempted. As I have suggested elsewhere (McAnany 1995), the farmlands of most Classic, Postclassic, and even early Colonial Maya peoples most likely were part of a kin-controlled fixed-plot system and were as carefully anchored in time and space as were Maya calendrics. A translation that might capture the true sentiment of the above testimony by Lorenzo Tus is as follows: "This, lord, is a fixed field that I inherited from my father and grandfather; at present it lies fallow."

Ancestors and Property

Many anthropologists have noted the complex interweave between restrictive forms of property relations and rituals of propitiation directed at specific ancestors (Fortes 1965, 1976; Freedman 1966; Goody 1962). Ancestors, it seems, give credence to the notion that a family, or a lineage, has preferential access to lands and other property claims. It is by means of ancestors, furthermore, that resource inequalities are transmitted generationally. Thus, it is somewhat ironic that the practice of ancestor veneration—which is highly conservative and heavily vested in precedent—is also at the base of dramatic social transformation.

In the Maya region, ancestors define a notion of place, of residential centrality, both in the past and today. For instance, Shelton Davis (1970: 80) describes residential units among K'anjobal-speaking Mam of Huehuetenango in highland Guatemala as having an unusually large or prominent structure called *yatut jichmam* ("house of the ancestor"). Within land-holdings, or *tx'otx jichmam*, which Davis (1970: 84) refers to as ancestor estates, "residents were joined together in a single religious community wherein prayer to the dead ancestors perpetuated the fertility of lands which the living gained through inheritance." Thus, among these highland Maya people, home is integrally related to land-holdings, and ancestors dwell metaphorically in the former and safeguard the latter. The principle that ancestors are the guardians of fields and forests as well as the continued occupants of residential structures is also prevalent among the Quiche, who maintain lineage shrines (Bunzel 1952; Carmack 1981; Tedlock 1982), and among the Tzotzil Maya, who venerate ancestors at shrines strategically positioned on the landscape (Vogt 1969, 1976)

The house, the place of the ancestors, is the heart and the nucleus of a tropical farming system. Handed down from generation to generation, the domicile was often perceived as belonging to the ancestors (Bunzel 1952). During the Classic period, pyramidal structures also were named the *nah*, or house of specific royal ancestors (S. Houston and D. Stuart, personal communication 1994). During pre-Hispanic times, significant progenitors were buried under the floors of residences throughout the Maya region. We have reason to believe that this interment of ancestors within the construction mass of a dwelling not only cemented the transmission of property between generations but also provided "habeas corpus" proof of a history of use rights. As such, the treatment of ancestors—recoverable archaeologically—may be a key to understanding another domain—property relations—which cannot be directly recovered.

Formative-Period K'axob: An Archaeological Case Study

An archaeological investigation of the trajectory toward more restrictive patterns of property relations was undertaken at the Maya site of K'axob in Belize, Central America, during the years of 1990 to 1993 (fig. 1). Archaeological documentation of changes in house form, burial patterns, and macrobotanical remains was collected from deposits dating to the Formative period (800 B.C.-A.D. 250). These three classes of information, it was reasoned, might be sensitive to changes in patterns of land use and inheritance. For many archaeological sites in the Maya lowlands, one can argue that the prior history of construction strongly affected the nature and composition of later architecture. At K'axob, the platforms which attain the greatest size and elaboration during the Classic period are those with Formative-period cores. For instance, a large, 6 x 8 m excavation in front of Structure 18 (fig. 2) uncovered nearly 2000 years of construction activity as represented by three meters of sequential floor and platform constructions. This area is the ancestral core of K'axob. The earliest levels, dating to ca. 700 B.C., contained a series of domestic structures and facilities: a house with an adjacent kitchen, sherd-lined

Figure 1. The Maya region showing the location of K'axob and other selected archaeological sites, Mayan language groups (in italics), and historically known Maya political provinces (boldface italics).

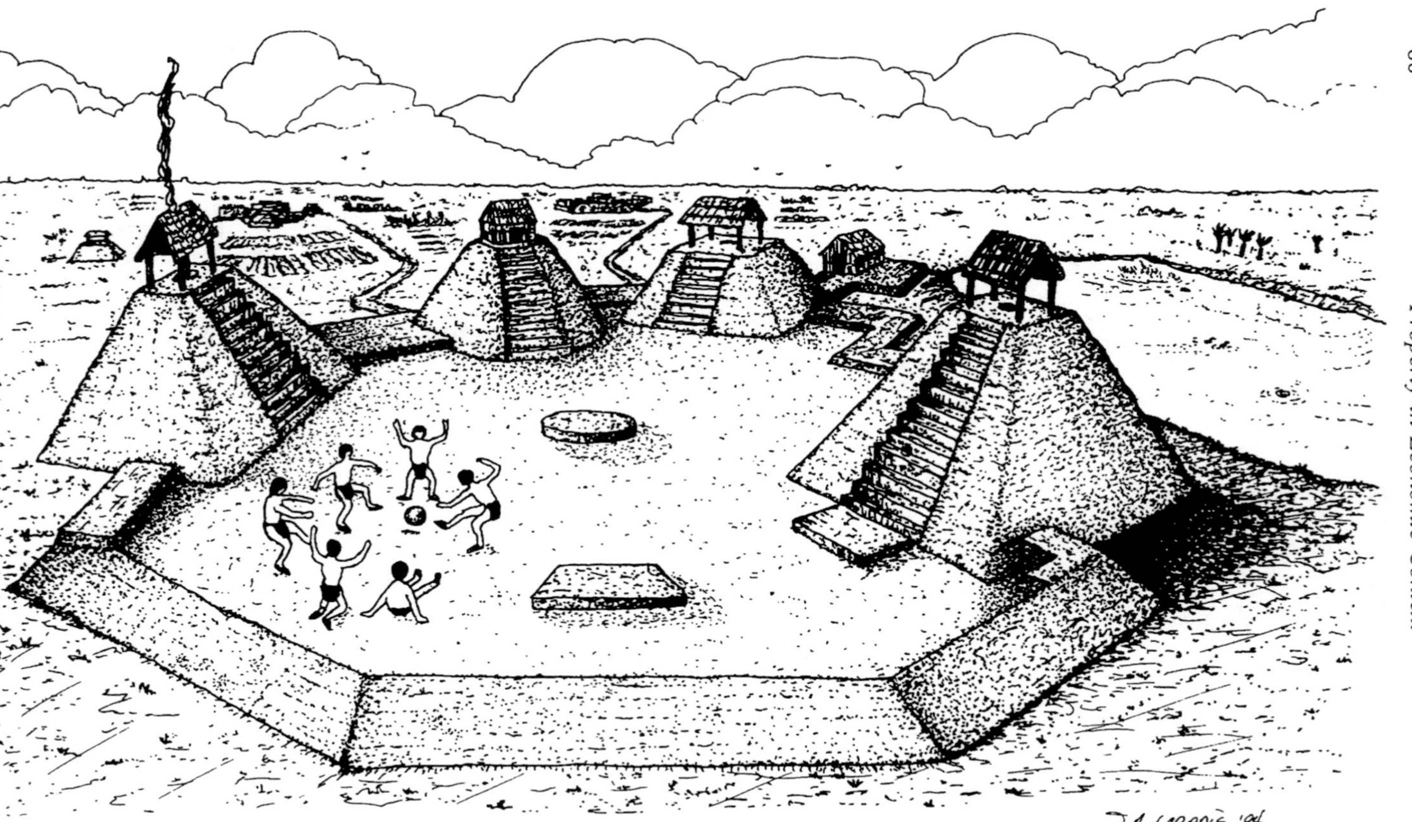

Figure 2. K'axob, Plaza B, as it may have looked during the Late Classic. The pyramid on the right side is Structure 18 under which the ancestral core of K'axob was found (drawing by John A. Labadie).

cooking-pits, midden deposits, and simple extended burials. As time went by, more individuals were interred under the floors of sequential structures at this location.

Around 200 B.C., this locale became less residential and more ritualistic. A platform was built to replace the ground-level structures, there were fewer sherd-lined pits, and individuals increasingly were buried in a tightly flexed position in small, circular pits. The small, well-made, and intricately decorated serving vessels of earlier times gave way to simpler and larger vessels with softer paste. Detailed decoration of ceramics was replaced by flamboyant shapes and striking decoration, such as large flat-bottomed flaring-rim bowls painted with a simple cross on the vessel base. One receives the impression that the social context in which these vessels were used had changed from small-group to large-group interaction.

Around 100 B.C., the Formative-period floor units and platforms were sealed by the construction of a thick plaza floor into which a burial pit was intruded. Repeated reopening of this place of interment is indicated by the disturbed condition of the "collar" which lined the pit. At some point, a low altar or shrine was built over the grave. Ultimately, this context contained seven individuals who spanned a range of ages; most of them had been added as secondary interments (fig. 3). This shrine appears to be a family burial crypt—possibly an example of what Southall (1988: 65) would term "kinship elites." Later, a Classic-period pyramid was built over this "layer cake" of house constructions and ancestor interments.

Other excavations at K'axob have revealed Late Formative "burials" that are so temporally and contextually connected with the raising of a new structure that their stratigraphic position is between an old and a new building (Henderson 1994; McCormack 1994). Burial of ancestors, therefore, seems to have been used to mark the termination of an older structure's use life and the commencement of a new one, creating a genealogy of place (de Certeau 1984) that may be directly linked to the transmission of resources between generations.

When these architectural and burial patterns are viewed against macrobotanical remains, an interesting trend is revealed. Preliminary results of wood charcoal remains from Formative contexts at K'axob indicate that wholesale removal of the climax rain forest probably did not occur until the end of the Middle Formative, or around 400 B.C. (Muhl Davis 1994). That is, climax and late successional tree species

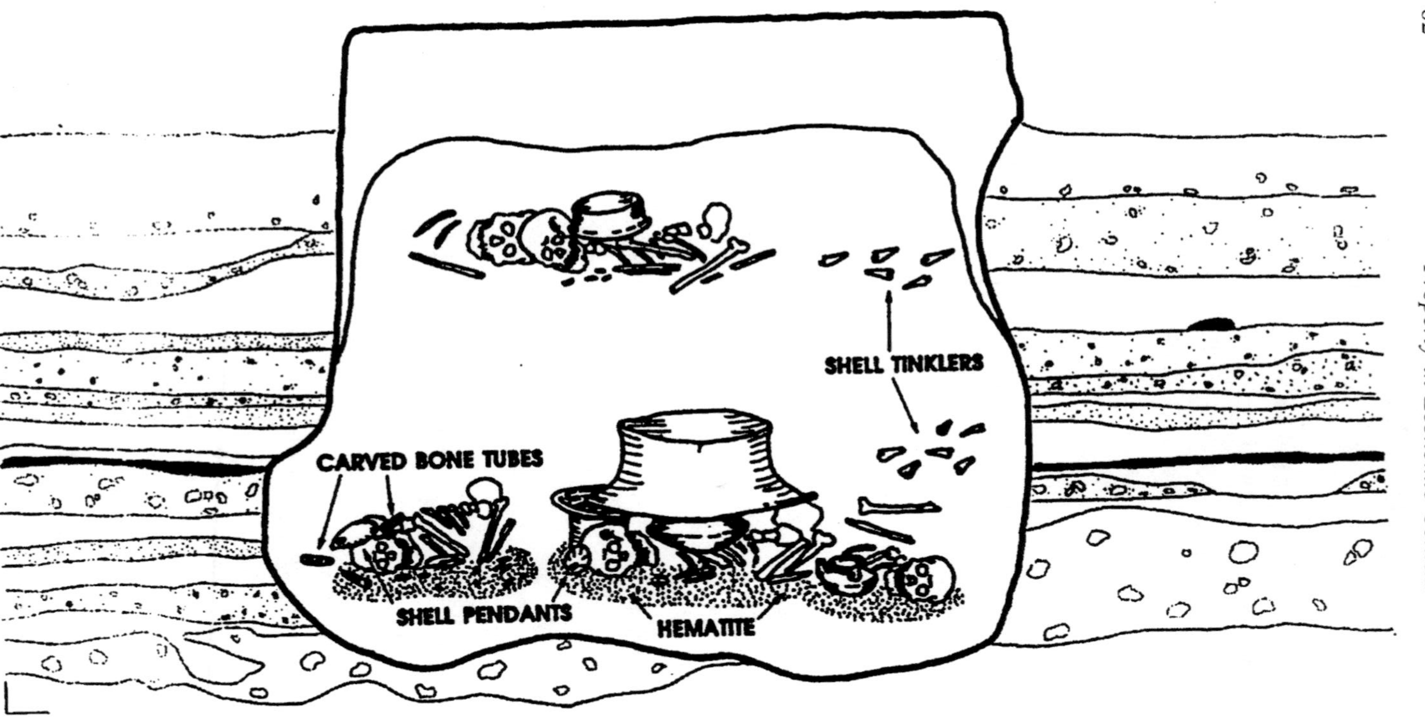

Figure 3. Idealized cross-section of a multiple-burial interment burial shrine from K'axob (drawing by John Walkey).

were present throughout Middle Formative times. On the other hand, firewood collected from nearby swamp, savannas, and economic tree species were dominant during Late Formative times. While we cannot be certain, it does seem probable that the disappearance of climax species wood charcoal from the macrobotanical record signals the onset of a short-fallow, fixed-plot agrarian system. Approximately 200 years elapsed between this environmental transition and the architectural transition to status-linked platform construction; almost 300 years passed until the first clearly identifiable ancestor shrine was constructed. Such constructions may be thought of as proxy indicators of social and economic inequality, or minimally of differentiation, within the settlement of Formative K'axob. They occur primarily at the ancestral core of K'axob beneath the large plaza of a Late Classic pyramid group (see fig. 2). The temporal precedence of the wholesale clearing of the ambient forest lands suggests that the restructuring of property relations into more restrictive forms is a measured response to a tropical-style "closure" of common lands.

Discussion

The manner in which the living relate to the dead is dependent upon the needs of society within a specific place and time. For the pre-Roman Iron Age of Europe, Pearson (1993) has suggested that the increasing incorporation of the dead into the world of the living indicates a growing concern with lineage and individual status. Elsewhere, Morris (1991) has reviewed Saxe's claim that the emergence of formal cemeteries corresponds to the appearance of agnatic lineages monopolizing vital resources through inheritance. Here, I suggest that significant changes in patterns of burial and architecture presage the formalization of a restricted form of resource control and of changes in property relations that increasingly placed inherited use rights in the "hands" of specific families. This societal transformation is one pathway to inequality.

This scenario is bolstered by ethnohistoric sources which indicate the extent to which restrictive forms of land tenure and inherited property existed historically in Yucatec Maya society (even though forested fields have not always been identified as farm plots). Ethnographic accounts, furthermore, point to the inextricable linkage between the creation of ancestors and the tradition of inherited property. Finally, recently unearthed excavation data from K'axob reveal the deep roots of this tradition and its linkage to emergent inequality. Whether by scholarly misperception or by the natural process of re-vegetation of an abandoned pre-Hispanic Maya village, property relations in Maya society truly have been obscured by the forest.

Acknowledgments

Field research at K'axob was supported by National Science Foundation Grant BNS-9112310 and the College of Liberal Arts and Office of International Programs at Boston University. I am immensely grateful to all who worked on the excavation and analysis of K'axob materials. Interpretations of the material are my own, however, and I accept full responsibility for any errors or misperceptions.

References Cited

Barrera Vásquez, A. (ed.)
1980 *Diccionario Maya Cordemex*. Mérida: Ediciones Cordemex.

Braudel, F.
1980 *On History*. Chicago: University of Chicago Press.

Bunzel, R.
1952 *Chichicastenango: A Guatemalan Village* (Publications of the American Ethnological Society. 12). Seattle: University of Washington Press.

Carmack, R.M.
1981 *The Quiche Mayas of Utatlan*. Norman: University of Oklahoma Press.

Davis, S.H.
1970 Land of Our Ancestors: A Study of Land Tenure and Inheritance in the Highlands of Guatemala. Unpublished Ph.D. dissertation, Harvard University.

de Certeau, M.
1984 *The Practice of Everyday Life*. Berkeley: University of California Press.

Fedick, S.L.
1994 Ancient Maya agricultural terracing in the upper Belize River area: computer-aided modeling and the results of initial field investigations. *Ancient Mesoamerica* 5(1):107-27.

Fortes, M.
1965 Some reflections on ancestor worship. In M. Fortes & G. Dieterlen (eds.), *African Systems of Thought*, pp. 122-44. London: Oxford University Press.
1976 An introductory commentary. In W.H. Newell (ed.), *Ancestors*, pp. 1-16. Paris: Mouton.

Freedman, M.
1966 *Chinese Lineage and Society: Fukien and Kwangtung* (London School of Economics, Monographs on Social Anthropology, 33). New York: Athlone Press.

Gómez-Pompa, A., J. Salvador Flores, & M. Aliphat Fernández
1990 The sacred cacao groves of the Maya. *Latin American Antiquity* 1:247-57.

Goody, J.
1962 *Death, Property and the Ancestors: A Study of the Mortuary Customs of the LoDagaa of West Africa*. London: Tavistock Publications.

Harrison, P.D., & B.L. Turner II (eds.)
1978 *Pre-Hispanic Maya Agriculture*. Albuquerque: University of New Mexico Press.

Henderson, H.H.
1994 Operation XII excavation report, the 1993 winter season at K'axob, Belize. MS in possession of author.

Martínez Hernández, J.
1929 *Diccionario de Motul: Maya Español*. Mérida: Compañía Tipográfica Yucateca.

McAnany, P.A.
1995 *Living with the Ancestors: Kinship and Kingship in Ancient Maya Society*. Austin: University of Texas Press.

McCormack, V.
1994 Field report of excavations at Operation XI, K'axob project. MS in possession of author.

Morris, I.
1991 The archaeology of ancestors: the Saxe/Goldstein hypothesis revisited. *Cambridge Archaeological Journal* 1(2):147-69.

Muhl Davis, M.
1994 The preliminary analysis of wood charcoal from the Maya site of K'axob. MS in possession of author.

Pearson, M.P.
1993 The powerful dead: archaeological relationships between the living and the dead. *Cambridge Archaeological Journal* 3(2):203-29.

Pohl, M.D. (ed.)
1990 *Ancient Maya Wetland Agriculture: Excavations on Albion Island, Northern Belize*. Boulder: Westview Press.

Roys, R.L.
1939 *The Titles of Ebtun* (Carnegie Institution of Washington, Publication 505). Washington: Carnegie Institution of Washington.
1943 *The Indian Background of Colonial Yucatan*. (Carnegie Institution of Washington, Publication 548). Washington: Carnegie Institution of Washington.

Southall, A.
1988 The segmentary state in Africa and Asia. *Comparative Studies in Society and History* 30:52-82.

Tedlock, B.
1982 *Time and the Highland Maya*. Albuquerque: University of New Mexico Press.

Turner II, B.L.

1978 The development and demise of the swidden thesis of Maya agriculture. In P.D. Harrison and B.L. Turner II (eds.), *Pre-Hispanic Maya Agriculture*, pp. 13-22. Albuquerque: University of New Mexico Press.

1983 *Once Beneath the Forest: Prehistoric Terracing in the Rio Bec Region of the Maya Lowlands*. Dellplain Latin American Studies, 13. Boulder: Westview.

Vogt, E.Z.

1969 *Zinacantan: A Maya Community in the Highlands of Chiapas*. Cambridge, MA: Belknap Press.

1976 *Tortillas for the Gods: A Symbolic Analysis of Zinacanteco Rituals*. Cambridge, MA: Harvard University Press.

Chapter Seven

Property Rights and the Evolution of Hawaiian Chiefdoms

Timothy Earle

Rights in property and people underlie the evolution of human society. Complex social institutions depend on a political economy to finance their operation. Mobilization for the political economy in return requires institutions to control human labor, and the simplest and most direct means to do this is through a system of land tenure that designates productive lands as chiefly property. Elementally a commoner family must have access to a farming plot (or other subsistence resource) that they can work for sustenance. If an emerging elite gains control over these resources, the lord can direct the lives of dependent commoners. In the Hawaiian chiefdoms, for example, the chief's land managers (*konohiki*) frequently spoke of "putting to work" the ordinary people (*maka'ainana*). A simple "reciprocity," of sorts, was established that allocated use rights in subsistence plots in exchange for tribute in products or corvée labor.

A system of land allocation directed by a ruling elite is fundamental to many chiefdoms and states (Earle 1991b). The emergence of the complex Hawaiian chiefdoms illustrates how hierarchical allocation of use rights constitutes the dimension of property basic to the emergence of political power. The long-term evolutionary dynamic created new relations of production based on these property rights. The simple question that I seek to answer in this paper is: how can elites, counter to the inherent interests of the numerically dominant commoner segment, assert ownership over land and other resources needed for the commoner's very life?

A Matter of Definitions

The 1994 Spring Meeting of the Society for Economic Anthropology reevaluated key concepts related to property. *Webster's Third New International Dictionary* provides two definitions; (1) a property is a quality of an object or land; (2) a property is the object or estate that is owned by individuals or groups. The first definition emphasizes the character of things that determines how they act or function. In this sense, property in human society is often viewed as a jural principle governing the relationship between people and things. The second definition emphasizes the things themselves, wealth and estates, that are possessed by people. Both definitions stress a dynamic interplay between people and things, but differ in the importance they place on the primary determinant of the relationship, either the society (or social structure) or the things themselves. From the difference in emphasis within anthropology have emerged divergent structuralist and materialist perspectives on property.

Following a structuralist, or legalist, tradition, Duran Bell (in this volume) draws a critical distinction between rights of person, such as citizenship, which are considered inalienable, and rights of property, such as house ownership, which are alienable. As he sees it, traditional societies (all noncapitalist societies) emphasize social relationships between people defining rights in objects and land. With the rise of capitalism and its commoditization of objects, things become separated from people and transferable in market transactions. For him, and for others at the 1994 SEA meeting, property (or private property) is a product of the new social relationships of capitalism. This simple distinction between traditional and modern societies and economies harks back to the structuralist position of Polanyi's (1944) *Great Transformation*.

Following a materialist, or evolutionary, position, I emphasize that properties are cultural things created as products of human economies and that they have potential attributes linked to the evolving nature of the human economy and the society which produce them. Except in the smallest-scale societies, things take on a critical role as the physical manifestation of social relationships and the rights entailed. Therefore, the changing character of things in human society must be considered when viewing the evolution of a concept such as property. In turn, as the nature of things (property) is transformed, dynamics of the economy change correspondingly. I start with the premise that property (the bundle of rights related to and materialized in things) is deeply rooted in human history and that the evolution of property rights is closely tied to the evolution of the political economy and to the organization of human societies and politics more broadly.

In the discussion, I concentrate on rights in productive resources (land) necessary for a human group's livelihood. Property can be conceived as possessing four attributes of "ownership" as follows: the right to use a resource, the right to inherit it in a socially determined manner, the right to allocate its use to others, and the right to alienate or transfer all rights to another. These rights associate as attributes of four ideal land tenure types that lie along a continuum: open access, commons, fief, and private property. These may be associated fairly directly with evolutionary levels of sociopolitical integration: family level, local groups, chiefdom, and nation state (Table 1).

Table 1
Types of Property (Land Tenure) and Their Associated Rights

PROPERTY TYPES	use	inheritance	allocation	alienability	**SOCIETAL TYPE**
open access	+				family level
commons	+	+			local group
fief	+	+	+		chiefdom/ state
private	+	+	+	+	nation state

An *open access resource* is simply that, open to anyone who comes to use it. It is often considered "natural," little modified or improved by human use. A *commons* is a resource held for use by members of a group "in common" and inherited within the structure that determines the social group's membership. Commons are minimally modified and subdivided lands, but they are frequently defined in the landscape by walls or recognized landmarks. A *fief* is held by a individual or institution that receives the fief through allocation or inheritance. The owner of a fief has the right to allocate use rights to others, characteristically in a hierarchical and overlapping fashion. The land is characteristically tied to the political or religious institutions of society. Land is usually carefully measured such that the boundaries are definite and marked in the landscape. Internally it is subdivided and often includes substantial capital improvements such as walls, prepared fields, terraces, and irrigation systems. A *private property* is held by an individual, or institution, who has the rights to use, bequeath, allocate, give, and sell the resource. In contrast to a fief, the ability to alienate the land through exchange is the defining attribute. Private property carries with it a legal document declaring exclusive ownership rights.

The association of these forms of property with different evolutionary types, economies, and political organizations, can be illustrated within the framework of increasing levels of integration: family level, local group, regional chiefdom and state, and modern nation state (Johnson & Earle 1987). The *family level*, as typified by the !Kung San (Lee 1979) and the Machiguenga (Johnson & Earle 1987: 65-83), contains highly flexible family clusters that position themselves opportunistically in the environment as resource availability changes. Family-level groups are not associated with marked and delimited resources; they are associated with repeatedly used home ranges. By and large resources are minimally modified and unrestricted, open to families or individuals who come by. Although an individual must establish a kin (or fictive kin) bond to some member of a resident camp or hamlet, social networks are sufficiently extensive and overlapping that use rights are open to all from a large region.

The *local group*, as typified by the Yanomamö (Chagnon 1968) or the Tsembaga Maring (Rappaport 1967), consists of settled villages or hamlet clusters. These enduring settlements are positioned close to their fields of shifting cultivation and other subsistence resources. The local group's territory is typically a commons held by the group or subgroup clan.

These territories are often marked off, as in the famous planting of the rumbim along the Tsembaga boundaries. Individuals retain personal use rights to plots within the territory as long as the plots are being farmed, but any group member can claim use of land not being actively cultivated. When the fields return to fallow, "ownership" reverts to the commons. This land-tenure system characterizes many agricultural populations that are organized along egalitarian principles. Group territories (clan or lineage lands) may be a response to intergroup competition and the need to exclude nonmembers from limited productive land. Increasing definition of individually held plots reflects the degree of intensification of land use; as fallows are eliminated, land never reverts to the commons, but is inherited individually by families (see Brown, in this volume).

The *chiefdom*, as exemplified by the Trobriand Islanders (Malinowski 1935) and Polynesian societies (Sahlins 1958; Kirch 1984), is a regionally organized political entity characterized by emergent stratification. Characteristically a community's land is similar to the commons held by a group and used by individual families. However, it becomes closely associated with the community leader (or chief), who retains rights to allocate the land to individuals (Earle 1991a). In return for use rights on the land, farmers provide a portion of their harvest, as in first fruits, or labor, to the chief. Often these lands have been significantly improved with facilities such as irrigation systems and these are in constant production. In complex chiefdoms, paramounts allocate community lands as fiefs to support high-ranking chiefs. As will be discussed for Hawaii, this land system underlies a tributary economy used by chiefs to finance the operation of the chiefdom.

The *state* covers a multiplicity of political forms, from the city states of the ancient Near East and the grand empires of the Old and New World to the nation states of the capitalist world. As would be expected, the nature of land tenure and property is variable both between and within the various types of states. Some states, such as the Inka, Near Eastern hydraulic states, feudal Europe, or even the former Soviet Union, retained a highly structured institutional form of land tenure as the basis for their tributary economies. Property can be used, inherited, and allocated, but not alienated; it is "owned" by institutions, not individuals.

But private property in land predated capitalism in many states where writing and formal legal systems were present. In the Middle East, in the heartland of hydraulic states, private lands and land transfers were apparently quite important (Adams 1984). As seen in the power struggles of medieval states, private ownership became a critical element in attempts by individual lords and factions to counter the central powers of the king. With the decentralization of economic power under European mercantilism and capitalism, individuals asserted specific rights in private property within the formal legal codes of emerging nation states. Private property, with rights of alienation, seems less a product of capitalism than a part of the formal legal systems with systems of writing used for contracts. The rights in lands existed on paper (or clay tablet) and were guaranteed by the state legal system; their defense no longer needed to be guaranteed by institutional ferocity. These properties, such as the industrial firms of British entrepreneurs or colonists' farms carved out of the forests of the New World, were idealized as things created by personal initiative and held exclusively by the individual.

In terms of the dichotomy made by Bell (this volume), the evolution of larger, more complex social forms is associated with a greater emphasis on the rights of property as opposed to the rights of person. In terms familiar to anthropologists, this transition shifted the nature of rights from those vested in a social persona (and determined by the roles and statuses that an individual holds within a social structure) to those vested in material things (firms, estates, and wealth). In fact, this transition is not a replacement of one system of rights by another but the creation of additional rights that become attached to property that can be transferred by allocation or alienation.

Why should this be? This paper explores why material things partly supersede persons as the repositories for rights in resources. Counter to Polanyi (1944) and, more immediately, to Bell, I do not see this change as caused by a one-time historical event, namely the rise of capitalism. Rather, capitalism is a continuation of long-term processes of social, political, and economic change. These processes involve the intensification of resource use, the institutionalizing of groups, the emergence of stratification, and the creation of large-scale polities. Increasingly rights vested in things became salient for these processes. As the landscape became increasingly transformed into a cultural artifact, property, as things, materialized the social and political system open to direct and strategic manipulation by individuals and social segments in their quests for power and political domination (De Marrais et al. 1996).

Some Theoretical Background

The central question is to explain the role of property rights in the evolutionary process. As part of my basic assumption, elaborated elsewhere, I see social stratification and larger-scale polities emerging as social segments concentrate control of power. The primary source of social power rests in control over the subsistence economy that permits the creation of a political economy used to finance emerging elite institutions (Earle 1987, 1991a, 1994).

My analysis begins with general theories of the political economy that see economic power emanating from ownership of land and capital. For England in the 19th century, Ricardo (1821) envisioned three social segments: workers, landowners, and capitalists. The lot of the working poor was desperate indeed. Competing with each other for limited jobs, their incomes were forced inexorably towards a base level adequate only to keep them alive (the Ricardian wage). Workers earned only enough to buy their bread and the meanest housing; they owned nothing. The other segments, the landed gentry and the capitalists, controlled their respective economic sectors through ownership, which permitted them to enrich themselves with material possessions and to maintain a high life style.

In *The German Ideology*, Marx and Engels (1965) assert that private ownership of productive resources, capital, gave industrialists a stranglehold on the political process. Ownership translated into an ability to alienate the surplus, beyond the Ricardian wage, from workers and then use these "profits" for class privilege, including the political domination of society. Thus ownership of the technology within an industrial economy translated directly into political control of society. For Marx, and many Marxists, the worst evils of human society stemmed from capitalism, namely restricted ownership of the new critical factor of production, capital technology.

The theory developed by Marx and Engels may have quite general evolutionary significance. The first principle, on which their analysis rests, can be extended broadly to understand the emergence of leadership among chiefdoms and nonindustrial states. Marx himself recognized this in part; feudalism was based on an explicit system of land ownership whereby serfs were tied to lordly lands. I argue that central power, whether comparatively strong or weak, derives in large measure from tenure restrictions ("ownership") on land and productive technology.

An example of this phenomenon is the "caging" effect of irrigation. In his comprehensive review of the sources of social power, Mann (1986) recognizes the importance of economic power, especially as seen in the hydraulic states of the Middle East. Here by irrigating the deserts, emerging ruling institutions provided productive farm lands to peasants. The construction of irrigation systems provided great opportunities for settlement and farming, but the institutional ownership of the land formed the foundation for a system of economic expropriation. Peasants had few opportunities for subsistence except through the plots provided by ruling institutions in return for their corvée labor.

In "An essay concerning the true origin, extent, and end of civil government," Locke (1947) conceived natural resources as open to all until an individual had improved them. Property was created by human labor, cutting the fields from the forest and enclosing it with fences. Ownership of property then rested with the person whose labor transformed the resource from nature to cultural thing. Locke held the ideal of private property, involving rights to inherit and alienate, against any governmental rights of the monarch or his government to co-opt or seize the land of individuals. The principle of private property, as articulated by Locke, was based on a simple theory that human labor invested in an object created ownership; as I will argue, similar ideals exist in many societies and help define the nature of social things.

As a very general principle in human societies, social labor creates property rights; the ownership of property rests within the individual or institution that makes a field, irrigation system, or monument. In fact, I believe that the transformed landscape of fields and monuments becomes a social map, or physical contract, that materializes relationships on which human societies become structured. Prior to the existence of written contracts, legal rights in land may have been literally sculpted on the land surface itself. *"Improvements" create cultural things that are handled in a cultural manner and provide the basis for economic power in a stratified society.*

But why does a culturally specific concept such as 'improvement' translate into a more broadly applicable principle for human societies? Quite simply, the technological improvement of the resource does two things. First, the improvements radically differentiate land in terms of quality. When specific lands are improved, they become much more productive and desirable than other locations in the same region. By financing the construction of the irrigation canals and maintaining warriors to defend them, ruling elites became the owners of the most productive lands. As Gilman (1976) argues for the emergence of social stratification in southeastern Spain, farmers became tethered to their land by the irrigation ditches and terraces that have improved the land and that would have been costly to replicate. Tied to their farms, commoners were subject to supervision and control by the regional elites, who could threaten eviction for nonpayment of tribute in labor and goods.

Second, land improvements evidently delimit and mark the resource in ways that can be easily represented, recognized, monitored, and defended. The walls, terraces, and ditches materialize the division of the landscape and form the basis of a cultural system of land ownership comparable to written contracts. The relationships between people are mapped onto the landscape in ways created and maintained by social labor organized within institutional settings. The physical landscape is difficult to change. It freezes relationships in ways that benefit the leaders and are constantly experienced in everyday life.

The Hawaiian Case

The Hawaiian Islands are a string of volcanic peaks, isolated from all other lands deep in the Pacific Ocean. The environment is a tropical paradise with warm weather and dramatic scenery. Hills support lush vegetation and tracery waterfalls. The sun is warm, cooled only by the trade winds.

At the time of first contact with the West, the political organization of the Hawaiian Islands was composed of competing complex chiefdoms (Earle 1978). Hawaiian society was rigidly divided into classes. The commoners were the rural farmers, fishermen, and craft producers. They lived in local communities (*ahupua'a*) that were often a river valley running from the mountains to the sea. Men toiled in the irrigated taro fields on the valley floors, worked the fishponds along the coast, and netted fish on the inner shore; women collected a wide range of wild foods and prepared the tapa cloth. Commoner genealogies were short, known only up to the grandparents. The basic social unit appears to have been the household with its house, fields, and family gear positioned within the local community.

The chiefs, in contrast, were organized hierarchically into ruling lineages from Kaua'i, Oahu, Maui, and Hawai'i. The paramount chief for an island was its sovereign. When he took office, by inheritance or through wars of succession, the paramount allotted the *ahupua'a* communities as fiefs to his supporting chiefs, usually close relatives or military supporters. Each community chief lived off the produce of his/her fief, and lower-ranked chiefs served as land managers (*konohiki*). While not required by the simple technology of the subsistence farmers, these managers organized on a daily basis the economic activities of the community. If an irrigation system needed construction or repair, the *konohiki*, as representative of the community's chief, organized the work project and the feast to follow. The *konohiki* also mobilized labor to collect the goods given annually to the paramount, representing the god Lono at the annual Makahiki ceremony that guaranteed the fertility of the soil and its people.

During the late 18th and early 19th centuries, Western explorers and merchants described irrigation systems along the valley streams of the Hawaiian Islands. The Russian explorer Kotzebue (1821: 340) was impressed:

> The artificial taro fields . . . excited my attention. Each of them forms a regular square of 160 feet, and is enclosed with stone all around like a basin. This field, or rather this pond, for such it really may be called, contains two feet of water, in the slimy bottom of which the taro is planted . . . ; each pond has two sluices, to let in the water on one side, and out again at the other, into the next field, and so on. The fields are gradually lower, and the same water which is led from a high spring or rivulet, can water a large plantation. . . . In the spaces between the fields, which are from three to six feet broad, there are very pleasant shady avenues, and on both sides banana and sugar-canes are planted. The taro fields afford another advantage; for the fish which are caught in distant streams thrive admirably when put in them.

As described by Menzies (1920: 29), botanist with George Vancouver, "the whole plantation is laid out with great neatness and is intersected by small banks." The technical sophistication and the orderliness of these irrigation systems evidently appealed immensely to the European sense of an organized landscape.

A typical irrigation system, some of which continued in use until recently, can be reconstructed as follows (fig. 1): Dams of loose stream cobbles and boulders were thrown up across the stream. Water backed

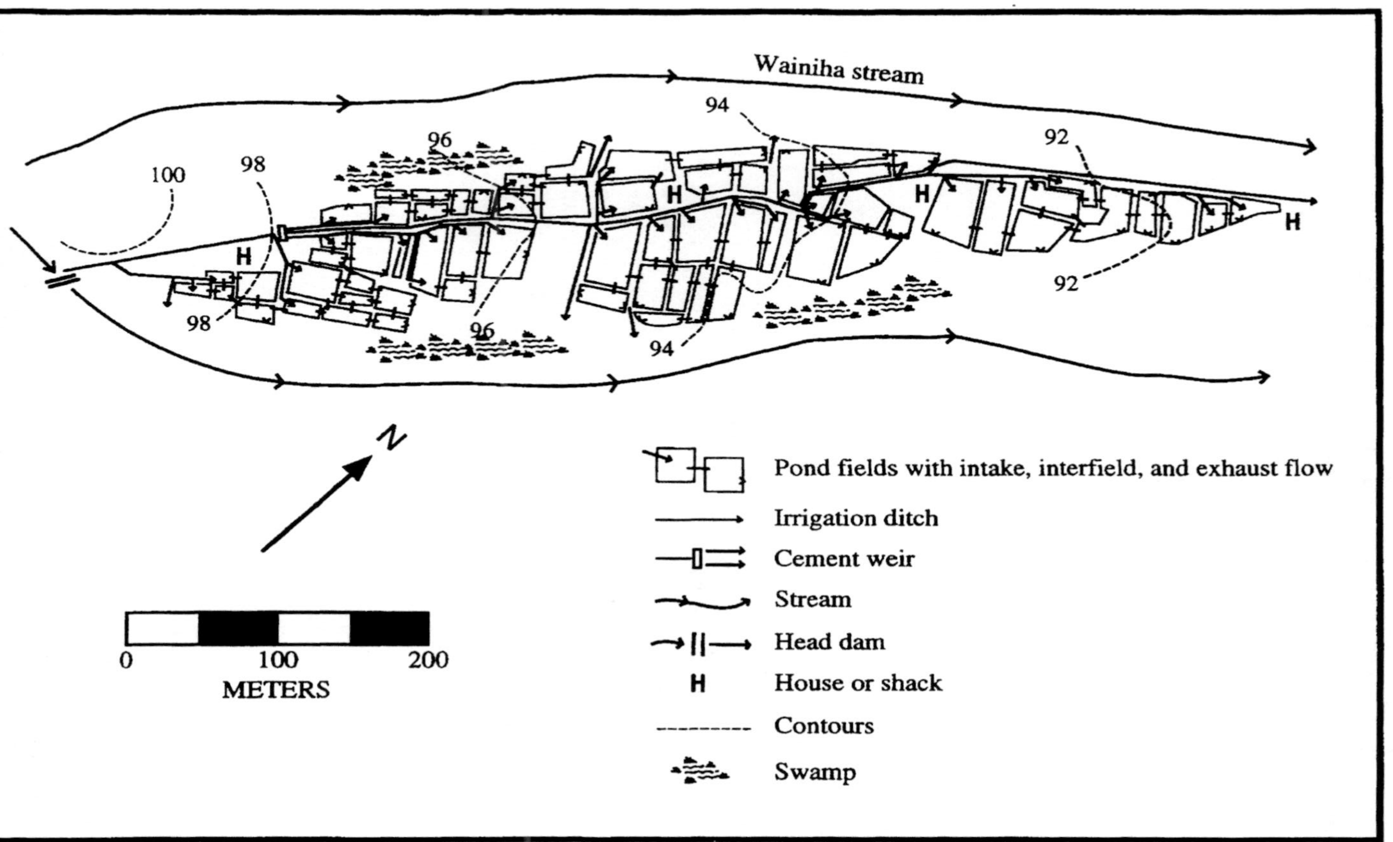

Figure 1. A traditional Hawaiian irrigation system in Wainiha, Kaua'i, as operating in 1972 (Earle 1978: Fig. 5.5).

up behind the percolation dam and was diverted into the main earthen ditch, which carried water 100 m or so to the fields. Water was then delivered to a pond field (*lo'i*) either directly from the central ditch or from a short secondary ditch. Each field was banked by an earthen bund, often reinforced with a stone retaining wall. Water was kept constantly flowing through the pond field and down the stair-stepped terraces, eventually returning to the stream. Taro, one of the world's most productive root crops, was planted in the pond. In the larger ponds at the base of an irrigation system, or in separate artificial ponds, fish were raised from fry. The overall agricultural technology was ingenious but technically uncomplicated.

Despite the fact that the small scale and elemental technology of these irrigation systems require little central management (Earle 1980), the Hawaiian *konohiki* oversaw construction, maintenance, and planting on them. Many accounts (Corney 1896; Stewart 1970: 142; I'i 1959: 68; Kamakau 1976: 34) describe the work crews that constructed the pond fields and prepared them for planting.

> "Food" and "fish" were brought to the scene of labor. . . . When the men had gathered—perhaps . . . several hundred—most of them were lined up at the lower bank of the patch. If the patch was 40 *anana* [40 m] in length, they were perhaps in two or three rows. Along the two shorter sides there might also be two or three rows [of men]. Then the embankments, the *kuauna*, were raised by heaping up dirt from below. . . . They heaped up the dirt to raise the embankment. . . . They stamped the sides facing the *lo'i* with their feet to straighten them, then beat in sugar cane tops. . . . To make firm the foundation underneath, they pounded in large flat rocks. . . . On the day of treading, the *lo'i* was filled with water, and the owner of the patch made ready plenty of "food" (poi), pork, and "fish." It was a great day for men, women, and children . . . [who] bedecked [themselves] with greenery and worked with all might. . . . This treading was done so that the water would not sink into the soil, and to allow the taro to grow. (Kamakau 1976: 34)

The important point is that the pond fields and ditches were a product of social labor; they were built up and maintained by community work parties traditionally organized by the chief's *konohiki*. The systems as constructed and used embodied the essence of the social structure of the chiefdom, and the *konohiki* allocated their limited use right to community members who had participated in their construction (Nakuina 1894).

"In the native Hawaiian conception land was inalienable; use right was acquired through a hierarchy of land-giver/tenant relationships, from higher to lesser chiefs to local land supervisors and hence to commoners" (Linnekin 1987: 15). Legal documents of the Great Mahele provide many details concerning traditional land-tenure rules in Hawaii. During the middle of the 19th century, the land-tenure system was remodeled to become based on principles of Western private property; each individual's rights to individual land plots were assigned based on the traditional land-use system (Earle 1978; Linnekin 1987; Sahlins 1992). A claimant came forward to describe his/her *kuleana*, lands to which he (or she) held prior use rights. In a typical claim, the farmer recounted the original allocation from a *konohiki* and the tract's continued use. Land-use right in subsistence plots descended in the male line, passing almost exclusively patrilineally, from father to son, or paternal grandfather to grandson (Linnekin 1987).

This "patrilineal" inheritance of traditional use rights, I argue (Earle 1978, contra Linnekin 1987), reflects the place that the land held in the system of staple finance. Land was given to men, who in compensation worked as corvée on the chief's land and on projects organized by the *konohiki*. As the Mahele proceeded, and more died from European diseases, Linnekin describes how females began to be more common as claimants; traditionally women were only placeholders in transfers from one man to another. Thus when a woman inherited rights from her dead husband, she evidently remarried immediately to retain her rights through her new husband. An alternative was to transfer use rights to a son, but this transfer would deprive her of direct rights in the land that she enjoyed as wife.

The land-use rights of the male commoner evidently rested on the required corvée labor contribution to his chief. To understand the nature of land holding, the Mahele records provide cases in which an individual's claim is contested because the use right had been revoked by the *konohiki* when he failed to contribute corvée labor. For example, "*konohiki* took away [tract] numbers 3 and 4 on the grounds that the claimant was getting old and his labor on the *konohiki* days of little worth" [LCA 10313] (Earle 1978: 187). A farmer's right to a subsistence plot, on which he and his family relied, depended on his laboring for the *konohiki*. The land-tenure system thus mobilized commoner labor and lay at the base of the tributary economy.

Staple finance is a tributary economy in which staples are collected from subsistence producers and used to compensate those working for the financing institutions (Earle & D'Altroy 1982). The chief received taro that was to be used to support political activities. As described vividly in the early quotations from Kamakau, the feasts provided by the chiefly owners compensated work crews on an irrigation system or other projects using social labor. The staples also supported the specialists, attached to the chiefs, who included the *konohiki* himself, warriors, and craft specialists. The community labor raised pigs, maintained fish ponds, collected special products from the mountains, and built religious monuments, trails, and other things. By controlling the commoners' labor through control of use right in subsistence resources, the chiefs derived the resources to finance other sources of power.

The irrigation systems, in particular, provided the opportunity for control over the commoners' subsistence and labor. Irrigated land was not an abstract resource. The essence of an irrigation system was its physical character; it was a cultural landscape of ditches, terraces, fields, and walls. The agricultural system included the facilities of agricultural production and an evident division into discrete, yet interdependent units. Units of land use—the individual irrigated field (*lo'i*)—were entities of social production. The field borders, pounded into place by work teams directed by the *konohiki*, marked off segments of subsistence production.

An irrigation system provided the perfect means to materialize power relations within the Hawaiian chiefdoms. Water, the life-giving essence of agricultural production, flowed through the canals built under chiefly supervision and thus considered chiefly property. The local structure of the ditch network can be interpreted as a map of the social relations of the group. Spriggs and Kirch (1992: 154-57) argue that it is sociology, not simple hydrology, that determines the specific layout of a Hawaiian ditch network. Access to water was the economic realization of the social relationships within a community. To this I would add that, more than sociology, the ditch maps power dependencies. The pattern of distribution of water was a dendritic network, and as such it could solidify the hierarchical relationships of a chiefdom.

The irrigation systems that blanketed the Hawaiian valleys created the ordered world that so appealed to the Western explorers. The taro plantations "are laid out in a variety of forms, according to the fancy of their owners, whose various shares are marked out with the most scrupulous exactness" (Dixon 1789: 131). To claim rights or responsibilities in an irrigated field was a specific legal action formalized by the products of social labor. Control was easily exercised concretely through allocating specific marked plots, the water to farm the plots, and the labor organized in their productive cycle. The ditches and earth embankments materialized, in fact *were*, the structure of rights and obligations within the local community.

The historic landscape documented and described the order of the traditional Hawaiian economy. In the community of Waioli on the northern coast of Kaua'i (fig. 2), the house lots (*pahale*) were scattered along the beach and less commonly among the irrigation systems. *Pahale* means literally fenced house, and we know them archaeologically by the enclosing stone wall that sets off a private yard and paved platform. The main irrigation ditch for the large System 22 came off the Waioli stream in the narrow upper valley and carried water to the subsistence taro plots along the stream and on the coastal plain. These were divided into individual *apana*, sections assigned to specific farmers. Mixed among these subsistence farms were sections of *ko'ele*. *Ko'ele* farms were set aside by the *konohiki* to produce staples for the community chief; each community farmer had to work the *ko'ele* land in return for continued use right on the irrigation system. On the northern coast of Kaua'i during the historic period, the *ko'ele* lands were widely distributed close to the subsistence farms (Earle 1978: 188). As seen in figure 2, the chief's lots were intermixed among, and closely correlated with, the distribution of commoner plots. On average, there was a *ko'ele* plot for each five farmers on an irrigation ditch, and virtually all irrigation systems with more than three farmers had at least one *ko'ele* piece. Even the dryland farms (*kula*) were most commonly simply attachments to the structured irrigation facilities.

Kirch (1982, 1994; contra Earle 1978) has criticized the argument that irrigation, and its ownership, was basic to the evolution of Hawaiian chiefdom. He points out correctly that, on the Big Island of Hawai'i where the largest chiefdoms developed, irrigation systems were highly localized and comparatively unimportant (see Earle 1980: fig. 1). But Kirch's exception may help prove the rule. According to tradition, Liloa, father of the great paramount chief Umi who unified the island chiefdom of Hawai'i, lived in Waipio Valley "that was the land on which the ruling chiefs lived in ancient times" (Kamakau 1961: 2). Waipio is a deeply cut valley with a well-developed stream system that watered extensive irrigation complexes.

When Umi conquered the whole island of Hawai'i, he moved his residence to Kailua on the west coast where few streams existed to irrigate

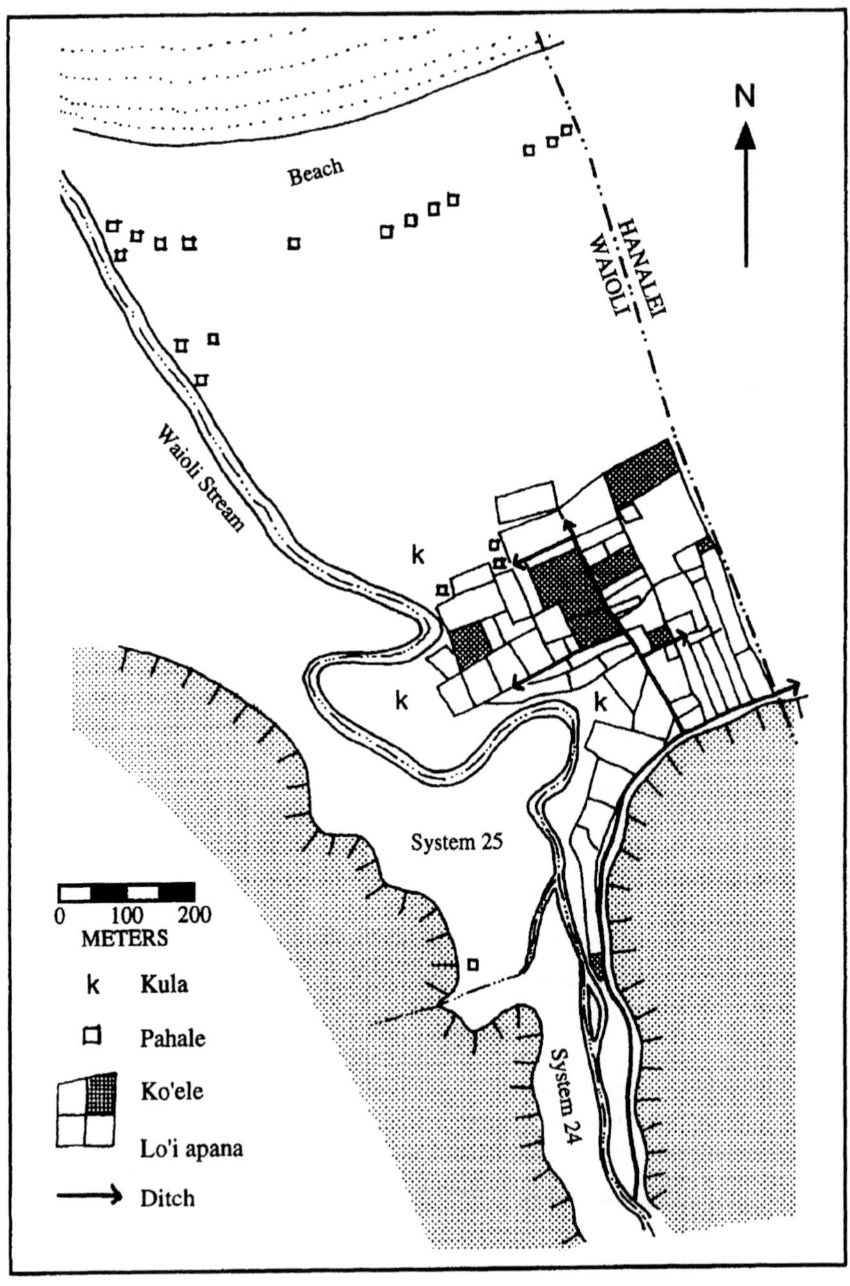

Figure 2. Historical land-use pattern, Waioli, Kaua'i, as reconstructed from the Mahele land records (Earle 1978: Fig. 8.1).

fields of taro. Does the absence of irrigation here at the new seat of power disprove the linked between the physical facilities of irrigation and the emergent political economy? I think not. Dryland field systems were constructed throughout Hawai'i and the eastern half of Maui, where the absence of streams restricted an irrigation technology. Instead of irrigation facilities, the chiefs of Hawai'i constructed elaborate dryland field complexes.

The fields of Lapakahi, located on the western North Kohala coast of Hawai'i, have been studied most extensively by archaeologists (Rosendahl 1972; Kirch 1984, 1985). Here land slopes down from the Kohala Mountains to the coast, unbroken by valleys. The *ahupua'a* communities were arbitrary land strips that ran from coast to mountains with trails and stone markers designating the community territory. Within the community, Hawaiian cultivators built extensive fields in a zone suitable for rainfall agriculture. Permanent fields were constructed of low stone walls that created narrow, contoured terraces, and the fields were divided into sections by a regular pattern of trails laid out up and down slope (fig. 3).

Within Lapakahi, "the field borders and trails break up the agricultural landscape into a regular grid with individual field units of rectangular shape" (Kirch 1984: 182). These complexes of dryland fields, terraces, borders, boundary walls, and trails were, like the irrigation systems, a physically constructed landscape in which the subdivided agricultural facility created very specific units of production on which use rights could be allocated and monitored. The intensified dryland farming areas were functionally equivalent in terms of the land-tenure system to irrigation facilities. Ownership by the chiefly hierarchy of the developed facilities of irrigated and dryland fields permitted control over the subsistence economy and the commoners' labors.

The Historical Sequence Considered

From the historical records and late period archaeology, the basis of power for Hawaiian chiefs was their control over commoner labor exercised through the system of land tenure embodied in the facilities of intensive agriculture. I consider here how the pattern of land use and tenure developed through Hawaiian prehistory as part of the emerging political economy. Kirch (1994) discusses how, throughout Polynesia,

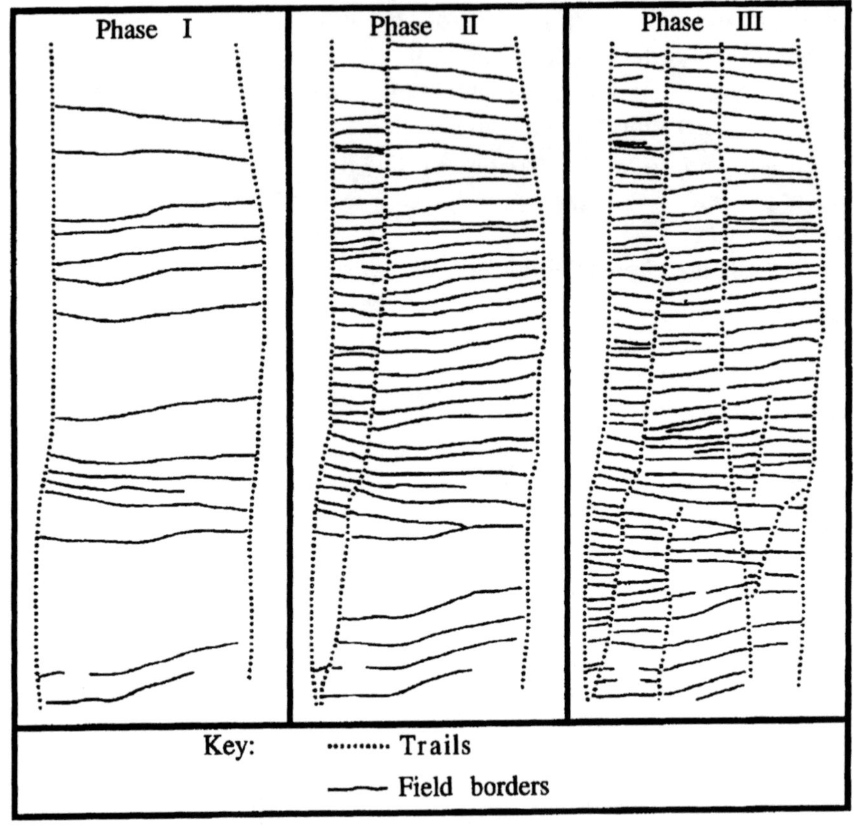

Figure 3. The developmental sequence for agricultural field walls and trails in the *ahupua'a* of Lapakahi, Hawai'i (after Kirch 1984: Fig. 60).

population and politics together drove agricultural intensification with the creation of an artificial landscape of capital improvements. The landscape that Captain James Cook and subsequent explorers observed was a cultural artifact created during the previous 1400 years, following colonization by Polynesian voyagers.

Early Settlement (A.D. 400-1200)

When the Hawaiian Islands were first settled, sometime before A.D. 400, they were forested with stands of *ohia* and *koa*. The Polynesian colonists brought with them the full range of plant and animal species, which they introduced to establish an economically viable resource base. Kirch (1984: 135-46) refers to the historic Polynesia as a "transported landscape," transformed by the introduction and husbanding of the economically useful species replacing endemic fauna and flora. The colonists evidently carried with them knowledge of irrigation technologies. Similar practices of taro pond field agriculture were practiced ethnographically and historically across the Pacific (Kirch 1984: 171), and seven radiocarbon determinations date pond field use in Hawaii prior to A.D. 1200 (Allen 1992: 53). The early population of Hawaii apparently used both irrigated and dry agricultural methods scattered through the newly colonized islands.

Formation of Hawaiian Chiefdoms (A.D. 1200-1400)

After a long period during which the initial colonists became established, population grew rapidly during A.D. 1200-1400 (Dye & Komori 1992). The numbers of agricultural features dated to this time period increased rapidly, corresponding well with the increasing population (Allen 1992: fig. 3). The forests must have been cut down, as both dryland and irrigation agriculture changed the landscape. It appears as if expansion in dryland agriculture was particularly significant. One apparent result may have been increased erosion of the upland soils and resulting sedimentation; this sedimentation would have created new alluvial bottom lands ideal for intensive irrigated farming (Spriggs 1985). The fragility of the upland soils may have triggered expansionist warfare as a means to seize more surplus (Kirch 1994). The oral histories tell of an emerging stratified society, as chiefly lines become clearly differentiated (Kolb 1994). Regional chiefdoms were apparently fighting intensely with each other, and the first religious shrines were constructed. The evident conclusion is that the initial institutionalization of chiefdoms in Hawaii was *not* tied to major agricultural facilities.

Consolidation and Unification of Island Chiefdoms (A.D. 1400-1650)

Rapid population growth continued early in this time period, peaking about 1450; growth then appears to have stalled as numbers leveled off (Dye & Komori 1992: fig. 3). The largest number of radiocarbon dates for agricultural features also comes from this period: construction of the major irrigation systems peaks about AD 1500 (Allen 1992: fig. 3). The dryland complex at Lapakahi was apparently also begun at this time (Rosendahl 1972). Oral histories tell of the development of large competing regional chiefdoms. Polities controlling east and west Maui were locked in war, resolved by an unstable unification during the 16th century (Kolb 1994). Umi, the first paramount chief of all of the Big Island, was born about A.D. 1570 (Hommon 1976: 124). Early in this period, prior to unification of the island polities, chiefs organized large constructions of religious monuments (*heiau*), but, following unification, *heiau* construction declined (Kolb 1994: fig. 7). The religious monuments were apparently a critical tool in the materialization of the complex ideology of the Hawaiian chiefdoms. Following unification, construction activity may have shifted more towards the irrigation complexes and the staple finance systems on which they were founded.

Conquest Chiefdoms and the Formation of the Hawaiian State (A.D. 1650-1825)

During the protohistoric and historic periods, the island paramount chiefs attempted to conquer neighboring island chiefdoms and bring them under their sway. Smaller islands such as Ni'ihau, Molokai, Lanai, and Kaho'olawe were incorporated into the larger neighboring chiefdoms. Maui and Hawai'i were locked in war with reciprocal invasions; the eastern section of Maui was temporarily annexed by the Hawaiian chiefs. The coming of the Europeans with their large ships and guns broke the stalemate, and Kamehameha, the young paramount of Hawai'i, quickly conquered the western islands to mold the new Hawaiian state.

State formation was apparently a time of rapid expansion in the use of large irrigation systems throughout the Hawaiian Islands. Some of these irrigation complexes were constructed during the early historical period directly to support the conquests by Kamehameha. The combined historical and archaeological investigation of the Anahulu Valley on Oahu demonstrates that the primary development there, at least in the upper valley section, dated to the invasion by Kamehameha. The irrigated taro fields were constructed to support his army, 7000 strong, and to finance his planned invasion of Kaua'i (Kirch 1990, 1992).

The dryland field complexes on the Big Island of Hawai'i may have been expanded extensively at this time. Kirch (1984: 182-92) describes how the demands on the political economy caused a rapid expansion and restructuring of the dryland agricultural systems. Working from Rosendahl's original data for the dryland complexes in Lapakahi, Kirch (1984: 185) has reconstructed the sequence by which the field complex was built up (fig. 3). During Phase I, probably starting about A.D. 1450, the upland area was terraced and subdivided by trails into long vertical swaths, probably corresponding to community territories. Through Phases II and III up to perhaps A.D. 1800, the original broadly defined field areas were successively parceled out into smaller components, and the original community territory was subdivided by new trails into three vertical areas. The agricultural development of the dryland regions created an increasingly dissected landscape representing the division into subsistence plots allocated to local farmers in return for their corvée labor obligations to the *konohiki*. The Lalmilo-Waimea field complex, also on Hawai'i, included both permanent fields and irrigation for intermittent water flows; it was constructed between 1790 and 1794, when Kamehameha was consolidating his regional power base and conquering Maui (Reeve 1983).

The construction of agricultural facilities at the beginning of the 19th century was a means to expand the staple finance system based on intensive agricultural production. It appears to have been part of the political strategy to increase surplus production and evidently not a response to population growth (Dye & Komori 1992).

In addition to increasing the productive capacity for staples, the construction of the organized agricultural complexes had a second outcome of potentially greater significance. The new, permanent facilities physically structured the landscape into the neatly divided units of subsistence, given by the *konohiki* in return for labor contributions. It was the cultural landscape of land ownership which created the property relationships of the expanding complex chiefdoms and incipient state for the islands.

Rights in Persons and Property

I began by referring to Bell's (this volume) distinction between rights of person and rights of property. In relatively small-scale, egalitarian societies, rights are especially vested in the person and his/her social position. In such societies, individuals are known on a personal, face-to-face basis. Who a person is and what rights and obligations he/she holds are evident. One need not dispute whether a person is an adult member of a clan and justified in using an agricultural plot in the group's commons. That is a fact of history generally known. A person who is unknown has no rights.

With the creation of larger-scale polities, i.e., chiefdoms and states, two changes are immediately important. Introduced into the social and political equations are 1) conflicting group interests and 2) a mass of people such that individuals may be unknown to other members of the polity. Who these people are and what their rights are within the social system may no longer be obvious. It must be answered by positioning the person within the social structure or, more precisely, within the social history of the polity. Rights are based on sequences of events (including genealogies) that extend back over generations.

These structures of historical knowledge must be remembered and presented in a convincing way. In our own legal system, written documentation (wills, deeds, etc.) define rights in property and other things. But in a nonliterate culture, histories were written on the landscape. Physical manifestations in the landscape encapsulate social relations or, more precisely, the historical events that defined those relations. Thus the building of an irrigation system fundamentally changed the landscape and rights within it, now vested in the property and its history of use.

On the Hawaiian Islands, the building of the agricultural facilities with their ditches, terraces, and enclosing walls created a physical history of land use and the hierarchy of rights that attached to them. Although not alienable, in a market sense, the rights could be seized in battle, inherited through political succession, allocated to supporters through the chiefly hierarchy, and eventually farmed by the commoner for his family support and his chief's finance. The constructed landscape defined property in land attached to and supporting the political economy.

Property is defined in objects as well as land. With emerging complexity, a strong connection exists between objects, persons, and status. The object and the person become one. In Hawai'i, feather cloaks draped the backs of chiefs in battle, during ceremonies, and on public occasions (Earle 1990). Cloaks of rare and dramatic yellow and red feathers were the clothing of gods, signifying that the chief was a god (Cummins 1984). The cloak symbolized the rainbow that always marked the presence of a god. This was the ultimate dressing for power, part of the chief's sacred and potent persona.

Obviously the cloak's power made it dangerous. Its manufacture, presentation, and use were carefully controlled. The cloaks were manufactured from feathers collected for the paramount chief at the Makahiki ceremony. They were then tied laboriously onto a woven mat by craft specialists attached to the high chief and supported by his staples mobilized in the political economy. The cloaks could be given by the paramount to his supporting chiefs, and they were removed from him when defeated. As I have argued elsewhere (Earle 1990), cloaks were handled in the same ways as land. During the original ceremonial dealings between Western explorers and the Hawaiians, the paramount chiefs gave cloaks to the Westerners. It appears that these cloaks had been taken in the recent battles of conquest, and the cloaks, like the land, were handed over to the victorious paramount chief, who would then distribute them to his supporters. I believe that rights within the political system were made manifest by the giving, receiving, and wearing of the cloaks. Thus the political institutions became formalized in the prestige objects of the chiefdom. Ownership of the highly personalized objects defined a person's position and rights within the political hierarchy. The most important of these rights would be possession of a fief, the income from which supported the chiefs and financed their political endeavors.

Conclusions

The evolution of the complex Hawaiian chiefdoms involved the creation of island-wide and inter-island polities with tens of thousands of people brought together under a sovereign. Such a large polity would have contained within it many histories and interests that set people off against each other. Part of the evolution of these formidable political institutions involved the formalization of rights and obligations within the polity. But such rights could not simply be known and recognized. The institutional formations must have been materialized and presented in readily recognizable ways that themselves were difficult to fake. This paper has described two ways that social and economic rights were materialized within the Hawaiian chiefdoms.

First, within the cultural landscape, property rights in land became formalized, given permanency, in the constructed, productive facilities: the irrigation systems, the fish ponds, and the fenced house lots. The landscape was carefully marked by the walls and other constructions built by social labor organized by the chiefs' managers. The managers then allocated use rights in these very specific facilities of production. Who a person was, how he supported his family, and how he sustained his chiefs were written in the landscape by the community's own labor activities. The symbolic order was grounded and subsumed within the everyday practice of subsistence labor in the fields of the chiefs. Land tenure was transformed by the control over social labor used to construct a cultural landscape.

Second, the identity and corresponding political rights of these chiefs were bound up in objects, frequently called "prestige goods." These goods were manufactured and distributed within the political economy, which was closely controlled by the ruling paramount. The ownership and wearing of goods such as the feathered cloaks defined the political status of a person and correspondingly the person's rights and obligations within the chiefdom. Access to the status objects and to the institutionalization of hierarchical relationships became controlled through the political economy. The social relations of the chiefdom were transformed by control over attached specialists and the symbolic products of their labor.

With the emergence of complex societies such as the Hawaiian chiefdoms, rights in person became formalized in rights in land and in objects that materialized and extended broadly the political institutions. Person and thing were joined, and people could be controlled through the economic processes by which the facilities and goods were produced (De Marrais et al. 1996).

Acknowledgments

The first draft of this paper was prepared for the Spring Meeting of the Society for Economic Anthropology, Notre Dame University, March 1994. The revisions have benefited from heated discussions at this meeting and from useful comments by Elizabeth De Marrais, Eliza Earle, and Antonio Gilman. My research on Hawaiian irrigation was conducted during the early 1970s on a project directed by Marshall Sahlins and funded by the National Science Foundation (GS-28718X1). My ideas have developed over the years through a long and valued dialogue with Patrick Kirch.

References Cited

Adams, R. McC.

1984 Mesopotamian social evolution: old outlooks, new goals. In T. Earle (ed.), *On the Evolution of Complex Societies*, pp. 79-129. Malibu: Undena.

Allen, J.

1992 Farming in Hawai'i from colonisation to contact: radiocarbon chronology and implications for cultural change. *New Zealand Journal of Archaeology* 14:45-66.

Chagnon, N.

1968 *Yanomamö: The Fierce People*. New York: Holt, Reinhart & Winston.

Corney, P.

1896 *Voyages in the Northern Pacific: Narratives from Several Trading Voyages from 1813-1818*. Honolulu: Thrum. Original 1819.

Cummins, T.

1984 Kinshape: the design of the Hawaiian feather cloak. *Art History* 7:1-20.

De Marrais, E., L.J. Castillo, & T. Earle

1996 Ideology, materialization, and power strategies. *Current Anthropology* 37:15-31.

Dixon, G.

1789 *A Voyage round the World, in 1785, 1786, 1787*. London: Goulding.

Dye, T., & E. Komori

1992 A Pre-censal population history of Hawai'i. *New Zealand Journal of Archaeology* 14:113-28.

Earle, T.

1978 *Economic and Social Organization of a Complex Chiefdom, the Halelea District, Kaua'i, Hawaii* (Museum of Anthropology, Anthropological Papers, 63). Ann Arbor: University of Michigan.

1980 Prehistoric irrigation in the Hawaiian Islands: an evaluation of evolutionary significance. *Archaeology and Physical Anthropology in Oceania* 15:1-28.

1987 Chiefdoms in archaeological and ethnohistorical perspectives. *Annual Review of Anthropology* 16:279-308.

1990 Style and iconography as legitimation in complex chiefdoms. In M. Conkey & C. Hastorf (eds.), *The Uses of Style in Archaeology*, pp. 73- 81. Cambridge: Cambridge University Press.

1991a Property rights and the evolution of chiefdoms. In T. Earle (ed.), *Chiefdoms: Power, Economy, and Ideology*, pp. 71-99. Cambridge: Cambridge University Press.

1991b (ed.) *Chiefdoms: Power, Economy, and Ideology*. Cambridge: Cambridge University Press.

1994 Political domination and social evolution. In T. Ingold (ed.), *Companion Encyclopedia of Anthropology*, pp. 940-61. London: Routledge.

Earle, T., & T. D'Altroy

1982 Storage facilities and state finance in the Upper Mantaro Valley, Peru. In J. Ericson & T. Earle (eds.), *Contexts for Prehistoric Exchange*, pp. 265-91. New York: Academic Press.

Gilman, A.

1976 Bronze Age dynamics in southeastern Spain. *Dialectical Anthropology* 1:307-19.

Hommon, R.J.

1976 The Formation of Primitive States in Precontact Hawaii. Unpublished Ph.D. dissertation, Department of Anthropology, University of Arizona.

I'i, J.P.

1959 *Fragments of Hawaiian History*. Honolulu: B.P. Bishop Museum Press.

Johnson, A., & T. Earle

1987 *The Evolution of Human Societies*. Cambridge: Cambridge University Press.

Kamakau, S.

1961 *Ruling Chiefs of Hawaii*. Honolulu: Kamehameha School Press.

1976 *The Works of People of Old* (B.P. Bishop Museum Special Publication, 61). Honolulu: B.P. Bishop Museum Press.

Kirch, P.V.

1982 Advances in Polynesian prehistory: three decades in review. *Advances in World Archaeology* 1:51-97.

1984 *The Evolution of Polynesian Chiefdoms*. Cambridge: Cambridge University Press.

1985 Intensive agriculture in prehistoric Hawai'i: the wet and the dry. In I.S. Farrington (ed.), *Prehistoric Intensive Agriculture in the Tropics*, pp. 435-54. BAR International Series 237. Oxford: British Archaelogical Reports.

1990 The evolution of socio-political complexity in prehistoric Hawai'i: an assessment of the archaeological evidence. *Journal of World Prehistory* 4:311-45.

1992 (ed.) *Anahulu: The Anthropology of History in the Kingdom of Hawaii*, Volume 2. Chicago: University of Chicago Press.

1994 *The Wet and the Dry*. Chicago: University of Chicago Press.

Kolb, M.

1994 Monumentality and the rise of religious authority in precontact Hawai'i. *Current Anthropology* 34:521-47.

Kotzebue, O. von

1821 *A Voyage of Discovery into the South Seas . . . in the Years 1815-1818*, 3 vols. London: Longman et al.

Lee, R.

1979 *The !Kung San*. Cambridge: Cambridge University Press.

Linnekin, J.

1987 Statistical analysis of the Great Mahele: some preliminary findings. *Journal of Pacific History* 22:15-33.

Locke, J.

1947 The second treatise of civil government. In T. Cook (ed.), *Two Treatises of Government*, pp. 133-46. New York: Hafnir Press. First published 1690.

Malinowski, B.

1935 *Coral Gardens and Their Magic*. London: Allen & Unwin.

Mann, M.

1986 *The Sources of Social Power*, Volume 1. Cambridge: Cambridge University Press.

Marx, K., & F. Engels

1965 The German ideology. In E. Hobsbawm (ed.), *Precapitalist Economic Formations*, pp. 121-39. New York: International Publishers. Original 1846.

Menzies, A.

1920 *Hawaii nei 128 Years Ago*. Honolulu: W.F. Wilson.

Nakuina, E.M.B.

1894 Ancient Hawaiian water rights. *Hawaiian Annual* 20:79-84.

Polanyi, K.

1944 *The Great Transformation*. New York: Farrar & Rinehart.

Rappaport, R.

1967 *Pigs for the Ancestors*. New Haven: Yale University Press.

Reeve, R.

1983 Archaeological investigations in Section three. In J.T. Clark & P.V. Kirch (eds.), *Archaeological Investigations of the Mudlane-Waimea- Kawaihae Road Corridor, Island of Hawaii, Report 83-1*, pp. 181-239. Honolulu: B.P. Bishop Museum Press.

Ricardo, D.

1821 *On the Principles of Political Economy and Taxation*. London: J. Murray.

Rosendahl, P.
1972 Aboriginal Agriculture and Residential Patterns in Upland Lapakahi, Hawaii. Unpublished Ph.D. dissertation, Department of Anthropology, University of Hawaii.

Sahlins, M.
1958 *Social Stratification in Polynesia*. Seattle: University of Washington Press.
1992 *Anahulu: The Anthropology of History in the Kingdom of Hawaii*, Volume 1. Chicago: University of Chicago Press.

Spriggs, M.
1985 Why irrigation matters in Pacific prehistory. *Journal of Pacific Prehistory* 20:23-41.

Spriggs, M., & P.V. Kirch
1992 'Auwai, kanawai, and waiwai: irrigation in Kawailoa-Uka. In P.V. Kirch (ed.), *Anahulu: The Anthropology of History in the Kingdom of Hawaii*, Volume 2, pp. 118-164. Chicago: University of Chicago Press.

Stewart, C.
1970 *Journal of a Residence in Sandwich Islands during the Years 1823, 1824, 1825*. Honolulu: University of Hawaii Press. Original 1830.

Chapter Eight

Concepts of Property and Access to Nonagricultural Resources in the Inka Empire

Cathy Lynne Costin

In this essay I deal, not with a theoretical discussion of property, but rather present a substantive discussion of how resources—specifically the raw materials used in craft production—were claimed and allocated among various social segments within the Inka empire. Such a study contributes broadly to our understanding of the nature and structure of such claims and access, to the study of the evolution of political finance systems, and specifically to the structure of the economy of the Inka empire.

The Inka empire dominated the Andean Highlands and Pacific Coast of South America from roughly A.D. 1400 until they were conquered by the Spanish in A.D. 1533. The empire incorporated some 80 different ethnic groups with a total population of eight to twelve million people. The military and civilian bureaucracies controlled and integrated this large, diverse population without true writing, money, the wheel, or markets.

At the time of the Spanish conquest, the Inka empire was undergoing a series of structural and organizational economic changes. These included shifts from staple to wealth finance in the political economy (D'Altroy & Earle 1985), corvée to retainership as the dominant mode of securing labor to produce goods for state institutions and elite patrons (Murra 1975, 1980; Rowe 1982), and the development of privately/individually held productive resources at the expense of communal *and* state control of productive resources. All of these changes entailed a realignment of property rights and patterns of access to productive resources.

Given these dynamic conditions, it is not surprising that documentary evidence from the early colonial period suggests that at the time of Spanish conquest, three systems of real property ownership and access to subsistence were in place in the territories administered by the Inka empire. First was the presumed indigenous system of communal ownership, a system in which a localized corporate kin group called the *ayllu* controlled an "archipelago" of resources spanning multiple environmental zones (Murra 1975; Masuda et al. 1985, Stanish 1992). Such spatially complex structures of resource control are believed to have promoted community self-sufficiency in subsistence production as well as to have ensured emerging local elites access to relatively rare and valuable exotic goods. Second was a system of ostensible state ownership of all productive resources. When the Inka conquered an area, they nominally "regularized" ownership of and access to resources by declaring state ownership of all productive resources and reapportioning partial usufruct rights back to local communities while retaining significant rights to mobilize labor, raw materials, and finished goods for the use of bureaucratic, military, and religious institutions within the political economy. Third, the growing practice of allocating land and other resources to individuals as a prerogative of rank and as reward for service to the empire resulted in a expanding body of property held by individuals. Fundamentally, these systems defined three classes of interests in productive resources: communal, institutional, and individual.

The colonial documents discuss most often rights in agricultural land and raw materials used to make sumptuary goods such as fine textiles and precious metal objects. In considering the constitution of property more broadly in the Inka empire, two related questions arise: (1) Does the reconstruction from the colonial documents fully and accurately reflect the way resources were controlled and allocated in the pre-hispanic empire? and (2) Were more mundane, utilitarian nonagricultural resources perceived and treated in ways similar to those for which the state had a direct and proximate use?

Our primary textual sources of information about property in the Inka empire consist of chronicles, court documents, and government censuses compiled in the early colonial period. These documentary sources are problematic for a number of reasons. Most importantly, in the colonial era local communities, local elites, Inka elites, and Spanish colonials vied for control over lucrative agricultural and nonagricultural resources. The documents—some written by Spaniards, some by descendants of the native populations—reflect the diverse property interests of the various colonial factions, rather than record directly the pre-Colonial pattern. Given the likely complexity and flux within property relations at the time of the conquest, it is not surprising that informants and litigants would represent the tenure system to Spanish government representatives in a way which would support their own claims for control over productive resources.

Yet despite potential distortions and biases, the documents clearly point to a series of relationships and structures that might stand as a *model* of property relations which can be tested with other data, specifically with the material, or archaeological, remains of Inka society. In this paper, I review the archaeological evidence for resource use in the Inka empire as means of inferring property rights. The archaeological data are particularly useful for several reasons. First, their distributions and patterns are presumed independent of the colonial textual record, in no small measure because the two data sets were created by different means and at different points in time. Second, archaeological data and their interpretations are subject to sorts of biases quite different than those inherent in the colonial documents. Finally, archaeological data are more likely to reflect elements of society that were either relatively ignored by the various factions who contributed to the documentary sources or who were least powerful within Inka and colonial society, and therefore most likely to have their interests distorted during the social upheavals of the Inka and Spanish conquests.

The archaeological data do present the challenge of developing methodologies for identifying intangible concepts such as property generally, and distinguishing between title or rights in usufruct specifically. In some ways, this latter distinction may not be critical, at least for the

Andean world. We must remember the limited utility of distinguishing between title and usufruct rights in the Inka system. "Title" could not protect local communities from state seizure of their property. And unlike other pre-capitalist states such as Rome and the various Mesopotamian polities, there was no open "market" for real property and resources and thus there was no mechanism other than government alienation and reallocation for "transacting" or transfering title among real property-holding entities.

In her seminal study, *Power and Property in Inca Peru*, Sally Falk Moore (1959: 46- 47) has discussed the problem of distinguishing between title and usufruct rights to resources from the documentary evidence. She argues that while claims of universal Inka ownership of productive resources were a strong symbol of state sovereignty and domination, the key issue was not who held title (community or state) but the fact that operationally the local communities and state held concurrent interests in resources. While I agree with Moore that the distinction between title and usufruct may not have even applied in the Andean world view, I disagree with her interpretation that various parties held concurrent interests in all resources. Rather, I will argue that the three classes of property holders maintained and exploited resources relatively independently of one another, and that a key principal was the operational detachment of the various property holders.

I suggest here that patterns of raw material use can inform us of patterns of usufruct rights, if not title to real property. I by no means intend to imply that all producers owned or even controlled the resources they used. However, I do believe that patterns in resource utilization will strongly reflect resource control for several reasons. First, in the Andean system, a fundamental principle in production was that patrons supplied raw materials and tools to the producers who worked for them (Murra 1980; Julien 1988: 264). Thus, in elite-sponsored production, we can infer that the consumers controlled the resources used in the fabrication of the craft goods they consumed. Similarly, a lack of formal markets and a deemphasis on exchange more generally (e.g., Lalone 1978; Earle 1998) suggests that artisans producing within the local economy would have either unobstructed access to or direct control over the raw materials they employed in their crafts.

In this paper, I review the evidence for the use of nonagricultural resources in craft production and architectural construction to investigate the three fundamental distinctions in property control abstracted from the documentary evidence: (1) the contrast between state and local resources; (2) the differentiation among state institutions; and (3) the separation of some "elite" resources into institutional and personal property.

State and Community/Nonstate

One of the fundamental distinctions made in the ethnohistoric documents is between lands and other productive resources that pertained to local communities and those that pertained to the various elite institutions such as the political bureaucracy and the state religion.

The state apparently had the capacity to alienate resources from indigenous populations after conquest and reallocate them to the institutions and populations of their choosing. Many chroniclers describe how the Inka divided resources among state religious institutions, the secular government, and the local population after an area was brought under imperial domination. According to Cobo (cited in Niles 1987: 165), the boundaries of agricultural land pertaining to different interest groups were clearly marked. No archaeological evidence for such boundaries is explicitly discussed in the literature, but Niles (1987: 168) conjectures that "in an area where major rural agricultural works were built new by the Inkas, difference styles of terracing and waterworks might well be part of the delineation of the different kinds of fields." She argues specifically that more carefully constructed, fitted stone terraces were associated with state-controlled production.

In considering the relationship between the state and local community in regards to real property, a key issue is determining the extent to which the state alienated existing productive property from conquered communities, and the extent to which the state essentially added to the property stock in conquered regions by developing previously unexploited resources. Property, generally, is a tangible good with productive potential. The amount of property is expandable, because what is nonproductive under one technological regime can become highly productive, hence property, under another. It seems likely that whenever feasible, the state developed new resources—in essence, creating its own property *de novo*. The state would likely develop and utilize new or different resources for three reasons. First, there were many resources with productive potential which could only be exploited with the large labor pool that state institutions could command. In fact, in his chronicle, Garcilaso (Niles 1987: 165-66) comments that the produce of agricultural terrace systems pertained to religious and administrative institutions, since they largely sponsored construction of these terraces, hence expanding the resource base. Second, the state likely distinguished activities associated with the state political economy from those of the local, subsistence economies in part by exploiting readily distinguishable raw materials (and technologies) in state crafts and architecture. As a corallary of this argument, I suggest that in highly complex systems such as the Inka, multiple resources might be developed to distinguish not only the monolithic "state" from the local community, but also to keep the various institutions that comprised the state operationally and ideologically separate. Third, those responsible for managing the "state" economy likely recognized that it was in their and the state's best interest to avoid disrupting the local economic base upon which the stability of the empire ultimately depended. In sum, I suggest that the state seized existing resources and disrupted existing property regimes only if doing so directly served their interests in ways that could not be accomplished by developing parallel property.

Data on two nonagricultural resources—ceramics and metals—provide evidence for the degree of separation between state institutional and local community resources. These materials are particularly useful because (1) their material composition can be analyzed to distinguished among raw materials sources and (2) we can readily distinguish among "state" Inka-style goods and local-style goods.

Prior to the Inka hegemony in the Andes, each region and/or ethnic group had distinctive forms and styles of pottery, most of which continued to be made and used in their traditional domestic cooking, storage, and serving functions after the Inka conquest. Added to the local ceramic assemblages in conquered provinces was pottery manufactured and decorated in the imperial Inka style. These distinctive vessels were used initially in specific state activities such a storage, feasting, and the distribution of valued commodities such as maize and *chicha* (corn beer), although they eventually came to be widely distributed in local settlements in at least some parts of the empire.

Inka style pottery was manufactured throughout the empire by artisans working for the state. How were these state artisans supplied with clay and aplastics? If the state alienated all property—including seizing existing clay mines and sources of temper—and reallocated some or parts of some back to local communities, I would expect that Inka-style vessels would be compositionally similar to local wares made before the Inka conquest and those made contemporaneously with the Inka occupation. In contrast, if the Inka developed and maintained new resources apart from traditional community property, then I would expect Inka-style vessels to be compositionally distinct from local-style vessels made before and after the conquest.

My own research (Costin 1986, 1998) conducted in the Yanamarca Valley in the Central Andean highlands—an area conquered by the Inka in A.D. 1460 or 1470—supports strongly the second scenario, in which the state developed new resources for craft production. Petrographic and mineralogical analyses (Costin 1986, 1998) demonstrate that separate resources were used to fabricate vessels in the local and Inka styles. The local cooking jars were fabricated of a highly micaceous clay; local-style decorated bowls and storage jars were fabricated of a sedimentary clay; and most stylistically Inka bowls, plates, and jars were fabricated of a sedimentary clay visually and microscopically distinguishable from the clay used to make local-style vessels. Interestingly, we recovered a small number of Inka cooking forms fabricated in a clay compositionally indistinguishable from the micaceous clay used to make the local cooking vessels.

D'Altroy and Bishop (1990) analyzed a smaller sample of local and Inka sherds from the Yanamarca using Instrumental Neutron Activation Analysis to test for compositional homogeneity. In their results, there was no compositional overlap between local style and Inka sherds. Their study, then, strengthens the conclusion that local potters and state artisans utilized separate resources in pottery manufacture.

My analyses further demonstrated that the clays used to produce the local types during the Inka occupation—the sedimentary used for local wares and the micaceous clay sources—were similar to or the same as some of those used to fabricate pottery in the immediately pre-Inka period. Importantly, one clay source used in the pre-Inka period fell into disuse by local potters after the Inka conquest, but was not used in the production of Inka-style wares, either. (The abandonment of this source seems tied directly to the abandonment of the pottery-producing community that had exploited it.) Rather, the sedimentary clay source used to produce Inka style wares was one which was apparently not utilized at all in the pre-Inka period. Thus, the ceramics suggest some continuity in community ceramic resource utilization, and likely continuity in de facto property regimes. In both the pre-Inka and Inka periods, the pottery was made at local communities within the research area. We have not yet identified the locales where Inka style pottery was produced; they may be as yet undiscovered or they may lie just outside our research area.

Whether the state prospected new clay sources within the Yanamarca or imported raw materials or finished pottery from nearby the study area, in ceramic manufacture the state minimized disruption to the existing system of resource allocation where technologically equivalent clays existed. The fact that a small number of Inka style cooking vessels were manufactured of the same clays used to manufacture local-style cooking vessels supports the contention that the state coopted resources/property only in cases where functional equivalents or technological substitutes were not available. An alternate explanation is that local potters making cooking wares copied Inka forms in clays to which they had access.

Data from northwestern Argentina support conclusions drawn from the Yanamarca data that an observable distinction was made between resources pertaining to state institutions and those of local inhabitants. As in the Yanamarca, Inka-style vessels were compositionally distinct from local-style vessels, indicating exploitation of separate sources for local and state production.

These ceramic data from the Argentinean administrative center of Potrero-Chaquiago also illuminate the property relationship between the state and non-Inka populations forcibly resettled into the area to produce for the state. These laborers, called *mitmaqkuna*, were kin-based groups of craft or agricultural specialists removed from their natal lands and resettled into new communities to establish or expand production in areas which the state desired to develop economically. Although they were severed from their traditional community rights to natural resources, the ethnohistoric documents inform us that mitmaqkuna communities were given lands—presumably alienated from the indigenous populations of the areas in which they were resettled—so that they might become self-sustaining, rather than be supported from state stores (Lalone and Lalone 1987). It has been posited that the Potrero-Chaquiago area was settled in part by mitmaqkuna from several ethnic and geographic backgrounds (Lorandi 1983). The ceramic evidence from Potrero-Chaquiago suggests that among the resources the resettled populations were allocated were the raw materials necessary to produce their own craft goods. Mineralogical analyses of sherds and X-ray diffraction analyses of possible clay sources indicate that clays and inclusions used to fabricate pottery in the Inka and many non-Inka styles used in the region were quarried in separate locations. Importantly, the stylistically diverse, non-Inka ceramic types were fabricated of materials—clays and aplastics—distinguishable from each other, from Inka style pottery and from the ceramic wares believed produced by the indigenous populations (D'Altroy et al. 1994). The vessels used by the settlers were not imported. Rather, populations resettled into the area made pottery that reflected their traditional types both stylistically and technically. For example, transplanted puna residents not only continued to manufacture pottery in their customary styles, but went so far as to attempt to replicate the look of the paste of the pottery made in their natal communities—which had white inclusions of lutite and slate—by adding granules of light colored volcanic glass, a raw material available locally in their new settlements (ibid.). Interestingly, the Inka style pottery also shows resource diversity, suggesting that each potting group working for the state may have been supplied from separate resources.

General descriptions of the pottery recovered at the Inka provincial administrative center of Huánuco Pampa and surrounding indigenous local communities suggest that distinctive resources were also extracted for the production of state and local ceramic wares in this northern province of the empire. Chupaychu potters used a number of clay sources to make local style pottery, including a distinctive micaceous clay. This paste was not used to make Inka-style pottery; the only vessels recovered at Chupaychu and Inka administrative settlements fabricated of this clay were Chupaychu forms (Morris & Thompson 1985: 148).

This same pattern of resource tenure—with clear distinctions made between local and state sources—holds for other nonagricultural resources as well, including precious and semi-precious metals. Berthelot (1989) has demonstrated that gold and silver mines were held by both the state and the local communities in Bolivia (although in the latter case it seems likely that while ostensibly pertaining to the community as a whole, they primarily benefitted the leaders of those communities). Berthelot argues that the "community" mines—like agricultural land—were expropriated by the state upon conquest, but then granted back to local control. Interestingly, the "Inka" exploited the larger, centralized mines, while community resources were small and scattered across the landscape. Community mines consisted of river deposits which could be easily sifted and washed to extract the metal. In contrast, the Inka's mines consisted of tunnels and galleries dug into sedimentary deposits up to 65 meters deep. These state mines were worked by a more sophisticated process that required the construction of galleries, channels for carrying water, and construction of special washing surfaces to catch the gold extracted from the mud. While requiring more labor to construct and work, the Inka gallery mines were considerably more productive than the community stream deposits.

The principles of resource tenure I have outlined here may help explain the heretofore enigmatic distribution of tin bronze during the Late Horizon in the Andes. Copper and bronze were widely distributed in the Andes, used in both utilitarian and display objects in elite and commoner contexts. Andean smiths regularly used copper mixed with either tin or arsenic. Both tin and arsenic lower the melting point of copper and improved the workability of the metal to about the same degree. According to Lechtman (1976, 1981), the arsenic in the copper alloys occurred naturally in the ores smelted by pre-Inka metallurgists. As such, its relative quantity was not and could not be controlled. In contrast, tin was consciously added to the copper, and thus gave greater control to metal workers.

Prior to the consolidation of the Inka empire, arsenic bronzes were widely distributed throughout the northern and central portion of the Andes; tin bronzes were generally restricted to the south-central and southern portions of the highlands and coast. During the Late Horizon, tin bronze became generally and widely distributed throughout the empire, in large measure replacing arsenical bronzes.

The usual explanation for the sudden, widespread appearance of tin bronze is that the state controlled the mining and distribution of tin from mines in Bolivia (e.g., Owen 1986, Rutledge & Gordon 1987). Lechtman (1976) has dubbed tin bronze an "Imperial Alloy" and has argued that the Late Horizon constituted a tin-bronze horizon. She (Lechtman 1979) further argues that the state "imposed" tin bronze on conquered populations as a sign of imperial sovereignty. Yet despite this apparent resource homogeneity, there is little stylistic or technological homogeneity among bronze items in the empire. In a survey of metal objects from late prehispanic contexts, Owen discerned no identifiable, widespread Inka stylistic or formal influence on local metal industries (Owen 1986: 24). Because the tin bronze objects recovered from Late Horizon contexts are not stylistically homogeneous they likely did not serve as symbolic referents of the state (cf. Owen 1986). Thus, we must ask why the state would become involved in the extraction, distribution, and possibly processing of this resource. To understand, we must look at the use of bronze in its more general metallurgical context.

In the Yanamarca, the small amounts of copper used to fabricate utilization and decorative items in the pre-Inka period were relatively pure, unalloyed copper. Specifically, all eight analyzed pieces of finished copper from pre-Inka contexts contained no or only minuscule (<.05%) amounts of tin (Owen 1986: 50). The quantity of copper—or more correctly bronze—quadrupled after the Inka conquest, in part because it replaced silver as the common form of ornament (Owen 1998) and in part because there is a large increase in the use of utilitarian bronze items such as needles (Costin 1993).

In contrast with the pre-Inka period, 88% of the "copper" items recovered in Late Horizon contexts are tin bronze. At least some of the bronze objects used by the Xauxa after the Inka conquest were fabricated by local artisans, as evidenced by the recovery of small amounts of ore and production scrap in local contexts. Owen (1989; cf. Costin et al. 1989) has identified an "Inka" bronze technology used in the fabrication of some items, but at the level of analysis reported, these items do not appear to be compositionally distinct from local style objects.

Copper initially seems counter to the pattern of resource tenure suggested for agricultural land, precious metals, and ceramic resources in that local and state artisans apparently exploited the same resources. However, if we examine access to copper in the broader context of all metals, then the principles of resource tenure I have outlined hold. *Copper ore* has a fairly wide distribution throughout the Andes (Lechtman 1976), and thus local communities could hold their own resources in this metal. However, tin, or the casserite ore from which it was extracted, was relatively spatially restricted in the empire. It is in the control and distribution of tin resources that we see played out one of the fundamental principles of the control of resources—and the workings of the political economy more broadly—in the Inka state.

Tin was a substance with spatially restricted availability but high potential utility in the Andes. Access to tin improved the predictability and consistency of "copper" working by increasing control and predictability and lowering production risk. Thus, it indirectly served state interests to increase its availability, to facilitate the local adoption of bronze as a replacement for the silver coopted by the state. While the state seemed content to allow bronze fabrication in local hands—since copper bronze held little economic and symbolic value for the central bureaucracy—unregulated long-distance trade in tin to supply local artisans would entail economic relationships outside the state spheres and would run counter to state policies of limiting interregional interaction (Costin & Earle 1989; Costin 1998). Thus, it was necessary for the state to directly supply tin to local artisans. State-sponsored distribution of tin expanded the entire metal resource base, but in this case—unlike agricultural terraces and ceramic materials—the new resource went to the locals, because it was existing resources (silver and gold) that were valuable, powerful symbolic referents the state sought to control.

Elite Institutions

The chroniclers maintain a consistent distinction between resources controlled by the secular bureaucracies (military and civilian administrations—which are often not readily distinguished)—and those pertaining to the "Sun" and other religious institutions. This focus on the distinction reflects, I believe, the growing secularization of power during the Inka expansion, and administrative strategies for delimiting—and thereby limiting—the religious hierarchy's access to productive resources.

Is this distinction, made so consistently in the documentary evidence, recognizable in the archaeological record? I would answer this question with a qualified, "yes." Unfortunately, we do not have fine-grained enough compositional analysis of ceramics and metals from clearly secular and religious contexts to distinguish among these goods in the way that we can distinguish more generally between state and local craft resources.

However, architecture may hold a clue. A wide range of construction techniques and building materials was used in buildings and features ostensibly in the Inka "style" (Gasparini & Margolies 1980; Protzen 1993). Protzen (1993) argues that Imperial Inka architecture was not as standardized as usually portrayed in literature. This would follow if the sponsors and inhabitants of functionally distinct structures each controlled their own resources and own labor force.

Most Inka-style architecture was constructed of semi-cut or unworked fieldstone set in mortar or made of adobe brick or tapia. Finely cut and fitted stone was used in only small percentage of Inka style structures. Variability among materials and construction techniques at both the intra- and inter-site level reflects a complex set of criteria: material availability and suitability, the status and importance of the building and its occupants, and the ability to mobilize and control skilled and unskilled labor (Kendall

1985; Morris & Thompson 1985; Niles 1987; Protzen 1993). I suggest that consistently made choices among functionally and technologically equivalent materials may reflect control over resources.

To control for variability reflecting status and importance, here I consider only cut and fitted stone. Although today we marvel at the artistry and technical proficiency of Inka fine masonry, Protzen (1993: 217) suggests that at least some cut stone masonry was plastered. If buildings were to be plastered, then choices of raw materials were less likely to be aesthetic (e.g., based on color, texture and other visual attributes) and more reflective of access to raw materials.

While quite a bit of attention has been paid to Inka construction technology, little work has been published that systematically identifies the types of stone used in buildings. What little material is available, however, is highly suggestive of the patterns expected if different institutions controlled separate resources. For example, Jose Gonzales Corrales (cited in Kendall 1985: 49) has identified at least four types of stone used in cut and fitted masonry in Cuzco. These materials came from distinct quarries, and he suggests stones were brought from specific quarries to be used in the construction of particular buildings. Different buildings in the capital clearly pertained to different institutions, and likely to some individuals as well. Although more detailed work is clearly in order, the architectural evidence hints that different builders or sponsors utilized materials from different sources near the capital, suggesting that they controlled separate property.

"Public" and Private Holdings

I turn finally to an analysis of the degree to which a distinction was made between the resources utilized by state institutions and those used to meet the needs of noble and royal individuals. Such an analysis bears on the issue of whether state institutions and the elites who controlled them operated independently of one another. While we expect a high degree of interpenetration in actions and activities among state institutions and those who ran them, at the same time we need to expore the degree to which elites within the massive empire could and did continue to control the state as their personal fiefs, and the extent to which parallel political economies—institutional and individual—developed.

The distinction between holdings of state institutions and those of elites as private individuals is perhaps one of the most difficult distinctions to identify archaeologically. This is so in part because elites regularly commanded productive resources *as* public officials and as private individuals. Bureaucrats were entitled to some of the goods whose production they oversaw (Moore 1958); late in the empire these same elites likely also controlled resources for their own use.

Much of the land around Cuzco was held as private estates (e.g., Niles 1987). But title and usufruct within these tracts was complex. For example, at the emperor Huayna Capac's estate in the Urubamba Valley, a field-by-field description identifies many plots which pertained directly to the emperor and his descendants, while other plots or at least their produce were given over to his wives, mother, *aqllakuna*, and the state cult of the sun. Some lands within the boundaries of the estate were retained by the original inhabitants of the area, with no private or religious claims to them (Villanueva, cited in Niles 1987).

As with the analysis of institutional claims to resources, the architectural evidence currently provides the most compelling clues about distinctions between individual and institutional property.

The Inka constructions at Ollantaytambo were part of the royal estate of the emperor, Pachacuti, who conquered the region (Rostworowski 1970: 159, 253; Protzen 1993: 19). Based on colonial era court testimony, "the estate and its produce were the personal property of its royal owner, *distinct and apart* from the possessions of the state" (Protzen 1993: 27; emphasis in original). However, the settlement likely functioned secondarily as an administrative and religious center when the emperor was in residence.

The settlement is comprised of two sectors: the town itself and the area known as the "Temple Hill" or "Fortress." The town likely housed the personnel who worked on the estate in private agricultural and craft production for the emperor. In contrast, the Temple Hill houses many structures which may pertain more directly to the official workings of the empire as it was overseen by the emperor while he was in residence at the estate, rather than to the private production of the estate.

At Ollantaytambo, a variety of materials were used in construction: rose colored rhyolite for the Sun Temple, welded rhyolite tuff for the terrace walls on Temple Hill and the Enclosure of the Ten Niches, rhyolitic breccia for several buildings, as well as a strongly altered andesite, andesite, limestone, and ignibrite (Protzen 1993: 157). As at Cuzco, buildings of cut stone rarely mixed two or more rock types (Protzen 1993: 157, 251).

Protzen (1993) records several nearby locales and quarries where most stone types used in the construction could have been collected/ quarried. Highly organized quarrying operations at some locales—with clearly demarcated areas for extraction, storage and stone-cutting—attest to the level of control over architectural stone procurement. Protzen believes that several sources were quarried simultaneously. The scale of labor that was commanded to work some of the quarries precludes exploitation of these resources by certain classes of property holders. For example, Protzen (1993: 178-81) estimates that thousands of workers would be required to quarry and transport the rose colored rhyolite used in the Temple construction at Ollantaytambo. This is a number of workers that only the "state" as "state" would have the power to command, suggesting this was an institutional, rather than "private," operation.

The estate centered at the archaeological site of Callachaca was owned by Amaro Topa Inca, son of the emperor Pachacuti and full brother of Pachacuti's successor, Topa Inca. Because no ruler was ever in residence, the estate likely had a purely private function. Although there were structures identified as shrines at the estate (Niles 1987), there is no documentary, architectural or archaeological evidence that the institutional state religion established facilities on the estate. We know from the ethnohistoric documents that the nobility often took personal responsibility for the care and maintenance of local shrines on their estates, but here the support must need come from their personal holdings, and not state resources.

Most buildings at Callachaca were made of unworked fieldstones set in clay mortar; others of coursed and/or fitted limestone masonry (Niles 1987). A single material—pink limestone available on the estate—was used in all the construction at the site.

The estates of Ollantaytambo and Callachaca present an interesting and informative contrast because of the status differences between their owners and because of the different functions performed at the two estates. Callachaca was the relatively small estate of a nonpower wielding noble. As such, it represents a single class of property-holder. We find that a single type of stone—quarried at a single locale—was used in the construction of all the buildings at the site. In contrast, as part of the estate of a ruling *Inka*, the buildings at Ollantaytambo pertained not only to the workings of the private estate, but also to the workings of the state administration and the state religion. The fact that different stone resources were used in the construction of different buildings may reflect the fact that various state institutions—and perhaps other individuals—held pockets of resources within the larger boundaries of Pachacuti's "private" estate, which were exploited to support those institutional functions carried out at his estate (as we have documented in the court records for Huayna Capac's nearby estate).

Conclusions

In sum, we can identify complex, but highly structured patterns of access to and presumably control over nonagricultural resources. Resource utilization must stand for ownership in the archaeological case, where we cannot distinguish between title and usufruct rights.

Although the archaeological data are not as "fine-grained" as the documentary data, in many ways they are less ambiguous in the information they provide regarding the structure of property and access to resources in the Inka empire. The archaeological data suggest that indeed there were three classes of property holders—local communities, state institutions, and private individuals—who were kept operationally distinct from one another. Despite the rhetoric of state seizure and ownership, patterns of resource use as evidenced by the archaeological data indicate that rather than actually alienating resources from conquered populations, the state utilized its ability to harness capital and labor to expand the real property base in the territories it administered.

The Inka may not have had property in the capitalist sense of the term, but it is clear that use rights and interests were clearly defined and maintained prior to the Spanish conquest. The identification of the relative inalienability and nontranferability of such claims not only clarifies our understanding of the Inka "property" system, but it also should help in our explication of the Inka tax system, where our analyses are caught in a fundamental debate as to whether the state mobilized goods or labor. I leave a full discussion of this issue for another paper, but let me just say that the clear separation between state and local resources defined here strengthens the argument that the state had a call on the labor, and not the "property" or tangible goods which pertained to subject populations.

References Cited

Berthelot, J.

1986 The extraction of precious metals at the time of the Inka. In J. Murra, N. Wachtel, & J. Revel (eds.), *Anthropological History of Andean Polities*, pp. 68-88. Cambridge: Cambridge University Press.

Costin, C.

1986 From Chiefdom to Empire State: Ceramic Economy Among the Prehispanic Wanka of Highland Peru. Ph.D. dissertation, Department of Anthropology, University of California, Los Angeles. Ann Arbor: University Microfilms.

1993 Textiles, women and political economy in late Prehispanic Peru. *Research in Economic Anthropology* 14:3-28.

1998 Ceramic production and distribution. In T. D'Altroy & C. Hastorf (eds.), *Empire and Domestic Economy: Transformation in Household Economics of Xauxa Society under the Inkas*. Washington: Smithsonian Institution Press. In press.

Costin, C., & T. Earle

1989 Status distinction and legitimization of power as reflected in changing patterns of consumption in late Prehispanic Peru. *American Antiquity* 54:691-714.

Costin, C., T. Earle, B. Owen, & G. Russell

1989 Impact of Inka conquest on local technology in the upper Mantaro Valley, Peru. In S.E. van der Leeuw & R. Torrence (eds.), *What's New: A Closer Look at the Process of Innovation*, pp. 107-39. London: Unwin Hyman.

D'Altroy, T., & R. Bishop

1990 The provincial organization of Inka ceramic production. *American Antiquity* 55:120-38.

D'Altroy, T., & T. Earle

1985 Staple finance, wealth finance, and storage in the Inka political economy. *Current Anthropology* 26:187-206.

D'Altroy, T., A. Lorandi, & V. Williams

1994 Producción y uso de cerámica en la economía política Inka. In I. Shimada (ed.), *Tecnología y Organización de la Producción de Cerámica Prehispánica en los Andes*, pp. 395-443. Lima: Pontificia Universidad Católica del Perú, Fondo Editorial.

Earle, T.K.
1998 Exchange and social stratification in the Andes: the Wanka case. In T. D'Altroy & C. Hastorf (eds.), *Empire and Domestic Economy: Transformation in Household Economics of Xauxa Society under the Inkas*. Washington: Smithsonian Institution Press. In press.

Gasparini, G., & L. Margolies (trans. P. Lyon)
1980 *Inca Architecture*. Bloomington: Indiana University Press.

Julien, C.
1988 How Inca decimal administration worked. *Ethnohistory* 35:257-79.

Kendall, A.
1985 *Aspects of Inca Architecture: Description, Function, and Chronology*. Oxford: BAR International Series 242.

Lalone, D.
1978 Historical Contexts of Trade and Markets in the Peruvian Andes. Ph.D. dissertation, Department of Anthropology, University of Michigan. Ann Arbor: University Microfilms.

Lalone, M., & D. Lalone
1987 The Inka state in the southern highlands: state administrative and production enclaves. *Ethnohistory* 34:47-62.

Lechtman, H.
1976 A metallurgical site survey in the Peruvian Andes. *Journal of Field Archaeology* 3:1-42.
1979 Issues in Andean metallurgy. In E. Benson (ed.), *Pre-Columbian Metallurgy of South America*, pp. 1-40. Washington: Dumbarton Oaks.
1981 Copper-Arsenic Bronzes from the North Coast of Peru. *Annals of the New York Academy of Sciences* 376:77-121.

Lorandi, A.M.
1983 Mitayos y mitmaqkuna en el Tawantinsuyu meridional. *Histórica* 7(1):3-50.

Masuda, S., I. Shimada, & C. Morris (eds.)
1985 *Andean Ecology and Civilization: An Interdisciplinary Perspective on Andean Ecological Complementarity*. Tokyo: University of Tokyo Press.

Moore, S.F.
1959 *Power and Property in Inca Peru*. New York: Columbia University Press.

Morris, C., & D.E. Thompson
1985 *Huánuco Pampa: An Inca City and Its Hinterland*. London: Thames & Hudson.

Murra, J.V.

1975 *Formaciones Económicas y Políticas del Mundo Andino*. Lima: Instituto de Estudios Peruanos.

1980 *The Economic Organization of the Inca State*. Greenwich, CT: JAI Press.

Niles, S.

1987 *Callachaca: Style and Status in an Inca Community*. Iowa City: University of Iowa Press.

Owen, B.

1986 The Role of Common Metal Objects in the Inka State. Unpublished M.A. Paper, Department of Anthropology, University of California, Los Angeles.

1998 The economy of metal and shell wealth goods. In T. D'Altroy & C. Hastorf (eds.), *Empire and Domestic Economy: Transformation in Household Economics of Xauxa Society Under the Inkas*. Washington, DC: Smithsonian Institution Press. In press.

Protzen, J.-P.

1993 *Inca Architecture and Construction at Ollantaytambo*. New York: Oxford University Press.

Rostworowski de Díez Canseco, M.

1970 El repartimiento de doña Beatriz Coya en el valle de Yucay. *Historia y Cultura* 4:153-267.

Rowe, J.

1982 Inca policies and institutions relating to the cultural unification of the empire. In G.A. Collier, R.I. Rosaldo, & J.D. Wirth (eds.), *The Inca and Aztec States 1400-1800: Anthropology and History*, pp. 93-118. New York: Academic Press.

Rutledge, J., & R. Gordon

1987 The work of metallurgical artificers at Machu Picchu, Peru. *American Antiquity* 52:578-94.

Stanish, C.

1992 *Ancient Andean Political Economy*. Austin: University of Texas Press.

Chapter Nine

Private Landownership, Debt, and Fiscal Crisis in the Ancient Near East

Michael Hudson

Public obligations owed by landed property holders for military service or corvée labor have a pedigree going back at least to the third millennium B.C. in the Near East. Almost as old a phenomenon is the striving by rich and powerful families to avoid such obligations on their own holdings and to shift them onto less powerful groups and economic classes.

Prior to the development of a land market, private absentee landholdings were built up mainly through debt foreclosure. Transfers of hitherto communally allocated subsistence lands to large property owners helped consolidate a hereditary oligarchy whose interests came into conflict with those of the public authority that guaranteed the traditional privileges of citizens to the means of self-support on the land. This privatization of economic power threatened to strangle governments fiscally and militarily, leading to their political and economic collapse. Mesopotamian rulers countered this by periodically restoring "economic order" through Clean Slate proclamations. But after monarchies were overthrown, no central authority was left to override the assertiveness of private wealth.

Mikhail Rostovtzev (1926) has provided the classic description of how, during the early centuries of our modern era, Rome's wealthiest landowning families managed to throw taxes onto the classes below them. Much the same phenomenon is found in the East Roman (Byzantine) empire from the 9th through 11th centuries.

Social Functions of Archaic Land Tenure

Self-support was the key to the survival of archaic communities. The Bronze Age spirit was basically one of mutual aid in a militarized context. Citizens were assured the means of self-support on the land in return for providing military service in the draft, and often various types of seasonal corvée labor.

Precommercial land tenure is communally allocated. Citizenship status typically is defined by the allotment of land rights, so as to enable citizens to support their families. The objective was not to enable citizens to make money by leasing out the land for rent or to exploit it by hiring landless cultivators. Much less was it to let land pass into the hands of absentee creditors and other land-buyers. Rather, the objective was largely military. Armies were composed of all able adult males from the landed families. In addition to their military role, their labor might be requisitioned for communal tasks, such as building dikes or harvesting grain on public lands. Newcomers, refugees seeking asylum, and the growing domestic population were provided with their own land, became dependents in the households of landholding families, or had to emigrate to colonial offshoots.

Archaic communities restricted the sale or forfeiture of subsistence landholdings in order to preserve self-sufficiency for their members. Selling one's land, or even borrowing against it, would have impaired the ability of citizens to perform their communal duties, for it usually meant a loss of self-support. Archaic interest rates were very high, so that property, once mortgaged, was often lost. This is why Mesopotamian communities, where interest-bearing debt is first attested, long blocked land from being pledged and forfeited for more than merely temporary duration. If it had to be sold as a result of need, relatives or neighbors typically had the right of first refusal and the sale was only temporary, being subject to redemption. This preserved land in the hands of local communities and their kinship groupings rather than letting it be forfeited or sold to outsiders, including merchants and royal officials.

How the Sumerians Maintained Economic Balance in the Face of Privatized Land

Southern Mesopotamian land tenure involved numerous types of property. (Diakonoff [1982] provides the classic review.) Rural land was allocated to citizens as their means of self-support. Individual lots appear to have been redistributed periodically, normally to the heirs of their customary holders. These lots could be alienated temporarily as pledges for loans or other obligations, or even sold for emergency money, but they were expected to be redeemed by the debtor, his relatives, or neighbors as soon as economic conditions permitted. Failing such redemption, they were restored to their customary owners when rulers proclaimed "economic order" (*amargi* in Sumerian [Lambert 1972; Lemche 1979: 16; Charpin 1987: 39; Postgate 1992: 195], *andurarum* in Akkadian and Babylonian [Edzard 1957; Postgate 1969, 1973; Balkan 1974], *misharum* in Babylonian [Bottéro 1961; Finkelstein 1961, 1965, 1969; Kraus 1984], *shudutu* in Hurrian [Lacheman 1962]), a measure reflected in the *deror* legislation of Leviticus 25 (the Jubilee year: cf. Weinfeld 1982; Levine 1996; Hudson 1996).

Sumerian communities also set aside land in the form of perpetual holdings for their local temples to provide sustenance for their administrators and for the indigent (widows, orphans, the blind, etc.). Turning over this land, as well as herds of animals and other assets to city temples, enabled them to be self-supporting. This was the Sumerian alternative to taxation. The endowments were permanent, making their public institutional holders the first documented landlords, in the sense of absentee landlords collecting a net usufruct from the land. These temple and palace lands thus represent history's first documented "permanent" property devoted to producing a regular rent-usufruct. Most of this land was let out on a sharecropping basis, usually via palace managers as middlemen, settling at a third of the crop by the end of the third millennium. Widows and orphans were placed in handicraft workshops to weave textiles for export or perform other tasks compatible with their infirmities.

Whereas private land transfers were only temporary in duration, land transfers to the public sector were permanent. Temple lands could not be alienated, nor could those of the palaces. (These emerged after about 2750 B.C. in southern Mesopotamia.) Palace rulers purchased lands from the communal groupings (as documented, for instance, in the Stele of Manishtushu in the Akkadian period c. 2250 B.C.; see Gelb et al. 1991).

Merchants and other well-to-do citizens acquired town houses, which they could buy or sell freely without being subject to any repurchase options or other redistributive measures. Inasmuch as these properties were not part of the subsistence sector, there was no pressing need to redistribute them when rulers "proclaimed order." Their ownership was left intact, as were commercial silver debts as opposed to consumer barley debts. The overall economy thus was allowed to grow, while taking measures to prevent its wealth from being used in ways that would undercut the rural sector's long-term balance. *Only subsistence lands were protected from permanent alienation, so as to preserve a self-supporting rural population intact alongside a commercial urban economy.*

What concerned rulers was that in addition to being a misfortune for debtors (who typically lost their status as citizens when they lost their land), foreclosures caused fiscal problems for the public sector. Creditors wanted the land's usufruct, often at the expense of the palace (in the case of royal sharecropping lands leased in exchange for a third or more of the crop as rent). Debtors were tied to their creditors virtually as servants, and hence were not available to serve in the army or to provide labor services and pay fees. To rectify this situation, rulers cancelled back taxes (and the debts stemming from them) and also reversed forfeitures of personnel and land to collectors and other creditors. These "restorations of order" were proclaimed at least once each generation (when new rulers took the throne, when they celebrated their thirtieth anniversary of rule, or when economic and military conditions warranted).

Communal land tenure helped guarantee the supply of labor services to the public sector as part of the reciprocal responsibilities between community members, the palace, and its administrative bureaucracy. This reciprocity was interrupted by absentee land acquisition on the part of members of the royal bureaucracy. Merchants (*tamkaru*) collected taxes and in the process often established financial claims on community members by paying on their behalf the moneys due (arrears which mounted up at interest). Military disruption also disturbed the circular flow of products and money. When men were called away from their land to fight, or when fighting devastated the land, some families fell into arrears and ended up pledging their servant girls, children, wives, or cattle to creditors. In time they pledged their lands (or more accurately, their crop usufruct, for debtors were left on the land to plant and harvest the crops for their creditors).

The first response of Hammurapi and other Babylonian rulers to the land-foreclosure problem was to proclaim laws preventing creditors from interfering with the "originally" envisioned balanced order. Above all, they proclaimed *misharum* acts, that is, Clean Slates restoring the idealized and symmetrical "straight order," or at least the *status quo ante*, by returning to customary holders the lands that had been forfeited for debt or, what virtually was the same thing, sold below market price. This put local notables and members of Babylonia's royal bureaucracy in their place by taking away the land with which they had aggrandized themselves at the ultimate expense of the palace. Many of these lands had been foreclosed on in settlement of unpaid tax obligations. What was owed to the palace likewise was annulled, enabling a new, equitable, and debt-free fiscal and financial start to be made. This restored the ability of local communities to perform the military duties with which they were charged and on which the palace depended.

Public Temples as Communal Corporations

Ancient Mesopotamia throws light on the idea of the "tragedy of the commons" (Hardin 1968), according to which communal resource users are deemed unable to devise rules to restrain overgrazing and other selfish exploitation of communal resources. A corollary is that communal ownership is not conducive to capital investment. These ideas have been used to defend private property's natural superiority: if no workable means exist to allocate capital expenses communally, improvements on the land and the development of craft industries will occur only if communal use rights are replaced by a regime of private ownership.

Ancient economic history suggests the reverse of the Hardin thesis: *privatized property is what turns out to be unmanageable and inequitable!* In a nutshell, a narrowing layer of wealthy landowning families monopolize the economy's wealth and, in the political sphere, divest themselves of fiscal responsibility for their society's survival.

In early Mesopotamia large-scale capital investment necessarily was communal, if only because individual families lacked the means for major undertakings. Starting with the land, investment extended to irrigation and the building up of large herds, culminating in public-sector investment in craft production and transport systems (boats, canals, caravans). Citizens benefited from these investments and were obliged to provide reciprocal services (military duty, corvée labor) for their use. Sumer's endowment of city-temples with the means to pursue export production and related commercial surplus-generating activity was compatible with personal entrepreneurial drives: an individual's opportunity for gain typically followed from his status as a public servant.

These early public enterprises had checks and balances to prevent the mismanagement that Hardin and his fellow private-property ideologues insist will result from communally managed assets. (To be sure, Hardin [1991] has recanted!) Assyriologists such as Denise Schmandt-Besserat (1992), Hans Nissen, Peter Damerov, and Robert Englund (1993) have traced how the inception of writing was developed in response to the need for account keeping as a check on the behavior of public administrators. The auditing of annual balance sheets was part of an institutional complex that included annual meetings and their attendant festivities, the invention of standardized weights and measures, and the regularization of economic activity generally, so as to permit impersonal exchanges between all buyers and all sellers. Uniform rent and interest rates were established, incomes and professional fees for public servants were stipulated (as in Hammurapi's laws), and contracts were formalized. These products of the explosive florescence of Mesopotamian public enterprise transcended the limitations of primitive economic systems.

Looking at the long-term economic dynamics of Bronze Age Mesopotamia, one can see that privatizing the debt system and establishing monetary claims on property was the major lever that led to privatizing land ownership. As needy commoners came to pledge and forfeit their customary property rights as collateral for debts, these led to the irreversible conversion of the communal rights enjoyed by the many (the right to self-support on the land) into private property for a narrowing few. This dynamic brought anarchy and disorder, until the idea of order was itself redefined and, indeed, inverted from the traditional system.

The Idea of "Freedom"

Outright "free" landownership, in the sense of cultivators being able to alienate their lands free of communal restrictions, was slow to come into being. Bronze Age Mesopotamia's idea of freedom was not one of free markets but of protecting the rural community from the adverse effects of wealth and economic polarization. The idea of order was not one of freedom for creditors to foreclose irreversibly on the lands and bond pledges of the economically weak; it was one of rulers restoring economic order by annulling personal debts and reversing debtor forfeitures of family members and property. This restored the means of self-support on the land for the population at large.

In practice this concept of social order and liberty meant that the land—and hence the economic freedom to be self-sufficient—was inalienable, much as America's Bill of Rights holds up certain personal freedoms as being inalienable. Families could not sell their lands under duress without recourse nor could they forfeit them permanently to creditors. As a result, the earliest inroads to private absentee landlordship were only temporary, save for heads of state (beginning with members of Sargon's family, as shown by the Stele of Manishtushu [Gelb et al. 1991]).

The Idea of Property

The Middle Bronze Age—the half-millennium from 2100 to 1600 B.C.—is one of the most important transition periods in the history of civilization, precisely because it was a time of decentralization and breakdown. In such periods forward momentum is lost, creating a power vacuum which affords a flexible environment for new structures to emerge.

What gave this half-millennium its quality of "middleness" was the dissolution of centralized public ownership and direction of industry, which enabled enterprise to become increasingly private in character. Civilization's first "stock market" developed for shares in the revenue generated by temple properties. The rights to crop revenues on earmarked lands were inherited and subdivided, bought and sold. A real-estate market developed for town houses, and also for farmland.

Yet there are no words for property as such. Although there are terms and regulations for deposit, pledge, pawn, and so forth, according to Szlechter (1958: 121), "one will look in vain in the Babylonian sources for a general orderly definition of the notion of property. . . . Although the expressions *lugal* (in Sumerian) and *belum* (in Akkadian) are habitually translated as "proprietor," one does not find in the Sumerian and Akkadian vocabulary a term which designates "property" in the abstract sense of law of property." The closest the Middle Bronze Age came to using a term for property was what cuneiformists translate as "domain of the lord," indicating temples as the first permanent absentee owners.

Land tenure thus had not yet evolved into fully autonomous ownership as the modern world knows it. For one thing, Bronze Age property had too many public-service obligations attached to it to be deemed "private" in the modern sense of the term. It also lacked one of the most important hallmarks of private property: the ability to be freely sold or otherwise transferred outside of its local kinship grouping. "Without doubt," concludes Szlechter (1958: 135), "it is not merely a matter of chance or poverty of the Sumerian and Akkadian languages that has left us no term for property in the actual sense of the word. It really appears that this notion has not entirely disengaged itself to the degree found in Roman or modern law."

Military Acquisition of Land and Temple Enterprise by Palace Rulers and Warlords

Temple officials of the old order had been losing ground to the palace and its nominees at least since the 25th century B.C. About 2360, the ruler Lugalanda is found in control of the major Lagash temples, as was his successor, the reformer Urukagina. A generation later, the conqueror Sargon of Akkad placed members of his family (female as well as male) in key priesthood positions throughout southern Mesopotamia. His successors obtained title to large tracts of hitherto group-held land (Gelb et al. 1991: 16, 26). Subsequent rulers continued this practice.

Meanwhile, new sources of revenue developed in the wake of bureaucratic decentralization, leaving authority—and in time, property—in the hands of local administrators, chieftains, and notables. In a word, temple offices were privatized. With regard to the Inanna temple at Nippur, Zettler (1992: 441, 461) makes the point that "the family archive of the chief administrator is mixed in with records of the temple operations." Stone (1987: 17) finds that business was conducted increasingly in the private apartments of temple administrators, and adds that "a few offices had associated prebend fields," but the best estimate of their value "is that they entitled the owner to a share of the sacrifice." By the Isin-Larsa period (2000-1800 B.C.) these revenue flows "had become a kind of private property which could have been passed on to the heirs of the owner" (ibid.)

Temple offices and their revenues were being organized along the lines that modern economists would call profit centers. Each produced an earmarked usufruct. As this revenue was bequeathed to family members, it came to be subdivided into smaller and smaller units. The earliest contracts with regard to temple offices "record the control of whole or half offices," notes Stone (1987: 21), "suggesting that these offices had either only been in the family for a short period of time or that they were neither heritable nor divisible before the time of the first contracts." Her hypothesis is that "the offices became heritable and divisible at the time they were given to these families" (ibid.), whose possession of substantial agricultural land suggests a rural foundation.

As background for how this state of affairs may have come about, Stone observes that the *Lamentation over the Destruction of Nippur* describes how, during the reign of Ishme-Dagan (1953-1935 B.C.), active warfare swept the city. It was attacked, most likely by Amorite tribesmen who had entered from the northwestern Arabian-Syrian desert. (Their first incursions into Mesopotamia are cited during the reign of Shu-Sin [2037-2029 B.C.], who built a long fortified wall [the "Martu," or, Western wall] to keep them out, but it was breached by the Amorites in large numbers in 2022.)

What may have stopped the fighting, Stone (1987: 22) suggests, was the decision by palace rulers to buy off the leaders of these rural, tribal groups. To stem future rebellion, the king moved them into the city, assigned them a large area of urban real estate, and co-opted the leaders with gifts of temple offices. Probably Iddin-Dagan (1974-1954 BC) and his Isin successors "initiated a program designed to pacify the countryside. Like the British during the mandate period, they brought the tribal leaders into the cities where they could be controlled" (ibid.). The chieftains were given temple positions, or at least the prebend revenues traditionally attached to these positions.

One result was to divorce the flow of temple revenue from the actual performance of temple functions. Indeed, it would have been a travesty if each individual receiving temple income actually had tried to carry out the associated position for just a few days. Whereas there was only a single *ugula-e* (head administrator) receiving income from the Inanna temple in the Ur III period, by Old Babylonian times, when up to one hundred may have shared a single office, the ownership of an office can have had little to do with the bureaucratic activities implied by the title, for these titles remained indivisible. There was only one responsible functionary in any given period. Administrative functions thus became separated from the prebend income earmarked to support temple officials (see also Charpin 1986: 62). Ownership was divorced from management—precisely what Adolph Berle and Gardner Means described in the 1930s as representing the "new capitalism" of our modern epoch!

What was happening was that property, or at least the income associated with it, was passing out of the hands of public institutions to effectively private holders. Based on a study of the clergy of Ur in Hammurapi's dynasty, Charpin (1986: 260f.) likewise concludes that the subdivision of temple prebend incomes must have begun late in the Ur III period. He finds that after 180 to 200 years so many successive bequeathings and partitions of these prebends had occurred that some holders received only a few days' income per year. Typical revenue subdivisions appearing in the cuneiform records are 15 days (1/24th of the 360-day administrative Mesopotamian year), 7½ days (1/48th), 5 days (1/72nd), 3⅔ days, and just 1⅔ days per year. "The result, after a century and a half of successive divisions, is an extreme parcellisation of prebends: when we see an individual owning five days of service a year in the Nanna temple, we may conclude that this theoretically signifies that the income is divided among 71 other persons for that year" (ibid.). (The number depends on how many heirs were left by successive generations of each branch of the original family.) The result was an economic organization of temples "as a kind of joint-stock company whose shares have passed into the hands of the town notables" (ibid.). By the first millennium B.C. this became standard practice throughout the Near East.

Ownership of temple usufruct flows came to be sold with increasing liquidity. Stone (1987: 18) finds that after about 1800 B.C., temple offices "carried none of the alienation restrictions which applied to the more traditional kinds of property, i.e., fields and houses," for unlike the case with rural fields and properties, the sale of temple offices was not restricted to one's kinsmen. A new economic class thus came into being: a *rentier* class of temple prebend-holders, history's earliest attested sinecures and absentee owners.

How Land Transfers Occurred Through Creditor Foreclosure

It was largely through debt foreclosure that communal subsistence landholdings were privatized, passing into the hands of public collectors and merchants when cultivators ran into problems. These alienations occurred especially in times of flood or drought, pestilence, and (above all) war, when men were called away from the land to fight or when fighting devastated their own land. Most cultivators had little to pledge as collateral except for their family members—their wives, daughters, sons, or servants. As an alternative, cultivators looked for something else that could be pledged. The most desirable asset was land.

What creditors really wanted was the land's usufruct, which they took as interest. Cultivators continued to work lands that had been foreclosed. Without their labor, land rights would not have been very valuable to creditors, for in the early centuries of land mortgaging there was not yet a body of "free" (that is, disenfranchised) seasonal labor for hire.

When land passed out of the hands of the community into those of outside appropriators, the economy as a whole suffered. One of the first objectives of these rich and powerful individuals was to avoid paying taxes and related obligations. As they gained exemption from the traditional obligation to use their wealth to support the palace and other communal organs, the fiscal burden was thrown onto the community's poorer and less influential members. Absentee owners shed the communal duties that were part and parcel of communal landholding—military obligations, corvée duties, payment of fees, and the customary forms of mutual aid. This left a shortfall that had to be made up by the rural population at large.

The palace lost militarily, for outsiders were not subject to local military service. Indeed, their foreclosures removed the debtor's draft status, preventing communities from fielding their own armed force.

Most Babylonian debts were due in the barley-harvesting month, Simann—the third month of the year, corresponding to our own late May and early June. Just prior to the harvest, cultivators found their resources to be at their lowest ebb. Matters were especially serious if a drought or other natural disaster gave creditors reason to believe that debts were about to be cancelled, and they therefore tried to anticipate matters by extorting what they could. To prevent creditors from prematurely trying to collect their debts by coercing debtors to pay and then refusing to refund their money when *misharum* was proclaimed, the Edict of Ammisaduqa (§5) prescribed the death penalty for such acts: if a creditor "prematurely collected by means of pressure, he must refund all that he received through such collection or be put to death" (Pritchard 1975: 36).

As credit became more privatized, merchant-collectors and other lenders sought to make their financial claims immune from these royal restorations of economic order. Indeed, this seems to have become a major objective of aristocratic or oligarchic opposition to royal authority. Rulers for their part overrode such attempts, and in the early centuries they emerged victorious. One finds wealthy landowning creditor families emerging in most major towns, only to disappear again suddenly from the cuneiform record.

Clean-Slate Proclamations

The severe fiscal problems caused by absentee ownership gave rulers good reason to reinforce the traditional barriers to the land's alienability, and specifically to prevent its transfer to wealthy appropriators. This was particularly the case when the new owners were local officials or chieftains assembling power bases of their own. §37 of Hammurapi's laws annulled any sale of rural fields, orchards, or houses that belonged to soldiers, commissaries or feudatories. §38 prohibited these soldiers, commissaries, and feudatory tenants from pledging their fief-fields, orchards, and houses as collateral for any obligation, or deeding them to their wives or daughters. However, §39 permitted property that already had been bought for cash to be resold, pledged for debt, or deeded, evidently on the ground that such market property had passed out of the traditional communal or public sphere.

These restrictions against alienating the land were part of long-standing Mesopotamian tradition. Szlechter (1958: 133) points out that although pre-Sargonic records attest to land sales, "when the lease-fields become 'private property' they refer only to houses, orchards or fields, whose area is relatively small." The sellers were professional bodies, and the buyer invariably was the palace (Diakonoff 1982: 8-19, 36, 67). This is not the same thing as property being freely and autonomously transferred among individuals acting on their own account, following the dictates of market forces alone.

The most important royal proclamations deterring absentee landlords from evolving into a permanent wealthy aristocracy upheld the idea that the sale or forfeiture of such lands was only temporary, until the next *misharum* act restored the *status quo ante*. It seems that when rulers enacted *misharum*, all tax and debt tablets were supposed to be handed over to the authorities to be broken, along with all land-property contracts. "Astounding as it must appear to our normally skeptical eyes," concludes Finkelstein (1965: 244), instead of the *misharum* institution being "a pious but futile gesture," the fact is that "at the promulgation of the *misharum* formal commissions were established to review real-estate sales."

Finkelstein (1969: 58) comments on Ammisaduqa's edict and its predecessors that "the provisions of these acts anticipated a certain amount of skullduggery and fraud aimed at circumventing the effect of the edict." One creditor, for instance, tried to collect the amount nominally due on a debt tablet predating one of Hammurapi's four *misharum* acts. The debtor sued and won on the ground that *misharum* had been declared since the document was drawn up. The judges in this case symbolically broke a clod of earth in lieu of the tablet, so that the latter should be considered null and void if the creditor ever again tried to collect.

Another way in which creditors sought to evade the royal proclamations was simply to get debtors to waive their rights following a Clean Slate. A Mari text dated to the sixth year of one of Hammurapi's contemporaries, Zimri-Lim, stipulates that "if an *uddurarum* is instituted, this silver will not be subject to that measure" (ARM VIII 33 discussed by Lemche [1979: 17], Margueron & Durand [1982: 107], and Charpin [1987: 39]). By writing this clause the creditor got his debtor to formally renounce any benefit of the debt remission.

Julius Lewy (1958: 24) cites similar contractual clauses from another upstream town, Hana, during the reign of Kashtiliashu in the late 1700s. One contains "a brief reference to an oath pledging the contracting parties not to contest the validity of their agreement by raising claims against each other." If the complaining party seeks to recover his land, his head is to be "smeared with hot asphalt." Inasmuch as Kashtiliashu's date formulae indicates that he "established (social) justice" at least twice, Lewy infers that it was considered necessary to insert this clause into the contract because "without such a statement, the landed property . . . might have been liable to reversion to its former owner." Such clauses are banned in Ammisaduqa's edict of 1646, but are echoed finally in Rabbi Hillel's *prosbul* clause formulated nearly two thousand years later to circumvent the biblical Jubilee Year debt cancellations called for in Leviticus 25.

Anticipating that some creditors might try to perpetrate such deceptions by having their claims "drawn up as a sale or a bailment and then persist in taking interest" (§6), Ammisaduqa's edict voided such documents, thereby annulling the transfers. Creditors who attempted to "sue against the house of an Akkadian or an Amorite for whatever he had loaned him" were threatened with the death penalty, as in §5. (This was just the opposite of subsequent Roman law, which threatened only debtors with death, never creditors!) §7 laid down a similar punishment against creditors who claimed they had given barley or silver not as an interest-bearing loan but rather as an advance for purchases, or equity investment for mutual profit, or some similar form of credit exempted from debt cancellation in §8.

These Clean Slates restored liberty to bond-servants (while returning to their former owners house-born servants who had been pledged to creditors). Thus, not only the land was restored to its traditional equilibrium; so were household structures. But just as land tenure was undercut by the rural usury process, so were the customary family lineage structures.

The "Fictive Adoption" Loophole

Although absentee landlordism caused many social problems, it was intended to resolve an even worse problem. Prior to being able to mortgage their land rights, all that poor cultivators had to pledge was their family members, who became bond-servants to the creditors until the debt could be repaid. Inasmuch as interest rates typically mounted up at 33⅓ % per year by 2100 B.C., rural debtors often were unable to redeem these pledges. So disruptive was this loss of family members that the laws of Hammurapi dictated that bond-servants should be freed after three years, probably on the logic that creditors got their capital back in this time. Gradually, sanctions against pledging the land for a longer period of time were loosened, beginning with the "fictive adoptions" found in Babylonia by the 18th century B.C. and spreading upstream along the Euphrates to Nuzi by the 16th century.

It has become an axiom of history that wealthy individuals (usually creditors) tend to appropriate property by stratagems that public policy and laws have not anticipated. Under traditional Mesopotamian land-tenure arrangements, land could not be sold or pledged as collateral for debts, but could only be bequeathed to the heirs of its customary holders. Middle Bronze Age creditors thus could not purchase it directly or get it pledged as collateral for loans on more than a temporary basis. Their solution was to take a strategic detour, arranging to inherit the land upon the death of its seller/debtor, by being "adopted" as his legal son and heir. This ploy became one of history's first documented legal loopholes, opening the gates for major inroads to be made against the principle of self-sufficiency for landed kin-groupings.

The genius of this loophole was that it appeared to reconcile their radical objectives with the conservative force of communal traditions, with the compliance of debtors driven to the wall by economic need. In exchange for money to get by, debtors adopted their creditors as sons. Sometimes this entailed having one's daughter marry the creditor or his son. It probably was from such marriage and adoption arrangements that the Babylonian proverb arose, "A creditor has many relatives." When the debtor-landholder died, his adopted creditor-son inherited the land, to the exclusion of the natural sons.

In their study of *Adoption in Old Babylonian Nippur*, Stone and Owen (1991: 2-3) elaborate how Babylonia's "shallow patrilineal lineages" succumbed to the spread of inheritance contracts in which "the adoptee takes on the social role of the son or daughter," standing to receive property through inheritance, "while the adopter [that is, the debtor] may receive an adoption payment [the *de facto* loan], . . . the text may describe the monthly and annual rations which are to be delivered by the adoptee to support his new father until his death," these payments representing compensation for the rights to inherit the land. The witnesses to such contracts are listed, and "the penalties for breaking the contract are spelled out."

One such contract finds a debt-ridden cultivator, Ur-Lumma, unable to support himself, yet "prevented by contemporary alienation restrictions from converting his property into cash through sale." He solved the problem by adopting the well-to-do Lu-Bau, son of a prominent temple official, "as his heir in exchange for support. The text includes an oath in which Ur-Lumma and his heirs foreswear all claims to Lu-Bau's new inheritance." For Ur-Lumma, the only way to alienate his property to obtain cash and security in his old age was through the back door of adoption; for Lu-Bau, the only way to obtain good property was through this same route. As matters turned out, Lu-Bau died without issue. The natural sons of Ur-Lumma pressed their traditional claims to inherit the property and, "thanks to the accident of Lu-Bau's childlessness, they regained control" (ibid.: 9).

The effect was to concentrate property in the hands of an emerging oligarchy, at the expense of poorer lineages. Such arrangements signal the breakup of family-lineage equality of opportunity. Indeed, creditor values historically have been counterpoised to traditional family values; or rather, credit relations become the new basis for kinship arrangements.

The Emergence of a Landed Aristocracy

Hammurapi's feudal-type arrangements were a landmark in catalyzing the privatization and secularization of Babylonia's economy. To pursue his ambitious plans of conquest, he needed to win the adherence of local chieftains. His strategy was to co-opt them into the royal bureaucracy, at the price of delegating broad authority to them. According to Yoffee (1979: 13), "many of these new bureaucrats appear to have come from mid- to upper-level elites of the community who had certain connections to resources embedded in local organizations that the crown wished to mobilize." Thus, whereas centralization of the economic surplus in the public sector had characterized southern Mesopotamia in the third millennium, Hammurapi sponsored its decentralization. This was the essence of his "feudalism," placing authority and, in time, property in the hands of local administrators, chieftains, and headmen as the successors of the earlier temple and palace bureaucracies. In a nutshell, hitherto-public offices were privatized.

Many Babylonian mortgage holders were public officials, who obtained land, in effect, by paying the obligations of insolvent cultivators. What they needed to secure permanent rather than merely temporary title was to unseat rulers. This became easier as the palace delegated authority to local headmen through quasi-feudal arrangements. Concerned mainly with securing an overall income and source of soldiers, the palace levied obligations on local communities, to be apportioned by their headmen.

Feudalization of royal authority blurred the distinction between public and private. Rulers leased public land to well-placed individuals in the royal bureaucracy, and let local chieftains administer their territories on the condition that they turn over a specified yield (proto-taxes and contributions) to support the palace and its armed forces.

The idea was to make this decentralized enterprise yield as much to the palace as public enterprise would have done. This autonomy was part of the *quid pro quo* for getting chieftains and headmen to acquiesce in the palace's empire-building, allowing local headmen broad leeway as long as they provided the palace with the same flow of economic usufructs that would have obtained through its own direct management. Well-placed families thus served, in effect, as public proxies.

Economic polarization inevitably followed from the dynamics of extending local systems to imperial regionwide ones, going hand in hand with a "feudalization" of authority. The basic economic tension in Babylonia stemmed from the fact that despite the fact that most creditors were *tamkaru* serving in the royal bureaucracy, charged with acting in the public interest, they put their own interests above those of the palace, taking as payment for their own extension of credit the land's usufruct that formerly was available for taxes. Turning over crops to creditors thus prevented them from being paid as royal sharecropping rent or sold to the palace.

This was what Hammurapi's laws sought to restrict, forbidding *tamkaru* from taking land from the families of soldiers. Rulers periodically restored the *status quo ante* by annulling all claims denominated in barley, that is, personal debts owed by cultivators, including claims for payment by "ale-women" and other public or quasi-public officials, as distinct from the silver-debts owed by and among merchants.

The designers of this system did not plan for the gray area that developed as rural subsistence landholders pledged and forfeited their land-tenure rights to creditors after falling into debt arrears at archaic interest rates, whose exorbitance made them nearly impossible to pay in a near-subsistence economy.

Rulers took steps to counter this development, to the extent that they could do so in the weakening momentum of the Middle Bronze Age. This delegation of authority did not immediately bring into being an aristocratic ruling class, for, as just noted, wealthy families disappear after a few generations. Still, the seeds for such a class were being planted. Palace overrides were being undercut.

The logic underlying royal Clean Slates was never spelled out by Bronze Age rulers, but the Roman historian Diodorus (1.79), writing ca. 40-30 B.C., got to the heart of matters when he explained why the pharaoh Bocchoris abolished debt-servitude and cancelled undocumented debts by ruling "that the repayment of loans could be exacted only from a man's estate, and under no condition did he allow the debtor's person to be subject to seizure." The social context for this edict was the growing military threat from Ethiopia. According to Diodorus, Bocchoris's rationale was that "the bodies of citizens should belong to the state, to the end that it might avail itself of the services which its citizens owed it, in times of both war and peace. For he felt that it would be absurd for a soldier, perhaps at the moment when he was setting forth to fight for his fatherland, to be haled to prison by his creditor for an unpaid loan, and that the greed of private citizens should in this way endanger the safety of all."

This is much how Bronze Age rulers must have reasoned. Hammurapi's laws blocked creditors from taking for themselves the usufruct of tenants on royal and other public lands, and on communal lands that owed manpower and military service to the palace. Creditor attempts to take such lands for themselves threatened to strip the rural sector of its ability to fill the military draft, in an age when warfare was endemic and mercenary armies still lay largely in the future. Such privatization of hitherto communal or royal land thus threatened to bring about fiscal, economic, and military disorder in the rural subsistence economies of the Middle and Late Bronze Age. Palace rulers had not yet become economic predators of the land; that would come only with the first-millennium florescence, and it formed the crux of Israelite opposition to such rulers.

The Byzantine Collapse

It is instructive to compare the logic of Bronze Age Clean Slate decrees with those promulgated in the Byzantine agrarian state three millennia later. While the western half of the Roman empire fell into poverty after the imperial capital was shifted to Constantinople in 396, the East Roman Byzantine half regained its economic momentum and prosperity by the 7th century. Based on the preservation of rural stability, imperial policy sought to avoid a relapse resulting from the corrosive effects of usury. For many centuries royal rulings (Novels) prohibited mortgaging the land and its attendant monopolization by large landowners, on much the same rationale as the one that had motivated Bronze Age rulers: a military one. Just as Babylonia's army three thousand years earlier had been recruited from the ranks of peasant freeholders, so was the Byzantine army—and so, too, were the best emperors.

Basil I (r. A.D. 867-886), founder of the Macedonian dynasty, was the son of a peasant who had spent most of his life in modest circumstances before ascending quickly to reform Byzantium's fiscal and legal systems. He replenished the army's ranks by ordering that the vouchers of insolvent debtors be burned, and his lawbook, the *Epanagoge*, prohibited creditors from taking fields as collateral. To prevent the recurrence of rural instability, Basil banned agrarian lending at interest, save for the loophole of permitting the money of orphans and other minors to be lent out to provide an income for their support. His laws restricted alienation of the land "by giving the right of first refusal to the other members of the community, either individually or collectively" (Toynbee 1973: 147). However, his successor, Leo VI (r. A.D. 886-912), permitted interest of 5½% to be charged, claiming that the ban on rural mortgages burdened the economy. This and subsequent Novels opened the way for the large *dhynatoi* to re-appropriate the land. (Novel 114, for instance, removed the right of first refusal to local community members.)

What forced a reversal of Leo's "market-oriented" philosophy was a wave of rural credit disasters and famine. The need to raise troops to defend the empire's eastern front entailed the domestic danger of empowering landlords and the armies under their command to become an autonomous force threatening palace rule. After some years of turmoil following Leo's death, the imperial crown again passed to a man of lowly origin, Romanus I Lecapenus (r. A.D. 920-944). A soldier's son who had distinguished himself by his strength and bravery, he managed to surround himself with competent advisors.

Bréhier (1977: 111) describes Romanus as "the first emperor to take legislative measures to check the disturbing spread of large estates at the expense of smaller properties and to preserve the integrity of military properties, fundamental to the administration of the themes and the recruitment of an indigenous army." Toynbee (1973: 153) paraphrases one of his Novels, probably from the year A.D. 929, following Byzantium's victory on its eastern frontier. Famine had plagued the countryside during the winter of 927/928, forcing many peasants to mortgage their lands to wealthy creditors, who absorbed the properties into their own holdings and enserfed the former freeholders. With the memory of the rural credit disasters under Leo VI still fresh, the emperor wrote a preamble avowing that: "we have left nothing undone to liberate districts and villages and cities from the enemy. . . . Now that we have achieved these magnificent successes in putting an end to the aggression of the foreign enemy, what about the domestic enemy in our own household? How can we refrain from dealing severely with him?" (ibid.). This question might apply just as well to Babylonia three thousand years earlier. According to Bréhier (1977: 111), Romanus's Novel of 934,

> stigmatized the egoism of the powerful, and also, without actually ordering the general eviction of all proprietors who held properties belonging to the poor, annulled all transactions, gifts and legacies made after 922, and laid it down that any property which had been acquired for less than half the reasonable price should be handed back without indemnity. On the other hand, if the purchase had been fair, the property could be redeemed within three years provided the money paid for it was refunded. "The small property," wrote the emperor, "is particularly useful for the payment of taxes and the performance of military service. Everything would be imperilled if it disappeared." Romanus, who was himself the son of a holder of a military property, understood the danger which threatened the free peasantry, which was the best support of the state.

Subsequent emperors were not so strong. As creditors monopolized the land, they weakened the fiscal position and hence the ability to field a Byzantine army. Indeed, as tensions mounted between the emperors and large landholders, Byzantium cut off its nose to spite its face. To prevent warlords from emerging from the ranks of the large landowners (as local commanders) and turning their troops against Constantinople itself, the emperors avoided funding the army. In any event, collecting taxes became all but impossible as local autonomy increased. The landowners welcomed this warlord strife, for by countering royal power, it minimized the emperor's ability to collect taxes.

Matters were stabilized by the nearly fifty-year rule of Basil II (r. A.D. 976-1025), the longest in Byzantine history. At the start of his reign the military and landed aristocracy controlled the leading palace advisors, seeking above all (as aristocracies invariably do) to prevent the emergence of a strong emperor. However, as two warlords, Bardas Sclerus and Bardas Phocas, vied for control of the empire during the early 980s, the young emperor came to realize that to gain control of matters, he must enter a life-and-death fight against the landlords. This he achieved by rescuing the still-free peasantry from being reduced to serfdom and hence clientship to the large landholders. To reverse the wholesale forfeiture of lands that had taken place, Basil moved on New Year's Day 996 to abolish

> the law which prescribed a period of forty years of tenure before ownership of property could be established. Instead, he ruled that all lands which had been acquired since the first law of Romanus Lecapenus in 922 must be restored to their original owners without any indemnity, even those taken over by the Church. The preamble to this novel, regarded as a gloss added by Basil, protests indignantly against the scandal caused by important families such as the Phocae and the Maleini, who had kept unjustly acquired properties in their possession for more than a hundred years. This law was applied with extreme severity. Philokales, who had usurped a number of large properties and bought himself high palatine offices, was reduced to his original status of simple peasant, and the authorities even went so far as to destroy the buildings he had erected. (Bréhier 1977: 150)

Basil's "chief weapon against the maintenance of large properties was a reform of the so-called *allelengyon*. This system, whereby local communities were jointly responsible for an annual sum payable to the imperial fisc, was now altered in such a way that the financial burden fell solely on the owners of large estates, the poor being exempted" (ibid.). The leading landed families tried to get the patriarch Sergius to intervene on their behalf, but with little effect.

Basil II resembled Hammurapi, not only in his exceptionally long rule, but in the fact that he was obliged to establish a feudal-type system as the price for consolidating imperial power, rewarding supporters who were loyal with tax exemptions. This had the ultimate effect of weakening Byzantium's fiscal condition, while catalyzing a transition to feudalism in the sense of establishing personal loyalties to a ruler who could hand out financial favors or impose heavy burdens at his own personal discretion.

The Problem of Tax Exemption for Large Religious and Other Institutional Landholdings

The problem was by no means limited to large private landowners, but extended to the monasteries and other religious bodies which played an important role in the East Roman Empire (as they also did in the West, of course). For instance, when Byzantine officials descended on the empire's Bulgarian province after the region finally was conquered in 1018, Basil was obliged to "win the peace" by issuing *exkousseia*, "excusances." Their pedigree can be traced back to the Middle Babylonian *kudurrus* exempting local towns and temple precincts from royal taxation. Such privileges, writes Oikonomides (1988: 321), were distributed to quell the revolt of local potentates, by rewarding "those who remained faithful to the emperor in order to secure their support."

This was the root of feudal privileges: making local leaders—above all the clergy, in this case—dependent on the emperor's will, not *ipso facto* as a result of their belonging to a class of exempted properties. "What used to be a general privilege for all priests, now appears as a special favor granted to the archbishop, and concerns only a limited number of those under his jurisdiction. The privileges of Bari [in Grecian Italy] and Ohrid [in Bulgaria] are identical from that point of view" (ibid.: 322).

Down through the 10th century, emperors had sought "to contain the expansion of big landownership, including ecclesiastical, expecially under Nicephoros Phokas and Basil II in the early years of his reign," by abolishing the traditional ecclesiastical exemption from corvées and *leitourgoi*. This revived Byzantium's fiscal position, at the expense of the clergy and its traditional privileges. However, "the state, instead of abolishing the privilege completely, tried to control it by establishing limited numbers of exempt clerics for each diocese. It thus reserved to itself the right to increase the number when it so wished in order to win the favor of a prelate or of the inhabitants of a region" (ibid.: 323). Bishops, for instance, were allowed to distribute a specified number of exemptions to individuals within their sees. "Consequently, the new approach created automatically a client relationship between the prelates and their subordinates."

Actually, Oikonomides (ibid.: 324) points out: "What appears to us as a major gift, is in fact a limitation of pre-existing privileges," for there was a fundamental shift from the Late Roman situation.

> In the Late Roman Empire traditional privileges concerned a whole class of individuals, while the "gifts" of Basil II reflect all the characteristics of medieval privileges, i.e. exceptional treatment granted—or increased or diminished . . .—by the sovereign to individual cases in anticipation of, if not in exchange for, the favors of the recipient. The difference is essential. Moreover, what was initially, in the Byzantine case, a real limitation of the extent of the privilege, ended up by becoming a loosening by the institution of the tight structure of the monarchic state in favor of the centrifugal forces of the privileged aristocrats, among whom the church formed a part.

For in effect, the priestly hierarchy was filled mainly with scions of Byzantium's leading landed families. The Late Roman tax exemptions had been granted to the clergy and other public bodies across the board by virtue of their public roles. But in time their proliferation impaired state finances, a tendency made worse by the fact that "these privileges could easily be considered as hereditary, especially when granted to members of large and powerful families. They were easily granted and in large numbers in moments of political instability, when local magnates—or church representatives, like those who obtained Basil's exemptions—could influence or even bring pressure to bear on the central authority" (ibid.).

The benefits of such exemptions were passed on to tenants (*paroikoi*) at the expense of other landlords and the palace. By renting from the church, such tenants gained exemption from the royal land tax (*klerikotopion*). "Their exemption from certain fiscal burdens profited mainly the bishop, who received at least part of the exemption and who was thus in a better position to attract to his lands the manpower necessary for their cultivation, by offering prospective lessees more advantageous conditions than those of nonexempt landowners" (ibid.: 325).

Actually, large religious institutions have enjoyed fiscal exemption in nearly all known societies, reflecting their autonomous status on a par with the palace ("the state"). This did not create problems in Mesopotamia, for at the inception of the Bronze Age, Sumerians endowed their temple as surplus-creating centers, many centuries before taxation of the community at large developed (since there was as yet no substantial private-sector surplus to tax).

Matters were different in Egypt, where each pharaoh's soul was cared for by a cult incorporated upon his death—an entire funerary territory and population, cutting people and their economic energy out of society's commercial operations to support a public overhead which, in economic terms, was unproductive of any surplus. Via classical antiquity, when temples increasingly became purely religious institutions rather than commercially productive ones, the transition to feudal times in the Late Middle Ages saw these institutions become productive only in the spiritual world, not in that of commerce.

It also is significant that traditional communal inheritance laws were first loosened in medieval times by the Christian church. In contrast to the practice from Babylonia to Byzantium, it was no longer poor tenants who bequeathed their lands to creditors, but rather wealthy aristocrats who gave them to the church for the salvation of their souls. These properties thus passed out of the royal tax domain—until Henry VIII reversed the trend by breaking up England's monasteries in a pre-Thatcherite privatization.

Land Monopoly Leads to Byzantine Military Defeat

By the 11th century the Byzantine fiscal situation was so weakened that the empire no longer could defend itself. The last stand against the landlords—and enemies at the borders—was made by the Comnenus dynasty founded by Alexius I (r. A.D. 1081-1118). However, the dynasty's position was weak from the outset. "Since they belonged to the nobility, they abandoned the time-honored offensive of the central government against the great landowners and, to consolidate their dynasty's power, they favored the formation of large apanages and the unlimited increase of monastic properties, thus weakening the authority of the state" (Bréhier 1977: 202).

To be sure, in the year of his accession, Alexius "seized the goods of numerous noblemen convicted of conspiracy; he made grants or *charisticia* to the profit of individuals from the possessions of monasteries in exchange for the military services of their tenants (*paroikoi*); he tightened up taxation and debased the coinage"; but this made him so unpopular that "people in the provinces preferred barbarian to Byzantine rule, and in 1095 the towns of Thrace opened their gates to the Comans" (ibid.: 207).

Unable to raise taxes to fund a royal army and fearful of leaving troops in the hands of commanders drawn almost exclusively from the ranks of the upper aristocracy, the Byzantine emperors had few resources with which to counter the pressures from the Turks, who were gaining control in the eastern Arab states. Matters were complicated by the Normans pressing in from Italy, joining forces with of the navies Venice and Genoa. German emperors entered into a tenuous partnership with the papacy as the Crusades set vast troop movements in motion from western Europe across Byzantium to the Holy Land.

In 1204 Byzantium fell before the small army of Crusaders who looted Constantinople on behalf of their Venetian creditors, with whom they had reached a booty-sharing arrangement to finance the naval expedition against Byzantium. Actually, the sacking of Constantinople was an anticlimax, following the economy's erosion in the 11th century when the emperors followed the disastrous policy of throwing out the baby with the bathwater. They could not solve the problem of promoting wealth without letting economic polarization strengthen the nobility in its opposition to any centralized royal overrides to oligarchic wealth-seeking, land monopolization and, ultimately, regicide.

The Relevance of Bronze Age and Classical History for Today's Economic Crisis

This essay has examined Middle Bronze Age Mesopotamia (2000-1600 B.C.) and the Byzantine Empire (A.D. 330-1204) to trace how the corrosive dynamics of debt, absentee land-ownership, monopolization, and economic polarization have repeatedly destroyed societies throughout history. As private property threw off its originally public context and oversight, it undercut overall economic viability to the point where it destroyed entire civilizations.

Today's debt overhead once again is transferring real estate and farms, natural resources (oil and other minerals, and forest products), industry, and government-owned assets into the hands of a narrowing layer of bankers, bondholders, and other creditors. Over the past century, a major field for finance-capital has been the creation of railroads and exploitation of natural resources. In both cases, such capital has gained special tax breaks that have contributed to hoarding and other utilization of land. The oil industry's depletion allowance is the most notorious, but related tax breaks for mining, for real-estate depreciation, and indeed the interest deductibility for debt all represent equally serious concessions.

Matters have become expecially pronounced in Third World countries, whose governments, under pressure from the International Monetary

Fund and World Bank, and from the U.S. and European governments, have been urged to provide special concessions to foreign investors in an attempt to generate more foreign exchange, which in turn is used to service foreign debts or facilitate capital flight to offshore havens. The result leaves ostensibly resource-rich countries in debt beyond their capacity to pay, creating a permanent fiscal and foreign-exchange crisis.

At least in antiquity, governments were not debtors; more often, they were creditors. This condition no longer is true, making the modern crisis all the more serious. Today, government debt is responsible for generating interest payments that have come to equal the entire budget deficit, even in the United States. It is to curtail these deficits, and to raise funds to redeem some of the public debt while paying interest on the remaining indebtedness, that governments are privatizing their hitherto public resources, from land to public utilities.

Today's budget deficits and privatizations may be viewed as the price of refraining from taxing land and natural-resource ownership. Wealth-holders have broken free of taxation—and abolition of the capital-gains tax may crown this trend, inasmuch as most "capital gains" actually are land-value and real-estate gains.

A grand cycle is thus being closed, which this essay has described for the ancient Near East and Byzantium. Public obligations owed by landed property holders, above all for military service (and for corvée labor in the Near East), have a pedigree going back at least to Sumerian times in the third millennium B.C. Almost as old a phenomenon is the striving by rich and powerful families to avoid such obligations on their own holdings. Prior to the development of a land market, these holdings were built up mainly by foreclosing on collateral pledged by debtors.

The transfer of hitherto communally allocated subsistence lands to large property owners helped consolidate hereditary aristocracies and oligarchies to the point where their own power was able to undercut that of centralized authority. The ensuing privatization of economic power—and its associated displacement of rights-of-person by property rights—was achieved by strangling governments fiscally and militarily, leading to political and economic collapse.

Periodic restorations of order did not survive the Bronze Age outside of the Near East and Egypt. Instead of creating corporately autonomous public sectors, Greece and Rome concentrated the focus of enterprise, land-rent, and interest-bearing debt in the households of local chieftains. There was no palace or temple authority to be undercut in the classical

Aegean and Italy; only southern Mesopotamia had created the strong centralized public-sector traditions that gradually diffused throughout the Near East. The Mycenaean palaces were a hybrid "mixed" form, and in any case did not survive after 1200 B.C. Where local chieftain-kings emerged in the Dark Age of 1200-750 B.C. in Greece and southern Italy, they ended up being unseated by landed aristocracies, much as England's aristocracy curtailed royal power from the 13th century A.D. onward. For better or worse, these aristocracies replaced central power with their own economic control, leaving no central authority to restore economic balance and order once it was disturbed by the dynamics of debt and growing oligarchic power.

The widening polarization between rich and poor was expressed most characteristic-ally in the conflict between creditors and debtors, ending up as a polarization between large landowners and expropriated dependents and slaves. The biblical examples denounced by Isaiah 5:8-9 reflect a polarization that became most pronounced in Rome. Italy in fact was the westernmost peripheral area of the early first millennium B.C. that still was a viable part of the Levantine system. (Documents from Spain, Carthage, and other Phoenician colonies do not appear in the historical record until these regions are conquered by Rome.) Being peripheral, Rome never created the checks and balances that preserved self-sufficiency in Mesopotamia and the Levant. Debt-servitude was practiced from the outset.

Cicero (*De officiis* 2.78-80) reflected the spirit of his times in condemning the redistribution of land and cancellation of debts. The plebeians never were able to break the patricians' stranglehold on the economy. Matters were especially serious for soldiers called away from the land to engage in the almost constant fighting that enabled Rome to conquer central Italy. In effect the peasantry was fighting for its own expropriation. Their families were forced into debt and were absorbed (along with their lands) into the estates of their well-to-do creditors. The wealthiest families, for their part, managed ultimately to gain immunity from the public obligations which landholders traditionally had owed their communities. Taxes became regressive and the economy polarized between rich and poor, stifling society's fiscal position.

In each society the winning of tax-exemption by well-placed landholders and natural-resource appropriators appears as a singular, nearly accidental result of jockeying for position, but looking across the broad sweep of history, a common pattern emerges spanning over four thousand years, extending back to the Middle Bronze Age, 2000-1600 B.C. Typically a politically weak ruler is confronted with a strong aristocratic leader mobilizing the leading families behind him.

Mesopotamian rulers countered this by periodically restoring "economic order," that is, by issuing Clean Slate proclamations, but this practice did not survive into oligarchic Greek and Roman antiquity. In place of Clean Slates we find irreversible debt servitude. No economic-order proclamations cancelling debts are known, no time-limits to debt bondage or to the forfeiture of property to foreclosing creditors and other wealthy buyers. The result was that Rome became the most extreme and unmitigated oligarchy known in antiquity. The principle of linear economic progress had replaced that of "circular time," with its periodic restorations of order to undo what the emerging landholding and slaveholding oligarchies called progress.

References Cited

Balkan, K.

1974 Cancellation of debts in Cappadocian tablets from Kültepe. In K. Bittel, P.H.J. Houwink ten Cate, & E. Reiner (eds.), *Anatolian Studies Presented to Hans C. Guterbock on the Occasion of his 65th Birthday*, pp. 29-36. Istanbul: Nederlands Historisch-Archaeologisch Instituut in het Nabije Oosten.

Bottéro, J.

1961 Désordre économique et annulation des dettes en Mésopotamie a l'époque paléo-babylonienne. *Journal of the Economic and Social History of the Orient* 4:113-64.

Bréhier, L. (trans. M. Vaughan)

1977 *The Life and Death of Byzantium.* Amsterdam: Elsevier North-Holland.

Charpin, D.

1986 *Le Clergé d'Ur au siècle d'Hammurabi.* Geneva: Librairie Droz.

1987 Les décrets royaux à l'époque paléo-babylonienne, à propos d'un ouvrage récent. *Archiv für Orientforschung* 34:36-44.

Diakonoff, I.M.

1982 The structure of Near Eastern society before the middle of the second millennium B.C. *Oikumene* 3:7-100.

Edzard, D.O.

1957 *Die zweite Zwischenzeit Babyloniens.* Wiesbaden: O. Harrassowitz.

Finkelstein, J.J.

1961 Ammisaduqa's edict and the Babylonian "law codes." *Journal of Cuneiform Studies* 15:91-104.

1965 Some new *misharum* material and its implications. In *Studies in Honor of Benno Landsberger on His Seventy-Fifth Birthday*, Oriental Institute Assyriological Studies 16:233-46. Chicago: University of Chicago Press.

1969 The edict of Ammisaduqa: a new text. *Revue d'Assyriologie et Archéologie Orientale* 63:45-64.

Gelb, I., P. Steinkeller, & R.M. Whiting, Jr.

1991 *Earliest Land Tenure Systems in the Near East: Ancient Kudurrus* (Oriental Institute Publications, 104). Chicago: Oriental Institute.

Hardin, G.
1968 The tragedy of the commons. *Science* 162:1243-48.
1991 The tragedy of the unmanaged commons. In R.V. Andelson (ed.), *Commons Without Tragedy*, pp. 162-85. London: Shepheard-Walwyn.

Hudson, M., & B. Levine (eds.)
1996 *Privatization in the Ancient Near East and the Classical World: A Symposium Held at New York University, November 1994.* Cambridge, MA: Peabody Museum.

Kraus, F.R.
1984 *Königliche Verfügungen in altbabylonischer Zeit.* Studia et Documenta ad Jura Orientis Pertinentia, 11. Leiden: E.J. Brill.

Lacheman, E.R.
1962 The word *šudutu* in the Nuzi tablets. *Proceedings of the 25th International Congress of Orientalists (Moscow, 1960)*, Volume 1, pp. 233-38. Moscow.

Lambert, M.
1972 L'expansion de Lagash au temps d'Entemena. *Rivista degli Studi Orientali* 47:1-22.

Lemche, N.P.
1979 *Andurarum* and *mišarum*: comments on the problems of social edicts and their application in the ancient Near East. *Journal of Near Eastern Studies* 38:11-18.

Levine, B.
1996 Farewell to the ancient Near East: evaluating biblical references to ownership of land in comparative perspective. In M. Hudson & B. Levine (eds.), *Privatization in the Ancient Near East and the Classical World: A Symposium Held at New York University, November 1994*, pp. 223-52. Cambridge, MA: Peabody Museum.

Lewy, J.
1958 The biblical institution of *deror* in the light of Akkadian documents. *Eretz-Israel* 5.

Margueron, J., & J.-M. Durand
1982 *Mari, Annales de Recherches Interdisciplinaires*, Vol. 1. Paris: Éditions Recherches sur les Civilisations.

Nissen, H., P. Damerow, & R. Englund
1993 *Archaic Bookkeeping: Writing and Techniques of Economic Administration in the Ancient Near East.* Chicago: University of Chicago Press.

Oikonomides, N.
1988 Tax exemptions for the secular clergy under Basil II. In *Kathegretia: Essays Presented to Joan Hussey for Her 80th Birthday*, pp. 317-26. Camberley: Porphyrogenitus.

Postgate, J.N.
1969 *Neo-Assyrian Royal Grants and Decrees*. Studia Pohl, Series Maior, 1. Rome: Pontifical Bible Institute.
1992 *Early Mesopotamian Society and Economy at the Dawn of History*. London: Routledge.

Rostovtzev, M.
1926 *The Social and Economic History of the Roman Empire*. Oxford: Clarendon.

Schmandt-Besserat, D.
1992 *Before Writing: From Counting to Cuneiform*. Austin: University of Texas Press.

Stone, E.
1987 *Nippur Neighborhoods* (Studies in Ancient Oriental Civilization, 44). Chicago: Oriental Institute.

Stone, E., & D.I. Owen
1991 *Adoption in Old Babylonian Nippur and the Archive of Mannum-mešu-lissur*. Winona Lake: Eisenbrauns.

Szlechter, E.
1958 De quelques considérations sur l'origine de la propriété foncière privée dans l'ancien droit mésopotamien. *Revue Internationale des Droits de l'Antiquité* 5:121-36.

Toynbee, A.
1973 *Constantine Porphyrogenitus and His World*. London: Oxford University Press.

Weinfeld, M.
1982 "Justice and Righteousness" in ancient Israel against the background of "social reforms" in the Ancient Near East. In H.J. Nissen & J. Renger (eds.), *Mesopotamien und seine Nachbarn: politische und kulturelle wechselbeziehungen vom 4. bis 1. Jahrtausend*, Berliner Beiträge zum Vorderen Orient 1:490-519. Berlin: Dietrich Reimer.

Yoffee, N.
1979 The decline and rise of Mesopotamian civilization: an ethnoarchaeological perspective on the evolution of social complexity. *American Antiquity* 44:5-35.

Zettler, R.
1992 *The Ur III Temple of Inanna at Nippur: The Operation and Organization of Urban Religious Institutions in Mesopotamia in the Late Third Millennium B.C.* (Berliner Beiträge zum Vorderen Orient, 11). Berlin: Dietrich Reimer.

Chapter Ten

ജ്ഞ

Property, State, and Self-Destruction in Medieval Iceland

E. Paul Durrenberger

Ownership defines who may legitimately use what things in what ways. Property is that which is owned. Ownership defines differential access to resources and productive technology and thus embodies and enforces the social relations entailed in production. Because ownership defines relationships among people, it is a social relation, a characteristic of social systems. Fried (1967) argues that differential access to productive resources, the hallmark of stratification, can only be maintained by force organized in the form of state institutions to protect the claims of the "haves" against those of the "have-nots." In egalitarian societies, in contrast, all have equal access to productive resources, and ownership does not organize production.

Fried further argues that, without state institutions to enforce differential access to resources, those who are unprivileged will attempt to change political relations to egalitarian or rank ones so that they and everyone else share equal access to resources, and no one will be advantaged or disadvantaged by the social relations of property. Those who benefit from stratification, he argues, must develop state institutions to maintain their favored position.

Concepts and practices of ownership vary with types of social systems. As a socially meaningful category, any kind of property, including common property, enters some system of property relationships. The Lisu of northern Thailand clear swiddens wherever there is forest to clear. From their point of view, if not the Thai government's, the lands are not owned but are simply a productive resource that does not enter any system of ownership, collective or private. They have no notion of common property, nor of any kind of ownership of land.

Their Karen neighbors, in contrast, claim collective ownership of forests surrounding their irrigated fields. A major difference is that Karen have irrigated fields that can be owned whereas as traditionally Lisu had none. Karen use the nearby hillsides to supplement their irrigated rice harvests and consider the tracts of forests to be the common property of the village. Lisu, with no similar category of private ownership in land, have no opposed category of common property (Durrenberger & Pálsson 1987a). There are conflicts when the two systems, with their contrary definitions of property, meet. When Lisu begin to encroach on the common forest tracts of Karen villagers, Karen see an incursion into their common property by an alien group without rights to it, while Lisu see themselves as using a resource that no one can own or claim to own. Both of these systems are set in a larger and yet different social order of a Thai state with different concepts of property, resources, and forests.

Shan lowlanders in Thailand's northwestern province of Maehongson are not egalitarian, but they have long been organized as states and principalities in various combinations of alliance and conquest with other lowlanders, such as Thai, Burmans, and Chinese. In Maehongson they practiced a kind of agriculture similar to the Karen system until a third concept of property became salient (Durrenberger & Tannenbaum 1990, 1992). From the Thai government point of view, uncultivated forest is not common property, or village property, or any property at all, but royal property to be disposed of by the government (Jonsson 1991). The Thai government thus views the Karen and Lisu equally as interlopers in national forests.

This has not made much difference, except rhetorically, until recently (Jonsson 1991). Many Shan farmers have long relied on swiddens to produce the difference between what their irrigated fields can produce and what their household needs. When the Thai government granted teak harvesting permits to timber firms, the consequences for remote villages were both fast and positive: the construction of roads by timber firms to remove the logs provided villagers access to markets, health care, and other government services. Later, when swiddening was outlawed and reforestation programs were initiated to produce wood for paper firms, many villagers were cut off from an important means of subsistence. Concepts and practices of property made a great difference.

In stratified societies, with unequal access to resources enforced by the power of states, those who control the state define the terms of ownership. Governments create and enforce rights of ownership. State law and its enforcement define who can legitimately claim what and decide among competing claimants. Highly centralized states may claim ownership of every person and thing in their domains as, for example, in Tokugawa Japan (Durrenberger & Pálsson 1987b).

Medieval Iceland is interesting because it involved the conjunction of property and law with a stratified social order, but without state institutions to enforce them. The society was stratified and there was differential access to resources, but there was no state to define or enforce rights of ownership. Landowners extracted the product of dependents' labor by claiming ownership of the land they worked. Early in the medieval period they did this by claiming and enforcing ownership of individuals as slaves, later by means of seasonal labor and rental arrangements. The chieftains of medieval Iceland made the laws that defined their social order. Because the chieftains refused to entertain the idea of a state to protect their common interests, they could only enforce claims to ownership by force. Their own law was ineffective.

When they tried to expand their holdings, chieftains confronted other chieftains in violent conflicts until only one remained. He then ruled in the name of the king of Norway, thus radically changing the nature of social and political relations in Iceland. The chieftains destroyed their social order in a period of internecine strife known as the Sturlunga period, after the name of the strongest of the families during most of the 13th century. This strife illustrates the inherent contradiction in claiming both relations of property and no state. The example argues for the conclusion that there can be no property without a state to support it. It suggests, further, that property relations without states to enforce them are destructive of the social order. Thus, the stateless society of medieval Iceland destroyed itself.

History

The traditionally accepted date for the first permanent settlement of Iceland is 874 when chieftains from Norway began claiming land on the uninhabited island and establishing an agricultural economy based largely on grass for livestock management but supplemented significantly from hunting and fishing. Chieftains were the only ones in western Norway with sufficient means to sponsor sea voyages and settlement ventures.

Their motive for migration was to avoid the attempts of Harald Finehair to establish a kingdom in Norway. They framed their resistance in terms of their reluctance to pay taxes in return for nothing and their aversion to servility. They came to Iceland with their slaves and followers. One of their first acts, after claiming land, was to allocate it to their free followers of high rank with the understanding that such followers would support their chieftains against others. Thus, the idea of ownership of land and people was implicit from the beginning of the settlement of Iceland.

Harald had put together a coalition of Norwegian chieftains to form an aristocracy and gave the others the choice to fight, join, or flee. Those who were late to join or who resisted or who could not bring themselves to pay taxes to the new king left. Having left an emerging state, they had no inclination to establish a similar social order in their new land. They were familiar with kings, courts, aristocrats, and states as they traveled widely after the settlement. Part of young men's coming of age was typically a series of voyages to raid, trade, compose poetry, and visit the courts of northern Europe and the British Isles.

In addition to the settlement in 874, three other dates are important. The general assembly (*alþingi*) was founded in 930. That date is important chiefly because Icelandic sources say that the land was all claimed by 930, thus marking the end of the period of settlement. The fact that the land was all claimed is evidence of increased population since the first settlement. In the year 1000, by a compromise decision of a single arbiter selected at the *alþingi*, Christianity became the religion of Iceland. This was a turning point in Iceland, not because Christianity was adopted, but because about the same time, slave owners freed their slaves and began using seasonal labor from people who had insufficient means to support themselves through the year. With the less costly source of labor, those who claimed to own land could expand their holdings (Durrenberger 1992).

The third important date is 1264 when one chieftain, having defeated the rest, was appointed to rule Iceland in the name of the Norwegian king.

The Sturlunga Period

Late in the year 1241 a chieftain named Gissur, the son of Þorvaldur, had Snorri Sturlason, probably the most powerful and richest man in Iceland, stabbed to death. Snorri's son, Órækja, and his brother's son, Sturla Þórður's son, gathered their forces. With about five hundred men, the avengers rode toward Gissur's house where Gissur was holding a feast on the eighth day of Christmas. When he heard the news, Gissur and his men fled to the bishopric at Skálholt. The avengers attacked and the battle raged. Clad in full vestments, his miter on his head, crozier in one hand, and a bible and candle in the other, the bishop leapt up on the house beams and began to excommunicate Órækja and his followers. Órækja agreed to reconciliation, and after much commotion, the battle was stopped. Gissur then went to Norway and spent three years with the king in Norway, who assigned to him the whole northern quarter of Iceland. When he returned to Iceland and read the king's letter publicly, he was accepted as chieftain of the north.

Another group attacked Gissur in his house, burned the house and the people in it, killing his wife and son and a number of his followers. Gissur escaped death by hiding in a vat of sour whey sunk in the floor and covered with a lid. He gathered his forces again and began to hunt down and kill his attackers. Gissur again went to Norway where Hákon gave him the title of *jarl* (earl) and gave him the southern, northern, and western quarters of Iceland. After four years, he returned home to Iceland. Isolating and killing those who opposed him, he consolidated his holdings and power. Thus, for the first time in about four hundred years, was Iceland united under the rule of a single earl, appointed by and ruling on behalf of the king of Norway. The year was 1264.

Thus ended a period of bloody double crosses, burnings, maimings, mayhem, looting, and murders, a time of chaos that took its name, Sturlunga period, from Snorri's relatives, the descendants of Sturla, one of the most powerful and literary families in Icelandic history. The Snorri whom Gissur had killed had a brother whose son wrote the Saga of the Icelanders, which tells the names of men who fought on each side of each battle, the number of combatants, the names of people's fathers, mothers, wives, husbands, and paramours, the dreams they had, poems they wrote, the people they killed, and the people who killed them. Early in the 14th century this was assembled with a series of smaller sagas about individual chieftains and areas into a collection called the Sturlunga saga, the saga of the Sturlungs. During the same time, other Icelandic writers turned their attention to their past and wrote the Icelandic family sagas. Some writers recorded the law traditions, some wrote the sagas of the bishops. Together these writings provide a rich self-account of a stratified society without a state as it saw its own past and as it recorded its own demise (Durrenberger 1988, 1990).

Economic Dynamics

In the early period, when land was plentiful, labor limits put ceilings on production. One could not recruit labor outside the household. As long as there was land to be claimed, no one would work for someone else while it was possible to work for oneself and keep the product for one's own use. While slaves augmented the size of households so one could claim and work larger tracts of land with them than without them, they also proved a liability because they ate about as much as they produced. Productivity was low in this subarctic agricultural and hunting economy (McGovern et al. 1985, Gelsinger 1981). By A.D. 1000, because of population growth, some families were working land that was insufficient to meet their consumption needs.

Now control of land, rather than labor, became the major constraint. If one could control land, one could recruit seasonal laborers and not have to support them throughout the year. With such labor, landowning households could produce surpluses. Those with insufficient land, however, were in subsistence deficits because nothing had increased labor productivity. In fact, because of environmental degradation, it had decreased (McGovern et al. 1985). It was not possible to intensify production because the amount of grass, especially grass that one could save as hay to bring livestock through the winters, put an absolute limit on the number of livestock a household could maintain. Households with less than enough land could send some of their members to work at larger establishments in exchange for their keep during part of the year.

There was a congruent change in settlement pattern and class relations. Instead of large estates with their slaves and satellite estates of high-ranking clients, there developed landowning estates surrounded by dependent establishments worked by freed slaves. The product of their labor was extracted by rents or by supporting workers only during the period they worked rather than all year. The difference provided a surplus for landowning households but a deficit for working households. The gap between aristocrats and commoners widened. The titles used for aristocrats began to change from "chieftain" to "aristocrat." Chieftaincy was a formal status defined by law, but it could be bought, sold, or given away, so that it and aristocratic standing were subject to the same vagaries of possession and enforcement as any other kind of property.

When the chieftains enacted a tithe law in 1096, it provided that one-fourth of the revenues collected were to be used to support the poor of the communities from which they were collected. This law was enforced in the same way as any other law—by the personal force of chieftains and to their advantage. It was not universally enforced, and when revenues were collected, they did not necessarily go in the directions the law specified. The interesting observation is that local documents recognize a category of poor whose annual subsistence is in doubt. The law indicates that there were people who found it difficult to support themselves throughout the year and that the landowners—those chieftains and worthy men who made the laws—found it to their benefit in principle (in law) if not always in practice to maintain them, even to share out the cost of their maintenance, so that they would be available for labor when needed. This made less demand on the funds of landowning households than did the support of slaves, without affecting productivity.

Surplus that was not used to support the poor was available for alternate purposes, as it had been during the period of slavery. Large and powerful households could use it to sponsor periodic feasts, to present lavish gifts to others of the same class so as to cement alliances, or to pay large fines to avoid fights when they chose to. This "addition" to the funds of independent households provided an exploitable resource for chieftains.

With seasonal labor available, large landowners could expand their holdings, and thus increase their power not only by controlling land but through gifts, dowry and bride prices for marriages, and other distributions. They did this by gaining control of land from those who had insufficient land to support their households. Originally there had been owners of larger or smaller estates, slaves, and freedmen; now various other non-landowning categories developed. This system, in both its economic and political aspects, relied on the concept of property. Rents and recompense for labor, as well as differential access to land, depended on property relationships. Though the concept was defined in law, the law was ultimately unenforceable. There was no institutional form to enforce law, only the system of private vengeance which could receive public sanction through legal maneuverings at the various assemblies. There was no state to give institutional reality to the concept of property (Durrenberger 1992).

Political Dynamics

The principles of ownership of land and slaves were central from time of the settlement. From that time, too, there were local assemblies based on Norwegian models. The elite of a stratified society without a state must somehow cope with its fundamental contradiction: how to maintain its privileged differential access to basic resources without institutions to enforce or protect this, the essence of social stratification, i.e., without creating a state. Commonwealth chieftains attempted to do this by establishing a general assembly, *alþingi*, a legislative and juridical body, in 930.

Even though a complex system of courts evolved during the next decades, most disputes were not adjudicated (Jones 1935: 21). While the system seems conceptually rather neat, it apparently was not very tidy in practice. Of 520 cases of feud recounted in the Icelandic family sagas, fewer than a tenth (50) came to any legal settlement. More than half were handled by private actions of vengeance (297), a fifth were settled by agreement (104), and another tenth started as legal procedures but were arbitrated or settled by agreement (60). Nine were legal cases that could not be concluded (ibid.). Violence was an important "dispute-processing mode and . . . outcomes reached by talk, although not rare, were neither easy to achieve, nor desired by most disputants" (Miller 1984: 100). Plaintiffs had to execute any legal judgments in their favor by holding what were called "courts of execution" at the farms of the defendants. Plaintiffs had to enforce any legal decisions that favored them, and if they could not, the decision was of no use. Attempts to execute legal decisions often led to violent clashes. The *alþingi* was not primarily a legal institution but an arena for building coalitions, for making, breaking, and testing connections that would be useful in such tests of personal strength either as a defendant or a plaintiff.

The social system and the system of extraction upon which it rested were based on concepts of property, of unequal access to resources, but there was no state to defend claims to ownership. One could maintain such claims only through coalitions of force which depended on being a member in good standing in some chiefly entourage or developing some personal power base for oneself by trying to head an entourage. Being a member or leader of an entourage was primarily a matter of social maneuver, generosity to one's following, arranging good marriages and foster relationships, holding feasts, winning important law cases at the *alþingi*, and winning fights.

If one were not a chieftain, one had to select some chieftain to follow. Likewise, relationships among chieftains were voluntary. There were two sorts of groups: the entourages of chieftains and coalitions of chieftains. Both shifted and changed membership through time. Parties to either kind of relationship had to see some advantage to maintaining it. Kinship played very little role (Rich 1976), and sagas (e.g., Víga Glúms saga, Gísli's saga, Laxdæla saga) detail feud relationships among members of what would be bilateral kindreds, had they existed (Phillpotts 1913).

There were about thirty-six chieftains. Chieftainship was defined as a kind of property, as power, but not wealth. It could be divided, sold, inherited, or assigned to others for various periods of time. As with other medieval Icelandic legal concepts, the practice was problematic. The titles changed from time to time, but, whatever the linguistic usages and the social and political realities, the significant dimension of the office remained the same throughout: the control of force through coalitions with other chieftains and entourages of followers.

As in other such systems of hierarchic entourage relationships, there are no egalitarian relationships. Authority rests on the assumption that the one in authority is a benefactor to the subordinate. Authority goes to the provider of benefits in hierarchical relationships. The greater the resources one has, the more reciprocal relationships he can form, the more enduring are the relationships, and entourage heads try to cultivate as many reciprocal relations as their resources allow. The most significant aspect of this system from its inception is that redress was left to the individual who won the case.

Stratification and States

There were chieftains, there was law, there were concepts of property, but there was no constituted authority. The legal decisions of the *alþingi* and other assemblies only added rhetorical weight to personal solutions. Law or no, assemblies or no, decisions or no, a man could only do as much as his influence, cunning, and power at arms allowed. The accounts in the saga of the Icelanders as well as in many family sagas of cases brought to local assemblies or the general assembly are more precise about the numbers of arms and men—who supported whom with what force—than about details of arguments and decisions. In the saga of Hvamm Sturla and the saga of the Icelanders, the results of cases are reported but nothing of the process except the strength of each side. Clearly the saga-men thought that the armed power each side of a case mustered was more significant than any niceties of procedure or argument. There was no state. It was just this aspect of the commonwealth that made it attractive to the chieftain-settlers. They perpetuated it as long as they could.

Morton Fried (1967: 231) argued that, in a state, a ruling class maintains its position through its monopoly of violence, which it exercises through formal and specialized social forms. Fried also pointed out that a stratified society without a state is one of the most unstable of social forms. Although he does not mention the Icelandic commonwealth, his speculations on the fate of such a society could stand as a thumbnail sketch of the Sturlunga period. The hallmark of stratified societies is unequal access to resources. Fried argues that the people who are denied access to resources would assert principles of equal access and institute egalitarian or rank forms of organization, or that those who claim privileged access would constitute state forms of control to insure their continued enjoyment of disproportionate shares of resources. It may take some centuries, as it did in Iceland, but ultimately, "the stratified society will face a magnitude of internal disputes, pressures, conflicts," and if "there is a partially congruent kin-organized system of restraints and balances, it is doomed to increasing incidence of failure if relied on to maintain the political integration of the society" (Fried 1967: 225). This process took four hundred years in Iceland, so Fried's judgment about "stability" is open to question. A system that lasts that long, even though it be at the cost of the misery of most of its people, may be said to be stable by some standards.

In medieval Iceland, there was a ruling class, but the law was not an instrument with the force of a state to insure the privileged position of the ruling class against other classes. Members of the elite did this individually by the force of their coalitions and followings. While the law specified more or less tidy rules for inheritance, sale, and other transfers of property, there were no state institutions to give practical meaning to it. Law had only the currency of the force of arms backing any particular interpretation. It could only be used for the framing of rhetorics of justification for acts of force. In spite of this contradiction, farmers had to rely on some chieftain in order to maintain their claims to land. While the inheritance customs codified in the lawbook, Grágás, seem quite orderly in Hastrup's (1985) analysis, inheritance of land is often hotly disputed in the saga of the Icelanders. One who wanted another's land could often find a third party with some inheritance claim and acquire the claim on which to base a legitimation for taking the land.

Chapter 28 of Hvamm Sturla's saga tells of a chieftain who concocts a spurious inheritance claim to get a farmer's land. The farmer gives his farm to a competing chieftain in return for protection. The dispute seemed closed, but Chapter 2 of the saga of the Icelanders takes up the story and tells us that when the protecting chieftain dies, the other one reasserts his claim. The sons of the farmer, defending their land and stock, injure the chieftain when he tries to take over their farm, and he dies of his wounds. As a result, the followers of the chieftain whom the boys killed win an assembly case against the farmers' sons, the chieftain's killers, and they are outlawed and have to leave Iceland. A powerful chieftain is held at bay by another for a while. But then he justifies a land grab by driving less powerful people from their land. The chieftain dies of an unfortunate mishap in the process, but his followers continue the process and use legal justifications to get the claimants banished and open the way to their own use of the land.

Recruiting support before he took the case to the assembly, one of the kinsmen of the chieftain who had been killed asked Jón Loftsson, the most respected man in Iceland at that time, to help him with the case. The response is indicative of the nature of class relations. Jón, chapter 3 of the saga tells us, replied: "But it seems to me matters have become hopeless if it shall not be righted when no-account men [the farmer's sons] kill an aristocrat [the chieftain who was trying to take over their land] and I want to promise you my support in this case when it comes to assembly."

The offense of a working person defending claims to property was worse than any attempt of an aristocrat to take the land that someone else claimed. Notice that the grounds for the case shifts from claims to ownership to claims about what members of one class can do to members of another. Notice also that the decision was not one of law as such, but rather that the kinsmen of the chieftain who was killed had to muster superior force at the assembly to win the case in the first place and to enforce it afterwards by making the sentence of outlawry meaningful. They could and would kill the farmer's sons if they did not leave the land. Claims of inheritance were only worth as much as the armed support behind them. This follows from the fact that claims to ownership, property, were only worth as much as the armed support behind them. This meant that to assert any claim to ownership, whether by inheritance or any other means, one had to back the claim with armed force. Chieftains were focal points for concentrating force to protect and to forward claims to property.

There is no state, chieftains take land when they can and want to, and farmers and others are free to resist these transgressions. No one knew better than the people who lived then that their stratified society without a state was unstable, because they did everything they could to stabilize it to make it conform to their ideas of a stable social order. They standardized the law and founded the general assembly sixty years after they settled the land, and, about seventy years later, even accepted Christianity to try to unify the law into a single system. After these 130 years of settlement the balance was beginning to shift. It took another 120 years to reach the breakdown proportions that Fried discusses (1967) and enter the age of the Sturlunga when the sagas were written.

Conclusions

In commonwealth Iceland a system of extraction was based on claims to ownership of property, on concepts of the unproblematic differential access to resources in favor of a chieftainly class, and on the unwillingness of those chieftains to subordinate themselves to state institutions to protect their privileged positions. This entailed the contradiction of an economic system based on property relationships without a congruent institutional system to enforce them: stratification without a state. Ownership was as sound as the force one could muster to defend it. There was a complex system of law, but it was all so many rhetorical labyrinths in the face of the stark realities of the decisions by power that in fact prevailed. As slavery diminished and claimants to land enlarged their holdings by using seasonal labor and tenancy arrangements to work them, they had to enlarge their circle of power by enlarging their entourages. About A.D. 1000, when the ceiling on the size of holdings was removed by the availability of seasonal labor, large landowners began to expand their holdings. There was no state to guarantee differential access to resources, but the system of appropriation of wealth was based on concepts of property. Thus individuals had to enforce their own claims to ownership by force. As they began to expand their holdings, these claims more and more frequently clashed, and force was more frequently used.

Chieftains' increasing demands for demonstrations of force in support of claims to ownership conflicted with the subsistence demands, the economic roles, of farmers. Chieftains sometimes used coercion against their own followers to insure support. In spite of this contradiction, farmers had to rely on some chieftain in order to maintain their claims to land. Chieftains were dependent on farmers for support—to feed their increasingly large personal followings or armies, to support them at assemblies, to accompany them on raids on other chieftains or their followers, and to defend them from such raids. Without such support and the ability to amass force, claims to ownership of land, which defined the class system as well as the forms of appropriation, were void. Farmers had to rely on some chieftain to be able to defend their claims to property, though this might lead in the end to the loss of the property to their own chieftain. Chieftains had to rely on farmers to enforce their followers' claims and their own as well as to expand their territories into others' and to defend themselves.

So chieftains recruited and maintained followings of farmers, farmers relied on chieftains to enforce their claims to land with but indifferent success since a chieftain might turn on a reluctant follower, and chieftains tried to expand their holdings at the expense of others. This was the basis of the conflict of the Sturlunga period, and it provided much of the dramatic material of the sagas of that time.

Though it neatly defined property, the jural system—the system of assemblies, law making, and case hearing that the chieftains developed—did not determine access to property. That was the paradox, the contradiction, of this system that lead to its downfall. Personal force decided issues, not laws or legal decisions. Legal decisions could be used as rhetorics of justification, but even those decisions were determined by force, not legal argument or evidence. After a single aristocrat defeated the competing chieftains and became the earl of the king of Norway, the jural system changed. The law now came from the king of Norway. The system of chieftains and assemblies was replaced by territorial divisions and an administrative system that culminated in the king of Norway. The violence ceased. Iceland was incorporated into a state system with its attendant law and order.

This did not usher in a golden age of tranquility and prosperity. In fact, there were natural disasters and plagues as well as restrictive trade policies that ravaged the land until the 19th century when many Icelanders despaired of ever gaining independence or prosperity and emigrated to North America. Then the internecine violence of the medieval period came into focus as a heroic period of independence and entered the imagery of the Icelandic independence movement. The ideologists of the independence movement portrayed the medieval period, not as a period of economic misery and political oppression of the many by the few, but as a period of heroic individuals to be emulated in the present. But that, as they say, is another saga (see Durrenberger 1996).

Because they did not institute their own state system to enforce their claims to ownership of productive resources, chieftains fought each other, and finally one won over the others and turned to the king of Norway for ratification of his license to rule, and Iceland became absorbed into Norwegian hegemony. From then on, the laws came from Norway, and after Norway joined Denmark, from that king. Iceland did not become independent until 1944 when Denmark was occupied by Nazis and Iceland was occupied by the Allies.

Because they established a system of extraction that relied on property, and because they refused to establish state institutions, the chieftains of Iceland destroyed their social order.

References Cited

Durrenberger, E.P.

1988 Chiefly consumption in commonwealth Iceland. *Northern Studies* 25:108-20.

1990 Production in medieval Iceland. *Acta Archaeologica* 61:14-21.

1992 *The Dynamics of Medieval Iceland: Political Economy and Literature*. Iowa City: University of Iowa Press.

1996 Every Icelander a special case. In G. Pálsson & E.P. Durrenberger (eds.), *Images of Contemporary Iceland*, pp. 171-90. Iowa City: University of Iowa Press.

Durrenberger, E. P., & G. Pálsson

1987a The "grassroots" and the state: resource management in Icelandic fishing. In B.J. McCay & J.M. Acheson (eds.), *The Question of the Commons: The Culture and Ecology of Communal Resources*, pp. 370-92. Tucson: University of Arizona Press.

1987b Ownership at sea: fishing territories and access to sea resources. *American Ethnologist* 14:508-22.

Durrenberger, E.P., & N. Tannenbaum

1990 *Analytical Perspectives on Shan Agriculture and Village Economics* (Yale University Southeast Asian Studies, 37). New Haven: Yale University Center for Southeast Asia Studies.

1992 Household economy, political economy, and ideology: peasants and the state in Southeast Asia. *American Anthropologist* 94:74-89.

Fried, M.

1967 *The Evolution of Political Society*. New York: Random House.

Gelsinger, B.E.

1981 *Icelandic Enterprise: Commerce and Economy in the Middle Ages*. Columbia: University of South Carolina Press.

Hastrup, K.

1985 *Culture and History in Medieval Iceland*. Oxford: Clarendon.

Jones, G.

1935 *Four Icelandic Sagas*. Princeton: Princeton University Press.

Jonsson, H.

1991 Foreigners in our forests: Thai states and the definition of upland groups. Paper presented at the 90th meeting of the American Anthropological Association, Chicago.

McGovern, T.H., G. Bigelow, & D. Russell
1985 Northern islands, human error, and environmental degradation: a view of social and ecological change in the medieval North Atlantic. *Human Ecology* 16:225-70.

Miller, W.I.
1984 Avoiding legal judgment: the submission of disputes to arbitration in medieval Iceland. *American Journal of Legal History* 28:95-134.

Phillpotts, B.S.
1913 *Kindred and Clan in the Middle Ages and After: A Study in the Sociology of the Teutonic Races*. Cambridge: Cambridge University Press.

Rich, G.
1976 Changing Icelandic kinship. *Ethnology* 15:1-20.

Chapter Eleven

The Changing Commons: The Case of Swaledale (England)

Andrew Fleming

Collective Resource Management and Game Theory

Few subjects can be of more vital interest to humanity than the management of collectively owned resources. In the final analysis, we are all commoners of the planet Earth: the majesty of the law, the defense of national interest, the logic of political ideology will avail us nothing unless we remember that and take appropriate action. At a smaller geographical scale, collective resource management is also a serious subject for sociopolitical debate. It is implicated in the conservation and administration of some of the world's resources, such as deep-sea fish, and collectivities of various kinds are found in the modern world, both in "traditional" and "advanced" societies. If commons are the domain of political and social scientists, they are also an area of interest for prehistorians such as myself. It is true that there is a school of "economic prehistorians" who are prepared to discuss the "economic strategy" of Neolithic peoples in terms of the perceptions of a 20th century agricultural adviser. But for many of us, these issues cannot be tackled without modeling the sociopolitical context. The occupancy of the land and how it is "exploited" are inextricably bound up with people's perception of social relations and the recursive relationship between their sense of moral order and the ordering of the landscape.

More simply, it seems intuitively likely that early human groups, living at low densities among abundant resources, would have had no concept of property in land, but a relaxed approach to the "defense" of their home ranges, or "territories." So prehistorians (e.g., Fleming 1985) have started to think about collective land occupancy (a word which neatly avoids the terms "use" and "ownership") and to consider the implications of such occupancy, and how it might have been eventually subverted. My own discussion of the social context of systems of prehistoric land boundaries in south-west England (Fleming 1988) was influenced by the concept of "the tragedy of the commons"—effectively, the over-use of a collective resource by individuals legitimately but disastrously exercising their common rights (Hardin 1968). Cass and Edney later argued (1978) that the tragedy of the commons could be averted by partitioning the resource or by making resource levels more visible; they used game theory, simulating the playing strategies of commoners in varying states of knowledge. Subsequently Ostrom, in *Governing the Commons* (1990), has extended this approach. She argues that solutions to the problems of collective resource management are to be sought neither in privatization and the operation of the market nor in public ownership in the sense of state control. Instead, she advocates the study of systems of collective resource management in the world today and offers an analysis of the reasons for their long-term success or failure.

Using game theory allows us to assess the "pay-offs" of various playing strategies and the effects of changing the rules of the game. In confusing real-world situations, this kind of analysis may help us to identify the key organizational elements which sustain systems of collective resource management in the longer term. But from an anthropological or historical point of view, it oversimplifies the situation. Commoners are treated as players involved in a competitive, Monopoly-like game in which the players eventually have to formulate rules, a) to make each other settle for lower gains in order to secure the long-term stability of the resource (or at any rate its much slower decline) and b) to prevent each other from cheating even after the need for a) has been accepted.

Clearly, however, this approach takes a one-dimensional view of human motivation, rooted in the ideology associated with the rise of Western capitalism.

In reality, the contexts in which commoners make their decisions, as individuals or as a management team, must vary considerably. I do not wish to labor this point for anthropological readers, but a few reminders may be useful. Leaving aside the consequences of the varying management regulations which they have themselves devised, the following influences on the decision-making environment should be borne in mind:

Eco-demographic Pressures. The relationship between the carrying capacity of the common and the population which depends upon it may vary considerably, with the common under light or heavy pressure, and commoners in varying states of awareness of the ecological situation.

Incentives for Productivity. Commoners may depend on the common for their basic subsistence needs, but a range of other factors may make them seek to increase production, such as taxes, rents, tribute, bridewealth payments, involvement in gift exchange, participation in a market system, and so on.

Role of the Commons in the Total Economy. Many of a community's resources may be collectively controlled, so that individual players are caught up in the collective; at the other end of the scale, the common may be of peripheral importance, perhaps a residual feature of a once more collectivist system. Equally, there may be an alternative sphere of economic activity, such as mining, and the possibility of emigration may or may not be present.

Social Structure in the Collective. There may be considerable variation in the number, size, and type of households using the common. On some commons the distribution of power and wealth among participant households may vary considerably, on others it may be much more uniform. The size of the community in relation to the size of the common may affect the extent and nature of managerial control. Inheritance customs may allow all or most members of the community a share in its resources, but there may be impartible inheritance, with the expectation that some junior family members may seek their fortune elsewhere.

The Ethic and Tradition of the Collective. Different historical trajectories may have determined whether the decision-making atmosphere is relatively relaxed, egalitarian, flexible, and collectivist in spirit, or highly competitive, with a constant struggle between cheats and whistleblowers, and a complex set of rules with powerful groups trying to use their political muscle to circumvent them.

Thus many variations are possible among peoples sharing resources.

Toward a Historical Sequence for the Commons

In some parts of the world it may be possible to improve our insight into the problems and opportunities associated with collective resource management by adding a historical dimension, demonstrating how commoners have responded to internally and externally generated change. We must try to avoid circular argument here. Models for change in the past are likely to have been derived from ideas generated by the study of present-day commoners. Independent data from the past are clearly important. At present this probably implies the study of communities where written records or reliable oral histories are available; it is not clear how far the unaided archaeological record can take us.

The agrarian history of England has obvious potential for the development of a historical sequence for commons management. The English Middle Ages are conventionally dated from A.D. 410 to A.D. 1485. The nucleated villages and associated open-field systems which developed in the later Middle Ages are still a major determinant of landscape character in a broad belt of central England (Rackham 1976: fig. 1). Their origins are not very well known, although most commentators suggest that they developed in the 9th or 10th centuries and in some cases perhaps as late as the early 12th century, after the Norman conquest and the introduction of feudalism. The origins of the nucleated village/open-field complex constitute a major topic of debate for medieval historians (e.g., Williamson 1988). In much of the broad belt of central England where they are dominant it may well be that these "planned landscapes" essentially were imposed, rather than developing "naturally" within a typology of commons management. If this was the case, then from the point of view of commons analysis origins may be less interesting than their later histories, which are in any case much better documented. It is suggested (Williamson & Bellamy 1987: 40) that the Norman lords and their successors tended to leave the management of agrarian production to the villagers, who negotiated their rights, duties, and financial relationships with the lords through the manorial courts. Manor court proceedings record many regulations and customary practices relating to

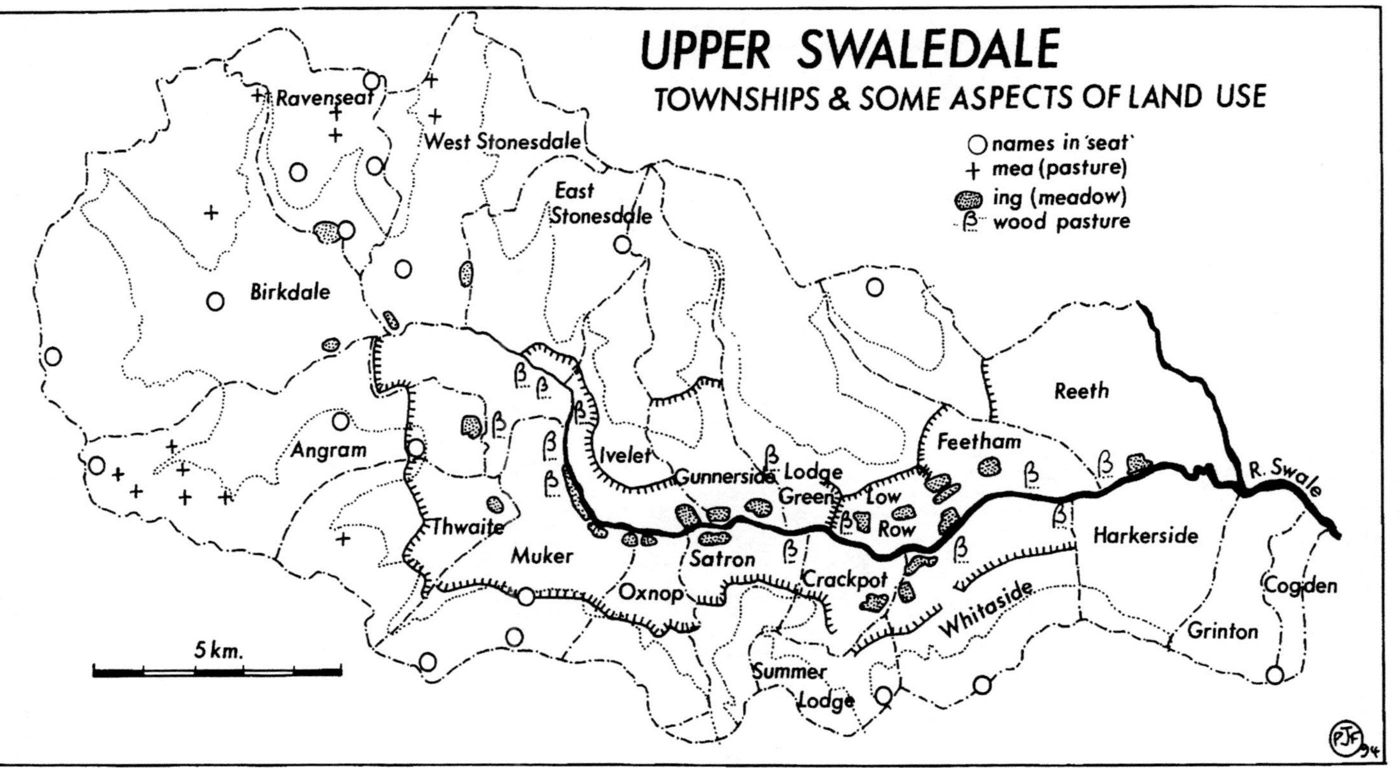

Figure 1. Map of Upper Swaledale, showing boundaries of townships and some aspects of land use. The names in "seat" correspond to Norse *saetr*—upland pastures, mostly distant from the homestead. Contour at 500 m.

the exercise and management of common rights; these have sometimes formed the basis of general accounts of village self-government (e.g., Ault 1972). However, historians have written much more about the decline of the open-field system in the later Middle Ages and afterwards. It started with piecemeal enclosure by agreement among the peasants themselves, and by landlords, especially after the economic depression of the 14th century. A landless proletariat developed. Later, into the first half of the 19th century, enclosure by Act of Parliament was widespread. Often this led to the demise of common land, usually by now on poorer-quality soils, and remaining rights of common. The human misery which accompanied these changes has been well documented and was the subject of trenchant comment at the time. Some historians argue, as "improvers" did at the time, that social justice was well worth sacrificing on the altar of a more efficient, productive agriculture and greater national wealth.

Others, however, contend that the "inefficiency" of open-field agriculture has been exaggerated and that the system has various advantages, notably potential economies of scale (e.g., Dahlman 1980). These commentators face an uphill struggle, given the bias of the documentary record. By the later Middle Ages, the commons were probably well past their heyday. When the commoners appear in the written record, they are defending their rights against predatory manorial lords. Juries of older men argued from precedent, insisting that certain rules and management practices had been in operation since "time out of mind." They could not admit that the system was anything other than traditional and unchanging. To do this would have been problematic for various reasons: it might have implied, in front of powerful seigneurial interests, the possibility of future change which might threaten important aspects of the system. Thus it is not surprising that both 16th-century landowners and modern historians have tended to regard commoners as deeply "unprogressive." For this reason, in England, it is not too easy for us to recognize potential variability and historical dynamism within societies involved in the management of collective resources.

However, we know from the work of theorists such as Ostrom that change in management practice does have to occur from time to time, and that the administration of commons involves not only rules, but also rules about how to change the rules (Ostrom 1990: 51). So we can contemplate the possibility of medieval common people making their own history and doing so, to some extent at least, in circumstances of their own choosing. We cannot afford to take the documents at face value; they may be interpreted at more than one level. As Britton has pointed out, the nature of the written record has meant that "most historians have tended to treat medieval England as a land of manors rather than of villages" (1977: 2).

It is worth considering the implications of placing commons systems on a single axis of variation. At one end of the scale are relatively relaxed, co-operative systems with virtually free access to resources. Rights are more conspicuous than restrictions. In a sense, they hardly need to be defined as rights; they are exercised, rather than asserted. At the other end of the scale are much more competitive systems, with more complex systems of rules, which restrict both how the common may be used and who is entitled to use it. There is a perpetual struggle between those who try to cheat and those charged with policing the system, and also between relatively powerful groups who are manipulating the system to their advantage and the other commoners, whose desperation stems from the knowledge that the importance of their stake is out of all proportion to its size. Sharp practice and political maneuvers become more effective courses of action than attempts to work within the framework of the rules, or to change them by argument and consent. The impartiality of umpires and officials cannot be counted upon. The collectivist ethic itself may well be subject to an increasingly hostile critique: in England, early post-medieval witchcraft accusations have been interpreted in this light (MacFarlane 1970). Although I have described these two forms of commons as two ends of a continuum, there is an important difference between them. The "competitive" form is relatively unstable, with a much more powerful built-in dynamic for change, so that it may well break down altogether, and we may no longer be able to speak meaningfully of collective resource management. In other words, with the competitive commons, positive feedback is dominant, or may well become so, whereas negative feedback is more likely to prevail in the more stable atmosphere of the co-operative commons.

Various forms of the commons could have existed side by side, an obvious source of variation being relative population density. But the variation may also be treated as a historical sequence, with three "stages" through which commons have passed. The middle stage is the most problematic one, since it is involved with the processes which "explain" the flip-over from co-operative to competitive and the creation of conditions where positive feedback increasingly threatens the survival of the system. Intuitively, one may characterize this stage as the "regulated" commons. It must be obvious that the passage from stage one to stage three should be characterized by more reglementation, whatever else is happening at the time. I should stress that the sequence from co-operative to regulated to competitive is suggested as a model which may be heuristically useful; it is not proposed as a universal or inevitable trajectory for the commons. There may well be a case for seeking other developmental sequences and other approaches.

The sequence offered here takes no view on the relative importance of endogenous change or internal contradictions, on one hand, and the impact of external forces, on the other. It may be appropriate to emphasize the centrality of the producers, the people who occupy a particular terrain over a long time period, shaping traditions and creating the landscape. It may also seem that the model assumes population growth if not population pressure as an independent variable and a recurrent cause of systemic change. This is not so. Pressures tending to increase competition among a roughly constant number of commoners could arise from a number of causes other than population growth. In the specific case of the late medieval period in England, however, there is little doubt that population rose substantially between the 11th and 14th centuries (Russell 1948).

Although the model tends to counteract the view which sees the commons as unchanging, the high levels of activity and systemic change which characterize a commons community at stage three inevitably obscure the character of earlier stages of the sequence. Features of the commons community as it was in earlier times may be hard to identify, and their survival chances will be patchy. In what follows, I take the case of Swaledale, in northern England, as an example of a partial reconstruction, to some extent ongoing, of earlier features of a collective resource management system. It depends partly upon the tension between the historian's approach to local history and the approach of a landscape archaeologist trained as a prehistorian. Unless the historical analysis is penetrating and seeks to pursue very specific themes, written histories of localities such as Swaledale tend to feed too directly off the documentary sources. The result is a history of the inheritance and disposal of property, and of financial relationships—a history told from the perspective of the wealthy and powerful, with ordinary people emerging anecdotally. The archaeologist, partly from force of habit, seeks to engage with the landscapes of the past, to identify a spatial pattern of communities, rather than individuals, and to work out how they used the land in an economic sense. If he or she is willing to operate in a text-aided period, picking up crucial detail from documentary sources, a richer synthesis should be achievable.

In this particular study, we are dealing with an archaeology of names. Conventional English local history has a long tradition of seeking patterns in place-names and using them to deduce sequences of Anglo-Saxon or Scandinavian settlement. In Swaledale I have also been concerned to deal with the historical significance of two or more alternative names for the same place, with the corruption of names in the long term as they become casualties of everyday speech, and with patterns of name replacement.

Swaledale: Historical Introduction

Swaledale is situated in the county of North Yorkshire, in northern England. The course of the river Swale runs from west to east for about forty km through the sedimentary sandstones and limestones of the Pennine hills before flowing out into the flatter, fertile vale of Mowbray. The hills reach heights of some 450-700 m above sea level. The upper Swale has reputedly the steepest gradient of any English river of comparable length (about 1 in 160), and its (English) name means rushing or torrential. The valley was probably quite densely occupied by the Iron Age (after c. 500 B.C.). Field boundaries and settlement sites dating from this period and the succeeding Romano-British period (A.D. 43-410) are quite well preserved on the valley sides, among the present-day walled fields, most of which now provide grass, hay, and silage for milking cows and sheep. Ancient ruined walls also survive on the heather-clad moors above the enclosed land. The moorlands are mostly the subject of common grazing rights, though landowners make a good income charging fees for grouse shooting in late summer and fall.

The genesis of the ancient land divisions is largely a matter for archaeological and palaeobotanical investigation. Most of them are of coaxial type (Fleming 1987), the main boundaries being laid out roughly parallel to one another according to a prevailing but not inflexible axis of orientation. On the moors, few definitely identifiable settlement sites can be located, and the main boundaries are widely spaced; on the dalesides there are numerous settlement sites, and a much denser network of ancient boundaries, creating squarish or rectangular field which have clearly been plowed, though medieval re-use of these land parcels has created problems for the landscape archaeologist.

I have published elsewhere a reconstruction of the early medieval polities of Swaledale (Fleming 1994). Early in the post-Roman period, three large earthworks were dug across the Swale valley, "defending" the western two-thirds of the dale against potential attackers from further east. Evidently this was a small British polity, probably at some stage part of the rather shadowy realm of Rheged. At this time the British occupants of the Pennine dales were potentially threatened by English-speaking Anglians (Higham 1993). Eventually, around or shortly after A.D. 600, some Anglians occupied the dale, perhaps a small warrior group taking over and imposing their language and major aspects of their culture, according to an influential account of this process (Higham 1992: chapter 7). The early English settlers may have re-used the earthworks. A few English place-names survive, some potentially from this early period. There is reason to believe that the polity during its English phase was called something like Swar, following the classic early English usage where people and polity take the name of the local river.

In the 10th and 11th centuries, Norse speakers from northwest England settled in the western, upper part of the dale, which they called something like "Swadal." Norse place-names now predominate here, though not in Lower Swaledale, to the east of the earthworks. The Norse language contributed to the developing dialect of northern Middle English. Then came the Norman Conquest of 1066. Shortly after 1100 the old Swaledale, namely the long-established polity west of the earthworks, became the feudal manor of Healaugh and the ecclesiastical parish of Grinton, as well as a Forest—that is, a game reserve subject to special regulations. Analysis of pollen and place-names tells us that the valley was quite well wooded at this time; shortly afterwards, several vaccaries or dairy-farms were established here, some belonging to distant monasteries. For various reasons, we can deduce that lead was being extracted from the adjacent moors and side valleys before the Norman conquest; there is a little evidence for Roman lead-mining before that.

Reconstructing the Late Medieval and Postmedieval Commons

Apart from a few references to tenants' rights in 12th- and 13th-century documents, the tradition of collective resource management has to be reconstructed from post-medieval documents and from what can be seen in the landscape. At the present time, thousands of acres of moorland are still subject to common grazing rights. From the first edition of the Six Inch to One Mile Ordnance Survey map (1857), from the Tithe Maps of ca. 1840, and from other documents, it is possible to reconstruct a pattern of "townships" within Upper Swaledale (fig. 1). Not all of these were formally townships in the 19th century, but with well-understood exceptions, each township marked on the map can be shown to have had, at some stage in the past, its own common moor on the hills and its own common cow pasture on the daleside; additionally, its name has been persistently used in written records to define the location of tenements. There is chronological depth in this pattern, as there is among the hamlets and single farms in Upper Swaledale; a full account is given elsewhere (Fleming 1996). From east to west, the townships are the following: Cogden is small in size, but its independence goes back at least as far as the 16th century. Summer Lodge is apparently a late medieval interpolation; it is not a true township, though it has its own moor. Lodge Green, with its indicative alternative name of Little Rowleth, is obviously a late intrusion, though it existed in the 16th century. Keld, too, has a double name and a suspiciously small territory with a very small moorland pasture; it may well be intrusive, though within the medieval period. Stonesdale, its sparsely populated neighbor, has probably been little more than a kind of "federal" moor-sharing arrangement between East Stonesdale, West Stonesdale, and Crackpot Hall, each of which in recent times had its own cow pasture and local moor. Birkdale, likewise, has always been a sparsely populated township with no nucleated settlement or common cow pasture, its individual farms taking up land in small parcels. Birkdale forms a kind of residual territory for the wild, harsh country of the Swale headwaters.

In the 16th century, when the documentary record becomes more detailed, the tenant farmers of Swaledale were engaged in a series of largely successful legal actions to prevent rent rises and to maintain the continuance of customary law (Fieldhouse & Jennings 1978). Contemporary rentals list the number of "beast-gates" in the possession of each individual. The common moors (used for summer grazing) and the common cow pastures were stinted—that is, the number of livestock which could be kept on them by one individual was limited by the number of beast-gates for which he or she had paid. As on other traditional British stinted commons, a formula, which in principle could be adjusted, defined how many of each livestock category made up one beast-gate. Another rule, also widespread in north European commons and documented for the 14th century in Swaledale, was that individuals must not keep more stock on the moors in summer than they could feed over the winter.

The commons management regime can be understood in simple terms from documentary references and from the landscape. A general account can be derived from various sources from the past two or three centuries. In Swaledale, livestock were driven onto the common moors for the growing season; they arrived on a specific date in April and spent the summer there, returning at a specific date in November. Some parts of the moors have names which reflect their past use as shielings: Rogan's Seat, Rayseat, and so on, from the Norse word *saetr*. There were also "seat houses" or "lodges," one or two of which are marked on 19th-century maps. Nowadays, drystone walls, mostly running along the contour, separate the cow pastures from the moors. These were built or rebuilt at varying dates. The earliest, which require more frequent repair than the later ones, perhaps date from the 16th century, if later written accounts can be trusted (Whitaker 1823: 310); many are probably from the 19th century in their present form. Most of these "top walls" have vertical "joints" known as "ekes" in the stonework at intervals, marking the divisions between zones which different individuals had to maintain; at present, the Gunnerside top wall has sets of initials painted in white on each side of these joints. The gateways between cow pastures and the moors are few in number (there is normally only one per township) and little more than 1.5 m wide, facilitating close surveillance and enumeration of animals and people passing through them.

The daleside cow pastures are more complex. Unlike the moors, most of the former cow pastures are now wholly or partly subdivided into walled fields, rented or owned by individuals; groups of adjacent fields form a fairly coherent farm unit as elsewhere in Britain. These fields vary in character. Sometimes the irregularity of the boundaries of groups of adjacent fields suggests that they must have been cut piecemeal from woodland or scrub; sometimes this seems to apply to individual enclosed parcels. Some walls are straight and parallel, forming rectangular fields which are evidently planned subdivisions of open pastures. Finally, there are the "allotments" resulting from enclosure by Act of Parliament around 1800, where the old top wall, running sinuously along the contour, is met at right angles by ruler-straight walls laid out by professional surveyors. The whole cow pasture, or what remained of it after earlier piecemeal enclosure, was apportioned to different claimants in this way. Now, much of the cow pasture survives at Ivelet, quite a lot at Gunnerside, rather less at Feetham and Low Row. In summary, and leaving aside late Parliamentary enclosure, the open daleside commons have been enclosed, by individual families or groups (presumably in most cases by agreement with the commoners) or by the community as a planned land-division program. Much of this enclosure and subdivision seems to have occurred from the 13th to the 17th century, when various pressures on the older commons system were operating.

Reconstructing the Earlier Medieval Commons

Despite the decline of the older, more collective system, it is possible to work out roughly how it was organized, spatially and in terms of communal control.

Reconstruction of Former Wood-pasture Zones. Rackham (1976: 135-41) has emphasized the link between the commons and wood pasture as a form of land use. In Swaledale, the daleside commons all included pastured woodland, and for many townships it is still possible to pinpoint the zone where wood pasture survived into relatively recent times (Fleming 1997). Low Row, for instance, still has a large grazed wood (Great Rowleth Wood) on its cow pasture, and there are some fine old alder pollards on Ivelet Common (pollards are trees lopped at head height for wood, or, in some cases, for leaf fodder). The lord of the manor took almost all of Feetham's wood pasture for a deer park (perhaps allowing the continued exercise of some established rights), but to this day a fragment of woodland just outside one corner of the park, on a precipitous slope just above the river, carries the name "Feetham Wood;" thus the name of the community's wood pasture has been perpetuated. Usually the woodland has survived on slopes too steep to do much else with, as in the case of Great Rowleth Wood. These post-medieval wood pastures are essentially remnants of a much wider distribution of early wood pasture, however. Place names suggest that before and around the time of the Norman Conquest, when tree cover was much more extensive, there were shielings on the daleside, in zones of wood pasture at some distance from the main settlements. One was Satron—"at the *saetr,*" originally an outpost of the Norse settlement at Muker.

Vegetational Zones on the Commons. Where economic strategy is primarily a matter for the community, and individuals operate within communal principles of organization, it is natural to allocate broad zones within the community's territory to various areas of economic activity. In Swaledale, field names provide a great deal of information about these community land-use zones. For the years around 1840 the fields are named on the Tithe Maps. Many of these names have not changed since the time when they were given to fields when they were first enclosed, in the 16th or 17th century or sometimes earlier. Many of them are called "closes" or "intakes," and usually each has what is nowadays called a "haybarn," showing signs of having been built or refurbished in the 19th century; its predecessor was called a cow house or a laithe.

The names of some of these "closes" show that a township's land was zoned, and originally undivided. A few examples will make the point. Reeth, at the eastern end of old Swaledale (figs. 2 and 3), had a significant amount of permanent arable land, in two subdivided open fields. Its pasture land was also in two very distinct zones, each now occupied by a coaxial field system whose fields share a "zonal" name. Thus fields in one system are called Low Sleets, High Sleets, East Sleets, etc. (meaning "the smooth or level place"—the name is used ironically). In the other system the zonal name is Mill Holme, which probably comes from Middle or Mel Holme, the meadow island between [the rivers]; "holme" is the word usually applied to meadows on the flood plain of the river—as opposed to "ing," the usual Norse word for a meadow. Muker, the major township of western Upper Swaledale (fig. 4), had three of these zonal meadows—Long Ing, Gun Ing (the name deriving from a Norse personal name such as Gunnar) and Foal Ing (foal meadow).

These "ings" were dedicated to the production of hay; they were often on flattish benches of land just above the flood plain of the Swale. These meadow zones were originally open and undivided. It is not simply just a matter of zonal names—"Low Gun Ing," "West Gun Ing," and so on. A further indication is provided by the word "dale," used quite frequently as a field name; here we are dealing with an Old English word meaning a share in the common land. It tends to be used in a parcel of

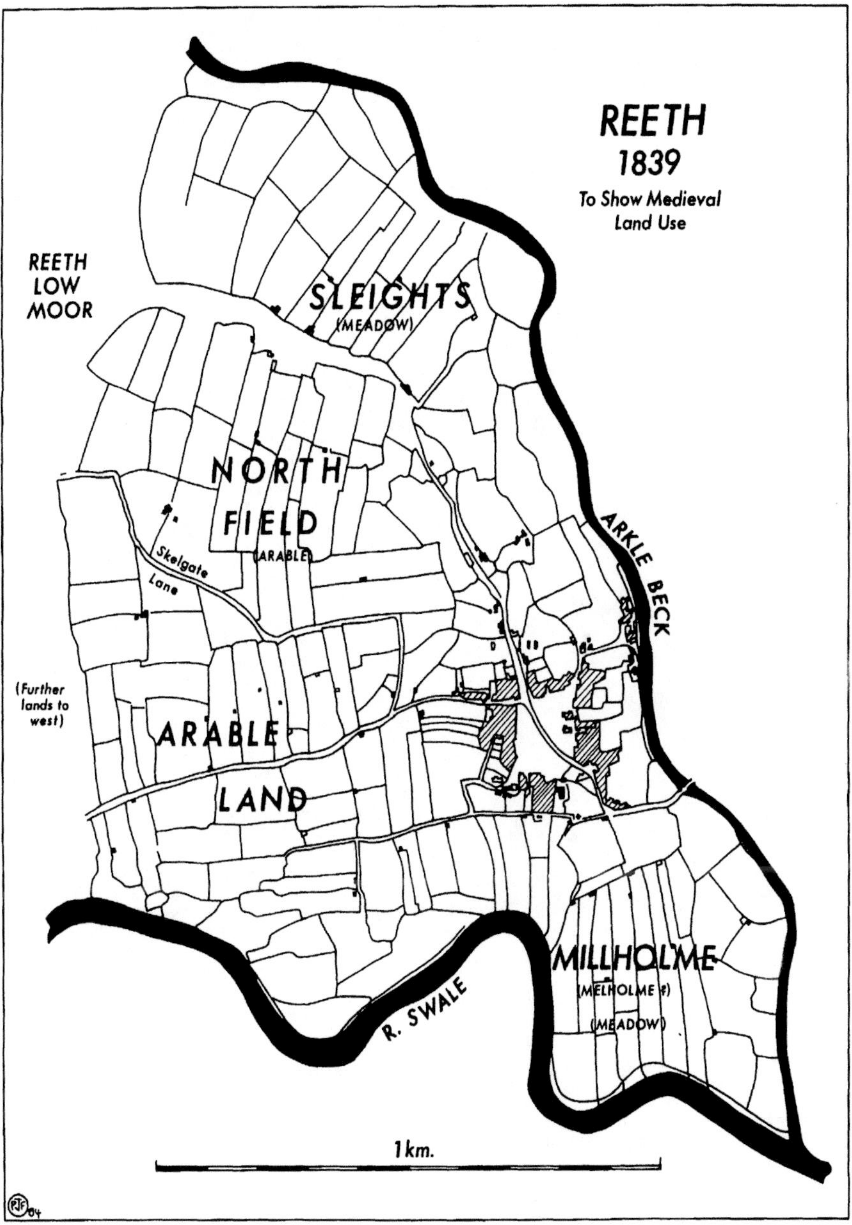

Figure 2. Reeth and its surroundings, showing major land-use zones of the medieval period. The long, striplike parcels within these zones would once have been available for re-allocation; now they are properties with fixed boundaries. The planning of the village around a large square green is almost certainly a post-medieval development.

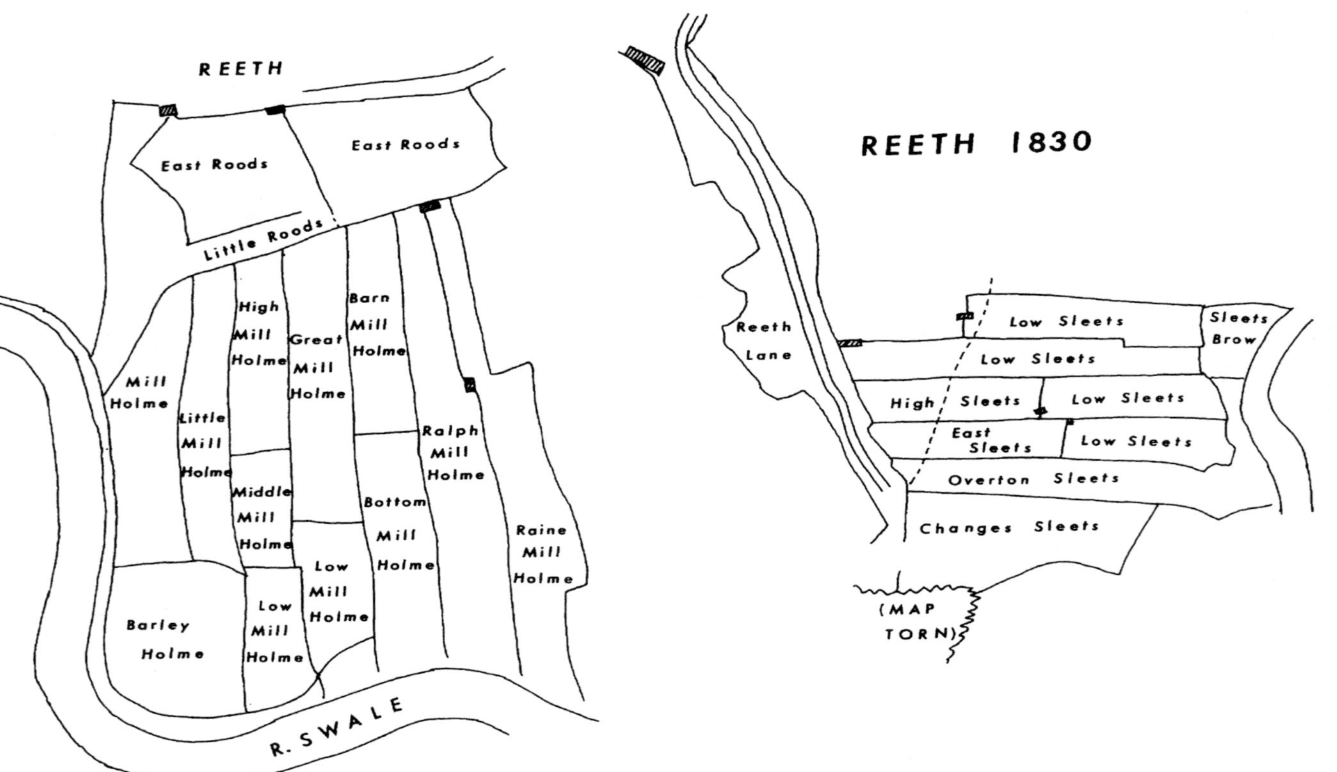

Figure 3. Two of Reeth's old communal meadow zones show how their original character was reflected by the nineteenth-century field names. "Mill Holme" was probably Mel Holme, the meadow between (the rivers); "Sleights" meaning a level area is used ironically.

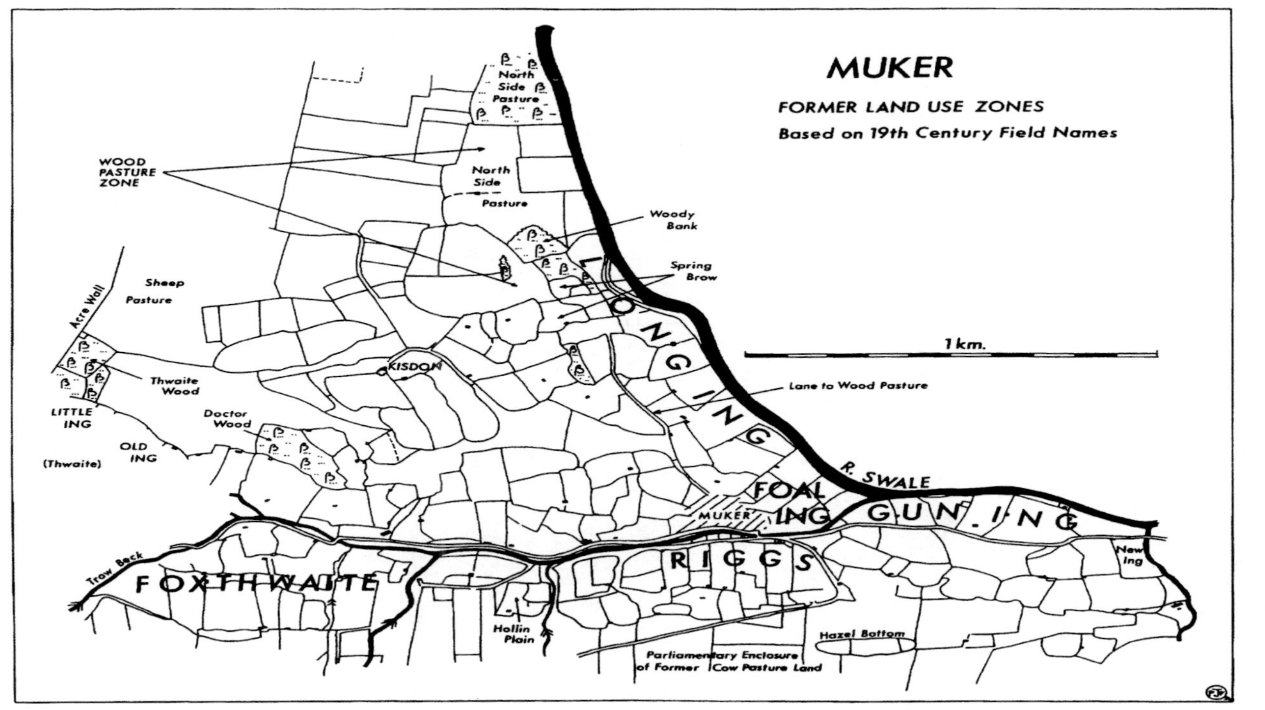

Figure 4. A nineteenth-century map of the area around Muker (Norse, "the narrow cultivated acre") shows the zonal character of medieval land use. Wood pasture survived longest on the steep slopes above the Swale. The ings are the major hay production zones, with large named parcels like Foxthwaite and Riggs suggesting communal clearance and subsequent subdivision. "Hollin Plain" probably related to an old clearing in which holly for winter feeding was maintained.

land with coaxial subdivisions. The subdivision sequence is well shown at two places in particular, Ravenseat and Low Row (fig. 5). At Ravenseat, the fields named "East Dale" and "Bob Dale" are shares, but elsewhere in this subdivided parcel the name "Old Ing" refers to the fact that this was once an undivided "ing."

The sequence is plain. At Low Row, the names and shapes of a group of rectangular fields show that there was a larger Foal Ing here once, and a Wardale, itself later subdivided. Elsewhere in Swaledale, we come across the name "Wandale" or "Wandells," indicating dales marked out with wands or rods, an intermediate stage between an open meadow and one subdivided by stone walls. A fine example of these general principles is provided by the field names from Crackpot, a small community on the southern side of Swaledale (fig. 6). North of the settlement, the old ing/cow pasture distinction is noteworthy, as well as the evidence for late subdivision of both zones. South of the settlement, the ing has been divided into dales; the "old ing" is close to the settlement. (The north wall of High Close is part of the boundary of a medieval deer park).

The converse of subdivision is piecemeal, small-scale enclosure; at Lodge Green, one of the townships which can be shown to be a late interpolation, the parcels of land are of the piecemeal-enclosure type (fig. 7). In several regions of England, the place name "green" indicates a late, small, secondary common, used both by smallholders and by those with little or no land. At this stage the commons were being enclosed; the green was essentially residual, and organization was more concerned with managing enterprise and competition than with the continuance of an essentially collectivist system.

Grazing Zones. To the ings and the partially wooded cow pastures we may sometimes add zones dedicated to the provision of grazing for particular animals; there are names such as "Foal Ing" and "Horse Pasture." At Keld there were two moorland pastures, on Kisdon Hill and on Keldside, and a distinction was made between "sheep gates" on Kisdon and "cattle gates" on Keldside, suggesting that the two zones were designated for different livestock. One is tempted also to bring the field-name "Bull Park" into this discussion. A Derbyshire farmer suggested to me that a "Bull Park" ought to be a slightly sloping field, in order to give the bull a better purchase during the performance of his duties. However, most fields in Swaledale would have given the bull no anxieties in this regard. From a township point of view, the availability

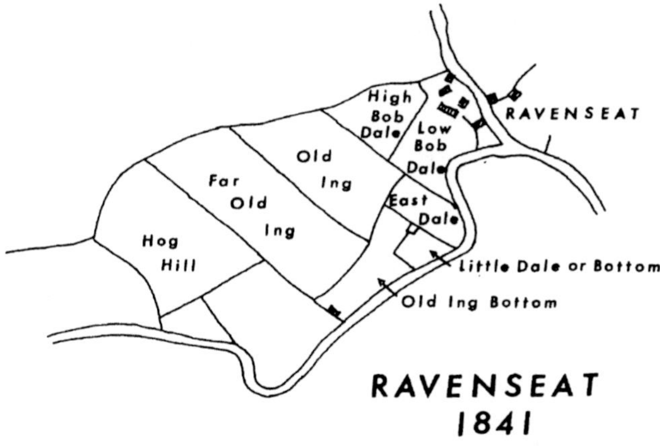

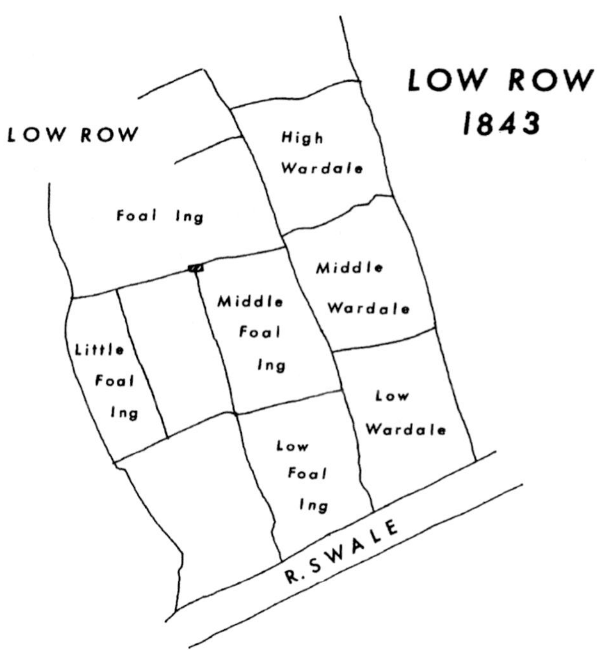

Figure 5. Subdivision of old communal meadows at Ravenseat ("Hrafn's *saetr*") and Low Row ("The Wra," a nook or secluded place), as exemplified on a nineteenth-century map. The evidence is supplied by common names for neighbouring parcels and by the name "dale" meaning share (cf. dole). There are several "Foal Ings" in Swaledale, as well as the odd "Horse Pasture," suggesting that animals were segregated in some situations, presumably under a communal herd (cf. the medieval surname "Calf-herd" now present in the dale as Calvert).

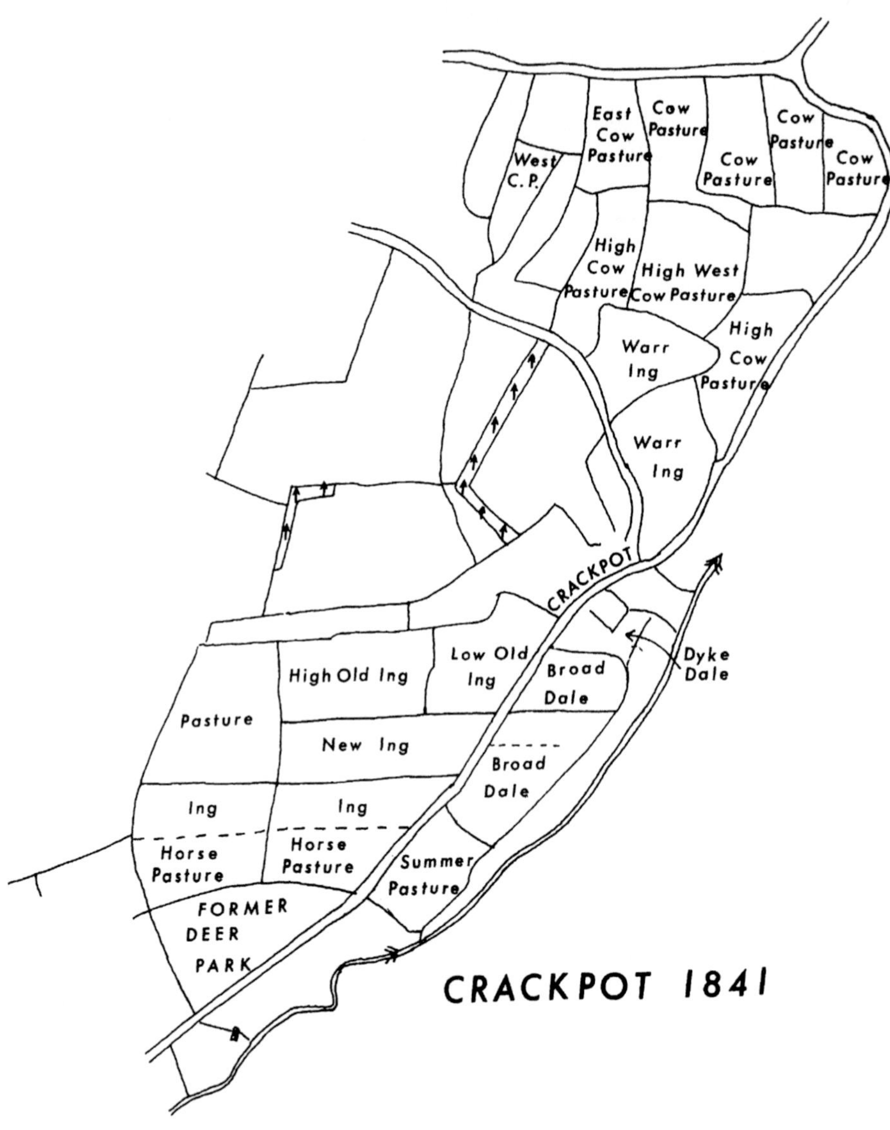

Figure 6. Crackpot in the 19th century shows the subdivision on what was once a large open cow pasture, as well as the "ing" (meadow) land with its characteristic late subdivisions.

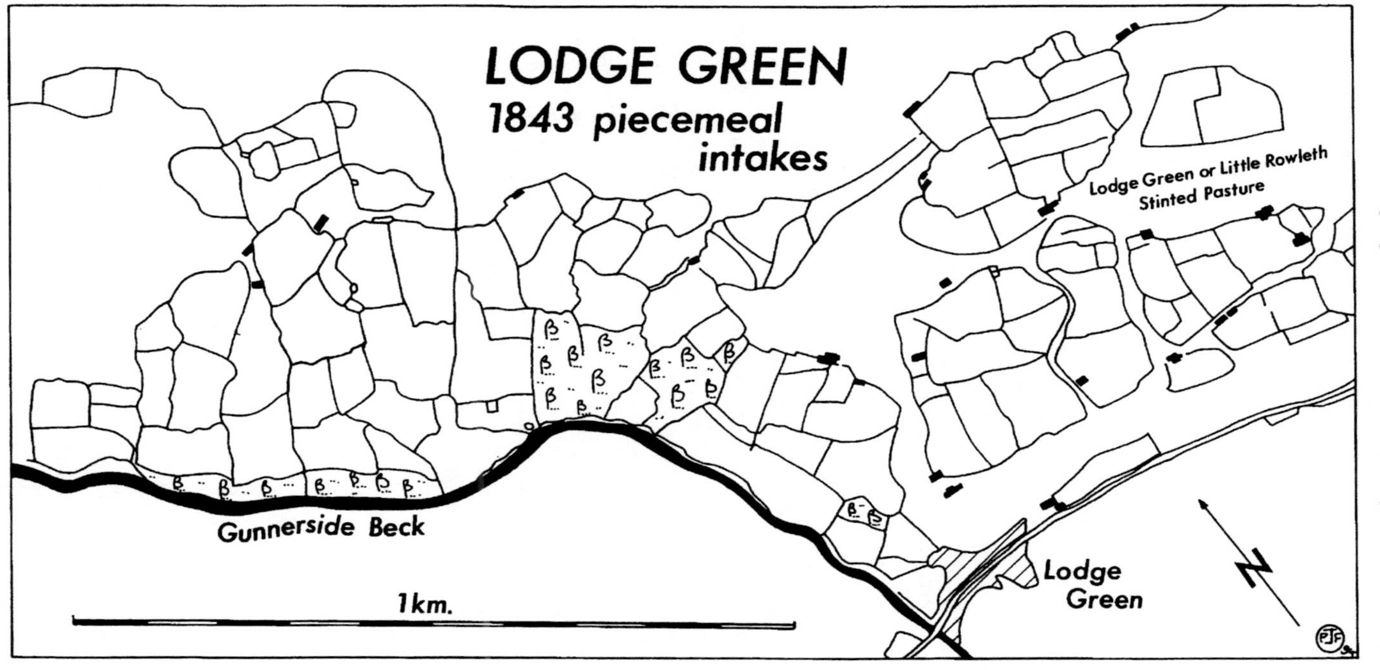

Figure 7. Lodge Green in the 19th century. In contrast to the coaxial subdivisions illustrated in figs. 5 and 6, the enclosures to the NE of Lodge Green were taken out of a common cow pasture known as Lodge Green or Little Rowleth Cow Pasture (presumably by agreement; note how access lanes to what remained of the common have been left between these "intakes"). Further west, parcels have been cut out piecemeal from old wood pasture, as the field shapes show.

and management of the bull was a serious matter. A document of 1790 is a memorandum of an agreement between Richard Guy and the inhabitants of Muker. Guy, "in consideration of his having and receiving the rents and profits of the Bull Pasture, and the sum of forty shillings a year, to furnish and supply the aforesaid inhabitants with two good and sufficient bulls . . . during the time that the cows are upon the pasture, and one bull . . . for the remainder of the year. . . . All cows which are kept to graze in the inclosed pastures belonging to the Town, to be allowed to be bulled with the Pasture Bulls, as they can agree with the Master of the Bulls." Going to fetch bulls, making them available, sorting out payments, stopping them getting out, and bringing them back when they did, were part and parcel of community life.

Community Officials. Commons theorists remind us that a successful commons has to be properly regulated. This usually means choosing officials trusted for their sense of justice and responsibility; but such officials should also be properly rewarded, as was the Master of the Bulls at Muker. In Muker two "bylawmen" were appointed annually, and this entitled them to an extra cattle gate on the stinted pasture. Further information comes from field names. In several townships, we find the names "Barnward Ing," "Midwood Close," or "Midward Close." We can rule out the notion that they refer to people's surnames (although the current local vicar is called Midwood!); according to the parish registers, neither Barnward nor Medward/Midwood are old Swaledale surnames. The names refer to commons officials, people who guarded or watched over the community's barns and their meadow land (Midwood is a corruption of Medward). These field names are post-medieval, but it is also clear from a 12th-century document (Lancaster 1912: 249) that the name Haverdale comes from "hayward's dale." These field names may imply that officials were rewarded for carrying out their duties by having access to designated parcels of land; theorists emphasize the importance of proper incentives for those who were expected to oversee the system (e.g., Ostrom 1990). When the wood pastures were extensive, there should also have been woodwards, and the existence of pinfolds (pounds for stray animals) in the dale suggests another category of official, the pinder; Pounder was once a Swaledale surname. The main point here is that these officials were administering resources on behalf of the community. Other medieval surnames, such as Wetherhird, may also relate to specialists appointed by communities. The place name Calvert Houses is interesting here; at first sight it simply incorporates the Swaledale surname Calvert. However, this name means "calf herd," and when one recalls that maps and documents also refer to the place as "Cawenerdhouse" (cow-herd house), "Coverley" or "Calverley" House (cow-herd's clearing house), or even "Calsett" (calves' fold), it becomes clear that the place was referred to either by its most important land-use characteristic or by the name of the "specialist" involved. In other parts of England it might be possible to argue that these officials and specialists were appointed or employed primarily by the manor, but here, with numerous townships in a large, extensively wooded manor with an absentee lord, it is much more likely that these were commons officials.

Evidence for Share-farming. Historians (Fieldhouse & Jennings 1978) have noted the occurrence of partible inheritance in Swaledale, and neighboring Wensleydale, and they have tended to treat it as an essentially maladaptive cultural trait which must have had the unfortunate consequences of splitting farms to the point of inviability. It is argued that strategic marriages would have been necessary to re-aggregate the land. It is true that the late-17th century manor court records show rent being paid on "the fifth part of a messuage," and property can be divided into as many as forty-two parts. But it is wrong, I believe, to regard this as an "inheritance custom," and to infer that Swaledale's traditional land-use system trapped people into salami-slicing individual farms, fields, and buildings. In their study of two Tyrolese communities, favoring partible and impartible inheritance respectively, Cole and Wolf (1974: 176-81) noted that the number of "estates" did not remain the same under the impartible system, as one might expect; nor did the partible system result in the predicted decline of estate size to a point below the threshold of viability. As they put it, both of the prevalent ideologies of inheritance were honored more in the breach than in the observance.

In Swaledale we need to do more detailed, document-based work on inheritance within individual communities to find out how far—on the Tyrolean analogy—the system tried to maintain "estates," or how far the ideology was that all kin group members (at whatever level) should have access to land or some means of subsistence which did not involve emigration. The latter seems more likely in the Swaledale case, which is complicated, however, by the existence of lead-mining in the locality. What we are seeing in Swaledale, probably, are the dying traces of a system of share-farming, with land and some facilities being shared among all those entitled to them, though not necessarily equally, and at a family/household level to be investigated. Responsibility for any tax and tribute levied from land or people would have to be shared. The written records are no doubt documenting the legal and financial independence of some farming families, but "partible inheritance" must surely be a phrase which encapsulates the encounter between an old share-farming system and the demands of landlord, clerks, and lawyers. Responsibilities shared at the extended-family level had to be translated into a system of obligations for individuals. Vertical wall joints (ekes) denoting maintenance responsibilities are found in the enclosed land too (Phillips 1984), though repairs by individual farmers who now have less reason to maintain the ekes make them hard to see nowadays in many places.

Swaledale: Reconstructing the Historical Origins of the Commons

In various ways, then, it is possible to discern the basic elements of an older system of commons management in Swaledale, a system much closer to the "collective" stage than to the "competitive" phase, in terms of the developmental sequence suggested earlier. The Swaledale sequence seems to support the concept of changing commons management, and it would be interesting to make a closer analysis of the well-documented post-medieval period.

In terms of recent archaeological theory, the argument developed has been a "processual" one. In trying to make the point that, in a games-theory approach, not all commons can be treated as the same, I have put forward a general model and illustrated it with a case study. In most processual arguments of this type, the implication is that the model is of widespread applicability, and in my opinion there is nothing wrong with making this kind of assertion. "Post-processual" theorists of the 1980s, however, argue that such an approach writes history as social science, privileging abstract, deterministic forces over the critical historical detail of particular cases, and denying human beings the credit for making their own history.

In the case of Swaledale, an interesting historical question must be the relationship between the commons tradition and the customary life-ways of the different ethnic groups who have settled in the dale. The inhabitants of the "British" polity here, speaking Old Welsh and steeped in whatever customary way of life may be envisaged for a hill tribe only just inside the borders of the late Roman Empire, were eventually subjugated by what may have been quite a small group of incoming, English-speaking Anglian warriors. Later, speakers of Old Norse came in from the west, making an impact on the place-names of the western part of the dale and a distinctive contribution to the local dialect of northern Middle English. Even if each of these ethnic groups was committed to a communal approach to the distribution of land and the utilization of labor, it is hard to accept that their cultural attitudes would have been identical. What conclusions can we reach concerning this question?

Of the three groups, it seems that the Norse were somewhat different from the English/British. The latter are notoriously difficult to distinguish, because although speakers of Old Welsh seem fairly readily to have adopted the English language, it looks as if "British" customs survived rather well, if the carefully documented "multiple-estate" hypothesis is accepted (e.g., Jones 1965). In the case of the Swaledale commons, common cow pastures and beast-gates occur in Lower Swaledale, well outside the area of Norse immigration, which makes it seems that these are "English" institutions. The same impression is given by the names of the commons officials. Bylawmen should be of Scandinavian origin, but meadow-wards, barn-wards and hay-wards are all English words; we do not hear of ingwards or laithwards. The word "dale" in the sense of a dole or share is also English. There is also a difference in surname adoption. The people of the western, Norse end of the dale went in for patronymics (Alderson, Hodgson, Clarkson, etc.), while those further east tended to name themselves after places—Kearton, Feetham, Raw (after Low Row), and Harker (after Hercay, modern Harkerside). In the Middle Ages they also called themselves after the district—de Swale (English) or de Swaledale (Norse). Furthermore, in the Norse part of the dale, the *saetr* (later the "seat") now tend to be named after people; for example there is Rogan's Seat, Alderson's Seat, Ravenseat (after Hrafn), and Gunnersett (now Gunnerside), the *saetr* of Gunnar (see fig. 1).

The impression gained from these observations is that the basic commons structure and ethic, as it emerged in the later Middle Ages, was "English" (or at least in part "British," translated after the 7th-century takeover) and that there was a kind of place loyalty among the "English." Possibly this had to do with the multiple-estate ethic, or had been encouraged by the melding of British and English traditions in earlier centuries. Perhaps the English involvement in the organizational complexities of open-field systems, in subdivided arable land, and in nucleated settlement had inculcated an ethic of place loyalty; the individual or the household may have become more committed to the maintenance of land rights within heavily contested territories, rather than to a more flexible system of alliances of the kind described by Durrenberger for medieval Iceland (this volume). Perhaps the Norse, with a more pastoral economy in the wilder uplands of western Swaledale, were more inclined to emphasize kin-group and family loyalties, and grazing grounds occupied by reference to noted or half-mythical ancestors. Perhaps this is the ethic of an earlier stage of development than the communal, where, at low population densities, the concept of territory recedes into the background, and human social interaction is more important than any collective resolve to manage a territory.

Conclusion

I have argued that the attitudes of commoners to management problems, and the contexts in which they attempt to solve these problems, cannot be treated as uniform or as a term whose value may be quickly determined and inserted into a games theory framework. I suggest that there may be a typology of commons, arranged along a cooperative/competitive axis, and that this typology may correspond to a historical sequence. This may be investigated through well-documented historical cases. These ought to include that of the medieval open-field system in England, even if the latter's genesis does not seem to result from an unbroken natural development from pristine early origins. However, a rather different commons system in the more pastoral northern English uplands, where for various reasons "mainstream" open field ideology does not seem to have held much sway, appears to provide an opportunity for reconstructing a commons typology more like the one suggested. But I would not wish this to be interpreted too literally, as a kind of universal framework, to be sought and found everywhere. As usual, it would be more interesting to study divergent and contradictory cases!

References Cited

Ault, W.O.
1972 *Open-field Farming in Medieval England.* London: George Allen & Unwin.

Britton, E.
1977 *The Community of the Vill: A Study in the History of the Family and the Village in Fourteenth Century England.* Toronto: Macmillan of Canada.

Cass, R.C., & J.J. Edney
1978 The commons dilemma: a simulation testing the effects of resource visibility and territorial division. *Human Ecology* 6:371-84.

Cole, J.W., & E.R. Wolf
1974 *The Hidden Frontier: Ecology and Ethnicity in an Alpine Valley.* New York: Academic Press.

Dahlman, C.T.
1980 *The Open Field System and Beyond.* Cambridge: Cambridge University Press.

Fieldhouse, R., & B. Jennings
1978 *A History of Richmond and Swaledale.* Chichester: Phillimore.

Fleming, A.
1985 Land tenure, productivity and field systems. In G. Barker & C. Gamble (eds.), *Beyond Domestication in Prehistoric Europe*, pp. 129-46. London: Academic Press.
1987 Coaxial field systems: some questions of time and space. *Antiquity* 61:188-201.
1988 *The Dartmoor Reaves.* London: Batsford.
1994 Swadal, Swar (and Erechwydd?): early medieval polities in Upper Swaledale. *Landscape History* 16:17-30.
1996 Patterns of names, patterns of places: medieval political geography in Swaledale (England). *Archaeological Dialogues.* In press.
1997 Towards a history of wood pasture in Swaledale (North Yorkshire). *Landscape History* 17. In press.

Hardin, G.
1968 The tragedy of the commons. *Science* 162:1243-48.

Higham, N.
1992 *Rome, Britain and the Anglo-Saxons.* London: Seaby.
1993 *The Kingdom of Northumbria, AD 350-1100.* Stroud: Allan Sutton.

Jones, G.R.J.
1965 Early territorial organisation in northern England and its bearing on the Scandinavian settlement. In A. Small (ed.), *The Fourth Viking Congress*, pp. 67-84. Edinburgh: Oliver & Boyd.

Lancaster, W.T. (ed.)
1912 *The Chartulary of Bridlington Priory*. Leeds: Yorkshire Archaeological Society.

Macfarlane, A.
1970 *Witchcraft in Tudor and Stuart England*. London: Routledge & Kegan Paul.

Ostrom, E.
1990 *Governing the Commons*. Cambridge: Cambridge University Press.

Phillips, S.K.
1984 Encoded in stone: neighbouring relationships and the organisation of stone walls among Yorkshire Dales farmers. *Journal of the Anthropological Society of Oxford* 15(3):235-42.

Rackham, O.
1976 *Trees and Woodland in the British Landscape*. London: Dent.

Russell, J.C.
1948 *British Medieval Population*. Albuquerque: University of New Mexico Press.

Whitaker, T.D.
1823 *An History of Richmondshire*. London: Longman, Hurst, Rees, Orme & Brown.

Williamson, T.
1988 Explaining regional landscapes: woodland and champion in southern and eastern England. *Landscape History* 10:5-13.

Williamson, T., & L. Bellamy
1987 *Property and Landscape*. London: George Philip.

Chapter Twelve

ꕤ

Reconstructing Property Systems from Archaeological Evidence

Antonio Gilman

The most positive feature of the "new" processual archaeology of the 1960s and early 1970s was its methodological optimism. Instead of accepting the evident limitations of the available record and, thus, resigning themselves to practicing an archaeology that in its most conservative forms resembled philately, processualists set out to develop methods ("middle range theories," as these came to be known) that could link the material remains of the past to the underlying causes that generated their variability. These theoretical efforts were not altogether successful, perhaps, and the last fifteen years has seen something of a resurgence of methodological pessimism, but in their heyday the processualists produced an archaeology considerably more interesting than that of their normativist predecessors. All the same, the methodological ambitions of the New Archaeology have stopped well short of addressing ancient property regimes. Why?

The dominant current within processualism has been ecological functionalism, according to which "culture" is a system of homeostatic regulation which governs the relation between human organisms and their environment. Accordingly, cultural change must be produced by environmental or demographic imbalances external to the cultural system, since the position of a mechanism that seeks its own balance cannot be accounted for internally. The most ambitious and comprehensive variant of this approach identified population pressure as the principal cause of first the Neolithic and then the Urban revolutions and led to research programs to develop concrete measures of this essentially relational concept.[1] That these admirable methodological efforts have failed to persuade skeptics (demonstration that significant demographic imbalances preceded major socioeconomic transformations has proven difficult) might best be taken as illustrating the weakness of the underlying theory that guided them, but the difficulty processualists have had in developing testable, mechanistic links between the archaeological record and the social dynamics that produced it has led to a qualified renewal of archaeological pessimism. Archaeologists of my generation were told by their seniors to delay historical speculation "until the facts were in;" those of the present generation are warned to wait until more effective middle range theories are developed (e.g., Binford 1980).

From a materialist perspective more historical and less reductive than cultural ecology, the principal factors that would explain large-scale changes in the archaeological record would be the economic relations within and between human social groups, that is to say, relations expressed in terms of property rights. Processualist archaeologists have devoted a great deal of attention to the development of methods for identifying and analyzing production specialization and systems of exchange, but they have rarely discussed explicitly what the patterns they identified implied in terms of degree of property relations (see Earle [1977] for a notable exception). Likewise, processualists devoted much attention to developing methods for reconstructing how humans exploited plants and animals, but rarely considered what these techniques implied in terms of land tenure. This was not for want of distinguished examples they might have followed: Childe (1951, 1964) and Adams (1966) had made property relations central to their accounts of social evolutionary process, and behind them, of course, were Marx and Engels. Outside the old Soviet sphere, however, marxism has found few adherents, most of whom have been attracted to its nonprocessual, hegelian aspects (e.g., McGuire 1992). An emphasis on property relations on the lines of Marx's (1967: 791) admonition that "it is always the relationship of the owners . . . to the direct producers . . . which reveals the innermost secret, the hidden basis of the entire social structure" would involve a distinctly harder line.

Processual archaeologists have also been reluctant to develop the study of property systems because of the presumed difficulty of the task. In the historical and ethnological discussions that define the problem for archaeologists, the jural aspects of property predominate. (Hunt's paper in this volume is a good example of this.) It is not immediately apparent how paired distinctions of rights and duties, such as those between demand-right and duty, privilege-right and no-demand-right, etc., are to be given operational equivalents in the garbage, ruins, etc., that archaeologists must deal with. At a detailed level, furthermore, the complex of regulations and customs by which a society regulates access to resources is only comprehensible within the framework of its historical development, and this level of analysis is one which the New Archaeology has deliberately avoided. Although processualists (e.g., Binford 1968: 21) have taken pains to denounce Hawkes's (1954) ladder of inference,[2] with respect to property they have largely accepted it.

All the same, the difficulties an object of study such as property may present renders it no less important. In all societies studied by archaeologists as wholes, the land is the basis of the economic structure, and differential access to the land the basis of social inequalities. Accordingly, we must do our best, however difficult the topic may be. My purpose here is not to present any novel breakthroughs, but to suggest that the available literature, not least the archaeological contributions to this volume, contains a variety of useful approaches to the problem and that greater methodological optimism on this matter may be warranted.

An Evolutionary Framework

As Earle argues in this volume, one can develop a general overview of the development of land tenure systems in prehistoric societies based on evolutionist comparative ethnology. Schemes along these lines go back to the 19th century, of course, but more recently the syntheses which give greatest weight to property as a key of social organization are those of Fried (1967) and, more recently, Johnson and Earle (1987). Using Service's (1962) evolutionary classification as a series of simplifying signposts, the following sequence emerges:

Bands. These consist of gatherers and hunters in environments of low natural productivity, where there do not exist zones with a richness and concentration of resources that would permit a group that committed itself to their exclusive possession to live off of them as well. Generally speaking, the natural resources exploited by such groups cannot be controlled by them, and so cannot be claimed as property. If there exist fixed, concentrated, valuable resources (say, permanent waterholes or productive groves of trees), more limited social segments may claim title to them, but these "owners" do not attempt to establish rights to their exclusive use, because such exclusive possession would enter into conflict with the principles of reciprocity essential to long-term survival. Consequently, "private" property is limited essentially to personal effects, and land as such is a *res nullius*. Such a property system is sometimes associated (e.g., Lee 1990) with Engels's notion of "primitive communism."

Tribes. Tribal societies can establish themselves on various types of production: gathering and hunting in territories with relatively abundant resources, extensive crop cultivation (using, say, slash-and-burn methods), livestock-raising, or some combination of the above. In such a society corporate groups organized on the basis of kinship (clans or lineages) possess a common territory which they defend collectively, because exploitation of the fields, pastures, and so on, it contains can produce enough to sustain the group over the long term. Inside this territory, particular households of producers will establish exclusive claims (i.e., usufruct rights) to the parcels they exploit during the period of that exploitation and, of course, to the stored surplus arising from it as well. (These stores may be direct accumulations of surplus produce and so on or may be concentrated by dint of labor into less perishable forms, i.e., be transformed into valuables, but in any event they usually are not freely transferable from one household to another.) In such societies there are usually headmen or other persons of importance who direct the productive or conflictive activities of their followings, but the simple, direct, and unintensive character of the system of production impedes such leaders from exploiting the led, since these, as Carneiro (1970) has shown, can abandon would-be exploiters and establish new, independent communities with relative ease.

Chiefdoms. Here crop and livestock raising (or in certain exceptional cases, such as on the Northwest Coast of North America, fishing) is intensified thanks to investments of labor whose productivity and permanence limit the capacity of fission of subgroups within the social whole. Irrigation systems, tree cultivation, livestock raising oriented towards secondary products, and other like improvements increase the long term production of the households that have made the necessary investments, but these create differentiated productivity that comes into conflict with communal access to resources. Under these circumstances leaders can consolidate their power and establish their dominion over the long term. As far as land tenure arrangements are concerned, this hegemony can have quite different consequences. In some cases, such as Medieval Iceland in the period of the "Free State," discussed by Durrenberger in this volume (cf. Byock 1988; Miller 1990), the chiefs are the direct proprietors of the most productive resource spaces and use the surplus these parcels generate to provide credit to (and foment the dependence of) poorer producers. In others, communal property is maintained in theory, but the heads of corporate kinship groups succeed in converting their positions into hereditary ones supported by obligatory contributions from their dependents. In yet others, as in Hawaii as described by Earle in this volume chiefs in principle own all lands and allocate territories to subchiefs who in turn offered plots to households in exchange for labor services and crop shares. Here all the essential characteristics of a tributary society are in evidence.

State. In classic evolutionary typologies this term is reserved for class societies which have developed formal institutions—ideological (a clergy), military (an army), and fiscal (a bureaucracy)—that maintain the differentiated power and property of their subjects. All states are characterized by an intensified production economy, and in all of them land can in principle be held as alienable, private property (although not all such real estate will be so held). These societies are usually not prehistoric (except, of course, in the cases where we cannot read their texts), since writing systems develop in the context of the fiscal and legal management of private property. Among the first written texts recovered in Sumer are the *kudurrus*, inscribed boundary stones recording the sale of plots to individuals (Gelb et al. 1991). Now it is clear that in precapitalist agrarian societies, privately owned land coexists with land which is still held under communal legal arrangements. A Castilian peasant of the 16th century A.D. might own some plots, pay dues to a lord for permission to farm others, and at the same time, as a member of his community, have access to *dehesas* (common pasture), *ejidos* (common farmland) and wastelands, and have the right at certain times of year to graze his animals on the stubble of the private plots of others (under the so-called *derrota de mieses*) (Vassberg 1984). It is only under capitalism that enclosure and Blackstonian private property becomes the norm, but as the kudurrus demonstrate, in the earliest state societies the nucleus of exclusive landholding already exists from which broader enclosure can develop.

From Morgan on, then, the implicit starting point for an evolutionist analysis of property is Locke's (1960: 19-20) definition of the term: "Whatsoever . . . [man] removes out of the state that nature hath provided and left it in, he hath mixed his labour with it, and joined to it something that is his own, and thereby makes it his property. It being by him removed from the common state nature placed it in, it hath by this labour something annexed to it that excludes the common right of other men." This definition has the virtue that it permits us systematically to link a juridical concept to forms of production. If, as Netting (1990: 47) says, "when land is brought into regular use by invested labor (as in heavy, specialized fertilization, terracing, leveling, or irrigation) or when it can produce consistent crops of grain, fruit, nuts, or hay because of special conditions of soil or moisture, there will be a system of enduring claims by households or individuals," then the material evidence developed by archaeologists for such intensified agricultural production can by extension be used to argue for the existence of demand-rights/duties with respect to some tracts of land between members of the society that generated that evidence. To put it another way, two generalizations with systematic implications for property relations can be drawn with reasonable confidence from our historical and ethnographic experience: first, that individuals or groups who have access to or have created a resource that yields a high, stable income will seek to retain that resource for their own use; second, that individuals or groups committed to the exploitation of such a resource can in turn be exploited (i.e., serve as a source of income for other individuals or groups). The principle of "sweat equity" permits one to link systems of property (a juridical concept whose reading in the archaeological record is obviously problematic) to systems of production (material facts whose archaeological interpretation is less problematical). The evolutionary schema presents a progressive scale according to which, as production becomes intensified, private property comes to encompass a broader range of objects.

Difficulties

Now, the use of ethnological generalizations as analogies can give one an initial, rather static impression of the broad character of prehistoric property systems, but it cannot tell much about how the prehistoric past differed from the present. If we simply apply to the prehistoric past the not unreasonable conclusions we can draw from comparative ethnology, we learn nothing new about the past. How, then, can we make the prehistoric past speak to us, as it were, with its own voice about the property systems that characterized it? It is clear that one reason why processual archaeologists have avoided this issue is that the rather narrow positivism characteristic of their point of view prevents them from thinking about an issue unless they possess a substantial quantity of clearly relevant information about the subject.

It is apparent that direct archaeological evidence bearing on the nature of agrarian property is scarce and often ambiguous. In some places there exist fossil landscapes where the boundaries of the fields once cultivated within it are preserved. This is the case of the famous Dartmoor "reaves" studied by Fleming (1988). These systems of parallel walls and hedges were constructed during the Bronze Age and covered very large areas: the Rippon Tor complex may have covered as much as 4500 hectares. Similar cases are documented in other areas of Great Britain, and dispersed instances of so-called Celtic fields have a broad distribution in northwestern Europe. It is obvious that archaeologists cannot count on direct evidence of this kind, but even when they have it, its interpretation presents considerable difficulties. In general terms it seems reasonable to suppose that a system of boundaries following a uniform plan reflects the existence of a hierarchical society, even when the peasants themselves are responsible for its organization on the ground. Fleming (1988: 122) argues, for example, that "the greatest degree of self-organisation, in matters of land use, would have been achieved within stratified societies, as commoners coped with the demands of an exploitative elite." But the layout of the fields are in themselves ambiguous. As Fleming warns, "the outward form of a field system does not correlate very well with the social organisation which helped bring it into being; in the middle ages, carefully subdivided field systems are associated with relatively autonomous peasant communities as well as with more hierarchical, coercive forms of social organization" (ibid.). For deep prehistory we lack, so to speak, the bilingual texts with which to decipher the multiple possible meanings of, and thereby make a positive social reconstruction of, such systems.

Ethnohistorical evidence, if it is available, is invaluable in establishing a baseline from which to evaluate archaeological evidence, and indeed all the archaeological contributions to this volume are assisted by such evidence. The fossil fields of Great Britain are of various ages, Bronze Age and subsequent, and Fleming's more recent research (reported on this volume) in Swaledale shows how they can be linked to historically documented systems. There as in Hawaii (Earle), the Andean highlands (Costin), and the Maya lowlands (McAnany), knowing what the prehistoric system of property relations developed into obviously helps us interpret the antecedent trajectory for which we only have material evidence.

Progress Against Difficulties

The direct historical approach is not available for deep prehistory, of course, but recent work demonstrates, I believe, that we can make substantial progress. To advance over this difficult terrain what is required is to establish indirect measures of how tenure is exercised over resources, measures which can then be evaluated against the nature and degree of intensification of various forms of production (the latter being relatively accessible to archaeological reconstruction). One line of attack on the problem might be to study the pattern of large-scale expenditures by which rulers make their power manifest. Elites derive their status from preferential access to productive resources (because they are able to impose duties on their subordinates). As De Marrais et al. (1996) indicate, their power must be materialized: the elite's conspicuous consumption of the labor of commoners in the form of sumptuary displays, public ceremonies, monument building, and so on, all serve to show who is boss and why. It seems reasonable to suppose, therefore, that changes in the patterns of these expenditures would be related to changes in the structuring of the elite's preferential access to resources and to the labor of commoners. Accordingly, controlled comparisons of the contents of the archaeological record, where these expenditures are more or less prominently preserved, can give us indications about the systems of property that supported them. Such an approach underlies McAnany's treatment (in this volume) of the burial evidence from Formative K'axob.

Recent publications by Bradley (1984) and Earle (1991) on the intertwined development of systems of monumental construction and forms of land tenure in Wessex provide a further example of the application of this idea. During the earlier Neolithic the social expenditures most salient in the archaeological record involve the construction of collective burial monuments (long barrows), ritual enclosures (causewayed camps), and large earthworks (cursus monuments). These would be the materializations by which corporate kin groups demarcated the territories they claimed as their own.

During the later Neolithic and the earlier Bronze Age, the amount of labor dedicated to construction increases and is devoted to large ritual monuments (such as Stonehenge and Silbury Hill) some of which are aligned to heavenly bodies, and to groups of burial mounds associated with these monuments, mounds in which individuals are buried with luxurious grave goods. Earle interprets these changes as indications that a chiefly stratum had separated itself from commoners and declared their possession of the whole territory through prominent religious sites that identified the elite with the forces of nature.

In the later Bronze Age and the Iron Age, labor devoted to public works diminished and was dedicated to the fortification of hill top settlements and to building coaxial field systems. In this last phase we see the establishment of a mature tributary system that detaches itself from the ritual apparatus which justified its formation. This development occurs in conjunction with a progressive intensification of cultivation and livestock-raising oriented towards secondary products.

Changes in land tenure of a similar kind can be seen behind the transformations over the course of the Copper and Bronze Ages in the southeast of the Iberian Peninsula (Gilman 1976; Gilman & Thornes 1995; Chapman 1990). In that region about 3000 B.C. or perhaps somewhat earlier, there are established small settlements whose long occupations imply a relatively intensive cultivation of the soil, in a pattern which begins to approach the Mediterranean polyculture of the historical period. The degree of intensification appears to increase over time and to be greater the more arid the region of settlement is. Within the general evolutionary schema I have outlined, one might expect, therefore, more frequent claims to exclusive rights over resources, and a greater potential for exploiting one's fellows, over time and in the areas of greater aridity. During this period the dead are buried in collective chamber tombs of various types with grave goods consisting predominantly of ritual fetishes and utilitarian artifacts (sometimes rendered in valuable raw materials). This burial rite must interpreted as a reflection of the collective values of the community, but the greater elaboration of tombs and differentiation of grave goods in the arid zones lends some support to the idea that where agriculture would be more intensive there were limited social segments which had a greater capacity of accumulation and expenditure for the ritual display that would affirm their privileged standing.

Towards the end of the third millennium B.C. the southeast sees an apparently fairly abrupt transition from the Millaran Copper Age to the Argaric Bronze Age. Two changes appear to me to be particularly suggestive with respect to property systems. First, Bronze Age settlements are almost all new foundations in extreme defensive emplacements, which suggests exacerbated competition between social groups for resources and surpluses. Second, the ritual communalism of the previous period is abandoned for a strongly marked individualism: single (or at times double) burials are placed underneath the houses of the settlements and accompanied by differing levels of personal wealth. Once again the arid areas of the southeast, where greater investments would be required to attain the levels of agricultural performance in more favored regions, show greater differentiation in grave goods. It does not seem unreasonable to interpret these patterns in terms of the establishment of more exclusive property rights over agrarian resources.

Likewise, differences in the way in which surpluses are accumulated and concentrated into wealth (a subject amenable to archaeological study) should reflect differences in property relations. Surplus agricultural production may be used to support the labor required to procure exotic goods or to manufacture items of concentrated value. The entire initial development of copper and bronze metallurgy is in the context of the manufacture of valuables. Small scale metallurgical production of individual, unstandardized objects, such as that predominates in the Copper and Bronze Ages of Iberia (Montero Ruiz 1993), may indicate that the potential of such valuables to influence primary production has not been realized, but when metal objects are standardized in shape and weight, the process of monetization (culminating in the development of coinage) is well under way. Michael Hudson in this volume discusses the attendant effects on property relations: peasants can endebt themselves (and cede rights to primary resources) to those who have access to monetized goods (cf. Engels 1973: 173ff.). That the copper ingots used in the Late Bronze Age metal trade of the eastern and central Mediterranean had the shape of oxhides demonstrates elegantly the linkages that exist between the production of transferable valuables, agricultural production, and in the end land tenure.

The avenues we have just been exploring examine systems of ownership, as it were, from the top down, by looking at the expenditures and wealth finance strategies of the elites. They should be complemented from the bottom up by comparative studies of household organization. The overall evolutionary model within which we have been operating predicts that households in societies at the simpler end of the scale, with more open land tenure systems, will also be engaged in broader webs of cooperation with one another, while at least some households in societies at the more complex end of the scale will make exclusive claims to land and establish more restricted alliances. The degree of cooperation and mutual assistance between households is open to comparative assessment by archaeological means. Jean Hudson, an ethnoarchaeologist and faunal analyst at UCLA, has recently proposed, for example, that in sites occupied for short time spans comparison of the minimum number of individual animals of various species in spatial subsectors of the site and in the site as a whole would provide a reasonable measure of food sharing: as the MNI in each subdivision approached the MNI in the site as a whole, sharing would be more pervasive (Hudson 1995). In principle, then, we could test our expectations concerning the household cooperativeness (a feature logically related to the exclusivity of claims on resources).

A good example of what can be done in this regard has recently been provided by Bernbeck's (1995) comparative analysis of Hassunan and Samarran household organization in sixth-millennium B.C. Mesopotamia at well-known sites such as Yarim Tepe and Tell es-Sawwan, respectively. In the former, household compounds are more simply constructed (out of pisé) and smaller; there are communal storage facilities and more elaborately prepared public spaces; and villages are apparently unfortified. In the latter, household compounds are larger and more elaborately built (of mudbrick); storage facilities are inside household compounds; and villages are fortified. As Bernbeck puts it, "one can . . . conclude from a comparison of village layouts that social distance was not only greater within Samarran villages but between them as well." These contrasts correspond to differences in production strategies: Hassunan villages are distributed in areas where dry farming prevails, while Samarran ones are located outside the limits of rain-fed farming in areas where irrigation is mandatory. As Bernbeck indicates, these contrasts would correlate with differences in land tenure: where irrigation is practiced, "cultivable land becomes a much more valuable means of production because its availability is no longer quasi-unlimited. . . . Strong pressure can be expected for the single household to keep its land together by mechanisms like inheritance or marriage rules." Bernbeck's account of the contrasts in Hassunan and Samarran property regimes confirms evolutionary expectations, but the results could have gone the other way.[3] It is by exploiting the tension between results and expectations that we can progress.

In the above-mentioned case of southeast Spain, for example, there is a largely tacit consensus that the record confirms evolutionary expectations on changing property relations: the changing pattern of elite expenditures, in conjunction with the intensification of production, would indicate the presence of exploiting and exploited classes at least by Argaric times. If this consensus view is correct, then examination of contrasting patterns of consumption should be present within domestic contexts: as Costin (this volume) notes, usufruct is a reasonable proxy for property rights. An evaluation of property relations through the study of household consumption and organization, the bottom-up approach, is scarcely possible for later prehistoric southeast Spain, however. Functionally oriented excavations have only been initiated in the southeast in the past twenty years and have been described only in preliminary or very partial publications. As a result, no systematic evaluation of the degree to which differences in consumption and household organization existed within and between sites is possible. We have to rely on the inevitably impressionistic accounts of excavators who have not yet analyzed their own materials systematically, whose positive evaluations are subject to revision, and whose silences may reflect either the evidence or the progress of their analyses.

All the same, the absence of claims for social stratification based on the evidence recovered from habitational contexts is notable. Hernando Gonzalo (1987) has noted the relative uniformity of Copper Age settlements (Los Millares aside). Much the same is true of the Bronze Age. The remarkable rectangular structures, O and H, on the uppermost platform at Fuente Álamo (Schubart et al. 1985: 72-78) have no reported analogues at other sites, and the excavators' evaluation of their functions is indecisive. The interpretation of such unique cases inevitably presents difficulties, of course, but the general run of Bronze Age habitation sites shows little obvious differentiation in their architecture. Thus, the social analysis of the Argaric site of Peñalosa by Contreras Cortés et al. (1995) relies on the human burials and faunal remains, not on architecture, for their conclusion that class divisions are attested at the site: the richer burials and the preponderance of horse and cattle remains are found in the occupational units in the middle and upper terraces of the site.[4] It is worth noting, however, that metal production and grain storage is distributed on all three terraces. If the pattern at Peñalosa were to be confirmed at other sites, it would suggest that households enjoyed relative equality in their access to agricultural land and metal ore and that the greater wealth of the richer households depended on their holdings of livestock. Clearly, studies of the usufruct of various categories of resources within settlements, such as those that have been initiated at Peñalosa, have a great deal to tell us about the property arrangements of the Millaran and the Argaric. Whether such analyses will confirm the evolutionary story developed from the overall pattern of changes in burial and settlement patterns remains to be seen. As matters stand, the limited scale of contrasts in living arrangements within Bronze Age settlements casts significant doubt on the consensus view of emergent stratification many of us have espoused.

Discussion

I have raised these examples not with the intention of providing a systematic account of the ways in which the patterning of archaeological evidence can be related to patterns of property holding, but as examples of lines of investigation that clearly show promise of further development. I need not say that there are many others. Property relations affect the style and nature of material goods so pervasively that any exhaustive list of methodologies would be impossible. My purpose is simply to suggest that the methodological pessimism that prevails with respect to property is unjustified and to call for much more further work on this topic. The controlled comparative analysis of several lines of evidence (those mentioned and others) against one another and against the nature of the production economy should permit one to assess variation in property regimes in ways that will permit us to go beyond the imposition of ethnological patterns on the past.

As Fleming (1988) has pointed out, the nature of ancient property systems can only be assessed by comparting the nature and the contexts of multiple lines of evidence. This is true, of course, of almost all archaeological attempts to understand the past. Save in the occasional Pompeii or Cerén our evidence is too coarse-grained in terms of provenance and chronology to permit us to reconstruct the past in Ranke's sense, as it really happened. Comparatively controlled readings of the evidence from different areas and periods can, however, give one a sense of the significant contrasts in the evidence, contrasts that can be interpreted in terms of processual expectations. It is this last point, of course, that sets apart the sort of contextual archaeology I espouse here from that advocated by Ian Hodder and other post-processual, post-modern anti-scientists. Their laudable attempt to address issues of ideology has led them into an area in which expectations cannot be tested: to do full justice to ideological systems one must understand the meanings of the symbols through which such systems operate, and symbols by definition are arbitrary with respect to their referents. By contrast, the directionality of human social evolution provides us with a set of warranted expectations to which the archaeological record can respond. The responses can be surprising, and therein lies the interest of the enterprise.

Notes

1. To demonstrate that population pressure exists one must provide assessments both of the size of the population and of the resources available to it under the technological conditions of the time. These are hard to nail down in any given archaeological instance.
2. This is the common sense notion that, since the archaeological record consists of material remains, it must be relatively easy to reconstruct technology, harder to reconstruct social organization, and practically impossible to reconstruct ideology.
3. Thus, the development of irrigation systems may lead to the development of greater differences between households and to property rules that enshrine these inequalities or they may lead to intensified communalism so as to prevent such inequalities.
4. These conclusions can only be accepted provisionally, since the data behind them is presented as a narrative with partial and uneven reporting of critical details. It is apparent, for example, that the differences in the faunal assemblages are ones of degree, and in the absence of the minimum numbers of individuals of each species found in each habitational unit evaluation of the statistical significance of the contrasts is impossible. Likewise, three of the richer burials are found in the upper habitational terraces, but several other burials in this area are poor (Contreras Cortés et al. 1995: 103). In the absence of full reporting of the burial assemblages and the physical characteristics of each case, there is no evident reason to accept the conclusion that the poorer burials belonged to "serfs or nonwarrior levels of the population" (ibid.), as opposed, for example, to members of the same families who achieved lesser statuses in their lifetimes.

References Cited

Adams, R.McC.

1966 *The Evolution of Urban Society*. Chicago: Aldine.

Bernbeck, R.

1995 Lasting alliances and emerging competition: economic developments in early Mesopotamia. *Journal of Anthropological Archaeology* 14:1-25.

Binford, L.R.

1968 Archaeological perspectives. In S.R. Binford & L.R. Binford (eds.), *New Perspectives in Archaeology*, pp. 5-32. Chicago: Aldine.

1980 Willow smoke and dogs' tails: hunter-gatherer settlement systems and archaeological site formation. *American Antiquity* 45:4-20.

Bradley, R.

1984 *The Social Foundations of Prehistoric Britain*. London: Longman.

Byock, J.L.

1988 *Medieval Iceland: Society, Sagas, and Power*. Berkeley: University of California Press.

Carneiro, R.L.

1970 A theory of the origin of the state. *Science* 169:733-38.

Chapman, R.

1990 *Emerging Complexity: The Later Prehistory of South-East Spain, Iberia and the West Mediterranean*. Cambridge: Cambridge University Press.

Childe, V.G.

1951 *Man Makes Himself*. New York: Mentor. First published 1936.

1964 *What Happened in History*. Harmondsworth: Penguin. First published 1942.

Contreras Cortés, F., J.A. Cámara Serrano, R. Lizcano Prestel, C. Pérez Bareas, B. Robledo Sanz, & G. Trancho Gallo

1995 Enterramientos y diferenciación social I: el registro funerario del yacimiento de la Edad del Bronce de Peñalosa (Baños de la Encina, Jaén). *Trabajos de Prehistoria* 52(1):87-108.

De Marrais, E., L.J. Castillo, & T. Earle

1996 Ideology, materialization, and power strategies. *Current Anthropology* 37(1):15-31.

Earle, T.K.

1977 A reappraisal of redistribution: complex Hawaiian chiefdoms. In T.K. Earle & J. Ericson (eds.), *Exchange Systems in Prehistory*, pp. 213-29. New York: Academic Press.

1991 Property rights and the evolution of chiefdoms. In T. Earle (ed.), *Chiefdoms: Power, Economy, and Ideology*, pp. 71-99. Cambridge: Cambridge University Press.

Fleming, A.

1988 *The Dartmoor Reaves: Investigating Prehistoric Land Divisions*. London: B.T. Batsford.

Fried, M.H.

1967 *The Evolution of Political Society: An Essay in Political Anthropology*. New York: Random House.

Gelb, I.J., P. Steinkeller, & R.M. Whiting, Jr.

1991 *Earliest Land Tenure Systems in the Near East: Ancient Kudurrus* (The University of Chicago Oriental Institute Publications, 104). Chicago: Oriental Institute.

Gilman, A.

1976 Bronze Age dynamics in southeast Spain. *Dialectical Anthropology* 1:307-19.

Gilman, A., & J.B. Thornes

1985 *Land-Use and Prehistory in South-East Spain*. London: George Allen & Unwin.

Hawkes, C.C.

1954 Archaeological theory and method: some suggestions from the Old World. *American Anthropologist* 56:155-68.

Hernando Gonzalo, A.

1987 ¿Evolución cultural diferencial entre las zonas áridas y húmedas del Sureste español?. *Trabajos de Prehistoria* 44:171-200.

Hudson, J.

1995 Food sharing: how can we see it archaeologically? Lecture presented at UCLA Friday Research Seminars, Los Angeles, USA.

Johnson, A.W., & T. Earle

1987 *The Evolution of Human Societies: From Foraging Group to Agrarian State*. Stanford: Stanford University Press.

Lee, R.B.

1990 Primitive communism and the origin of social inequality. In S. Upham (ed.), *the Evolution of Political Systems: Sociopolitics in Small-scale Sedentary Societies*, pp. 225-46. Cambridge: Cambridge University Press.

Locke, J.
1960 An essay concerning the true original, extent and end of civil government. In E. Barker (ed.), *Social Contract: Essays by Locke, Hume, and Rousseau*, pp. 1-143. New York: Oxford University Press. First published 1690.

Marx, K.
1967 *Capital: A Critique of Political Economy*, Volume III: *The Process of Capitalist Production as a Whole*. New York: International Publishers. First published 1894.

McGuire, R.H.
1992 *A Marxist Archaeology*. San Diego: Academic Press.

Miller, W.I.
1990 *Bloodtaking and Peacemaking: Feud, Law, and Society in Saga Iceland*. Chicago: University of Chicago Press.

Montero Ruiz, I.
1993 Bronze Age metallurgy in southeast Spain. *Antiquity* 67:46-57.

Netting, R.McC.
1990 Population, permanent agriculture, and polities: unpacking the evolutionary portmanteau. In S. Upham (ed.), *The Evolution of Political Systems: Sociopolitics in Small-Scale Sedentary Societies*, pp. 21-61. Cambridge: Cambridge University Press.

Service, E.R.
1962 *Primitive Social Organization: An Evolutionary Perspective*. New York: Random House.

Schubart, H., O. Arteaga, & V. Pingel
1985 Fuente Alamo: informe preliminar sobre la excavación de 1985 en el poblado de la Edad del Bronce. *Empúries* 47:70-107.

Vassberg, D.E.
1984 *Land and Society in Golden Age Castile*. Cambridge: Cambridge University Press.

Part III

Modern Colonial Encounters

Chapter Thirteen

ᘓᘐ

Modern Colonial Encounters: Introduction

Robert C. Hunt

The papers in this part of our volume are all dealing with land as the object, with the development of property rights in land, under the circumstances of the expansion of the dominion of a nation-state. Each of these papers participates in at least two different discussions. One of those discussions is the subject of this volume. The others are largely offstage. In Bishop's case, for example, there is long scholarly debate among Morgan, Engels, Speck, Lowie, Leacock and Feit among many others, on land as property among northeastern Indians. Paula Brown is a noted contributor to our understanding of highland Papua New Guinea, and discussions of the impact of colonialism in that area are just barely offstage in her paper. Wolters brings us welcome information from the Dutch scholarly tradition. Colin works for ORSTOM, a French government research agency, which has invested in intensive local-scale social science research in the third world. The work of that institution is too little known in the anglophone world. The Wolters and Colin papers are both directed as much to discussions in New Institutional Economics as to Anthropology. Peters's paper invokes the literature on common property. Each of the papers is thus as much embedded in another discussion as in our theme of property in economic context. The consequence for this volume is that each of the papers needs to be read in two directions, one the subject of this volume, and the other which is particular to the paper.

Charles Bishop's article, geographically based on northeastern North America, is focused on the issues of foragers, egalitarian social structure, trade, and property. Leacock argued in 1954 that property in beaver was an outcome of European colonial operations in North America. Prior to the arrival of the Europeans there was no stratification, and no property. Bishop is concerned with stratification, and finds that trade and property are deeply involved. There are political and social contexts to property, as well as an economic context.

Bishop argues several things. First, there was a north-south flow of goods and probably mates between the fully agricultural societies to the south, and the completely foraging societies in the far north. Pottery and some grain went from south to north, and pelts (beaver, moose) and birchbark went from north to south. The exchanges were between adjacent societies (a form of down-the-line trade). The exchanges across society boundaries were managed by a single person, usually an elder, who Bishop calls a chief. The individual or family production was assigned to the chief, who would trade the goods with his counterparts in neighboring societies, and the relationships between producer and chief, and between chiefs, were ritually marked.

Second, there were are least two forms of property involved, exchange resources and exchange routes. The resources needed for subsistence were open to all. But in the north the resources that provided the exchange goods were under the control of the society, which did not give permission to exploit them to outsiders. Thus the right of exclusion was invoked. Since the same territory contained both subsistence and foreign trade goods, there was often suspicion about the activities of outsiders. The other form of property was the exchange route. Exchanges along the line were between neighboring groups. Any attempt to skip over a neighbor for exchange was a breach, and could result in conflict. It would seem that there was a demand right involved, that obliged any nearest neighbor to trade with you, and not go around you to trade with some group further away. Bishop thus does not hold that exchange in a market is a necessary condition for the existence of property.

Third, Bishop argues that this north-south exchange system existed long before the late 15th century advent of the Europeans. There is archaeological evidence of flows of goods. Bishop reasons that the complexity of the trade routes, and of the social relationships which existed in the trade context, was so developed that it could not have resulted solely from Colombian contact. Bishop concludes that aboriginal northeast North America contained foragers, producing for both subsistence and for exchange, organized into societies with chiefs and which excluded outsiders from exchange resources and from exchange routes. The social structure of these societies thus contained forms of property. Bishop argues that there was a continuum of stratified social structures, both in time, and across space. He finds, for North America, that there were two circumstances under which highly, or totally, egalitarian, bands could exist. One was produced by isolation. As bands moved into uninhabited terrain they could become isolated from other such bands, and from the more developed economies behind them. Opportunities for trade would decline and eventually disappear, and they would become concentrated on immediate return. The consequence is a pure egalitarian society. The second circumstance was provided by the European trade system. At the beginning, the Europeans occupied the complex end of the north-south trade, increasing the demand for furs at the southern end, and sending beads and guns north. But later the Europeans eliminated the long exchange lines by establishing fur buyers in permanent posts in the north (the Hudson Bay Trading Company is the major example.) As this developed, the Indians tried to reproduce the producer-chief relationship with the officials of the store. The stores were not interested, and eventually the stores came to monopolize the trade of furs for European goods. The Indian societies became smaller and more isolated. They became simpler—marginalized, in Bishop's words—and thus also more egalitarian.

Paula Brown's account of changes in Highland New Guinea property rules focuses mainly on land as the object. Prior to Australian penetration of the Simbu territory, the Simbu were organized in tribes (1-4,000 persons), and the tribes were organized in clans and subclans. There was tribal territory, and there was territory held by clans and subclans. The core of the territory held the sacred sites, cemeteries, men's houses, and other places important for the identity of the tribe and its members. On the borders with other tribes territory was often contested and far less densely occupied. Individuals would acquire spaces from their subclan or clan, clear fields, and mark the borders by various means including planting trees. Thereafter that field became the individual property of the developer and could be devolved to his sons. The produce of the field, produced with the labor of women, belonged to the woman who did the work.

The Simbu world was, and is, one where violence is a common means of creating claims to land. A group might be uprooted by losing a fight, and have to locate elsewhere. Groups also moved around the countryside in peace. There were institutions for how one acquired rights to land in these circumstances. The host had to agree, and the guest offered goods in exchange. These exchanges were long-term if not perpetual in design.

When the Australian administrators arrived in the 1930s they wanted to respect the local customs, and they also wanted to acquire land for patrol posts and other purposes. The Australians offered to "pay" for the land, and did. The Simbu version was that a permanent exchange relationship had been established, which of course was far from the idea that the Australian's had of the transaction. It might be the case that the traditional or customary relationship is more akin to rent than to alienation by sale. It appears to be the case that from the Simbu point of view, if the occupiers of the land cease to present goods in exchange, the rights to occupy the land have ceased as well.

When Papua New Guinea was created in 1975, the Australians wrote a constitution for it, and English Common Law became the national law. However, there was also a strong tendency to use local customary rules. There are hundreds of these local customs, and little or no codification, or perhaps even agreement, on them. The reason for this may well be that violence was a major part of local adjustments to constraints, and the PNG system was, like all major state systems, assuming that peace was a condition for jural relationships. In any case, the local conflicts have been very difficult to solve with the local customary rules.

As development has proceeded, with the planting of valuable long-lived trees such as coffee and coconut, the creation of commercial spaces, and the extraction of trees and minerals, and as market exchange has spread, land become much more valuable. Old agreements between guests and owners are being rethought, and the courts are one arena for renegotiation. There is a desire to escape some old exchange relationships as the property involved becomes more valuable. This seems to be a case not only of legal pluralism, but of legal uncertainty. Furthermore, the role of violence in managing land and relationships, in creating and settling disputes, not only has not disappeared with the appearance of States, but may have increased.

Willem Wolters' paper is a detailed examination of a primary proposition in the New Institutional Economics. That body of theory (see Acheson 1994) holds that the efficiency of markets depends upon clear-cut and effective rules about property rights. Private property sets fewer problems for the economy than does any other form of property. Wolters sets up a test of some of the propositions in the NIE model. He notes that "the institution of private property requires organizations such as laws, a legal system, a land register, a geodetical service and land surveyors, courts, sanctioning organizations, the maintenance of law and order, in short a functioning state reaching down to the local level, and maintaining its monopoly of violence."

Wolters' case study is of western Java between 1870 and the 1920s. During this time period population grew enormously, as did Dutch and native interest in the area. The Dutch extracted coffee with corvée labor, and attempted to lay down the organizational foundation for private property in land. There was no effective land register, geodetical service, or sanctioning organizations. In consequence many "natives" had no legal basis for using land as security for credit and there arose many money lenders, charging high rates of interest. Wolters concludes that the organizational foundation for private property rights in land were at best defective in Priangan. He also finds that economic activity grew quite vigorously. Thus, the effects of faulty private property upon economic activity, predicted by NIE, need to be rethought.

Jean-Philippe Colin represents a scholarly tradition too little read in the anglophone world. ORSTOM is a French Government agency specialized in basic research on agrarian matters in the third world. Colin conducted several years of ethnographic and economic research in the Ivory Coast. His paper presents part of the results of that research. Colin studied a pioneer plantation zone. The early immigrants came into unoccupied territory to plant coffee and cocoa. They were for the most part separated from their home territories by substantial distances. It is not clear how effective state institutions were in managing the local scene. By Colin's account, the pioneers themselves invented the institutions to manage access to land.

Colin's paper deals with property rights in land in this changing situation. The intellectual context, as with Wolters, is the New Institutional Economics. Colin finds that property rights did evolve, but that the path of that evolution has been complex: at the beginning, there was an open access condition for the early pioneers; only when scarcity became apparent were more rights, and exclusions, adopted. He finds that, contrary to NIE tenets, the early pioneers did not decide not to have individual property rights in land. Rather, it was unthinkable for them to think in that fashion. As scarcity emerged, and the original pioneers wanted to leave the area, various forms of exchange of rights to land emerged.

One of the more interesting phenomena in this case is that tree crops can be owned separately from the land under them. The right to land was originally established by planting something. Clearing the land gave no rights. But the rights to the land would last only as long as the plants were growing. In the case of sharecropping, the owner had an incentive to restrict the sharecroppers plants to annuals. Perennials had a very different meaning, for they implied a very long-term right of the sharecropper to the land.

Pauline Peters' paper is concerned with land in England and Africa, and with the problem of common property. She states that not all land management forms constitute property (see Bohannan 1963). The conclusion of her paper is that common property rights in land can only exist in the context of private property rights in land.

Peters presents a summary of the interpretation of the English enclosures. This was a case of conflict between the powerful and the weak. Enclosures worked by stripping away, and nullifying, the common rights of the weak, and elevating or creating private rights in the same territory. The common rights were stripped of their legal standing in the process. The dominant interpretation of this process, especially from the late 19th to the middle of the 20th centuries, was of the triumph of entrepreneurial virtue over the vice of commoners. The view that the commoners did not develop the land entered the literature and was converted to its negative, that the commoners degraded the land.

In Peters' analysis, the English colonial policy in Africa reflected this view of the consequences of communal rights in land in England. In

Botswana, where Peters did field work, there was complex interplay between English colonial policy, Tswana elite interests, and the development of the cattle economy. Bore-holes became central to the cattle industry, and the Tswana elite and the English made a strong push to make them into private property. Having succeeded, the grazing area around the boreholes, which had been under communal control, now began a drift towards becoming private property as well. Peters defines property rights in terms of legal standing in formal courts. Common rights were stripped of their jural standing by powerful elements in society.

References Cited

Acheson, J.M. (ed.)

1994 *Anthropology and Institutional Economics* (Monographs in Economic Anthropology, 12). Lanham, MD: University Press of America.

Bohannan, P.

1963 "Land," "tenure," and "land-tenure." In D. Biebuyck (ed.), *African Agrarian Systems*, pp. 101-15. Oxford: Oxford University Press.

Chapter Fourteen

ᘓᘎ

The Politics of Property among Northern Algonquians

Charles A. Bishop

Barnard and Woodburn remark that property rights, "arguably, are the foundation of hunter-gatherer society" (1988: 4). They mean by this that forms of property and property relations underlie other features of society, especially forms of power and ideology. Nevertheless, while studies show how property forms are related to power structures and ideology, exactly how these change remains poorly understood. Because it is often assumed that evolution must go from the simple to the complex, and because nonprocessual evolutionary models pigeonhole societies into discrete categories defined by identifiable traits, the simplest hunter-gatherers are treated as being primal rather than devolved or atypical. These assumptions are retained in Woodburn's division of hunter-gatherer societies according to whether they possess immediate-return economies and are egalitarian or delayed-return economies and are nonegalitarian (1982; 1988: 31-64). However, unlike earlier evolutionary models that emphasize social or political factors, Woodburn's division is based primarily on how hunter-gatherers treat property. Thus, among egalitarian hunter-gatherers with immediate return systems

> the ability of individuals to attach and to detach themselves at will from groupings and from relationships, to resist the imposition of authority by force, to use resources freely without reference to other people, to share as equals in game meat brought into camp, to obtain personal possessions without entering into dependent relationships—all these bring about one central aspect of this specific form of egalitarianism. *What it above all does is to disengage people from property, from the potentiality in property rights for creating dependency*. (Woodburn 1982: 445, emphasis in original)

Conversely, societies with delayed-return economies depend "for their effective operation on a set of ordered, differentiated, jurally-defined relationships through which crucial goods and services are transmitted. They imply binding commitments and dependencies between people" (Woodburn 1982: 433; 1988: 33). Here, a form of competitive equality exists which is maintained by the "equal exchange of things of the same class or of identical things" (Woodburn 1982: 446).

Woodburn is able to identify only seven egalitarian societies in recent times (1988: 35) but maintains that these are genuine and not simply the result of cultural breakdown stemming from attempts at domination by outsiders (Woodburn 1988). I take a contrary position arguing that further ethnohistorical and archaeological research will demonstrate that the egalitarianism of these groups can be explained by self-imposed isolation from more powerful neighbors. Deliberate efforts to avoid enclavement, I suggest, limited them to locally available materials and restricted their access to nonlocal ones. Usually this meant survival in marginal, often circumscribed, areas that necessitated mobility and inhibited material accumulation. Thus, it isn't surprising that leadership positions are described as being poorly developed and the few forms of property "communally" owned. They are indeed egalitarian, but their egalitarianism, I maintain, became a necessary or at least advantageous survival strategy, and was not some autochthonous state.

Although Woodburn would not accept this, we agree that how property is treated is basic and that political and economic autonomy or near autonomy is a necessary precondition for egalitarianism (Woodburn 1988: 62). We also concur that at various times in the past there were genuine examples of egalitarian societies.

I suggest that these emerged when new uninhabited regions of the world were being populated. Here, hunting bands came to have minimal contact with each other and even became temporarily isolated as they moved ever further. Relative isolation and mobility required small groups to have been consensual, cooperative and sharing of their few possessions. Except for items of personal adornment, property was necessarily limited to materials required for bodily protection and for food production and preparation. Surpluses of seasonally obtained foods were probably consumed within a few weeks. Egalitarian societies emerging from conditions of natural isolation would have been unusual in the past and atypical of the majority of hunter-gatherers that have existed for perhaps 25,000 years (see Soffer 1985).

The egalitarianism of these bands, I argue, would have lasted only as long as these conditions prevailed. Once groups settled in particular regions, they would establish regular relations with neighbors and begin to store foods and other materials for delayed consumption or exchange. As natural environmental restrictions selecting for egalitarianism disappeared, groups embellished their cultures and new sorts of property emerged in the process. The archaeological evidence indicates that these societies did not overtly reject new forms of property when the opportunity arose to obtain them, any more than did band societies reject European trade goods when first offered them. Hence, the overt rejection of property by modern egalitarian groups may be an attempt to avoid dependence in a hostile world.

To make a case that egalitarian societies of the sort described by Woodburn are atypical, it is first necessary to briefly distinguish the sorts of property possessed by hunter gatherers since it is argued that some sorts are more important than others in creating inequality.

Property is more than just things. It refers to bundles of attributes associated with varying degrees and forms of possession, use and ownership by individuals and groups and how they are related to each other. An important distinction is between personal property and common property since, unlike the situation among western capitalist societies, I will argue that it is common property that provides the basis for the development of inequality among hunter-gatherers.

All societies possess personal effects which can be said to be "owned," and which help distinguish the individuality of persons. Among the least complex hunter-gatherers, these might include tools, clothing, and items of adornment. Such goods are not accumulated beyond what is required for survival and are freely loaned when not in use to kinsmen who may need them. Hence, individually owned goods do not provide a means whereby social inequality can develop.

Some forms of common property do. Forms of common property, however, vary widely among hunter gatherers. A dwelling may be the common property of the residents but residency may be defined rather precisely. Common property, then, does not mean open access. Indeed, open access suggests that resources are not subject to any rules and hence are not property at all. Land itself, for instance, is rarely considered to be property among hunter gatherers because it can't be alienated. Nor are basic subsistence resources. Except among the most complex hunter gatherers, unharvested subsistence resources do not constitute property since they are available to all in need, including outsiders, access to them being almost never refused. Labor in their production, however, converts them to the property of the producing group. Because survival dictates that the basic necessities of life must be subject to the most generalized form of sharing, subsistence resources cannot provide a basis for the development of inequality.

In contrast, certain types of resources on the land that have exchange value do, I maintain, provide the basis for the development of inequality. Their importance may be reflected in the defence strategies of the owning group which carefully guards and manages them. These materials are often relatively scarce and unequally distributed in space contributing to their value. I maintain that it is because these forms of property have exchange value and are not usually necessary for survival (there are exceptions) that converts them into property thus providing the basis for the development of inequality.

Through acts of exchange between different groups, the status of the participants, particularly that of the chief representatives of those who are allied, is elevated. As the sociopolitical importance of alliances grows, rules of exclusivity come to be applied to both property that is exchanged and the membership of the groups that produces it. If the exchange of materials is regular and longstanding, group membership may come to be defined very precisely and leadership positions be transformed into offices. Usually such chiefs must labor as hard as their kinsmen and distribute the goods obtained from others to those who contributed wealth to the chief. Among the most egalitarian societies, the chief has no extra power or wealth apart from a few visible symbols of personal adornment. Because exchanges between different groups are delayed and because status differences exist that are not simply based upon age and sex, such societies are not egalitarian according to Woodburn's criteria. As argued, since all societies engage in exchange to varying degrees except for those who have become naturally isolated from others, there is a continuum of nonegalitarian types. Societies that have been marginalized through the outside undermining of their economies and/or who have deliberately isolated themselves in an effort to prevent dominance are spurious. Original egalitarian societies are rare, and their primal nature uncertain.

Property and Social Relations among Northeastern Algonquians

It is therefore more profitable to examine a situation where it is possible to observe how property rights develop among relatively egalitarian societies and how these affect and are affected by other features of socioculture. One region where this is possible is northeastern North America, home of various Algonquian-speaking peoples of the eastern Subarctic and adjacent Woodlands. Here, there are sufficient archaeological and ethnohistorical data to demonstrate a continuum of groups from those which were relatively egalitarian to others distinctly less so. Consecutive historical records also indicate that moderately egalitarian groups developed new forms of political and economic organization during historic times. Thus, spatiotemporal variation permits the documentation of processes and the critical role of property in these.

Subarctic Algonquians provide an appropriate place to begin discussion of property since it was among these peoples that Frank Speck (1915) first identified the family hunting territory system of proprietorship which he thought had existed from time immemorial. Robert Lowie (1920) and later Speck and others (Cooper 1939; Speck & Eiseley 1942; Hallowell 1949) employed this example to challenge Morgan's evolutionism and, either implicitly or directly, Engels's idea of the priority of primitive communism (see Feit 1991b). Thereafter, the aboriginality of the private family system of tenure was challenged by a sequence of scholars (Jenness 1935; Leacock 1954; Rogers 1963; Bailey 1969; Bishop 1970), who employed historical records to document and explain its emergence.

The post-contact origin of the family hunting territory system has remained the standard view in most circles. However, recently it has been challenged by Feit who suggests that family territories associated with beaver management practices may have been pre-contact (Feit 1991a, 1991b). Feit, however, relies mainly on recent field data and so the question of what existed prior to European influences remains open. Feit's argument merits consideration.

Eleanor Leacock, whose work is most frequently cited, assumed the existence of a communal mode of production characterized by generalized reciprocity in the context of egalitarian social relations (1954, 1981). In her view, evidence for communal sharing practices rendered precontact forms of nonpersonal property both private and common as being nonexistent. Examples of these and of nonegalitarian behavior were attributed to capitalist Euro-Canadian influences, especially the fur trade (Leacock 1954). Convinced of the validity of Marx's model which posited a state of primitive communism for early humans, the Montagnais became her prototype, one that she sometimes extended to neighboring Algonquians (Leacock 1981). Thus, any and all evidence that contradicted it was dismissed as being of post-contact origin. This is unfortunate since early historical data suggestive of territoriality, storage, chieftaincy, and in some areas, unilineal totemic groups, indicate that many of these traits were prehistoric, and that perhaps most Northern Algonquians do not fit the egalitarian mold, at least not in its extreme form (Bishop 1986; Morantz 1986; Feit 1991a, 1991b).

Although some of the most northerly groups in northern Quebec and near western Hudson Bay do appear to have been relatively egalitarian, a north-south gradient exists with the most southerly groups being markedly unegalitarian. These latter peoples engaged in organized and balanced exchanges of property with their neighbors and also in less equal exchanges with more remote, northerly groups. These exchanges were mediated by formally chosen, high status leaders. Further, some groups stored foods and trade materials, and hence in Woodburn's scheme, possessed delayed-return economies. While both the archaeological and early historical evidence suggests that these traits pre-date European influences, the historic fur trade led to their extension to and/or elaboration among more remote peoples and to the introduction of new property among them all.

Many southern groups of Northeastern Algonquians possessed pre-Columbian forms of common property subject to rules of exclusive access, and employed them in exchange relationships with neighbors. Common property consisted of materials used in trade and alliance-making. Usually subsistence resources were not exchanged between groups but there are exceptions. For example, the Nipissing traded moose hides and fish with the Iroquoian Hurons for corn. Once harvested, wild foods became property. Access to the areas containing common property could not be alienated but could be inherited in accordance with kinship practice. There were also various forms of personal property (tools, hunting and fishing equipment, canoes, clothing, and items of adornment) that could be shared or given away but not accumulated.

Forms of property were closely tied to features of social organization. Within a group's territory, the key exchange resources were controlled and managed by the elders whose senior member represented the band in formal and highly ritualized property exchanges with neighboring peoples. Because these rituals publicly confirmed and elevated the high status of the participant chiefs, the resources necessary for their maintenance were carefully guarded. Territorial infringement of a band's lands by an alien group without permission resulted in open conflict. Thus, although most subsistence materials needed for survival were available to all in need, because these might be found in the same areas as trade materials, it was usual for neighboring groups to ask permission to enter other groups' lands. It is important to note that a request was not to hunt and fish on a neighbor's lands but rather to enter the lands to do so. The two are quite distinct since things necessary to survival were available to all in accordance with principles of generalized reciprocity. In times of extreme stress, emergency needs rendered requests as unnecessary. It was, then, controlled access to common property employed in exchange that generated social inequality among Northeastern Algonquians.

Among many remote pre-contact groups in northern Quebec and northern Ontario, the exchange of materials among neighbors may have been relatively infrequent. The kinship system involving the practice of cross cousin marriage that extended the web of relationships, however, would have provided a basis for the exchange of material goods between related groups.

Further south along the major water ways, however, early historical records document the existence of strictly enforced band territorial rules not attributable to postcontact conditions. Nevertheless, even in those instances where these are clearly post-contact, cultural practices appear modelled after antecedent ones.

While the historical evidence for particular examples of proprietorship may reflect changes resulting from the European fur trade and other disruptive forces that occurred prior to the written observations, especially given that the earliest records postdate European influences by perhaps a century, the rules and relationships among various groups appear far too elaborate to have developed in all instances entirely from the contact situation. The influx of large quantities of new wealth obtained from Europeans, at least initially, simply seems to have led to the elaboration and extension of institutional practices already present. As such, they provide insights into pre-Columbian processes.

Moreover, band-owned common (exchange) property provided social and cognitive models for later, and well documented, family-owned property, the "family hunting territory system." Hence, given that a good case can be made for continuity, rather than seeing "contamination" as an impediment to understanding as is often the case, it can instead be viewed as an advantage. Also, since the first forms of contact with Europeans frequently involved trade or barter, this would have had the most direct effect on productive means and property concepts.

Common property is widespread among hunter-gatherers. What makes the Algonquian area so interesting is that it is possible to document processes that account for cultural elaboration thereby providing either insights into developments elsewhere or an exemplar for supporting, modifying or rejecting current arguments.

An understanding of how property forms develop requires a broad spatiotemporal perspective. The geographic focus is the entire region north of the upper Great Lakes, Lake Nipissing, and the Ottawa and St. Lawrence Rivers. Although my main concern is with non-food producers, some Algonquians on the southern margins cultivated small fields. Climate and soil conditions, however, prohibited primary dependence on these alone and so they are also included.

From west to east the peoples are the Cree of northern Ontario and northwestern Quebec, their Ojibwa neighbors northeast of Lakes Superior and Huron, the marginally horticultural Ottawa of the Georgian Bay area, the Nipissing around the lake of the same name, the Algonquin of the Ottawa River valley, and the Montagnais of Quebec north of the St. Lawrence River.

Such broad categories as Montagnais, Cree, and Ojibwa—employed today to encompass large numbers of people related by common language and custom—are a recent phenomenon. Although French writers used general terms for various similar bands (such as Ottawa), more frequently they identified by name particular villages or bands.

From 17th-century accounts, about twenty-five distinct, politically autonomous groups can be distinguished near or along the water route between Montreal and northern Lake Superior, each possessing its own name, chief or leader, and territory. Near the upper Great Lakes, groups bore totemic names and were structured unilineally. One such mid-17th century group numbering about 150 persons was designated Ojibwa, a name that later came to be extended to many other similar neighboring peoples. Although demographic data are scarce, the figure of 150 for groups in this area may have been fairly typical.

Further north lived mobile and seemingly smaller bands each of whom occupied a somewhat larger area and who later came to be designated Cree, Montagnais, or Naskapi. Except for a few groups near the southern margins who appear to have done some limited gardening, all these peoples lived mainly if not exclusively by hunting, gathering, and fishing. Because of the greater abundance and variety of foods, southern groups tended to be larger, more sedentary, and more closely spaced than those further north.

All of these peoples were influenced by their farming neighbors to the south. Nevertheless, although most lacked precisely defined farmland belonging to lineages, or villages as was the case among neighboring farmers, most occupied hunting ranges that in certain respects were similar to the farm lands of the latter except that they required little or no labor to maintain.

While seasonal and regional variations in subsistence practices among different Algonquians explain demographic and locational features, I maintain that they cannot account for certain social formations including property concepts.

Because subsistence practices are somewhat easier to document, especially in the archaeological record, than are the more abstract changes in property relations, the evolution of property is attributed to improved means of harvesting, storing, and managing the distribution of foods. But since the ethnographic evidence on hunter-gatherers indicates that the distribution of foodstuffs is usually characterized by the most generalized forms of reciprocity, it is unlikely that the narrowing of control over these basic resources explains how other property forms develop.

Moreover, in the case of Algonquians, the documents indicate that everyone had access to the most basic necessities of life even when access to other resources including fur bearers was rigidly restricted. Improved productive conditions and storage techniques may have indirectly contributed to the elaboration of property by permitting sedentism and the opportunity for accumulation. Also, the ability of certain Algonquian groups to control sections of the major water routes was a key factor. Thus, although geography for Algonquians was not a determining factor, it was a necessary pre-condition to an understanding of property forms.

Elaborate trade relations among many Algonquians and their neighbors appear to have been of considerable antiquity. During Late Woodland times, the last few centuries immediately preceding European contact, there is abundant evidence for communication between southern farmers and northern hunter-gatherers and also among peoples living along the Great Lakes-St. Lawrence waterway. An elaborate burial mound complex exists among hunter-gatherers in southwestern Ontario and adjacent Manitoba that is clearly related both in style and contents to late Mississippian cultures.

Further east on sites in the region north of Lakes Superior and Huron are found a variety of unrelated pottery types attributable to Algonquian peoples in Wisconsin and Michigan and to the various Ontario Iroquois (Wright 1981, 1994). Still further east in the region occupied by the Montagnais, late prehistoric sites contain pottery attributable to both St. Lawrence Iroquois and New York State Iroquois (Wright 1981: 95-96).

Wright, who has synthesized the archaeological evidence for the entire region, attributes the mixture of nonlocal pottery to intertribal marriage practices. The presence of other materials from the south also suggests that there was much trade going on. In sum, archaeological assemblages indicate that there was plenty of contact between northern hunters and southern farmers, contact that gives the appearance of having been cordial and frequent and involved the exchange of materials and/or mates.

Elsewhere I have argued that an elaborate system of ritual exchange extended from at least the Upper Great Lakes to the Gulf of St. Lawrence in late prehistoric-protohistoric times (Bishop 1986). It involved the exchange of foreign prestige goods as well as foods, household commodities, and spouses encompassing a great many different groups including some northern bands of Cree and Montagnais. Materials were obtained for the band by leaders through their participation in interband traffic in nonlocally available materials, ritually exchanged during prearranged multigroup gatherings.

Although groups spent most of their time in mundane household and community activities in relative isolation, it was in the context of multigroup gatherings that social relations were reified through the ritual giving of property. At these gatherings, which usually took place in summer when food was abundant and travel easy, alliances were cemented by marriages and the relatively balanced exchange of goods. Feasting, dancing, and games of skill or chance sometimes accompanied by solemn mourning rites commemorating the dead went on.

Deliberate public displays of generosity were not unlike those among Northwest Coast peoples. Thus, at a Nipissing Feast of the Dead held in 1641 and attended by some 2,000 persons, the chiefs of each visiting group flaunted their wealth by throwing it from their canoes for others to scramble for. Later on, they gave away beaver skins and moose hides "in order to make themselves known, and that they might be received with applause in their Offices" (Thwaites 1896 [23]: 217). The goods given away by the Nipissings at this feast were estimated to have been worth almost 50,000 francs.

While both the size of the gathering and the value of the goods distributed on this occasion reflected the influx of huge quantities of European goods, the event itself was probably no more than a magnified version of what had existed before contact. The desire to acquire these new goods may, however, have enhanced the tension between groups who in some cases appear to have been in a state of competitive opposition not unlike the situation involving competing potlatch groups during the 19th century. For instance, Nicolas Perrot commented on the manner in which the upper Great Lakes Algonquians treated guests: "Although such generosity may be astonishing, it must be admitted that ambition is more the motive for it than is charity. One hears them boast incessantly of the agreeable manner with which they receive people into their houses, and of the gifts that they bestow on their guests—although it is not denied that this is done smilingly and with all possible graciousness" (Blair 1969 [1]: 135).

Both nonlocal utilitarian and nonutilitarian goods were exchanged. In protohistoric times these included copper, precious stones, shell bead necklaces, lead, pigment, mats, birchbark, nets, pottery, pipestone, chert, and furs and hides, among other things. Some Algonquian groups exchanged fish and moose hides for pottery and corn produced by Iroquoian neighbors to the south. Shell bead collars or belts were a post-contact intrusion from the shores of New Jersey, there being no evidence of them on prehistoric sites. Their dispersal to northern regions as a sort of special purpose money was encouraged by the Dutch as a means of extending alliances and thereby tapping the rich fur resources among people then allied to the French. That they were moderately successful is suggested by a 1632 French statement indicating that among the Montagnais near Quebec these collars, or wampum belts as they later became designated, were the Indian equivalent of "gold and silver, their diamonds and pearls" (Thwaites 1896 [5]: 61).

In addition to being employed in alliance making, shell, and later glass bead, belts were given at rituals validating chiefly positions, especially at feasts of the dead. Although their presumed exchange value soon declined, their symbolic and political importance as mnemonic devices and in alliance making, especially with Europeans, continued for many years. Such corporately held property underwrote alliances and attendant exchanges of nonlocal resources. Strictly enforced band territorial rules protected both alliances and access to trade materials. The latter were sufficiently important that band leaders, as representatives of their groups in barter, held high status positions. Stable, regular relations among groups generated leadership positions and enhanced the corporate characteristics of bands including their control over property.

By the beginning of the 17th century, the most important sort of band-owned private property was fur bearing animals, especially beaver. These were the same animals that in later years came to be harvested by families within family-owned tracts of land, a form of tenure emerging out of historic fur trade conditions (Leacock 1954; Bishop 1970).

17th-century records indicate the presence of long standing and well developed relationships among bands who by priority had exclusive rights to deal only with certain specified others. Ritualized greetings between chiefly representatives of two Algonquian bands formally recognized their right to exchange goods while simultaneously and publicly elevating their status. These rituals were of great sociopolitical importance and were often extended to relationships with Europeans. At early 18th-century Hudson's Bay Company trading posts on James and Hudson Bay, traders reported that Cree band leaders or captains would refuse to trade with the post master until the appropriate greeting ritual that symbolically affirmed their equality and commitment to each other had been conducted. During these early years, there is no evidence that Europeans in any way were considered to have been superior to Indians.

The symbolic and sociopolitical, not to mention economic, significance of the inter-group alliance system required that there be established and well known territorial boundaries between groups which became manifest when threatened by trespass. In the context of established associations between groups, any attempt at circumvention to get to a more distant group was viewed as a serious threat to the alliance and its chief participants, one frequently resulting in open conflict. Conflict occurred with increasing frequency concomitant with the influx of European goods and a corresponding rise in the value of fur bearers to Indians, particularly beaver, needed to obtain these materials. Overharvesting of beaver had led to their virtual extermination near the major water routes by the late 1630s, thus providing a growing incentive to disregard the territorial rights of others who either held lands where beaver could still be found or who occupied a middleman position to others who had them.

Property rights were manifest in attempts to poach or to travel through another group's territory to reach a still more distant group for purposes of trade without first obtaining permission and giving the necessary gifts to the party whose lands were being traversed. The latter was tried if the neighboring group was thought to have had nothing of value to trade or if a better bargain could be obtained by avoiding the middleman. Whichever, it usually resulted in violence if discovered.

Historic examples may explain much prehistoric conflict. Permission to cross another's lands could be refused if the purpose was barter and/or if it was thought that this would undermine the relationship or the high status position of the chief. There is abundant evidence indicating that chiefs and their close kinsmen made every effort to maintain the sanctity of middleman relationships if at all feasible. Iroquois incursions, depopulation from disease, and the westward advance of the fur trade during the 17th century, however, destroyed forever relationships near the Great Lakes and account, in part, for subsequent Algonquian population movements to the west.

If the purpose of another group was to obtain food on the lands of a neighbor, refusal was unlikely unless devious motives were suspected. Even so, in the only explicit example that I have, of the several groups of Indians who congregated yearly at the famous whitefish fishery along the St. Mary's River, all but one, the Saulteurs, were said by the missionary to have been there as "borrowers," that is, as guests of the host group. This suggests that Indians distinguished materials required for survival and which should be shared with outsiders, from property that should only be exchanged in very precisely defined ways. It was purely coincidental that beaver flesh could be eaten and pelts traded. Territorial defence mechanisms were not designed to protect land itself since land being inalienable could not be owned. Rather it was specific sorts of resources contained within certain geographic areas which were the property of the group.

As I have noted (Bishop 1986), territorial practices had two primary functions. First, they protected the rights and sanctity of the social groups and their chief representatives who were involved in a particular transactional relationship. Second, they restricted access to certain key resources that were of exchange value to members of the group.

Among such groups as those who were later designated Ojibwa, Ottawa, and perhaps Nipissing, stable territories, social units, and alliances may have been of considerable antiquity. These peoples were organized into patrilineal totem groups (Hickerson 1962; Bishop 1989). Succession to chiefly offices was determined patrilineally and by primogeniture, although validation required that a feast honoring the deceased chief be given. Chiefs functioned as representatives of their group in matters of diplomacy and war.

Although the members of such groups need not, and in fact could not, have lived continually together all year, their common totemic identity which was of considerable emotional significance bestowed on them the right to function as a corporation in their dealings with others and gave them common access to the property within their territory. As anthropologists have shown, unilineal descent by restricting membership can be a very precise means of defining property rights (Morphy 1988; Johnson 1989). Long established exchange and marriage alliances, I argue, had become a means for defining group membership and associating it with property giving rise to the examples of unilineal totemism. Although this property was possessed by the group as a whole, it was administered, distributed and exchanged by the chief of the band whose status was elevated in the process.

Property obtained through ritual exchange or barter, or contained on the lands of a particular group, was not hoarded by any single individual but thought of as belonging to the members of the group as a whole. Items obtained directly through trade with Europeans or indirectly through Indian middlemen were quickly distributed to others by the chief or leader. This might include even the most valued of materials such as guns, kettles, knives, and hatchets.

All who contributed their labor or materials had a claim on the things obtained by chiefs. It is apparent that many of the items obtained from European traders by Cree captains were those specified by members of his band. In large measure, his status was dependent upon their willingness to contribute since he had no claims on their labor. To ensure their support, some Cree band leaders near Hudson Bay even gave away their red captain's coat embellished with brass buttons and frills, and symbolic of their high status, to lesser individuals as a token of generosity. Moreover, while individual households or lodge groups might produce foods individually, these too were shared by all present.

Within bands or groups, it is probable, then, that forms of generalized reciprocity prevailed. Relations with other groups were more balanced and designed both to enhance the status of the chief participants as well as to obtain foreign goods.

Algonquian peoples further north were not unaffected by events nearer the St. Lawrence and upper Great Lakes. It would be wrong to assume that prior to European contact these peoples were isolated. As noted, the presence of prehistoric pottery derived from the south demonstrates frequent contact. Further, birchbark necessary for canoe making had to come from the south, since trees of sufficient size do not grow in the most northerly regions occupied by Algonquians.

The *Jesuit Relations* of 1656-58 (Thwaites 1896 [44]: 239-43) describe no less than five different trade routes to James Bay used by different southern groups to reach northern peoples. One route was traversed annually during the early 17th century (and perhaps for a century or more before this) by the Nipissings who traded beaver pelts from the Cree. Prior to Samuel Champlain's visits to Huronia, these Nipissing traded their pelts to the Ottawa Valley Algonquins who in turn traded them to Europeans. The Algonquins told Champlain that the Nipissings were sorcerers, either to discourage him from bypassing the Algonquins to reach the Nipissings, or perhaps because the Nipissings, indeed, used sorcery as a device to prevent others from usurping their right to trade with the Cree.

There is also evidence indicating that some of these northern peoples attempted to defend the routes to even more distant groups. For example, the people near Lake Mistassini east of James Bay jealousy guarded the trade route to more northerly peoples during the mid-17th century. The early records note the location of some of the key rendezvous spots where groups met north of the St. Lawrence and Great Lakes as far as James Bay. There were, then, forms of property valued by both southern and northern peoples that could only be obtained through formalized barter relationships.

Although relations with more distant groups were in a sense balanced, the greater the distance from the source of valued trade items, the more valuable they became. The markup on European items was sometimes dramatic, amounting to as much as 1,000 percent when these were bartered by Great Lakes Algonquians to Assiniboine and western Cree.

The most northerly Algonquian peoples appear to have been in large measure egalitarian, or at least were much more so than their southern allies. They were more mobile traversing large areas that would have been difficult to defend. Groups fissioned into family units in winter and came together when food again became abundant. There was little opportunity for storage and hence property was limited to what could be carried by canoe or sled. This is reflected in the refusal of the Cree to trap more furs than was necessary to meet their immediate needs until well into the 18th century, thus frustrating the aims of Hudson's Bay Company traders. The precontact traffic in goods to northern regions may have been smaller then among southern peoples. Nevertheless, peoples such as the Cree were able to trade moose hides and fish to the Nipissings and Ottawa who, in turn, traded them to the growing Iroquoian communities which were beginning to lack sufficient quantities of meat and hides for apparel.

The prehistoric alliance system with northern groups was preadapted to the needs of the historic fur trade since in beaver the Cree possessed a highly desired commodity that grew ever scarcer to the south of them as the fur trade expanded. Thus, many, perhaps most, of these Northern Algonquians were already locked into a system which prepared them to supply furs to their southern middlemen partners and in turn act as middlemen to the most distant groups. Except during times of Iroquois raids, a system that remained relatively intact until the 1670s, when the Hudson's Bay Company established coastal posts along James and Hudson Bay.

The introduction and spread of large quantities of European goods obtainable in exchange for furs seems to have altered band allotment systems among remote groups where the beaver hunting lands of families were determined and administered by the elders and a chief or steward. Originally allotment may have simply been a form of resource management. However, as the resources came to take on exchange value, strict territorial rules against trespass came to be applied. Over each of these Northern Algonquian bands was a leader who seems to have retained his position for life. Such individuals represented their groups in matters of trade with other bands.

As beaver pelts grew increasingly important to the fur trade beginning in the late 16th century, these leaders, in consultation with other elders determined where the constituent families would trap. Leaders, in turn, would collect the pelts from trappers and represent the latter at trade fairs or later with Europeans. So long as conditions remained stable, evidence suggests that Indians could selectively harvest beaver.

The allotting of beaver tracts to families may have been precontact for the same reason that pre-horse Plains bison hunts were strictly regulated since northern hunters needed beaver pelts for coats worn during the cold Subarctic winter. Hence, the management of beaver tracts for the food and apparel needs of the band may indeed be ancient as Feit has suggested. I give a late 17th century example of the allotment system pertaining to the Attikameks who reside about 100 miles east of the Waswunipi studied by Feit: "It is the right of the head of the nation . . . to distribute the places of hunting to each individual. It is not permitted to any Indian to overstep the bounds and limits of the region which shall have been assigned to him in the assemblies of the elders. These are held in autumn and in spring expressly to make this assignment" (Le Clercq 1910 [2]: 237). There are other similar statements in the early literature.

This form of land distribution was widespread in the middle of the 17th century southwest and southeast of James Bay. The system broke down soon when trading posts were established in nearby regions. At first, Indian leaders welcomed the presence of traders, perhaps thinking their status would be enhanced through their access to larger, more readily available quantities of goods for distribution. However, when other Indians took the opportunity to bypass the leader in order to trade directly with the European traders, a practice, in fact, encouraged by the Europeans, it undermined the chief's authority.

The collapse of the alliance system isolated different groups which in a few decades were transformed into essentially egalitarian and marginalized trading post bands (Bishop 1984). What remained in place was an acephalous congeries of related families each of whom came to occupy on a relatively permanent basis its own family hunting territory, the same lands which had earlier been assigned them by the band captain and elders. The continual, annual association of the same families belonging to several pre-contact groups with a particular trading post gave rise to their identity as members of particular trading post bands. Although today territorial restrictions have declined, trappers have retained the knowledge of how to manage their resources and also of the importance of sharing with kinsmen what is possessed. It is in this context that Feit's argument regarding the antiquity of beaver management practices has some merit.

Discussion and Conclusions

I have suggested that formal and ritualized relationships between neighboring Northeastern Algonquian groups pre-dated European contact. These were a means whereby unavailable materials could be acquired on a regular basis thereby creating new forms of property. When the materials were highly valued and exchanged at predictable times, defensive tactics were employed to prevent violation of both the relationships and the resources. Under these conditions, the prestige of leaders was enhanced and in those situations where long term exchanges could be regularized and routinized, leadership positions were transformed into hereditary offices. Rules of succession to offices may have become the focus whereby certain kinsmen came to identify with the chief thereby giving rise to corporate unilineal groups. Such groups were distinctly territorial both with respect to their defense of positions in exchange networks, and also in regard to control over the resources of exchange.

Earlier, I stated that egalitarian societies were very rare existing under special sorts of conditions. To the criterion of isolation, I now add marginality as a key determinant of egalitarianism. In the case of Northern Algonquians, their long standing dependence on European goods unritualistically exchanged for fur pelts obtained by families within bounded regions, along with their relative social marginality at the bottom of a caste system, restricted the possibility for equal exchanges to members of the camp group. Sharing can continue to function nicely within these autonomous units long after formal relations with other groups and outsiders have been altered or severed and can be adaptive.

While isolation can create the illusion that such social formations are genuine, research reveals that their basically egalitarian social relations are, in large measure, a response over the past three centuries to a breakdown in a formerly symmetrical alliance system along with a growing dependence on new alien but vital forms of property. Thus, as in the past, their necessary attachment to property in large measure determined the characteristics of their society. It is in this context that I argue that other recent egalitarian societies with immediate-return economies may be seen as being the result of similar processes.

References Cited

Bailey, A.G.
1969 *The Conflict of European and Eastern Algonkian Cultures, 1504-1700.* Toronto: University of Toronto Press.

Barnard, A., & J. Woodburn
1988 Introduction. In T. Ingold, D. Riches, & J. Woodburn (eds.), *Hunters and Gatherers*, Volume II: *Property, Power, and Ideology*, pp. 4-31. New York: Berg.

Bishop, C.A.
1970 The emergence of hunting territories among the northern Ojibwa. *Ethnology* 9:1-15.
1984 The first century: adaptive changes among the western James Bay Cree between the early 17th and early 18th centuries. In S. Krech III (ed.), *The Subarctic Fur Trade: Native Social and Economic Adaptations*, pp. 21-53. Vancouver: University of British Columbia Press.
1986 Territoriality among northeastern Algonquians. *Anthropologica* 28(1- 2):37-63.
1989 The question of Ojibwa clans. In W. Cowan (ed.), *Papers of the Twentieth Algonquian Conference*, pp. 43-61. Ottawa: Carleton University.

Bishop, C.A., & T. Morantz (eds.)
1986 *Who Owns the Beaver? Northern Algonquian Land Tenure Reconsidered* Anthropologica 28(1-2).

Blair, E.H. (trans. & ed.)
1911 *The Indian Tribes of the Upper Mississippi Valley and the Region of the Great Lakes*, 2 vols. Cleveland: Arthur H. Clark.

Cooper, J.M.
1939 Is the Algonquian family hunting ground system pre-Columbian? *American Anthropologist* 41:66-90.

Feit, H.A.
1991a Gifts of the land: hunting territories, guaranteed incomes and the construction of social relations in James Bay Cree society. In N. Peterson & T. Matsuyama (eds.), *Cash, Commoditisation and Changing Foragers*, pp. 223-68. Osaka: Senri Ethnological Studies.
1991b The construction of Algonquian hunting territories: private property as moral lesson, policy advocacy, and ethnographic error. In G. Stocking (ed.), *Colonial Situations: Essays on the Contextualization of Ethnographic Knowledge*, History of Anthropology 7:109-34. Madison: University of Wisconsin Press.

Hallowell, A.I.
1949 The size of Algonkian hunting territories: a function of ecological adjustment. *American Anthropologist* 51:35-45.

Hickerson, H.
1962 *The Southwestern Chippewa: An Ethnohistorical Study* (American Anthropological Association, Memoir 92). Washington, D.C.: American Anthropological Association.

Jenness, D.
1935 *The Ojibwa Indians of Parry Island, Their Social and Religious Life* (National Museum of Canada, Bulletin 78). Ottawa: National Museum of Canada.

Johnson, A.
1989 Horticulturalists: economic behavior in tribes. In S. Plattner (ed.), *Economic Anthropology*, pp. 49-77. Stanford: Stanford University Press.

Leacock, E.B.
1954 *The Montagnais "Hunting Territory" and the Fur Trade* (American Anthropological Association, Memoir 78). Menasha: American Anthropological Association.
1981 *Myths of Male Dominance: Collected Articles on Women Cross- Culturally*. New York: Monthly Review Press.

Le Clercq, C. (trans. W.F. Ganong)
1910 *New Relation of Gaspesia, with the Customs and Religion of the Gaspesian Indians*. Toronto: The Champlain Society. First published 1691.

Lowie, R.
1920 *Primitive Society*. New York: Boni & Liveright.

Morantz, T.
1986 Historical perspectives on family hunting territories in eastern James Bay. *Anthropologica* 28(1-2): 64-91.

Morphy, H.
1988 Maintaining cosmic unity: ideology and the reproduction of Yolngu clans. In T. Ingold, D. Riches, & J. Woodburn (eds.), *Hunters and Gatherers*, Volume II: *Property, Power, and Ideology*, pp. 249-71. New York: Berg.

Rogers, E.S.
1963 *The Hunting Group-Hunting Territory Complex Among the Mistassini Indians* (National Museum of Canada, Bulletin 195). Ottawa: National Museum of Canada.

Speck, F.
1915 The family hunting band as the basis of Algonkian social organization. *American Anthropologist* 17:289-305.

Speck, F., & L.C. Eiseley
1942 Montagnais-Naskapi bands and family hunting districts of the central and southern Labrador peninsula. *Proceedings of the American Philosophical Society* 85:215-42.

Soffer, O.
1985 *The Upper Paleolithic of the Central Russian Plain*. Orlando: Academic Press.

Thwaites, R.G. (ed.)
1896-1901 *The Jesuit Relations and Allied Documents*. Cleveland: Burrows Brothers.

Woodburn, J.
1982 Egalitarian societies. *Man* 17(3):431-51.
1988 African hunter-gatherer social organization: is it best understood as a product of encapsulation? In T. Ingold, D. Riches, & J. Woodburn (eds.), *Hunters and Gatherers*, Volume I: *History, Evolution, and Social Change*, pp. 31-64. New York: Berg.

Wright, J.V.
1981 Prehistory of the Canadian shield. In J. Helm (ed.), *Handbook of North American Indians*, Volume VI: *Subarctic*, pp.86-96. Washington: Smithsonian Institution Press.
1994 Before European contact. In E.S. Rogers & D.B. Smith (eds.), *Aboriginal Ontario, Historical Perspectives on the First Nations*, pp. 21- 38. Toronto: Dundurn.

Chapter Fifteen

ᢒᢓ

Simbu Property

Paula Brown

The highlands of Papua New Guinea figure prominently in discussions of some economic issues, but rarely in discussions of property. This paper, then, aims to show the relations of land, territory, acquisition, ownership, inheritance, and assessment of property among Simbu,[1] where changes in practices and concepts under colonial rule and independence have occurred in the short space of 60 years. I shall discuss the way that Simbu conceive of their resources, territory, land, goods, how they protect their rights and deal with transfers and inheritance, and how these have changed.

Simbu ideas about land and property are rooted in their relation to their land and territory, the rights and identity of groups associated with places, and the human imprint (crop growing, pig breeding and raising) and manufacture which personalize resources and goods into property. The foundations of property law introduced by colonial Australia and the legal establishment of independent Papua New Guinea have effected some transformation of values and new concepts of property of individuals and groups in Simbu.

Legal and economic theories of property are usually developmental and evolutionary (North & Thomas 1977; Pryor 1973). In economic theory, property in primitive agricultural communities is communally regulated: rights of the group exclude outsiders and limit the exploitation of insiders. The community may be identified with its territory or land. In the next evolutionary stage, with population growth and dependence upon limited resources, land, or improved/arable land, becomes private. In evolutionary stage theory, population growth and resource limitation seem to dominate over technological change, which is usually seen as a result rather than a cause (Boserup 1981); the mechanism of transition is unexplained. The theory is strong on principles but weak on culture and technology. Bell's proviso (in this volume) that the right of alienation is a right of private property cannot be simply applied to the Simbu of past time. However, recent incidents and developments indicate that sale and transfer of property rights have entered Simbu understanding.

This simple unidirectional evolution to private property cannot account for the complexity of territorial community rights, ownership and personal property concepts, and the ways land and goods are transferred, given, sold, and repaid, as my Simbu example will show. A prominent Papua New Guinea legal scholar and commentator, Bernard Narokobi (1988), discusses ownership in Melanesia. He shows how customary definitions of property differ from those imposed by the colonial government and the laws of the independent state of Papua New Guinea. Papua New Guinea's regional diversity and multiplicity of cultural and language groups have produced many different rights and practices with regard to land and property. There are intricate relations of common or communal and individual property concepts; technology, population density and distribution are significant factors. This paper will for the most part limit its discussion to the Simbu, as they have been affected by changes in law and economy over the past 60 years.

Papua New Guinea

New Guinea peoples are known for exotic practices and exchange: colorful bird of paradise headdresses, periodic pig feasts, kula exchange rings, big men, ritual homosexuality. Discussions of the economy have centered around questions of reciprocity, exchange, and the predominance of the gift economy (Gregory 1982; Strathern 1988; Weiner 1992). This gift economy is one aspect of the group/individual integration that also underlies property concepts in Simbu. In Simbu, group and individual, big man and followers, jointly guide the economy. There is no separate polity; leadership and the exchange system are both political and economic. Property, and particularly land, is not simply a resource: territory, land, place names, and locations validate the identity of each tribe, clan, and individual.

Since anthropologists usually come to ethnographic study after the people have been through years (or centuries) of colonial rule, and nowadays some years too of independence with its constitution and law reforms, the study of property in a tribal community must take account of rules introduced by outside colonial and post-colonial legislators and interpreted by the courts. I therefore review the history of land policy and its administration.[2]

The German New Guinea Company in its charter of 1885 took rights over (what they saw as) ownerless land (*terra nullius*, vacant or waste) and assumed sovereignty according to Prussian law of 1872, supervised by the German Imperial Government. Private companies, some of which took large areas for plantations, missions, and government stations, acquired and registered land. Native land was never registered, although some claims to title were recognized, and the settlements, gardens, and land used by a community were not alienated. When the New Guinea Company ceased to administer the country in 1899, the German Empire took over these sovereign rights and the administration of various ordinances (Phillips 1969).

After World War I the Australian administration took over New Guinea, and applied British-derived concepts of common law. British New Guinea had become Australian Papua some years earlier. Both German and Australian land policy tended to commoditize land, to consider it as owned and alienable, generally by a group or clan rather than an individual. Australians assumed that apparently unoccupied land was ownerless and could be appropriated for government or private use, but required that the natives understood and agreed to the sale or lease. The Land Ordinance 1921-1929 protected native land against acquisition by private persons and gave the Administrator power to "purchase or lease land from native owners provided they are willing to dispose of it", and "the land is not required, or likely to be required, by the owners" (Phillips 1969: 245). In principle, then, native land was alienable; however, the rights of native owners were to be protected.

The discovery, pacification, and initial administration of the central highlands of what is now Papua New Guinea began in the 1920s and 1930s. Simbu saw their first patrol and first missionaries in 1933. New Guinea was then a League of Nations Mandated Territory, and after World War II a United Nations Trusteeship, with the Australians responsible for education, economic and political development, to prepare the people for independence.

Overall, the Australians continued to assume that land was held communally by clans and communities. Loans for development and individual enterprise were not permitted without security of individual land holdings, and the people were dependent upon government sponsored development programs. Indigenous economic development required the land owners to plant and maintain cash crops, and harvest the produce. The Administration felt that individual tenure would adapt to long term commercial cropping, since tree crops of coconut, cocoa, and coffee were developing. They believed that customary group tenure of agricultural land would discourage such development, and they wanted to introduce a single system of land holding regulated by the central government (James 1985). The land policy was seen by Fitzpatrick (1980) as controlling native enterprise and keeping the people in their place. In the 1950s, 1960s, and 1970s some attempts were made by Australian administrators to register land titles or demarcate territories and boundaries, but there was no overall registration (Crocombe & Hide 1971: 315-20; Howlett et al. 1976: 100-130), and none of these recommended procedures were implemented in Simbu.

Independence, in 1975, introduced a new constitution and plans for law reform, the training and authority of Australian and native legislators, jurists, magistrates, and administrators of every kind. There are conflicts of principle, method, and outcome with respect to land cases before the courts. Local land courts were introduced to mediate local disputes in terms of customary principles, while the National Court follows English common law principles (Zorn 1992).

The general principle of communal tenure persisted: no alienation was allowed without the full agreement of all members of the group concerned, individuals and families held usufruct rights, and there were multiple rights to collect firewood, gather, hunt, and fish. However, the hundreds of language/cultural groups in Papua New Guinea, most unstudied, seem to hold many different customary traditions on land and property[3] (cf. Brown 1978; Scaglion 1987). Also, new forms have been introduced (Ploeg 1971, 1972).

Simbu: Land and Territory

For the Simbu, land is not simply a resource: places are colonized, named, and populated by the patrilineal ancestors buried and the descendant people living there. They are there by right of myth, pioneering original settlement or conquest. Their ownership is validated by the ancestors' burial places, the pigs sacrificed, shrines and sacred grounds, the plants and marks at boundaries, houses at traditional sites, the labor invested and crops raised, the trees planted, the pigs browsing in the bush, the wild plants, fruits, and building materials that grow, the goods made and stored. It is the relation between the people, that is, individuals and groups, the resources they recognize and use, the structures, plants, animals, and objects they acquire, make, and raise, that composes what I may call property ideas for the Simbu.

My historical discussion of Simbu property concepts begins with the traditional system of understandings and practices, as far as they explain what property means to the people. Simbu are a tropical highland population who live and raise their food on intensively cultivated steep mountain slopes. Kuman Simbu, some fifty-five large tribes, each of 1000-4000 people, are densely settled on slopes and valleys at over 5000 feet in altitude. Each tribe's and clan's tradition claims sites and territories, documented by legend and history. Forest trees, game, and wild plants are resources for tribe, clan, or segment members. Some land and special sites with planted trees or improvements are communal. Land and group territory are part of the Simbu social and economic system of resource use, labor, production, exchange, payment, personal and intergroup relations. While land may be the main "property" to be discussed, rights in people, trees, crops, buildings, livestock, and goods, concepts of exchange, gifts, and returns, compensation for injury and loss must be considered, as all affect the rights, obligations, and relations of individuals and groups.

Each tribe had a large block of land and several ceremonial grounds shared by clans and subclans. Local clan and subclan traditions further assign places, cemeteries, ceremonial locales, settlement sites of men's houses. Simbu at the turn of the century, and until 1933, was a region of fiercely competitive tribes fighting over border lands and occupying land when the defeated enemy fled. Tribes are composed of several exogamous clans, so that marriages and kinship bind together clans in a tribe. Within protected territories clan segments and individual families enjoy fairly secure tenure over long periods, holding ceremonies and food distributions to honor obligations to kin and affines. The garden land is passed within patrilineal groups and given to friendly kin and affines; this transfer may be short or long term, the outcome depending upon relations among the people. When a group is ousted from its land it seeks sanctuary and help from friendly clansmen and kinsmen. A clan or segment may grant a tract of land to a friendly group in need of new land and refuge. The gift is acknowledged by a gift of food grown on the tract, and then the land can be permanently held, subdivided, and inherited by the recipients. The groups continue to marry, exchange gifts, and support one another in war.

Land is the foundation of group and individual status and accomplishment. Simbu have a strong attachment to sites that are named for important people and events associated with them. Their collective homeland in the Simbu valley, the place of the first man and woman, the first fight and eviction, locates a whole people. Simbu preserve their history in the names and stories of tribal and group territories. Tribal traditions are tales of movements, fights, conquests, forced migrations, finding unoccupied land and pioneer settlements: events that occurred in the past at a place. The place name identifies the participants and the event and supports the claim to land. Historical tales are validated by the name of a place and participants. Particular locations, the cemeteries, ceremonial grounds, notable trees and building sites, are precise markers for historical claims. The origin story of all Simbu has a second and third chapter in the story of origin, movements, migrations, settlements, wars of each tribe and group. Strong and persistent traditions of group settlements and movements are the basis of continued land and territorial disputes; loss and conquest of land or territory are not forgotten.

For example, Naregu origin and migration takes a historical form, when the Naregu are settled at Pari, in the Singga valley. Their defeat by Kamanegu, within the memory of our older informants in 1958, ties into detailed statements of settlement, land occupation, and recent land gifts, transfers, movements. These merge into our detailed data on land in the area of study where repeated land surveys confirm transfers (Brookfield & Brown 1963; Brown et al. 1990).[4]

Tribal territories were unstable, especially at the peripheries that were threatened. Families with valued land on the periphery might invite a relative—often a kinsman or affine of the neighboring tribe—to live and garden with them on their land. Then gardens of these relatives of different tribes and clans were interdigitated in tribal border areas (Brookfield & Brown 1963). This might serve as a protection against invasion by hostile members of that neighboring group.

The core area of a tribe is densely occupied with houses and garden land, but at some borders with other tribes—especially when relations are hostile—an unoccupied no-man's- land of forest, bush, and browsing land for pigs separates these. From time to time pig stealing, fights, conquests, migrations—as well as sharing among kin and affines that brought people and new settlements—change intertribal relations and redefine the borders of these marginal areas.

A comparative study of highlands peoples showed a correlation of population density and individualizing land tenure (Brown & Podolefsky 1976). The highland peoples with low population density and large tracts of unoccupied land between settlements hold bush and long fallow land in communal or clan tenure. There was little of this in northern Simbu Province. Intervillage and interclan enmity was heightened in competitive relations and disputes over people, land, livestock, and reputation. Highlands warfare aims at the destruction of people, crops, houses, trees, and might result in the defeated abandoning their land and holdings, at least temporarily. However, the occupation of such land by the victors and establishment of new home territories by those who lost their land was not common, even in Simbu where many groups tell of eviction and resettlement following a defeat. Reoccupation of the area some months or years later was more usual. Intertribal alliance is a temporary arrangement in a particular conflict between the tribe and an enemy.

Simbu: Land and Gardens

We may distinguish territory, site, different kinds of land, and rights held by groups and individuals. Tribes have a block of territory and specific sacred sites, some of which may be associated with segments. Clan land blocks are not all fully discrete within tribal territory. Land for men's houses and the forecourt of a men's house is shared by a small men's group—part of a subclan—with their guests, who come to visit, discuss a marriage, mourn a deceased member or plan an exchange. The land and trees of a cemetery and sections of the ceremonial ground are clan and subclan sacred places, where pigs are killed, cooked, and distributed. Houses for women and children—where pigs also sleep—are located in garden land. Labor and materials are required for houses, and trees are planted on land prepared by the group members. Members of the group take wood, reeds, grass, and so on from bush and forest land within their territory.

Our long-term study documents the tenacity of individual holdings in the tribal territorial center and changeable, larger group claims in the peripheries (Brown et al. 1990). The land in fallow blocks and pig browsing areas is claimed by subclan groups or segments. However, the land in current or recent cultivation in the tribal core area is individual or family property, and inheritable. The improvements, trees, houses, crops are private. Trespass and theft of crops are a source of accusations against neighbors and fights within and between groups.

Simbu agriculture is based upon sweet potatoes, tropical and subtropical subsidiary crops of vegetables and fruits, and domestic pigs. While most of Melanesia has a form of swidden agriculture at low population densities, Simbu agriculture is very highly intensified: population density reaches 200/km^2. Full garden clearing, tillage, fencing, water and soil control on steep slopes, short and long fallow are all adapted to a system that mixes communal—that is, subclan and clan segment land claims traditionally under the direction of a *magan nim* (ground father)—and individual/family land claims.

In newly occupied areas when a man prepares a plot for a family garden he fences it (that is, if it is not in an area enclosed by a group fence), marks the boundary with cordyline plants and trees, and plants casuarina trees as a fallow crop. That plot is his to recultivate, divide among his sons, or share with selected relatives. Rights to such land are considered permanent and individual.

Soil varieties and location, family and crop needs, and methods of preparation of land for a garden are carefully evaluated by Simbu agriculturalists. The work invested in the garden preparation is the basis of a man's claim to this land; planting and tending give a woman a claim to the crop. After one, two or three cultivation periods, varying with the soil conditions and crops grown, the plot is put into longer fallow, with any remaining plants, fences, and the growing casuarina and other long-term plants, as markers.

After a fallow period the land is replanted by the original gardener and his family or by his son or sons succeeding him: most land going to a close agnate or subclan member (Brown et al. 1990). Simbu favor, but are not limited to, patrilineal inheritance of land, and if a man dies without designating heirs, his brothers or subclan mates are land trustees and reallocate valued holdings (Wohlt & Goie 1984). Land granted to a relative may pass to his descendants, and some group land gifts cemented relations with friendly affinal groups. This flexible land holding and usufruct system provided refuge and opportunity for alliances.

Each family has several plots (five or six on average) in different land types, located in several parts of the clan and subclan territory: some would be in fallow, others being prepared, planted, harvested, replanted, etc. Once taken out of communal or family fallow and prepared for gardening, individual tenure prevails. Here property is the crop, and its destruction or theft is an offense against the owner.

Simbu: Property in Exchange

Intergroup gift celebrations involve feasts of highly valued food and pigs and gifts of rare shells, axes, and plumes. The foods and pigs are mostly produced on native land. Sometimes they are traded in from other areas, as are the valued goods. The land of the group, and labor of men and women to produce these gifts, determines the prestige of its leaders, the big men. Pigs are acquired by purchase, trade, gift or breeding, mainly by men, and it is usually said that they are the property of the men who decide when the pig is to be killed or given in exchange. Goods and the pigs and special foods that are the foundation of intertribal feasts have a dual meaning: they represent both the group that sponsors an occasion and the individual who gives the objects to celebrate it. Big men represent groups.

The complex exchange system of Simbu binds individuals and groups in an endless cycle of debts and obligations, goods and foods received. These are to be returned with increment to pay for allied aid in fights, for brides, for children, to assist relatives after a death, to pay for land loaned, to borrow or sell valuables. A person or group that does not repay in a reasonable time loses face, and group status is judged by the display of valuables, plumes, and foods at ceremonies. Indeed, without anything that might be called a governmental structure, Simbu maintain relations within and between clans and tribes through competition, war and ceremonial exchange of food and valuables. Shells, plumes, and some other goods are held for a short time and given for a debt; food and pigs are shared and consumed. There is a constant circulation of these products, which carry the memory and reputation of the donors and the debt. When a land gift is made between groups and confirmed in gifts of food and goods, this transaction serves as payment for land. It is not a final payment but introduces a new exchange relationship between the two. This requires continued exchange and negotiation.

Contact and Change

From the first sight of the white man, his wealth in the form of shells and the hitherto unknown steel and cloth created a new set of relationships and source of wealth. In the first years of relations with the Australian government and missions, Simbu offered land to them for settlements, roads, airstrips, agriculture, and building sites. The missions and government gave goods to the Simbu leaders and groups they understood to be property owners. However, there were very different views of the meaning of these transactions: from the viewpoint of the Europeans, this was a final sale, but for Simbu it was a phase of an exchange relationship. Simbu worked and provided building materials and food, receiving shells and other things in payment. When the buildings were not used and further payments or support against enemies were not forthcoming, Simbu concluded that the obligation was not recognized and the relationship broken. The property in their eyes was to revert to the original Simbu owners. Simbu desire for European goods led to theft from and killings of missionaries as they traveled through the area.

In their attempt to end tribal fighting and abolish war weapons, Australian officers of the 1930s instituted peace ceremonies and exchanges of food, pigs, and goods to confirm the end of hostilities. They required compensation for injuries and losses to enemies. These two introductions—new objects of value given by outsiders for land, for produce, for labor, and for sexual relations, and the practice of paying compensation to enemies and in accidental injuries—began a new era of property concepts. The white man's goods were incorporated into ceremonial display and payments: all exchange activities soon depended upon these new goods, and economic values were revised. There was inflation in ceremonial payments: some traditional goods were replaced by new imported steel and other objects of value, and later cash payments were introduced. These in time supplanted almost all exchange goods:

only pigs continue as valuables. Food and beer are purchased for ceremonial gifts. Wealth, with new valuables, continues as circulation of money and goods among individuals and as group prestige marks.

Before the end of the 1930s the tribes of north Simbu were mapped by government officers, and these boundaries, whether long established and traditional or newly conquered, became the territories accepted as demarcating fixed tribal areas by Australian administration and courts. They assumed that land was group or clan property. Many areas were under dispute before and after the Australians came: government officers, lands commissioners, lands courts and mediators have been unable to satisfy all parties, and disputes continue.

The Simbu tenure system—a fallow cycle for agricultural land with bushland for livestock grazing and wild products, with dispersed land claims that gave each household access to several kinds of land within group territory—does not readily accord with land title registration. Hide (1971, 1973) and Nilles (1974) comment on the difficulties and confusions of applying these principles and procedures in Simbu.

Since coffee was introduced in the 1950s coffee trees have been planted on land to which the gardener has a right by tradition, membership in the group, inheritance, or previous cultivation. They are tended and coffee is picked by the individual owner and his family. The more remote and higher altitude Simbu groups have very little land that can grow coffee successfully. Some of them now produce vegetables for sale in town markets, and marijuana is a new crop (P.K. Moore, personal communication, 1991). While the principles of land tenure have not changed, new values do affect the economy. In Papua New Guinea, disputes between members of clans and communities have arisen concerning claims and use of land for cash crops and commercial activities (see Ward n.d.: 253ff.). Trees and crops, long or short term, are the property of the one who plants; the highly valued coffee trees are taken over by his sons when the original owner ages or dies. With self-government came the beginning of government recognition of local customary law. However, there is no standard or accepted body of knowledge concerning such customary law. For example, Simbu long established practices that gave migrants and visitors rights to usufruct, and potential inheritance had an important place in inter- and intra-group relations. Tribal border territory was shared with friendly relatives in neighboring groups to defend land and settlements. They can hardly be codified or applied in court cases. Some government officials and judges assume that all native custom is the same, some turn to local leaders, and a few legally qualified native authorities become the wise men of the transition.

The Australian administration rule that territories should stand as at the time of contact, whether long occupied or newly conquered, was never accepted by Simbu in their land disputes. In the last few years the idea that customary practice should supplant the rulings imposed by foreigners has gained support. There are now three, often contradictory, principles of land ownership: original settlement, status at the time of contact, and current occupation. Each principle may be argued in court when intertribal or commercial cases are heard (Zorn 1991, 1992).

In rural and urban areas of conflicting land claims, these principles influence court decisions in opposing ways. Individual and group property and rights are not clearly distinguished, and when cases involve business organizations or different native groups, customary law cannot solve problems. In the highlands many families, especially Simbu from the densely populated and high altitude areas, have migrated to the less densely settled Wahgi valley region, but their tenure is insecure, and they mostly restrict their activities to short term crops and pig raising, rather than invest in long term cash crops such as coffee (Rambo 1993). Migrants to urban areas often settle in shanty towns of insecure tenure.

In some cases of land dispute settlement, when land occupied by one tribe is awarded by the court to another, the government assists in compensating the losers (as individuals) for the crops and coffee planted on this land, but not for the land itself. As disputes and fights between adjacent tribes have raged since independence, people once peacefully settled near borders have moved to more secure sites and the borderland, now needed for increased population and cash crops, is unoccupied. The situation remains volatile.

The general direction of change has been towards individuation and privatization. The *magan nim* is no longer a functionary, as most land—and particularly commercially valuable coffee land and roadside sites—is claimed and held by individuals and their heirs. Private shops and buildings are often built of permanent materials and have a high value. Goods and services are now subject to payment. The early institutionalization of payment by Europeans for goods and services was a beginning of this trend. Simbu is increasingly commoditized in exchange as well. The traditional large feasts organized and managed by big men have largely disappeared. Now massive food distributions and payments include money and purchased goods, and are held to celebrate political successes, to compensate a group for the death of a member in a road accident or to bestow a government or insurance payment.

Compensation payments are decreed by government and accepted by the Simbu as intergroup damages in accidents and injuries, thus converting life to property. Bride price and death payments have escalated, intensifying a monetary measure of the value of persons. A prominent area of dispute and claim for compensation is the damage to crops by pigs, where the maintenance of fences and control of pigs is disputed (Podolefsky 1992).

Legal Pluralism and the Simbu

The transfer of government to independent Papua New Guinea in 1975 began a new period in which law reform and the adaptation of customary law to national law began. James (1985), with extensive experience in the application of British common law in former African colonies, sees this as the proper way to develop land law. A recent review of Papua New Guinea courts (Zorn 1991, 1992) contrasts the principles. Local land courts follow local custom; they mediate, negotiate, and compromise within a flexible understanding of local custom. The National Court adjudicates with common law principles, applying substantive law and consistent rules to effect final settlement of disputes. The conflict of these two court systems continues. Narokobi (1988, 1989) voices objections to the control by central government, and especially to the ordinances that make water rights and mineral rights properties of the state rather than the community. He would localize customary law.

Simbu cannot find a solution to this division of principles. In their rural situation, they continue to dispute boundaries and decisions made by the Australian administrators and the law officers of the present Papua New Guinea government. They first accepted the presence and occupation of what had been their land by the government and the missions, organizations who gave them valued western goods. These to the Simbu began an alliance and exchange relationship (Brown 1970a, 1970b). In the eyes of the government or mission, this was purchase. However, the former land owners know that some sites now have a high commercial value. They take new opportunities to sue the government for land in townships, airstrips, roadside sites, and land used for health centres and schools in rural areas (Gigmai 1995). In their stories of the past Simbu continue to tell of their past occupation of this land, and often wish to reclaim land. Long after a transaction is completed, Simbu are dissatisfied and wish to renegotiate.

Simbu have been spared the loss of land and resources through alienation, and the government has never sanctioned the granting of native land in Simbu Province to outsiders. Their land disputes and intertribal conflicts are still rooted in tradition. If the proposed land reforms favor customary rights, they may never experience controversial principles at work in their rural area.

In July 1995 the International Monetary Fund and World Bank asked for changes in Papua New Guinea customary land ownership in order to permit further loans for logging and mining, and legislation was proposed to register rural land as a component of structural readjustment. Parliament's proposed legislation to comply with this requirement was opposed by large protests and demonstrations by Simbu and other peoples in July and August. The proposal was withdrawn.

Simbu understandings and rights of property have changed over 60 years. The most prominent direction of change is towards individuation: passing land in coffee to sons, private enterprise and shopkeeping, payment for goods and services. Land is not yet fully a commodity among Simbu. Registration of titles is limited to commercial sites. Government, town, and missions have acquired land for which the owners received compensation, and there is now occasional payment for land among Simbu, usually in such circumstances as a roadside shop site or a location for some special commercial activity among rural people. Now, land most suitable for a cash crop may be transferred for a payment.[5] This takes the traditional system of land grants to clansmen or kinsmen into a form of commoditization. At present, we can only note with Brookfield (1996) that the Simbu trajectory of change has not transformed the rural land economy. The future is, as always, uncertain.

Notes

1. Simbu is now the official name for the province and the people, and so I use it here. Chimbu is sometimes still seen in correspondence and papers, and was usual in previous writings. I refer specifically to Kuman, about 80,000 people in the northern and western areas of Simbu Province; other Simbu groups are similar in most respects. In this section I use the present tense, since these principles and practices have persisted in rural Simbu.
2. For an account of land policy history in the South Pacific (Vanuatu, Western Samoa, Tonga, Fiji), see Ward & Kingdon (1995).
3. The student authors of the studies for the Law Reform Commission report many differing statements of community land rules (Scaglion 1983).
4. Wamugl, a Sungwakani elder of Kombaku clan, Naregu tribe, on 6/13/1958 told a characteristic tale of origin and movements, identifying many places of settlement, gardens, fights, cemeteries, and ceremonial grounds familiar to his listeners.

> This land at Damar had no inhabitants. It was water. The Chimbu were at Wulim, Keglsugl, Wom. We came from Womatne, Gembogl, Kaire, in the mountains. Then the water drained from this valley. The Naregu went to Kurumugl and Pari, long ago. When I married I was at Singgare, where there was a big men's house. We were at Agl, Yugu, Kungare, Daruwa, Bandagl, and Yomba Yaundo. There was a burial ground at Tambagl for Naregu. That's where my father and ancestors were, and they all died there. After a fight with Kamanegu and Naregu, the Endugwa and Endugwa-Nauru left the area. Then there was a fight between Kamanegu and Naregu. The fight was over my pig. The Kamanegu stole it, killed it, and some men ate it. Everyone was angry, and in the fight, the Kamanegu chased the Naregu out. They stopped at Guye; the Sungwakani went to Gondomakane; the Domkani went to Agumbaya and the Komniambugo to Wayankemambuno. My father and I were at Yombakangwa and Dibinmugl where we had a house. We came here later. The Gamgane had left this place Damar; the ground was unoccupied. Wagai's father and Dogoba's father went to Mintima to find land, and many of the Sungwakani were still at Guye; they were asked by Wagai's father to come to Mintima and Dibinmugl. The Pentagu went to Wandi, Bindekombugl, Guye, Manga, Mi, Druamugl, Bongolungu, Duwagi, Kanindemambuno, Okenagoli, Darali. They all found land in all these places. The Pentagu, Bindegu, Toglkane, Kendagagu, Kigungaumo, Sumbaingaumo found land. They kept

> it and stayed. Then the Numambugu came, Gamgani and Kombaku made a line. They are not patrilineal fathers and sons (*nemangigl*), but brothers (*angigl*) here, all the Naregu. The others—Siambuga, Wauga, Gena, Kamanegu, Endugwa—are not brothers of Naregu.

This story was told by Wamugl in Kuman Simbu. The interview was in my first period in Simbu when I used a Pidgin interpreter and took this down in a combination of Pidgin and English, spelling Simbu place names as well as I could. The material was put into English later. See Brown (1995) for fuller discussion of traditional land claims.

5. Recent correspondence elaborates: "the people of Simbu (some) now are for economic reasons registering their traditional land to apply for bank loans to develop their area" (L. Gigmai, personal communication, 1995).

References Cited

Boserup, E.
1981 *Population and Technological Change*. Chicago: University of Chicago Press.

Brookfield, H.
1996 Untying the Chimbu circle: an essay in and on insight. In A. Ploeg & H. Levine (eds.), *Work in Progress: Essays in New Guinea Highlands Ethnography in Honour of Paula Brown Glick*, pp. 63-74. Frankfurt am Main: Peter Lang.

Brookfield, H., & P. Brown
1963 *Struggle for Land*. Melbourne: Oxford University Press.

Brown, P.
1970a Chimbu transactions. *Man* 5:88-117.
1970b Mingge-money: economic change in the New Guinea Highlands. *Southwestern Journal of Anthropology* 26:242-60.
1978 New Guinea: ecology, society, and culture. *Annual Review of Anthropology* 7:263-91.
1995 *Beyond a Mountain Valley: The Simbu of Papua New Guinea*. Honolulu: University of Hawai'i Press.

Brown, P., H. Brookfield, & R. Grau
1990 Land tenure and land transfer in Chimbu, Papua New Guinea, 1958- 1984: a study in continuity and change, accommodation and opportunism. *Human Ecology* 18:21-49.

Brown, P., & A. Podolefsky
1976 Population density, agricultural intensity, land tenure and group size in the New Guinea Highlands. *Ethnology* 15:211-38.

Crocombe, R., & R. Hide
1971 New Guinea: Unity in Diversity. In R. Crocombe (ed.), *Land Tenure in the Pacific*, pp. 292-333. Melbourne: Oxford University Press.

Fitzpatrick, P.
1980 *Law and State in Papua New Guinea*. London: Academic Press.

Gregory, C.A.
1982 *Gifts and Commodities*. London: Academic Press.

Hide, R.
1971 Land demarcation and disputes in the Chimbu district of the New Guinea Highlands. *New Guinea Research Bulletin* 40:37-61.

1973 *The Land Titles Commission in Chimbu* (New Guinea Research Bulletin, 50). Canberra: Australian National University.

Howlett, D., R. Hide, E. Young, J. Arba, H. Bi, & B. Kaman

1976 *Chimbu: Issues in Development*. Canberra: Development Studies Centre, Australian National University.

James, R.W.

1985 *Land Law and Policy in Papua New Guinea*. Port Moresby: Law Reform Commission, Papua New Guinea.

Narokobi, B.

1988 *Concept of Ownership in Melanesia* (Occasional Papers of the Melanesian Institute, 6). Goroka: Melanesian Institute.

1989 *Lo Belong Yumi Yet* (Melanesian Institute Point Series, 12). Goroka: Melanesian Institute.

Nilles, J.

1974 Law enforcement or land reforms. In P. Sack (ed.), *The Problem of Choice,* pp. 134-40. Canberra: Australian National University.

North, D., & R. Thomas

1977 The first economic revolution. *Economic History Review* 30:229-41.

Phillips, B.

1969 Native land under German and Australian law. In B.H. Brown (ed.), *Fashion of Law in New Guinea,* pp. 237-48. Sydney: Butterworths.

Ploeg, A.

1971 *The Situm and Gobari Ex-servicemen's Settlements* (New Guinea Research Bulletin, 39). Canberra: Australian National University.

1972 Sociological aspects of Kapore settlement. *New Guinea Research Bulletin* 49:21-118.

Podolefsky, A.

1992 *Simbu Law*. New York: Harcourt Brace Jovanovich.

Pryor, F.L.

1973 *Property and Industrial Organization in Communist and Capitalist Nations*. Bloomington: Indiana University Press.

Rambo, K.F.

1993 Economic change and differentiation in Kerowagi (Papua New Guinea). Ph.D. dissertation, Department of Anthropology, State University of New York-Stony Brook.

Scaglion, R. (ed.)

1983 *Customary Law in Papua New Guinea* (Law Reform Commission of Papua New Guinea, Monograph 2). Port Moresby: Law Reform Commission of Papua New Guinea.

Scaglion, R.
1987 Introduction. In R. Scaglion (ed.), *Customary Law and Legal Development in Papua New Guinea* (Anthropology, 6:1-2).

Strathern, M.
1988 *The Gender of the Gift*. Berkeley: University of California Press.

Ward, A.
n.d. Customary land, land registration, and social inequality. In D. Denoon & C. Snowden (eds.), *A Time to Plant and a Time to Uproot*, pp. 249- 64. Port Moresby: Institute of Papua and New Guinea Studies.

Ward, R.G., & E. Kingdon (eds.)
1995 *Land, Custom and Practice in the South Pacific*. Cambridge: Cambridge University Press.

Weiner, A.
1992 *Inalienable Possessions*. Berkeley, University of California Press.

Wohlt, P.B., & A. Goie
1986 *North Simbu Land Use* (Simbu Land Use Project, 5). Boroko: Papua New Guinea Institute of Applied Social and Economic Research.

Zorn, J.
1991 Making law in Papua New Guinea. *Pacific Studies* 14:1-34.
1992 *Graun bilong mipela*: local land courts and the changing customary law of Papua New Guinea. *Pacific Studies* 15:1-38.

Chapter Sixteen

Land, Property, and Credit Contracts in Priangan, West Java, 1870s Through the 1920s: Legal Framework and Private Ordering

Willem G. Wolters

The emergence of property rights is an old topic in the social and historical sciences. The second half of the 19th century saw a spate of publications on this issue. German historians studied changes in landownership from the Middle Ages till the present time; social historians in different countries wrote on the diversity of property rights among peoples in the world; British policymakers and scientists were interested in the nature of property rights in the British colonies and particularly in India. Authors like Maine and De Laveleye postulated a system of communal property rights in early time among many peoples in the world and a shift to individual property in recent times.

Among the colonial powers the interest in property rights was more than a purely academic exercise. Colonial rulers observed complex and confusing patterns of land rights among the native populations in their colonies, which hampered the levying of taxes and the introduction of modern agriculture. Commercial interests in the mother country were interwoven with political debates between liberals and conservatives on policy issues. Should indigenous social institutions give way to modern private enterprise and commercial initiatives, or should the colonial administration refrain from meddling with indigenous society in order to prevent the breakup of the traditional community and the disintegration of society?

It is difficult to link up this older historical literature with the more recent studies of neo-institutional economists on property rights regimes. Private property rights are a basic assumption in economic theory (Alchian 1992: 223). A key assumption is that effective markets require the establishment of well-specified, defendable, and transferable property rights (Anderson & Leal 1992: 20).

Neo-institutional economists use the term private property, as if the concept can be defined unambiguously. For instance, Alchian defines private property rights as "securely held in fee simple and exchangeable at will at mutually agreeable prices" (Alchian 1992: 223). Empirical research usually brings to light more complicated and ambiguous forms of property rights.

In order to function, institutions have to be supported by organizations. The institution of private property requires organizations such as laws, a legal system, a land register, a geodetical service and land surveyors, courts, sanctioning organizations, the maintenance of law and order, in short, a functioning state reaching down to the local level and maintaining its monopoly of violence. There are situations where private property rights exist, but where part of the organizational structure is deficient. The interesting question then is: what are the consequences of these deficiences for economic transactions and for the market?

Neo-institutional economists have attempted to present explanations for the emergence of private property rights. There are two models: a naive or simple model and a more complicated model. The simple model states that changes in relative scarcities and prices of production factors lead to a demand for an institution to define property rights in those factors and to govern their use. This demand for property rights will lead to the supply of a system of such rights, if it becomes worthwhile to incur the costs of devising such rights (Feeny 1988: 273; North 1990: 51). The driving force of the supply-and-demand model of induced institutional change is population growth.

The simple model has been used to analyze the emergence of exclusive rights among North American Indians (Demsetz 1967), the evolution of property rights on the American Frontier (Anderson & Leal 1991), changes in Asian agriculture (Hayami & Ruttan 1971), and the development of property rights in Thailand and other Asian countries (Feeny 1988).

The problem with the naive model is that the demand for institutional change may not automatically lead to the supply of that new institution (Bates 1988). It is assumed that the collectivity of participants or the state will create the general framework of property rights that will permit the individuals to maximize the society's welfare. However, there may be problems of collective action, or the state may pursue different interests.

An extension of the naive model is the interest-group theory of property rights (Eggertsson 1990: 271). The state is viewed as a party with its own interests, which may prefer the persistence of "inefficient" property rights (North 1990: 52). This extends the argument to the political arena and to the power relationships between sectors of the state and societal groups.

This paper will focus on West Java, and specifically on the Priangan region. This region shows a continuous process of emerging individual property rights in land during the 19th century. The contrasting case is Central and East Java, where large areas experienced a shift toward communal land rights in the first half of the 19th century, as a result of government pressure. In those areas the later return to individual property rights was a matter of untangling the knot of government taxes, labor services, land rights, the interests of the sugar companies, and colonial conservatism. West Java did not experience the phase of communalization, and land rights remained individual from the beginning.

In the early 20th century the system of individual land rights could have provided the proper underpinnings of well-functioning and efficient markets that economic theory assumes. However, the legal system in the Netherlands-Indies was dualistic, and a sharp distinction was made between private property according to European law and native property rights. The consequence was that Javanese farmers, with individual plots of land, were limited in the use of the land at their own discretion.

In this paper the emergence and institutionalization of individual property rights among the population in the Priangan region in West Java in the second half of the 19th century will be described. Within the legal framework of the Netherlands-Indies colonial state, these individual property rights were merely of a customary nature. They were not properly recorded in a cadastral system, and therefore not easily defendable in court. In other words there was a tension between customary notions of individual rights to land and the legal framework of the colonial state. The result was insecurity of land rights, litigation, and conflicts over land. After this exposé two questions will be asked, and an attempt will be made to provide answers. The first is what were the consequences of these insecure property rights for economic activities, such as access to credit and capital? The second question is: did these insecure land rights hamper agricultural development in the region?

Colonial Policy in the Netherlands-Indies

The wider framework of land rights in the Netherlands-Indies was provided by colonial legislation. In the second half of the 19th century Dutch colonial policy underwent a number of changes. For a long time the colony had yielded large profits to the Netherlands government, the product of government intervention in agricultural production and trade, the so-called Cultivation System. By the 1860s this system had come under fire from political liberals in the Dutch parliament and from European entrepreneurs eager to enter the colonial economy, not only in the sphere of the processing of agricultural produce, but also in the cultivation of cash crops. This meant that they needed land, labor, and capital. The land could be waste land, but it was more convenient to have land located close to populated areas, so that laborers could be recruited. Preferably the land should be held in some form of property, so that it could be mortgaged to the banks as a collateral for loans. The Netherlands government recognized the legitimacy of these claims, but had to balance them against the interests of the native population, because a disruption of the social fabric could cause unrest.

In 1870 the Dutch parliament passed the Agrarian Law, which brought new land-legislation for Java and Madura. The law was a compromise between the interests of Western entrepreneurs and those of native farmers. The main item was the announcement that uncultivated land could be given out in "long lease" to western entrepreneurs and that native farmers could let their land to these entrepreneurs.

The new law stipulated that all land on which others could not prove Western property rights (*eigendom*) was the domain of the state (the so-called *domeinverklaring* or domain doctrine). The law distinguished two categories of domain, a "free domain" on which no rights whatever were exercised by others, and an "unfree domain," also called "land rent area," on which natives could have "hereditary rights of possession" (*erfelijk individueel bezit*). This last right was meant to safeguard the interests of the native farmers.

In practice the demarcation between free and unfree domain was not sharp. In many parts of Java farmers still practiced slash-and-burn (*ladang*) cultivation in forest areas. In order to curtail slash-and-burn cultivation, the Netherlands government stipulated that only permanently cultivated lands could be counted in the "unfree domain," i.e., land possessed by natives.

Several legal issues were dealt with in special government ordinances. In 1874 the Governor General issued a Cultivation Ordinance to regulate access of indigenous people to the free domain and the right to open up new land. The ordinance stated that in order to open up domain land which did not belong to the village land, natives needed to ask permits from the local indigenous and Dutch officials. By opening up new land the cultivator could acquire native ownership (Kools 1935: 42).

In 1875 the Governor General issued another ordinance, the Alienation Prohibition, prohibiting the alienation of native land to foreigners. The purpose of this ordinance was to prevent the loss of land possessions by natives to nonnatives.

This legislation reinforced the existing dualistic land rights system. Western land rights were recognized as titled ownership or freehold (eigendom), governed by Western Civil Code. These rights were registered in the Land Registration Office (*kadaster*). Indigenous land rights were considered rights of possession, based on custom (*adat*), and generally not registered. The transfer of land was subject to restrictions. Land subject to Western law could be acquired by anyone; land subject to indigenous law could not be alienated to nonnatives (Pompe 1992: 178).

In the last decades of the 19th century Dutch ethnologists and lawyers undertook a more systematic study of the customary rights of the indigenous population in the Netherlands-Indies. In the Indonesian archipelago the Arab word *adat*, meaning customs, is used in most languages to indicate a variety of local rules, customs, and habits. The Dutch linguist and lawyer Snouck Hurgronje coined the word *adat* law (1906 I: 16) and the lawyer Van Vollenhoven (1918, 1928) made the study and systematization of Indonesian *adat* law his life's work. In the early decades of the 20th century the Netherlands government promoted *adat* law studies and attempted a more systematic introduction of *adat* law in the colonial administration of justice. In the 1920s a large number of Dutch legal experts, trained in *adat* law, entered the colonial administration.

Van Vollenhoven sought the locus of *adat* law in the village community, which he considered the true law-making community. He had observed striking similarities in agrarian customary arrangements all over the Indonesian archipelago, such as the village right of disposal of land, usufructury rights, rights of occupancy resulting in rights of possession (*hak milik*). These similarities would be incomprehensible if one started from the assumption that *adat* law had originally been based in the legal conceptions and institutions of the native rulers, who often designed their laws and regulations on outside examples. A relatively coherent system of *adat* law could only have arisen within local communities. By giving the village a prominent position in his theory, Van Vollenhoven aligned himself with the 19th-century European tendency to glorify the village community.

The *adat* law school had a peculiarly ambiguous position in the political spectrum of the late colonial period (see Burns 1989). On the one hand, *adat* law scholars defended the rights and interests of the indigenous population against misapprehensions from Netherlands politicians and colonial administrators. Van Vollenhoven (1919) severely criticized Dutch colonial policy during the 19th century, even talking about a "century of injustice." On the other hand, *adat* law scholars accepted the reality of the colonial state and the existing situation as the outcome of historical processes and worked within that framework. They advocated a degree of autonomy for the Indonesian population, but it was the autonomy of lower-level communities, not of the Indonesian state. After Indonesia's proclamation of independence in 1945, new land laws—particularly the Basic Agrarian Law of 1960—replaced the 1870 Agrarian Law and the *adat* law rules pertaining to land (Sudargo Gautama & Budi Harsono 1972). *Adat* law plays a less important role in present-day Indonesian society.

The Emergence of Property Rights in the Priangan Region

It was from the fortress and harbor of Batavia (the present Jakarta) that the Dutch East India Company gradually extended its territorial control over the island of Java, during the 17th and 18th centuries. West

Java with its mountains and extensive forests was then a thinly populated region. The East India Company did not establish direct administration over the southern part of West Java, the Priangan region. The area remained under the rule of the native chiefs, the *bupati,* or regents, who were obliged to recognize the sovereignty of the Company and to accept the system of forced deliveries. The Company required coffee, and for that reason coffee cultivation was introduced in the region in the beginning of the 18th century. The regents forced the people to cultivate the coffee trees, to harvest the coffee and to transport the commodity to the Company warehouses. It was then shipped to Batavia and shipped to Europe.

The people in the Priangan area belonged to the Sundanese ethnic-linguistic group and were predominantly engaged in shifting cultivation (slash and burn), carried out in primary forests, where rainfed rice fields were made (called in Sundanese *huma*, in Javanese *gaga*), or dry fields (in Indonesian *ladang*). In this system the cultivator selects a forest area, makes a clearing by cutting down the trees and smaller bushes and grasses, burns them, makes holes with the digging stick and plants seeds and roots. Fields were used for two consecutive years and then temporarily deserted, because of soil exhaustion.

Sometimes a shift occurred to more permanent agriculture on dry and unirrigated land (called in Sundanese *tipar*, in Javanese and Indonesian *tegal*). When swiddens have been deserted, the primary forest does not return, and land becomes overgrown with secondary forest. Usually after a lapse of time these fields were used again, this time for permanent agriculture. Once a clearing had been made, individual cultivation rights were established and families had acquired a right to these fields, even though they often did not use them for years.

Wet-rice (Indonesian: *sawah*) cultivation was introduced in the Priangan region late in the 18th century, probably under Javanese influence. Sawah cultivation is practiced on irrigated or inundated fields, along mountain slopes or in valleys or lowlands. A system of dams, waterworks, and smaller pipes brings the water to the field. In the Priangan region the indigenous rulers usually undertook the construction of the larger waterworks, while local population took care of the smaller pipes and ditches.

For a long time Sundanese people preferred shifting cultivation to wet-rice farming. In terms of production per hectare wet-rice farming yields a bigger harvest than shifting cultivation (in the magnitude of fifty to one). However, in terms of returns on labor the picture is different:

labor in shifting cultivation yields more than labour in irrigated rice. There was another reason why Sundanese farmers were reluctant to abandon shifting cultivation for a more intensive system. Wet-rice cultivation requires a settled population, and its sedentary character facilitates the imposition of taxes and corvée labor. People who wanted to escape these burdens could flee to the wilderness and take to shifting cultivation. The native rulers were hardly able to control and to tax shifting cultivators in the forests.

It is still a historical puzzle how the Priangan regents were able to force their Sundanese subjects to cultivate large numbers of coffee trees and to deliver the coffee to the Company. The officials in Batavia did not pay the farmers, they only paid the regents. There was no money incentive for the people to spend their labor on the cultivation, harvesting and delivery of coffee. The question is concisely formulated by the Dutch historian Van Klaveren: "It is surprising that the regents could succeed in applying compulsion to a moving ladang population in a country so thinly populated that they could easily dodge the regent's grip" (Van Klaveren 1953: 61). The riddle has not been satisfactorily solved.

There was a high level of mobility among the population. The regents were permanently worried that their subjects would run away. People often moved away from an area to escape from the heavy tax burdens and placed themselves under the protection of another ruler or went to the forests (De Haan 1910-12 I: 362, 376; III: 827). Europeans and the settled native population used a special term for human cultivators moving around in the mountains, namely *jalma burung*, or bird people (De Haan 1910-12 IV: 507).

Toward the end of the 18th century contemporary Dutch observers saw a link between the wet-rice cultivation and the corvée labor for the coffee cultivation. In the words of one of them, the Company official Engelhard: "no native can be brought to cultivate coffee, unless he should be supplied with sufficient sawah land" (De Haan 1910-12 IV: 463). Apparently the ownership of sawah land provided the incentive for farmers to assume the corvée labor for the coffee cultivation. While this incentive worked for the late 18th century, it does not explain the system in the early part of the century, because at that time there was very little sawah land in the Priangan regencies.

The system of forced coffee deliveries left a lasting imprint on Priangan social structure. The administrative system bore the stamp of the work organization for the coffee cultivation. The *desa* (municipal village) as an administrative unit did not play an important role. In fact there were two distinct types of organization. The first one was the *terup* (from the Dutch word *troep*, English troop), a band of farmers from various settlements in a certain area under a headman, in fact a local labor gang. The labor gang was obliged to cultivate certain coffee fields in the uplands. The headman received his orders from the higher officials, who in turn were beholden to the regional ruler. The second type of organization were the *kampongs* in which the farmers lived. These kampongs were small groups of houses, organized into larger villages under a village headman. The village headmen did not have much control over the farmers, who were mainly under the orders of the indigenous rulers. This meant that the higher officials did not interfere much with the local territorial organization. The location of dwellings, the clustering of residential units, the ownership of land, the irrigation system, and the local administration were left to the villagers. The village headman was not very powerful. Many administrative duties were performed by the local Islamic officials, the lower mosque personnel.

In 1870-71 the colonial government abolished the Priangan-system of coffee deliveries. The indigenous officials lost the right of taxation and the coffee payments, but received a salary instead. The payments for coffee deliveries by the farmers were increased. At the same time the colonial government introduced general taxation on land, the land rent. The consequence of this reorganization was that corvée labor was largely diminished. This lifted a heavy burden from the rice farmers. Before 1871 owners of wet-rice land (*sawah*) often abandoned their fields, because they had no time to carry out the labor obligations and preferred to cultivate upland fields. After the 1871 reorganization the price of irrigated rice land increased greatly, often tenfold. Another effect was that people increased their efforts to open up new land and to transform dry land into irrigated rice fields (De Haan 1910-12 IV: 463-64).

After the administrative reorganization, when the labor gang for the coffee cultivation was abolished, the village settlement was turned into a territorial unit, called *desa*, with a local administration under a village head, or *lurah*. The land registration within the village was officially the responsibility of the village administration, but traditionally the Islamic religious officials in the village took care of the land registration, in connection with the collection of the religious taxation, the *zakat*, from the farmers.

Under these conditions a system of individual property rights on land (*hak milik*) developed at the local level. The initial claim to land rights was the activity of opening up wasteland. As long as wasteland was available, people did not pay much attention to the ownership of dry land, but *sawah* land became increasingly valuable after the reorganization. The village municipality was a weak institution: any right of disposal over village land (a key feature in Central and East Java) was absent, and the headman had little power over the villagers. There were no inhibitions in the village against alienation of village land to outside owners.

The emergence of individual property rights was clearly pushed by population increase in the Priangan region. For 1825 a population figure of 250,000 is mentioned, in 1860 this had increased to 824,000, in 1880 to 1,594,000, in 1900 to 2,425,000, and the growth continued in the subsequent decades. The Dutch agriculturist Scheltema (1927-28), referring to contemporary Russian scholars, clearly postulates a causal connection between population growth, the increasing scarcity of land, and the emergence of individual property rights in land. Present-day neo-institutional economists hypothesizing this causal connection are clearly not the first ones to have done so.

A remarkable development in the last decades of the 19th century was the emergence of a system of large landownership. This originated in the laying out of irrigated rice fields, the appropriation of former coffee gardens, the opening of clandestine clearings in the mountains and the purchase of land. The new stratum of big landowners owning dozens of hectares of *sawah* land often used the credit mechanism to acquire land. The new landowners were Sundanese farmers, called *pribumi*, or children of the land, to distinguish them from the Chinese. They were pious Muslims, who often tried to make a pilgrimage to Mecca. Alongside this stratum of large landowners the Priangan region had a high percentage of landless households, on the order of 50% of the population (Scheltema 1927-28).

Dutch writers at the time were divided over whether ot not the emergence of large landownership was a good thing. In central and east Java where many villages still had a communal character, land was more of less equally distributed among the population. The colonial government found this convenient as it facilitated the imposition of taxes and labor services on the population. The growth of a group of large landowners in the Priangan region was applauded by the civil servant Kern (1904), who argued that these landowners were entrepreneurs, striving for the improvement of their economic conditions, and therefore constituting a progressive force in society. However, Scheltema (1927-28) viewed the emerging socio-economic inequality with apprehension, fearing political unrest as a result.

Land Conflicts and Insecure Property Rights in Priangan

In the second half of the 19th century private property rights became institutionalized among the population of the Priangan region. After the abolition of the forced coffee cultivation, when farmers had more time to work on their own fields, private land was valued more highly. The question now is: how were these property rights maintained?

As we have seen, the colonial state had adopted a dualistic legal system. Native property rights were recognized as rights of possession. The registration and maintenance of these rights was considered the duty of indigenous village communities. However, a proper system of land registration for indigenous landowners was lacking. The colonial state only had a land register for individual land owned as property under the Western legal system, i.e., owned by Europeans and Chinese, mostly in urban areas. Attempts at establishing a register for indigenous rights of possession were not successful during the 19th century.

Around the turn of the century several authors complained that a legally instituted register of indigenous rights on land was absent and that natives often appealed to *desa* registers, land rent assessment lists, which were not kept up to date. These complaints were still mentioned in the reports of the Declining Welfare Commission (Hasselman 1914: 213-15, 220-22).

The problem can be explained as follows. The establishment of a land register can be done with two different purposes in mind: as a public record for fiscal purposes or as a register for legal investigations. The fiscal, legal, and financial requirements of a land register are different. The tax department is mainly interested in basic information concerning land, such as the approximate size, in order to fix the levy, and in sufficient documentation to identify the holder who can be assessed as taxpayer. Lawyers want to have a legally acceptable description of real estate property, based on declarations of interested parties before legal authorities, in such a way that the documents are legally valid in court. Financial experts want a register that clearly establishes relationships between plots of land and owners, users, etc., enabling creditors quickly to ascertain for each plot the debts and levies imposed on it. The purpose is to provide legal security to owners of capital engaged in providing credit to landowners.

The colonial administration was mainly interested in establishing a land register of indigenous landholdings for fiscal purposes. During the 19th century the colonial government repeatedly started land surveys in Java, but each time these programs came to a halt for lack of trained personnel and funds. Another problem was the lack of cooperation between the civil service and the cadastral or topographical service.

In 1890 another attempt was made, and a pilot survey started in the Priangan region, carried out by the land registry office (cadastral service) and the civil service. The system of registration worked as follows. The surveyors started with maps on the district and village (desa) levels. They divided the land into two broad categories, namely wet-rice land and dry land. Then they delineated so-called land-rent parcels, i.e., parcels of relatively homogeneous land, surrounded by roads, rivers, or dikes. Then they surveyed these plots with the triangulation method. The parcels were numbered and the surfaces were calculated. Together with the *desa* map they designed a *desa* register, in which the parcel numbers were registered. Then the civil service entered the scene to carry out a survey of the land-rent parcels, in order to establish the boundaries of individual lots, their area size, ownership of the field, class of productivity, the estimation of the average yield, and finally the tax assessment as a percentage of the harvest (Polderman 1925: 9-13). The village chief was given the task of keeping account of changes in landownership and of keeping the village register up to date. This system, known as the Preanger land-rent ordinance, was introduced in the whole Priangan region in 1896 and carried out between that year and 1909. After that the system was introduced in the whole of Java and Madura. This work was completed in the late 1930s. The present-day land-tax system in Java is still based on these old cadastral surveys.

The Preanger land-rent system had spectacular results. The more precise survey had resulted in an increase in the area of taxable land, for wet-rice land with 35%, for dry land with 224%. The total area of taxable wet-rice land increased from 157,797 ha in 1897 to 241,363 ha in 1907, for dry land from 96,405 ha in 1897 to 312,656 ha in 1907. As a result the land rent increased significantly (Velders 1909a).

The inevitable conclusion was that the Priangan people had opened up large tracts of waste land during the last decades of the 19th century. Much of this land had been opened up "illegally," i.e., in violation of the cultivation ordinance of the colonial state. This pointed to a failure of the lowest echelon of the European civil service, i.e., the controllers.

They had not exerted sufficient control over the "illegal" occupation of wasteland by the indigenous population (Velders 1909a). The opening up of wasteland had been in accordance with *adat* law rules. That civil servants had condoned these activities shows that the political sympathies of many members of the civil service were more on the side of the indigenous population than on the side of the state and the Western entrepreneurs.

But the new land-rent registers were not adequate to provide information about land transactions, such as land pledging and mortgaging. And specific registers in the Priangan region were usually not kept up to date. Three reasons can be mentioned for this lack of legal documents. Firstly, negligence and lack of cooperation by the village officials; secondly, the fact that judges did not consider scribbled notes on transactions as valid documents in court; thirdly, many transactions had a private or hole-and-corner character, and were altogether unregistered (Hasselman 1914: 214).

Earlier in the 19th century land conflicts were often brought before the so-called priestly councils, more appropriately called *penghulu* courts. These courts, consisting of mosque personnel led by the *penghulu* or Islamic functionary, were primarily charged with the religious (Islamic) administration of justice. But in West Java they also decided disputes over land until 1866, when the colonial administration decreed that land disputes were outside the jurisdiction of the *penghulu* courts. Since that time these disputes are decided by the Superior Native Court (*landraad*) (De Klein 1931: 94).

The west Javanese Islamic scholar Haji Hasan Mustapa, who published a book on Sundanese *adat* law (1946 [orig. 1913]), tells that in earlier times the village head and the *patinggi* (head of a *terup*, or labour gang) did not know about the "legal" status of land. They knew only that whoever took the labor obligations that burdened a plot of wet-rice land could use that field. They did not keep track of the sale, pledging, sharecropping or lease of land. That was the reason many wet-rice fields were cultivated by people other than the original owners: the owner was no longer capable of performing the labor services. Later, the owner or his descendants could file a complaint against the cultivator with the *penghulu* court and claim back the land. According to Hasan Moestapa, the claimants were right according to the *adat*, and the *penghulu* courts recognized those rights. However, the government administration of justice around the turn of the century did not recognize these claims, as the legal proofs were usually lacking. This was the reason why in later years people in the fields revolted against the decisions of the courts and refused to recognize their legitimacy (Hasan Moestapa 1946: 113-14).

In his 1912 dissertation the *adat* law scholar Enthoven presented an overview of the jurisprudence of the Superior Native Courts (*landraden*) during the 1849-1912 period. According to the colonial constitution of 1854 (*Regerings Reglement*) the native courts had to base their judgments on *adat* law. However, on the basis of 296 cases Enthoven shows that the application of *adat* law turned out to be pure fiction. In many cases judges based their decisions on European law, although this explicitly did not apply to indigenous people. It is true that during this period *adat* law was uncodified and largely nonstatutory. The judges did not inquire whether the disputes brought before their court should be decided on the basis of local rules.

The *adat* law scholar Soepomo (1933) in his study on *adat* private law in West Java has tried to find out whether *adat* rules were applied in the judgments of native courts. He has formulated 151 rules on various topics. For a large number of rules any regular jurisprudence is lacking. He cannot find jurisprudence for rights on land, swidden cultivation, transactions concerning the harvest, etc. For other topics, such as sharecropping, sale of real estate, only a few cases can be found. Many of these judgments do not support the *adat* law rules, or even go against them. It is clear that the higher order organs, i.e., the government jurisdiction, did not fulfill the function of the formation and maintenance of *adat* law.

To what extent were the lower government units, the village communities, capable of maintaining *adat* law concerning land? This question is difficult to answer because we do not have any hard evidence concerning the administration of justice at the local level. What we do have is the emerging *adat* law literature from around 1910 onward. Van Vollenhoven (1918) has given an extensive description of *adat* law in West Java in his general overview of *adat* law in the Netherlands-Indies. However, this stylized account is much too general to give a picture of what really happened at the local level.

We can surmise that the administration of justice at the local level did not function well. In his description of West Java *adat* law, Van Vollenhoven emphasizes that in that province the village community and village leadership were both weak and that the village did not exercise any right of disposal over its territory. One can surmise that these weak organizations were not capable of strictly maintaining *adat* law rules.

The Diminishing Welfare Commission reported many objections to the civil procedures in court. Complaints involved the high costs of civil procedures, the witness money, formalities, laborious and time-consuming procedures, the passivity of the judges, the heavy requirements of legal proofs, and the fact that it took courts a long time to decide. Also the *penghulu* courts were criticized for high costs (OMW VIa: 35-57; VIIIa: 204-43).

A big problem was that the courts took a formal attitude concerning the validity of the means of evidence submitted to them, but that indigenous society lacked the proper institutions for providing legal assistance to authorize these means of evidence (Jaarsma 1918). Around the turn of the century several authors advocated the establishment of a simple, cheap, accessible indigenous notary public to enable the public to have legally valid documents made up by authorized officials (OMW VIa: 28, 45-50).

The Dutch civil servant Velders (1909b) has given an extensive report on a long-lasting court case in a town in the Priangan region. The case involved a conflict between the heirs of a deceased man and the brother of that man over sawah fields. The brother had appropriated the land, claiming that his brother had borrowed money from him, and that the land had become his property. The case was first brought before a *penghulu* court, which supported the heirs, but failed to implement the decision. After that the heirs turned to the Supreme Native Court, which turned them down, because proper documents were lacking. Finally the Dutch civil servant interfered, but he could not do much. In the end the heirs lost the case. The story is a sad case of the seizure of an inheritance, a phenomenon that occurred frequently in the region, according to the author.

Landownership in the Priangan region was insecure for two reasons. Firstly, the colonial legal system did not recognize indigenous inheritable possession as valid and defendable in court. Secondly, the courts were not capable of administering justice according to traditional *adat* law. In a legal sense the situation was one of confusion and uncertainty.

That landownership was insecure must have had an impact on the agricultural practices of the local farmers. One consequence was that individual private property did not provide a strong incentive to improve farmland. This is a complaint that one finds in the reports around the turn of the century: methods of agriculture were still traditional and negligent. Another consequence was that credit could not be based on private property as a right "securely held in fee simple." The effects can be predicted: if the formal system does not provide solutions, people will resort to informal arrangements. That is what happened in the Priangan region.

Land and Capital Markets

According to economic theory private property plays an important role in money markets. Credit institutions usually grant long-term loans only against mortgages on real property. Only real estate and agricultural land with registered titles can be used as collateral for loans. Borrowers may have a strong need for credit, but if they are unable to provide sufficient collateral, they do not have access to the formal money market. The alternative is the informal credit market, where financial transactions are much more risky, and where other risk-reducing arrangements are used, such as personal guarantees, and interlinked deals, i.e., transactions in which two or more independent exchanges are simultaneously agreed upon.

Under a system of legal dualism such as existed in Java and Madura, money markets tended to be fragmented rather than unified. On the one hand, there was the money market of Western commercial banks and trading firms, serving the needs of Western enterprises on the basis of real estate collateral or advances on plantation crops. On the other hand, there was the private money market of indigenous moneylenders working among the farmers and small traders, who did not have legally recognized property titles. The Chinese who did have Western titles, could operate in both worlds, both as clients of Western firms and as informal moneylenders in the indigenous sector.

This market fragmentation can be shown for the Priangan region. Two important effects stand out. In the first place, indigenous farmers and traders did not have access to bank credit or loans and advances from Western trading firms, as they could not offer property titles as collateral. This meant that they had to resort to the informal capital market, dominated by rich natives, Arabs, and Chinese, where interest rates were high. In the second place, the imperfect money market generated a number of new contracts in the field of agriculture, credit, and trade.

The report of the Diminishing Welfare Commission (OMW 1906-14) mentions for West Java the inadequate credit system as the main impediment to trade in the region. Traders in need of credit had no other source than moneylenders. The report pointed out that European trading firms and banks usually dealt with Chinese traders, not with native traders. The explanation was the fact that Chinese traders could offer real estate as collateral for loans, while native traders could not do so because their land was not legal property. European trading firms and banks emphasized that they had little grip on native traders, because of the absence of a registry of births, deaths and marriages, a register of land and the lack of bookkeeping in native firms, which was not required by law (OMW VIa: 37).

In the 1890s and early 1900s Dutch government officials had discovered the need for credit among the indigenous population. A spate of publications on the spread of usury in indigenous society underlined the general feeling that the Javanese population experienced "diminishing welfare" and even outright impoverization. Civil servants argued for the need for cheap government credit for the Javanese farming population. In several areas civil servants started experiments with savings associations and small banks, and in 1911 the state-supported People's Credit Organization (*Volkscredietwezen*) was started.

How did farmers get informal credit in the Priangan region around 1900? A number of credit arrangements were available: land pledging, indigenous mortgage, the security-for-credit arrangement (*credietverband*), sharecropping, and finally the advance on the harvest (*ijon*).

Land pledging was an old credit arrangement, recognized as an *adat*-law institution. This is a land transaction in which a landowner borrows money and transfers the land to the moneylender, who as the pledgee can derive full profit from the pledged land. The pledgee can till the land, live on it, sharecrop it. The borrower retains the right to recover the land upon payment of a sum equal to that loaned to him or her on the land. In principle there was no stipulation for redemption of the land, and the right to do so passes to the heir of the original owner. The transaction was known in various parts of Indonesia. In West Java the terms used in connection with land pledging are *gade* (pledge), *ngagade* (pledging), *jual gade* (borrowing with the promise to repay the money) (Van Vollenhoven 1918: 745-46; Galestin 1909; Kern 1912). Although land pledging was a traditional customary law arrangement, the pledging of sawah fields was rare in the Priangan region in the 1860s (Van Vollenhoven 1918: 746). In the 1890s it had become much more frequent.

Although the Priangan region still looked very traditional to spectators around the turn of the century, socio-economic changes were occurring.

Wet-rice land had become more valuable; cash cropping was on the rise; commercial activities increased; monetization of the economy increased; and individual private property rights were more strongly appreciated. Priangan society became commercially oriented. In this setting traditional *adat*-law rules, which had been weak anyway, no longer provided adequate guidelines and institutional arrangements for new economic activities. New contracts and arrangements had to be designed for the economic transactions that emerged.

This change can be seen clearly in the controversy over a new type of money contract usually referred to as native mortgage. In some respects native mortgage resembled the old pledging contract, but the emphasis was different. In the native mortgage transaction the money loan was central, and land was pledged with the condition that after a certain period of time the debt would be discharged through the execution of the sale of the land (Kern 1912). This transaction was sometimes called "sale with provision for repurchase." *Adat*-law specialists saw this concept as misleading and argued that it should be avoided because it suggests that land had been sold and could be "repurchased," while under *adat* law there was no loss of native ownership (Ter Haar 1948: 120-21).

The civil servant Kern (1912) has pointed out that it was often not clear what kind of transaction people had concluded. Also the Supreme Native Courts had difficulty figuring out what had transpired between the parties in front of them. Often a money loan was obscured behind a land pledging transaction, or the two parties differed in their interpretation of what had been agreed upon: borrowing or conditional sale. There were two reasons for obscuring a transaction. The first was that people wanted to bring matters in conformity with Islamic law and particularly the prohibition against interest-taking. By talking about "sale with the provision for repurchase," people tried to go around this provision. For the same reason a land transaction was faked, while in fact a cash loan had been concluded. The second reason was that the traditional *adat*-law rules did not provide sufficient security for the money-loan, forcing the lender to demand a greater degree of security, hence the provision that the land would be forfeited if the borrower defaulted. Kern also pointed out that people were afraid of the government administration of justice and tried as much as possible to avoid bringing their disputes to court.

In practice the land pledging and native mortgage were even more complicated because these transactions were combined with a sharecropping relationship. In the case of *jual gade* the landowner pledged the land to the moneylender but the latter immediately started a sharecropping relationship with the former. The pledger still worked the land, but now got only one half of the harvest under the sharecropping arrangement, the other half going to the moneylender. In this interlinked transaction the interest that the pledgee received for the money loan was hidden behind the harvest sharing. In the case of native mortgage the contract stated that in case of default the land would automatically become the property of the moneylender. While *adat*-law specialists emphasized the separate character of each contract type, in reality the types were interchangeable. It often happened that a *gade* contract was entered into, but that the credit taker wanted to increase the loan and agreed to convert the contract into a "sale with the provision of repurchase" contract (De Bie 1903). The issue of the different contracts continued to haunt the administration of justice. In the 1930s lawyers discussed the confusion between land pledging and mortgage, even calling the terminological switches "fictitious acts" or "simulations" (Ter Haar 1934).

In retrospect the controversy can be understood as a reflection of socio-economic changes in the region. Farmers were in greater need of money loans. Indigenous entrepreneurs had come up with sufficient capital to engage in money lending. The traditional form of land pledging did not provide sufficient security to moneylenders, as it depended on the goodwill of the farmers and their neighbors. For both moneylenders and borrowers the courts were too unpredictable to rely on for arbitration. Moneylenders actively wanted to take over the land, to enforce the terms of the contract.

Another means to get access to credit was the sharecropping (*maro* or *mertelu* in Indonesian) contract between a landowner who provides the land and a landless laboring household which provides the labor, while the harvest is divided in two parts, often on a fifty-fifty basis, but other arrangements were also reported (Scheltema 1931: 153-62). Before the reorganization of 1870 sharecropping was rare in the Priangan region, but a few years later this type of contract was common in the area (ibid.: 155).

Advances on the harvest were another means by which farmers could get loans. The usual interest rate was in the magnitude of fifty percent in six months. Chinese traders supplied advances for agricultural products such as cassava, peanut oil, tobacco and potatoes.

Who were the creditors? Several authors in the early 1900s have given information on the moneylenders who were depicted as usurers (De Wolff van Westerrode 1904). There were several categories: (1) Indigenous well-to-do landowners, often indicated as *haji*, because they were pious Muslims who used their funds to finance a pilgrimage to Mecca. They were engaged in moneylending, using the pledging and mortgage transactions to get control of farm land. They also bought land in the land market. Among them were mosque personnel and religious officials, as well as indigenous government officials. (2) Indigenous big traders in rice and paddy. (3) Members of the old aristocracy, the *menak*. (4) Foreign Orientals (Chinese and Arabs), particularly traders in rice and paddy. Chinese money owners sometimes used loans to get control of land. However, the Alienation Ordinance prohibited the transfer of indigenous property to nonindigenous parties. This meant that Chinese had to use indigenous straw men to appropriate the land.

Land was attractive as an investment object in the Priangan region around the turn of the century for economic and social reasons. Land prices were still low compared to leases and rents. If a person owned money, it was profitable to buy land and to have it sharecropped or leased, because the rentability of these transactions was high. In this way an investment in land yielded 10 to 20%, and sometimes even 40% per annum (Scheltema 1931: 322-23). There were social considerations as well: investing money in land proved an effective means of protection against claims from poor relatives asking for financial support or loans.

For farmers in need of credit, the existing credit contracts involved high interest rates, often on the order of 100 to 200% per annum. European observers at the time saw the high interest rates as usury and viewed the moneylenders with moral indignation. In retrospect this was unjust. There were good reasons for high interest rates. In the first place the indigenous credit market was small in scale, keeping the costs of capital high. In the second place interest rates were high because of the high risk premium. Without the backing of proper papers and legal sanctions, moneylenders ran the risk that farmers would default on the loans.

The Dutch lawyer Jaarsma (1918, 1936) has pointed out that the absence of a well-developed credit market for indigenous farmers had been caused by the deficient system of land laws and the absence of an adequate land register in the colony. Jaarsma stated: "The big money market is not open for native land credit. Consequently the money-market and the number of money lenders is very limited, which is also the case with native mortgage and land-pledging" (Jaarsma 1936: 53).

It is understandable that private money owners were hesitant to enter the credit market, for the absence of a land register made money-lending a risky operation. For native land possession legal documents, such as certificates of registry and ownership documents, were absent. The courts hardly accepted the informal notes and handwritten receipts from the transacting parties as legal documents. Under the existing system—i.e., without a land register, a registry office, an office of notary—it was virtually impossible to produce legally acceptable means of evidence in court (Jaarsma 1918). And the courts were quite unpredictable in their judgments: sometimes they followed European jurisprudence, sometimes *adat* law.

In the absence of legal institutions, money owners had to use informal means of control to supervise their credit operations. Lending took place on the basis of personal acquaintance, reputation, neighborhood and social control. These mechanisms worked well as long as lender and borrower belonged to the same local community. Outside moneylenders had to resort to stronger means of control, namely actual seizure of the property to enforce the money contract. Taking over the land, as was practiced under native mortgage, was probably the only way in which moneylenders could reduce the high transaction costs connected with their operations.

Indigenous Agriculture

The money market for indigenous farmers in the Priangan region was characterized by high interest rates. Did this have consequences for agricultural development in the region? This question is difficult to answer. There was a steady growth and diversification of agriculture in the region. The insecurity surrounding indigenous property rights did not cause definite stagnation. The question whether growth would have been higher if property rights would had more secure is counterfactual and cannot readily be answered.

According to official statistics the total planted area (both rice and second crops) in the Priangan region increased steadily, from about 120,000 ha in 1870 to 477,700 ha in 1900 and 682,300 ha in 1915 (Boomgaard & Van Zanden 1990).

In the 1880s rice was the dominant crop in the Priangan region, but the cultivation of secondary crops was spreading. Peanuts were widely grown, and there were dozens of small oil crushers in the region, mostly owned by both Chinese and Sundanese millers. The products of these mills—peanut oil and cakes—were partly consumed in the region, partly exported (De Bie 1888). A conspicuous development was the growth of people's tea gardens, alongside the European tea plantations, to which the native tea growers delivered their produce. Starting in the 1890s the cultivation of cassava increased as did the processing of cassava into tapioca, which was increasingly exported.

In the early 1900s the most important second crops were cassava, peanuts, potatoes, tobacco, and soybeans (De Bie 1903). Of growing importance was the production of fish in fishponds and in the rice fields (De Bie 1903). A survey of the harvested area of food crops in the Priangan area in 1925 shows that rice was still the crop occupying the largest land area, about 86% of the land, with cassava coming second with 3.4%, and peanuts third, with 1.5%. Other secondary crops, such as maize, soybeans, tubers occupied smaller surfaces. In the 1910s and 1920s the cultivation of garden crops—cabbage, onions, garlic, chilis, and other vegetables—became more important, though still on a small scale. In the subsequent years these crops gained in importance.

Agricultural practices improved over the years. Around 1900 observers noticed that both large landowners and smallholders cultivated their fields in the same traditional way. By the 1920s large landowners were involved in cashcropping, eagerly adopting new cultivation methods, for which they consulted the colonial agricultural extension service (Scheltema 1927-28: 318, 323).

We can conclude that the incomplete property rights in land did not constitute a serious constraint on agricultural production during the period from the 1890s to the 1920s. Sundanese farmers were agricultural entrepreneurs who responded to market opportunities.

Conclusions

During the 19th century the Priangan population adopted an increasingly stronger concept of individual property rights in connection with land. The driving force behind this development was population growth. In the beginning of the 19th century the area was thinly populated, and a large part of the population was engaged in shifting cultivation. The native rulers tried to recruit people for corvée labor in the coffee gardens by providing them with wet-rice fields. For a long time people had the option to escape from the burden of taxes and labor services and to adopt a wandering existence in the mountains as shifting cultivators.

After the abolition of the forced coffee cultivation in 1870, people became more inclined to settle permanently and to acquire land, either wet-rice or rainfed upland fields.

Individual land rights were originally rooted in *adat* law rules. People who had opened up wasteland had acquired property rights to those fields, recognized in the local setting. However the local village community was not strong enough to enforce these rights. Infringement of private property was possible and probably occurred more frequently when land became more valuable in the later decades of the 19th century.

The colonial legal system did not provide support for the property rights of the native population. The 1870 Agricultural Law and the subsequent government ordinances defined native property rights as "rights of possession," not backed by legally viable documents and records. Around the turn of the century the colonial court system was not able to maintain and defend individual property rights in native society. The absence of legally supported property rights in land also excluded indigenous farmers from access to the wider capital market of European banks and trading firms.

The effect was that people had to resort to what present-day scholars are calling private ordering, i.e., designing and enforcing contracts without recourse to the courts, but by avoidance, self-help, and informal arrangements (Galanter 1981). Most transactions concerning land and credit took place outside the state sphere. The traditional *adat*-law rules and arrangements were equally inadequate, as an increasingly large part of economic transactions took place in the sphere of commerce and trade. New types of contracts arose, and new ways of enforcement had to be designed.

Several interconnected developments took place. With land becoming more valuable and commercial agriculture becoming an option, indigenous entrepreneurs started to accumulate land. Large landownership often resulted from credit transactions. Between farmers in need of credit and entrepreneurs engaging in moneylending, credit contracts were negotiated with high interest rates.

Contemporary European observers looked at these developments with suspicion and moral indignation. At the turn of the century civil servants lamented the rise of what they called usury and the activities of greedy moneylenders. They advocated the creation of a government organization for cheap credit to farmers, a step which was actually taken in 1911. However, the amount of credit from the People's Credit Organization was so small that for many years this source of credit did not make a sizable contribution to solving the credit needs of farmers. In the 1920s scholars noticed with apprehension the growing socio-economic inequality in the region, the polarization, with on the one hand, a class of large landowners and, on the other one, of proletarians, a development which they feared could lead to revolution.

The insecurity of property rights in land and the difficulty with credit did not hamper agricultural development and diversification, at least not in an obvious way. Between the 1880s and the 1920s both the planted area and agricultural production expanded strongly, while agriculture became more diversified.

Apparently "private ordering," the creation of credit arrangements and contracts in the informal sphere, was sufficient to make this happen. By the 1910s large landowners were taking up commercial agriculture.

Several conclusions can be drawn with regard to the neo-institutional economist's property rights thesis. In the first place, the thesis concerning the connection between population growth and the emergence of private property also holds for the Priangan region, a fact which was already established by Scheltema. In the second place, the interest-group theory (North 1990) is also confirmed: the state may have an interest in maintaining "inefficient" property rights, in blocking the proper development of these rights, as in the case of the Dutch colonial state. In the third place, the Priangan case does not support the hypothesis that effective markets require the establishment of well-specified, defendable and transferable property rights. Both the market for agricultural credit and the one for money and capital in the Priangan region apparently functioned relatively well, although property rights in land were not sufficiently well specified to give the owner access to the wider capital market, were not defendable in court and were only transferable if sufficient pressure and possibly violence were exerted. The conclusion is that the neo-classical property rights thesis does not hold in situations where there is a gap between the state sphere and the indigenous sphere and where private ordering in the indigenous sphere provides solutions to the transaction problems.

References Cited

Alchian, A.A.
1992 Property rights. In P. Newman, M. Milgate, & J. Eatwell (eds.), *The New Palgrave Dictionary of Money and Finance* 3:223-26. London: Macmillan.

Anderson, T.L., & D.R. Leal
1992 *Free Market Environmentalism.* San Francisco: Research Center for Public Policy.

Bates, R.H.
1988 Contra contractarianism: some reflections on the New Institutionalism. *Politics and Society* 16:387-401.

Boomgaard, P., & J.L. van Zanden
1990 *Changing Economy in Indonesia*, Volume X, *Food Crops and Arable Lands, Java 1815-1942.* Amsterdam: Royal Tropical Institute.

Burns, P.
1989 The myth of *Adat. Journal of Legal Pluralism and Unofficial Law* 28:1- 127.

De Bie, H.
1888 Eenige mededeelingen aangaande katjang olieslagerijen in de afdeeling Bandoeng. *Tijdschrift Binnenlandsch Bestuur* 1(4):263-85.
1903 Beantwoording van de gestelde vraagpunten nopens het landbouwcrediet voorzover de residentie Preanger-regentschappen betreft. *Tijdschrift Binnenlandsch Bestuur* 25(1-6):399-439.

De Haan, F.
1910-12 *Priangan: De Preanger-Regentschappen onder het Nederlandsch Bestuur tot 1811*, Volumes I-IV. Batavia: G. Kolff.

De Klein, J.W.
1931 *Het Preangerstelsel (1677-1871): En Zijn Nawerking.* Delft: J.Waltman, Jr.

Demsetz, H.
1967 Toward a theory of property rights. *American Economic Review* 57:347- 73.

Enthoven, K.L.J.
1912 *Het Adatrecht der Inlanders in de Jurisprudentie (1849-1912).* Leiden: E.J. Brill.

Eggertsson, T.
1990 *Economic Behavior and Institutions.* Cambridge: Cambridge University Press.

Feeny, D.
1988 The development of property rights in land: a comparative study. In R.H. Bates (ed.), *Toward a Political Economy of Development: A Rational Choice Perspective*, pp. 272-99. Berkeley: University of California Press.

Galanter, A.A.
1981 Justice in many rooms: courts, private ordering and indigenous law. *Journal of Legal Pluralism and Unofficial Law* 19:1-47.

Galestin, A.A.
1909 Het gade-contract op West-Java. *Indische Gids* 31(1):25-39.

Hasan Moestapa, H.
1946 *Over de Gewoonten en Gebruiken der Soendanezen*. The Hague: Martinus Nijhoff.

Hasselman, C.J.
1914 *Algemeen Overzicht van de Uitkomsten van het Welvaart-Onderzoek gehouden op Java en Madoera*. The Hague: Martinus Nijhoff.

Hayami, Y., & V.W. Ruttan
1971 *Agricultural Development*. Baltimore: Johns Hopkins University Press.

Jaarsma, S.
1918 *Bewijsmiddelen van Recht op Grond in Nederlandsch-Indië*. Leiden: Eduard Ydo.
1936 *Grond voor de Nederlanders*. Soerabaja: Drukkerij De Toekomst.

Kern, R.A.
1904 Prijanganpsche toestanden: 't grootgrondbezit. *De Indische Gids* 26(2):1816-24.
1912 Ontwikkeling van't pandrecht in West-Java. *De Indische Gids* 34(2):158-68.

Kools, J.F.
1935 *Hoema's, Hoemablokken en Boschreserves in de Residentie Bantam*. Wageningen: H.Veenman & Zonen.

North, D.C.
1990 *Institutional Change and Economic Performance*. Cambridge: Cambridge University Press.

OMW
1906-11 *Onderzoek naar de Mindere Welvaart der Inlandsche Bevolking op Java en Madoera*, Volumes I-X. Batavia: H.M. van Dorp.

Polderman, L.C.F.
1925 Het kadaster in Nederlandsch-Indië. In *Indisch Genootschap: Verslagen der Vergaderingen over de Jaren 1921-1925, Vergadering van 23 Januari 1925*, pp. 1-29. The Hague: Martinus Nijhoff.

Pompe, S. (ed.)
1992 *Indonesian Law 1949-1989: A Bibliography of Foreign-Language Material with Brief Commentaries on the Law.* Dordrecht: Martinus Nijhoff.

Scheltema, A.M.P.A.
1927-28 De ontwikkeling van de agrarische toestanden in Priangan. *Landbouw* 3:271-305, 5:317-68.
1931 *Deelbouw in Nederlandsch-Indië.* Wageningen: H. Veenman & Zonen.

Snouck Hurgronje, C. (trans. A.W.S. O'Sullivan)
1906 *The Achehnese*, Volumes I, II. Leiden: E.J. Brill.

Soebroto
1925 Indonesische Sawah-Verpanding. Ph.D. dissertation, University of Leiden.

Soepomo, R.
1933 *Het Adatprivaatrecht van West-Java.* Batavia: Soekamiskin.

Sudargo Gautama & Budi Harsono
1972 *Survey of Indonesian Economic Law: Agrarian Law.* Lembaga Penelitian Hukum dan Kriminologi Fakultas Hukum Universitas Padjajaran. Bandung: Tjikapundung.

Ter Haar, B.
1934 Schijnhandelingen tot verkrijging van zekerheid op grond. *Indisch Tijdschrift van het Recht* 139(2):145-62.
1948 *Adat Law in Indonesia.* Djakarta: Bhratara.

Van Klaveren, J.J.
1953 *The Dutch Colonial System in the East-Indies.* The Hague: Martinus Nijhoff.

Van Vollenhoven, C.
1918 *Het Adatrecht van Nederlandsch-Indië*, Volumes I-III. Leiden: E.J. Brill.
1919 *De Indonesiër en Zijn Grond.* Leiden: E.J. Brill.
1928 *De Ontdekking van het Adatrecht.* Leiden: E.J. Brill.

Velders, A.F.
1909a Landrente-hermetingen in de Preanger. *Tijdschrift van het Binnenlands Bestuur* 37(3):129-40.
1909b Eenige aanteekeningen omtrent het grondbezit in de Preanger. *Tijdschrift van het Binnenlandsch Bestuur* 37(2):87-115.

De Wolff van Westerrode, W.P.D.
1904 *Rapport Betreffende het Landbouwcredietonderzoek in de Preanger Regentschappen.* Batavia: Landsdrukkerij.

Chapter Seventeen

ဢ

The Emergence of Private Property in Land and the Dynamics of Agricultural Production: A Case Study from the Ivory Coast

Jean-Philippe Colin

Economists usually explain the emergence of private property rights, especially since the publication of Demsetz's well-known paper (1967), as the result of a trade-off between the benefits and costs of exclusion of others from the use of the resource. It is assumed that an increase in the value of a resource will lead to exclusive individual rights; as put forward by North (1990), changes in relative prices or relative scarcities lead to the creation of private property rights when it becomes worthwhile to incur the costs of devising such rights. Regarding land, this means that as this resource becomes scarcer in relation to population pressure or due to an increase in the demand for crops, a system of private property rights will tend to develop from an initial situation of open access or common property. This statement demands closer empirical examination. This Ivorian case study will explore the way in which property rights have evolved as an institutional arrangement.[1]

First, I will outline the ideal type of traditional land tenure system and its evolution in southern Ivory Coast since the beginning of this century, and relate this trajectory to the development of a peasant plantation economy.[2] It will be shown that the Property Rights School (PRS) prediction has not (yet?) been completely fulfilled. I will then analyze the emergence and dynamics of land property rights in a pioneer area of the Lower Coast. This case will offer the rare opportunity to witness the emergence of property rights from an institutional vacuum.

Beforehand, it is useful to discuss the meanings given in this paper to the basic concepts of property, ownership and private property rights, on the one hand, and of common property, on the other hand.

In the French tradition, the concept of "property right" is restricted to the combination of the right to use an asset (*usus*), the right to earn income from an asset (*fructus*), and the right to alienate it (*abusus*). (The well-known 544 *Code civil* article states that "La propriété est le droit de jouir et de disposer des choses de la manière la plus absolue, pourvu qu'on n'en fasse pas un usage prohibé par la loi ou les règlements.") As defined by the PRS scholars, the concept has the much broader meaning of "a socially enforced right to select uses of an economic good" (Alchian 1987: 1031). This broad concept encompasses more specific rights, especially the possibility to alienate the asset. The bundle of *usus*, *fructus*, and *abusus* rights is then defined as "ownership right" by some authors (e.g., Furubotn & Pejovich 1972: 1140; Ryan 1987: 1029; Pejovich 1990: 27; Pearce 1992: 351) or as "private property right" by others (e.g., Alchian & Demsetz 1973; de Alessi 1983: 59; Alchian 1987: 1031), in the latter case sometimes with the condition that the right is held by individuals.

A huge diversity in the use of the concepts remains. Some authors use the word ownership (e.g., "common ownership") even if they describe a situation excluding the right to alienate (e.g., Eggertsson 1990; de Alessi 1983). Barzel (1989: 2) uses "property rights" as including the possibility of alienation, i.e., in a French acceptation. Libecap (1989: 1) states that "private ownership of these assets may involve a variety of rights, including the right to exclude nonowners from access, the right to appropriate the stream of rents from use of and from investments in the resource, and the right to sell or otherwise transfer the resource to others," suggesting that private ownership may not include the right of disposal, etc.

To avoid any misunderstanding, in this paper I will use the concept of "property rights" in its broad meaning, of "ownership right" as the right including the possibility of alienating the asset, and "private property right" when the holder of the ownership right is the individual.

Another risk of misunderstanding comes from the meaning given to the concept of common property. Some PRS scholars (see for example Demsetz [1967] and Alchian & Demsetz [1973]) implicitly liken common property and open access. Eggertsson (1990: 36) makes no distinction between common property and open access, but differentiates them explicitly from communal property, whereby a community controls access to a resource by excluding outsiders and regulating its use by insiders. Bromley (1989: 203-206) distinguishes open access (i.e., no property at all) from common property, where the endowed group has a right to exclude nonmembers and where members of the group have both rights and duties with respect to use of the resource.

In order not to add to the prevailing confusion, but to facilitate the understanding of the analysis, in this paper I have made the following choices. "Communal property" will designate a situation where a community has the right to exclude nonmembers, to regulate the access to the land communally held for its members, and to impose on them norms and (possibly collective) practices in its use. "Common property" will designate a situation where a community has the right to exclude nonmembers, to regulate the access to land for its members, but without imposing on them norms and (possibly collective) practices in the use of the resource. "Open access" means no property at all, as suggested by Bromley.[3]

From Usufruct to Private Property Rights in Land: An Ideal Type for the Southern Ivory Coast

This section discusses the traditional land tenure system and its evolution in the context of the southern Ivory Coast.

The Traditional Land System in the Southern Ivory Coast: Common Property, Communal Property?

The fundamental features of traditional land tenure systems (i.e., before the development of the peasant plantation economy) have been described by various authors.[4] At the risk of oversimplifying,[5] I will sketch them roughly, a detailed presentation being beyond the scope of this paper.

Traditionally, land was considered as a support of religious values. It was collectively appropriated—or, to phrase it more correctly, controlled—on a village or lineage basis. The fundamental principle was that every member of the group had the right to cultivate plots of land to insure his household's subsistence. The control maintained over the land by the community—usually through the *chef de terre*, the descendant of the first land-clearer—took on a religious meaning; sometimes the "chef de terre" agreement was not even asked for. "In fact, a contradiction appears between a norm, which grants land control to a local authority, and a practice, which allows individuals total freedom to do what they want," writes Gastellu (1982: 21) in his study of the Moronou Agni.

Merely a formality for the members of the community, this control remained effective regarding outsiders: "Everything is possible for the villagers, on condition that the piece of forest they are clearing has not been already appropriated; they have no permission to ask, no gift to offer; they are submitted to no restriction regarding the acreage they want to cultivate. Conversely, outsiders, Agni or foreigners, have to request the authorization of the *chef de terre* and offer him a symbolic gift; the place where they have to settle is clearly indicated" (ibid.).

The community control over land was in fact fully exercised over uncleared forests: the use right granted to a member of the community and formalized by the clearing of the forest gave him a pre-emptive right on the same plot after a lapse of fallow. So, the general cultivation right included more specific families' rights to cultivate a specific plot, a situation also described by E. Boserup (1970). It was possible to pass this right to one's heirs, but it was not possible, not even contemplated, to sell the land. As Posner (1980) defines it, it was a purely possessory right, a usufruct, which allowed the possessor to exclude people from the land only as long as he was actually working it (or if, as can be seen in this case, he had worked it at some time in the past.[6]

How to qualify these land rights? Was this common property or was this communal property as defined above? This land tenure system may be labelled common property: there was the possibility of preventing outsiders' access to land, but there were no resource management rules enacted by the community. However, the posing of this question in these terms, even if it does correspond to the current practice in economics, does not seem really satisfactory. Here we encounter the classificatory problem that frequently results from the use of concepts in historical and social contexts for which they might not be suited. To speak of property in land, whatever specific right one has in mind (private, common, state right, etc.), means to understand land as a thing, a good, which can be appropriated. But in an emic perspective and according to the prevailing social representations (which determined what was a good and defined its appropriation and the institutional arrangements for its management, land was definitely not a good.[7] It seems preferable to speak of management in terms of a use right, rather than to speak of appropriation (Karsanty 1992), since the problem of land control was not of a major economic concern.[8]

Referring to a similar situation, Demsetz (1967) states that property rights in land (i.e., private property rights) would require policing costs for several years during the fallow period, during which no sizable output would be obtained. But is this the major point? Basically, in a context characterized by a very low density of population, by land abundance, by slash and burn cultivation systems, by nonexistent or very limited markets for land products, and by zero or near-zero land opportunity cost, the land was not scarce, had no exchange value, and was not an economic good which might be appropriated. The fact that there was a regulated access to land for outsiders should not be interpreted economically but socially, settlement and cultivating being synonymous with integrating the community.

Some PRS economists offer a "consciousness argument" in order to explain the absence of private property rights in land in such a context. Barzel (1989: 65), for example, states that "What is found in the public domain . . . is what people have chosen not to claim;" but such a logic means that one already conceptualizes this thing as the potential object of a claim. It seems to me that the absence of private property rights in land in precolonial era comes neither from the difficulties nor from the costs of enforcing them, but from the fact that these rights had no significance in such a context. In other words, the point is not that people *could not* or *did not want to* enforce private property rights, but that they *did not even think* about establishing these rights.

PRS scholars also state that, in such a context, every person has the right to exploit the land and tends to overwork it because some of the costs of this practice are borne by others (i.e., the absence of private property results in great externalities). This analysis has been criticized on the grounds that this absence must not be confused with open access and the lack of rules (e.g., Randall 1978; Bromley 1989; Aguilera 1991). The Ivorian case of the pre-plantation economy phase does not verify the behavior prediction of overexploitation. However, this may be due less to the existence of strict rules of management for the community resource, than to the fact that under the cultivation system used, overworking the land would have been immediately translated in a drop in food-crop yields. Besides, the sustainable nature of the long tree-fallow system is widely accepted.

The Emergence of Private Property Rights in Land: A Muddled Process

In the forested area of the Ivory Coast, even the partial integration of the communities to the market economy, through the development of the peasant plantation economy, modified considerably the issue of property rights in land. Two interrelated factors of change in land property rights must be considered: the introduction of tree crops in the cultivation systems, and increased land scarcity related to a rise in land demand coming not only from native cultivators but also from immigrants.

The development of the peasant plantation economy came from the insertion of tree crops into the traditional food-cropping systems. Coffee and cocoa, unlike food crops, occupy land over a thirty to forty years time span.[9] The spread of tree crops introduced a significant potential force for the privatization of land rights, for two reasons. First, because traditionally crops are considered to be the personal property of the individual who planted them: tree crops legitimize permanent land control for a long time.[10] Second, trees are considered one's property and can be sold, which gives rise to confusion between a plantation sale and a land sale. The shift from rights in crops to rights in land has been widely documented; tree appropriation, which generally precedes land appropriation, can be understood as a by-product of plantation creation as long as there is no "land rush" (see below).

In terms of modern economic vocabulary, the introduction of tree crops—a kind of technological change—makes easier the exclusion of potential co-users of the land resource. The full effect of this exclusion technique (originally not viewed as such) arises with the perception of land scarcity. The extensive character of peasant plantation agriculture is usually explained by the combination of a strategy that optimizes labor (the scarcest resource) rather than land productivity with a land reserve strategy, in that the cultivator anticipates the foreseeable shortage of available land. This strategy gives way to a land rush, during which it is more important to mark the landscape by planting trees that secure and perpetuate the rights obtained (i.e., exclude others) than to manage the cleared area optimally. In this logic, the plantations can be considered, at least in part, as a by-product of a land appropriation strategy.[11]

With the development of the plantation economy, land became a source of market values, and demand for it increased sharply. This demand came from autochthonous cultivators and also from nonnative people attracted by the earnings provided by the plantations.

Regarding the former, an essential point to note is a trend toward the individualization of land control. With the fragmentation of traditional family structures into nuclear cells, and the possibility of diverting land from the lineage patrimony through planting (each native planter can claim a right over land obtained through lineage), the lineage control right over land tends to "blow up" in a multiplicity of individual or family appropriation rights.

The second component of the increase in land demand is the arrival of immigrants. The plantation economy expanded in areas of low population, and this expansion has to be explained, in part, by the sometimes massive arrival of immigrants coming from regions ecologically unsuited for coffee and cocoa cultivation (the center and northern savannah of Ivory Coast, and also Upper Volta and Mali). The conditions of land access for these immigrants have varied from one region to another, regarding the relationships established between native and outsider ethnic groups. Three main cases can be distinguished:

(1) The allocation of a use right, sometimes after a period of wage labor. During the pioneer phase of the plantation economy, land was not only the source of a tradable production, but it often became a means of access to labor, the scarce resource for native cultivators. Frequently, the immigrant's aim was to become a planter; working some time for a native planter was often the condition which would later allow him access to a plot conceded by his former employer. The very fact that the native planter had the right to land access, temporarily allowed him to take advantage of immigrant labor force through the creation of interlinked

(labor/land) markets. (See Chauveau & Richard [1983] for an excellent analysis of this process.) The attribution of land rights to outsiders initiated, in numerous cases, a loss of control by autochthonous groups over uncleared forest. Commonly, the first immigrants respected tradition and asked permission to settle from the native authorities; once established, the immigrants, acting as land authorities in the area they controlled, would give permissions on their own initiative to other newcomers. Ultimately, the weakening of the capacity of some communities to enforce rules regarding the use of their land resources might create situations of de facto open access on resources which previously would have been considered common property (Karsenty 1992). Often this was due to a tremendous demographic disequilibrium after a massive immigrant arrival, such as that which occurred in the southwest Ivory Coast (see Schwartz 1979).

(2) The purchase of black forest from native people, and particularly traditional land authorities. This has been mainly observed in the west-central part of the country, in the Bete and Gban areas. In this case, uncleared land was directly transformed into a "good" (Dozon 1977).

(3) The purchase of a plantation, sold in general by immigrant planters going back home, with the shift toward a land transaction significance as described above.

Faced with this trend toward the individualization, privatization, and monetarization of land rights, the legal apparatus remained unenforced. The state's attempts to redefine the structure of property rights in land were unsuccessful, expropriation measures aside. A 1935 decree gave to the state the control of all land unexploited for more than ten years. The law of 20 March 1963 laid down the principle that the state was the owner of all nonregistered land, with the exception of exploited land; its purpose was also to abolish customary tenures and to prohibit the collection of any land fee. But this law has never been promulgated, and land law remains governed by the 1935 decree, supplemented in 1971 by an additional decree stating that any land occupation requires a land title and that the sale of unregistered land is banned. This legislation is largely unenforced and the formal legal process is only exceptionally followed; the user is often the legislator, in Haeringer's (1982: 87) terms.

(See Blanc [1981] and Ley [1982] on Ivorian land legislation, and Coquery-Vidrovitch [1982] and Le Roy [1991] for a general assessment.) This situation is de facto legitimized by the "land to the tiller" presidential slogan, and recognized in the current administrative practices.

Land rights continue to rest on voluntary local agreements or power relations (especially embedded in interethnic relationships). This does not mean that the State's nonintervention has no effect: the "land to the tiller" slogan did facilitate challenges to traditional land rights, even within the communities. The slogan has strengthened the race for land of planters willing to consolidate their land rights and to mark their ownership by clearing the forest and planting quickly.

To sum up, the situation described above shows how institutional arrangements regarding land rights have changed in response to new conditions such as land scarcity linked to the increased demand for land, and changes in the cropping systems with the introduction of tree crops. The emergence of new property rights in land can be understood as a response to changes in relative prices—increasing land scarcity, increased market value of the product—and to technological change—long cropping cycles—but not to a shortening of fallow duration, as in Boserup's analysis. This conclusion seems closely akin with PRS analyses. However, things might be a bit more complicated, and it would be too simplistic to go no further than the black-and-white categories of use rights and private property rights. I will just mention some elements which suggest that the generalization of private property rights in land has not (yet?) been fully carried out in southern Ivory Coast:

(1) The monetization of land rights appeared between native and nonnative people, or between nonnative cultivators, but it is reported only sporadically between native people. This observation in the Ivorian case seems to refute the assertion by Binswanger et al. (1993) that, in communal systems, sales to outsiders are traditionally forbidden or restricted; the writers add that that the last vestiges of general cultivation rights are lost and private property rights are complete only when the right to sell includes sales to members outside the community. In this case, it might be just the contrary: the nonmonetization of land rights between native cultivators might reflect the rejection (at least temporarily) of a market coordination of intracommunity land relationships.

(2) A monetized land transaction between native and nonnative planters does not take on pure market transaction features: the buyer sometimes remains under an obligation to the seller (e.g., by helping the seller financially in case of necessity). This situation may be characterized as an "imperfect commoditization" of land.

(3) There often remain ambiguities surrounding land property rights because of different interpretations of the nature of the first access to land obtained through a "use right": was it the right to plant or was it an ownership right in land? The long cropping cycle of coffee and cocoa adds to the potential confusion and sometimes explains the reluctance to cut down an old, unproductive plantation, on account of a possible conflict with lineage members (in the case of a native planter) or with native people (in the case of a foreign planter) (Chaléard 1991). (See Berry [1988] for an analysis of the multiplication and overlapping of rights and right-holders in individual farms in the peasant plantation economy.)

(4) What seems to be the individualization of land rights may hide the persistence of a family right (often a nuclear family or lineage-fragment right rather than a lineage right) which might be "activated" in cases of inheritance or to secure land access to family members coming back to the village (Pescay 1994). In other words, some individual rights which seem to be well established can be questioned or renegotiated (Chauveau 1994), especially within the families.

In short, it is often difficult to delineate an indisputable boundary between use rights and ownership rights, and to define precisely the social unit owning this right—the individual, the nuclear family, the extended family, or the lineage.[12]

The rapid change of land rights, marked by the removal of the collective control over land, and an increasing autonomy of the land issue in farmers' practices, is unquestionable. The nature of interdependence among individuals has changed: earlier, the interdependence of people in regard to land access was mediated by means of the group decision process, and there was no land issue as such; now, interdependency lies more on interindividual or nuclear family relationships. However, the complete emergence of private property rights remains problematic, especially if one takes into account the numerous variations at national, regional and local scales, i.e., the great polymorphism of the Ivorian land tenure situation (see Pescay 1994). The originality of the land rights issue in this context is precisely that these rights are and have been for years in a process of transition, meaning that things are changing, without any deterministic prediction regarding the result of the change. The methodological difficulty of checking PRS predictions—as well as their opponents' refutations—stems from the length of this transitional process.[13]

This "transitional stage" makes it possible (or necessary) for economic actors to legitimize their land rights playing on various registers, with all their associated transaction costs. This may involve appeal to traditional custom (often rebuilt and manipulated by modern economic actors to support their interests, as Coquery-Vidovitch [1982] and Dozon [1982] have pointed out), appeal to particular modern principles (such as "land to the tiller" logic) or appeal to the legal apparatus. The way is open for opportunistic individual land strategies. The "land rights game" is open, its rules are multiple and its issue remains largely indeterminate (see Chauveau 1994).

Open Access to Private Property: Land Rights Emergence and Changes in a Pioneer Area

This brief account of the evolution of land rights in the southern Ivory Coast suggests the need for local empirical studies in the context of the post-pioneer phase of the plantation economy. The field research results to be presented now focus on a pioneer region of the Lower Coast. Accordingly, the purpose will not be to analyze the evolution of land rights starting from traditional conditions, but—and this is quite an exceptional opportunity—to describe and analyze the emergence of land rights from a real institutional vacuum.

The region studied is located in the Lower Coast, between Samo and Adiake, in the Adiake subprefecture. The population of this agro-ecologically homogeneous region is mainly nonnative. The fieldwork has been realized in five villages: Djimini-Koffikro, Kongodjan, Assé-Maffia, Amangare, and Aboutou.[14]

The Pioneer Phase (1915-1955): From Res Nullius *to Private Property*

The study of the pioneer phase[15] of the plantation economy in this region provides the opportunity to document the shift from property rights over crops to land property rights, from *res nullius* to private property,[16] from an open access, free-for-all resource, to a socially recognized system of land property.

From No-Man's-Land to "Regulated Open Access"

The five villages studied are located at the furthermost bounds of the Agni Kingdom of Sanwi, in the Eotile vassal territory, and not far from the Aboure country. The Eotiles, fishermen people, have been, together with the Agouas, the first historical inhabitants of the Sanwi Kingdom. At the dawn of the 17th century, their settlements lined the banks of the Aby and Tendo lagoons, while the interior of the country was neglected (Rougerie 1957). The Sanwi Kingdom was built between 1740 and 1823 by the Agni people who came from the North, members of the great Akan Group. The Agnis absorbed the Agouas, and extended their sovereignty over the Eotile, Essouma, and Nzima peoples, politically controlling regions that they did not populate. The western region of the kingdom remained unoccupied, as before. "The kingdom is surrounded everywhere by deserted borders, cutting it off from its neighbors. . . . These are not slightly exploited spaces, not even hunting-gathering areas; the country is completely abandoned to the forest" (Rougerie 1957: 140).

According to Dupire (1960), the southwestern border of the Agni kingdom, which isolated it from the Aboure country, began to be occupied by immigrants coming from various regions of the Ivory Coast, Upper Volta and Mali, during the Agni exodus to Gold Coast, from 1913 to 1917. This infiltration of immigrants began along the Bonoua-Aboisso colonial track, and their numbers reached a real regional significance as early as 1935. After World War II, it turned into a migrational rush, converting the region for some time into a "Far West," to use Rougerie's expression.

How did property rights over land appear and evolve within this context? The Djimini-Koffikro village monograph will provide us a good illustration of this process. The data regarding Djimini-Koffikro, collected over a three year period in the village using of a variety of field research tools,[17] are much more precise than those regarding the four other villages where a simple one-shot formal questionnaire survey was administered; however, the comparison with Djimini-Koffikro will be of interest. The analysis will remain qualitative (see Colin [1990] for the quantitative data).

The first occupant of this region, at that time unexploited, was an Aboure who settled there around 1915. From 1920 and due largely to the completion of the Bonoua-Adiake colonial track, several immigrant groups arrived (mainly Baoules and Agnis, but also Gagous, Yacoubas, Nzimas). Some were fleeing the colonial forced labor in their native countries; others, on the other hand, were brought to the region for these very same constrained enrollments. Some worked in the lumbering industry, others in roadwork. The abundance of "black forest" and game incited them to settle there to create plantations. The first Voltaic settler (a Senoufo) arrived in 1933. He founded an encampment (Kongodjan, "remote plot") a few kilometers from Djimini-Koffikro which was later settled by the Dioulas—in the southern Ivory Coast, people from Mali and the northern Ivory Coast are all called "Dioula"—and the Voltaic Senoufos. Kongodjan is nowadays an independent village. At the beginning of the 1970s, a second wave of migration began, with the arrival of the Voltaics and the Malians who were drawn by the development of pineapple cultivation. These different migrational floods created a genuine melting pot: at present of every two inhabitants, one is a foreigner, and sixteen Ivorian ethnic groups are represented in the village.[18]

As a first step, the Aboure planter, who was the first to arrive, set up the first newcomers in different areas. They, in turn, began to allocate "use rights" to the latecomers, each one in his respective sector. The entire western part of what is now the village territory had been distributed by two Agni planters, the southeastern part by three Baoules, the northeastern part by a Nzima planter, and the northern part directly by the first Aboure immigrant and subsequently by his heirs. A break in the homogeneity of these ethnic blocs resulted from a late exploitation of some areas, which had been neglected for a long time as the result of not being suitable for the cultivation of coffee and cocoa.

Once he arrived, the newcomer generally found hospitality with a planter of his own ethnic group. The place where he could clear was designated by this planter or more commonly by one of the earlier settlers who were now acknowledged as "administrators" of the land access control. Then, the clearing of the forest was sufficient to insure one's uncontested individual right over the land. Therefore, even if the entire area was previously uncontrolled, and even if the first immigrants did not have the possibility of excluding others (see below), one cannot qualify land access as completely open, since this social land access regulation had been established to avoid conflicts. I characterize this situation as "regulated open access."

Was land access conditioned on previous labor for a planter?[19] This practice has not been mentioned, at least regarding the first decades of the pioneer phase. All the old planters said that at that time, "the land belonged to nobody." In the specific context of a pioneers' village—without any traditional, customary control over land—it apparently would have been inconceivable to prohibit land access to a newcomer or to condition it on previous work.

In such a melting pot it was inconceivable to establish and enforce exclusive rights over land so as to cut off a reserve for one's own benefit and/or create a "social land scarcity" in order to constrain others to sell their labor (so as to get access to land later). It wouldn't have occurred to the newcomers because land was not perceived as a scarce resource, and the arrival of new pioneers was welcomed in order to break the loneliness of a small pioneer settlement camp in a great forested area. The aim was more to attract newcomers than to condition their settlement. During his stay with his "guardian," the newcomer contributed through agricultural labor to his host's plots, and enjoyed a near family-member status.[20] However, this practice was considered as reciprocity for being lodged and fed, not as a condition for land access. Later, at the end of the pioneer phase, when land scarcity emerged, some planters who had succeeded in the constitution of land reserves through appropriate forest clearing techniques[21] did, as a result of that labor, constrain access to land by others.

As long as the forest was abundant, the delimitation of each planter's plot to be cleared was not a major concern. The newcomer was set up in the forest, at such a distance from other planters that he could not jeopardize an expected expansion of his neighbors' plantations. The limit was defined only when two clearing fronts came close, in order to avoid conflicts ("the use creating the boundary stone" [Lesourd 1982]). In the land and social context of Djimini-Koffikro, it was ruled out that some planters constitute land reserves by simply sectioning up the forest, nor could they limit the plot size of the newcomers. As seen above, clearing techniques aimed at isolating a reserve had been used, especially by the Aboure planters, but they remained exceptional.

This situation changed when the last of the pioneer phase immigrants arrived. The limits were then clearly indicated by the planter who was settling the newcomer, as the pressure of land scarcity led to more attention being given to the conditions of the new settlements. With the end of the era of abundance, it became necessary, and socially admissible, to manage newcomers' land access more parsimoniously.

The last cases of land access through this type of "use rights" in Djimini-Koffikro go back to the beginning of the 1950s. Around 1955, all the limits of the land patrimonies were clearly defined and even if there was still some forest to clear, the pioneer phase had ended.

The other villages studied share with Djimini-Koffikro the characteristic of being outsiders' villages. In no case was land traditionally controlled at the beginning of the century, not even around what is now Aboutou, which was located close to the Aby lagoon, and was under the control of the Eotiles in the North and the Essoumas in the South. No traditional right being exercised, access to land has been direct for the first immigrants in Assé-Maffia and Aboutou. In Kongodjan, the first immigrant was set up by a planter from Djimini-Koffikro. In Amangare, the village founder obtained permission to settle in Kakoukro village, in exchange for the symbolic gift of a bottle of gin. As in Djimini-Koffikro, the founder of the village indicated to the first newcomers where they could start to clear the forest. The same ethnic polarization occurred; the first to arrive of each ethnic group became the administrator of land access in his sector where the latecomers of the same ethnic group later gathered.

Creating Legitimate Exclusion

We saw that in Djimini-Koffikro "the use created the boundary stone." The same process happened in the other villages, with the interesting exception of Amangare. This village (in fact, a succession of encampments along a track) was created more recently than the others (1950), at a time when land scarcity could be anticipated. All the planters are Aboure. The plantations had been developed as family blocs, generally by brothers working together, and then shared on a core family base. In almost all cases, the limits between each family bloc had not been defined by the junction of the clearing fronts, as in the other villages, but marked right out in the forest after an agreement was reached between each family and in the presence of a representative of the Aboure king.

Such a sharing of the forest required anticipation of land scarcity to motivate it, and a collective acknowledgment of the limits as defined, to enforce it. Among the Aboure, this condition was fulfilled by appealing to a legitimate arbitration authority, the king's representative. In fashionable economic terms, we could say that this arbitration lowered the transaction costs related to the establishment of land rights. This practice has been successful only because the arrival of non-Aboure planters was blocked by the control that the Aboure maintained over the track, the northern and southern encampments along the track having been created at the same time. In this case, ethnicity can be understood as a means to create, in a new context, a legitimacy to enforce exclusive rights on uncleared forest.

The Distribution of Land Property at the End of the Pioneer Phase: A Product of the "First in Time, First in Right" Logic?

Schmid (1987: 20) stresses economists' lack of interest regarding the manner of appropriation of new resources, even if this issue contributes largely to explain differences in the distribution of wealth. In the case under study, it has been possible to reconstruct land distribution in Djimini-Koffiko at the end of the pioneer phase and to bring to the foreground the major factors of differentiation in land property. This land property distribution came from the combination of three factors: (a) the arrival time of the planter, (b) his capacity to mobilize family labor, and (c) the productive potential of the soil as perceived by the planters.

The arrival time in the village did play a role in land possession, but not as expected from a "first in time, first in right" logic. As we observed, that a person was one of the first immigrants in the village did not permit his claim on uncleared land. But by starting the clearing of the forest and the planting of coffee and cocoa early on, this planter had a potentially better possibility than a latecomer to accumulate land rights for more extensive acreage; the use made the right, in the context studied. It was observed that, at the end of the pioneer phase, eight of the twelve patrimonies larger than twenty hectares were controlled by planters who had arrived with the first migration wave. However, this condition was not sufficient. In order to take advantage of this early arrival, the settler had to have a good access to the labor of junior or subordinate kinsmen, for all work had to be done by family labor force until the trees were mature enough to enter a share-cropping arrangement. The effectiveness of these criteria have been verified in other areas where soil is considered equally favorable for coffee and cocoa trees. The lack of interest in small savannah zones allowed some latecomers to control a fair amount of acreage; the constitution of three of these land patrimonies, which were larger than twenty hectares at the end of the pioneer phase, can be explained in this way. These landlords had never been leading coffee or cocoa planters, but control of such acreage turned out to be particularly profitable when the introduction of new crops such as the oil palm tree or pineapple enhanced the value of these soils.

The Time of Pioneers' Relief (1955-): The Rise of Land Markets

With the end of the pioneer phase, regulated free access to land no longer operated. Land was completely appropriated; land rights were acknowledged; the limits of the patrimonies were well defined. From an open-access situation with an institutional vacuum, a new institutional arrangement had emerged: private property in land. The focus of this analysis shifts from the constitution of property rights to their transmission through inheritance, *inter vivos* donations or purchase, as well as to the conditions of access to the land resource for those who have no land ownership right. Some major points in this development will be touched on here: the breaking of traditional inheritance rules; a shift, in some cases, from individual private property to family ownership; the development of a land market; and the emergence of land tenancy and of a group of landless cultivators.

Inheritance and **Inter Vivos** *Donations*

The guidance principles of the customary devolution rules in southern Ivorian ethnic groups are well known (see for example SEDES 1967): the devolution is limited to one (agnatic or uterine) line; the properties are not divided up when their owner dies, a unique heir being designated; each generation is "exhausted" before transmission to another generation (the succession of generation principle), each elder having the priority in each branch (the primogeniture principle); men inherit from men, women inherit from women (the "homosexuality" rule); inter vivos donations are admitted but restricted to one's own personal property, i.e., noncustomary inheritance.

Two facts predominate in land property rights transmission in Djimini-Koffikro: the lack of respect for the customary inheritance rules and the importance of *inter vivos* donations.

The infringement of the customary inheritance rules is primarily concerned with the succession of generations and the devolution in uterine line in the case of matrilineal ethnic groups. This mutation regarding the traditional model has been facilitated—sometimes even after violent palavers—by the geographic distance between the planter and his legitimate heirs; patrilocality induces a strong reinforcement of the father-son group. It has also been facilitated by the fact that at the time of a pioneer's death, the transmission concerned a property created by his own labor, and not a customary inheritance.

The results of the research done in the other villages relativize and at the same time reinforce this analysis. The customary rules of inheritance have been far more respected than in Djimini-Koffikro. This fact has to be linked with the relative weight of the Aboure, Essouma and Eotile ethnic groups in the population of these villages: the proximity of the native village facilitated the social control for traditional rule enforcement during the inheritance process.[22] The transgression of customary inheritance rules remains the norm for people coming from other regions.

Can heirs be regarded as holding private property rights in land? In various cases, the heirs have to be considered as administrators of a family land patrimony. They have the usufruct; they manage it as they want and for their own profit; but they could not sell a plot on their own authority; and they may have to redistribute part of the land patrimony to family members (especially young brothers). This reveals an evolution from the unquestionable pioneer's land ownership right towards a family jointly-held land property (as in Ghana: P. Hill, quoted by Sautter [1968]).

Inter vivos donations of plantations or fallow lands have been frequent in Djimini- Koffikro as in the other villages, especially Amangare and Assé-Maffia. In general they have been beneficial for the planters' children. Frequently these donations correspond to an anticipated diversion of a future customary inheritance such as in the case of the Aboures, where social pressure due to the proximity of Bonoua facilitates the traditional matrilineage inheritance. This way, the planter's son(s) can create plantations during his (their) father's lifetime. The heir—a uterine brother, cousin, or nephew—will later receive the land which has remained under the planter's responsibility until his death.

The beneficiary of the donation cannot be considered as having full private property rights over land as long as the donor is alive; the sale of the land would not be permissible. Nevertheless, after the donor's death his property right seems undeniable; no heir's contestation has been reported during the surveys.

The Emergence of a Land Market

Land transactions have been frequent in Djimini- Koffikro: one third of the village territory has been sold at least once. Some of the oldest transactions concerned productive plantations. Originally then, land transaction was a by-product of a transaction on productive vegetable capital; "in the past, one bought the plantation, not really the land," comment the oldest planters. But in the beginning of the 1960's, it was the land itself which found a market value, through the sale of fallow land plots or of old unproductive plantations. (The same logic has been observed in the other villages studied, with a shift from the sale of plantations to the sale of land.)

Land was sold by planters leaving the village to go back home or by planters' heirs unwilling to settle in Djimini-Koffikro. Sometimes also planters living in the village would sell a part of their land patrimony for urgent money needs. With the exception of the Aboures, all ethnic groups have participated in land transactions. This ethnic exception (Amangare shows the same Aboure specificity in regard to the constitution of the land market) can be explained by the proximity of the Aboures' fief of Bonoua. An Aboure planter would never find himself in the dilemma of selling his plantation in Djimini-Koffikro in order to return to his native community (Bonoua), because of the close proximity of the two villages. In addition, his family would disapprove of his selling the land when there was such a scarcity of it in Bonoua: Aboures are traditionally referred to as 'Ehounva' (men without land) by their neighbors (Rougerie 1957).

This process of transformation of a use value of land to a market value came from the impossibility of gaining access to land through a simple regulated free access, once the pioneer phase was over. It should be stressed that in this case, the land scarcity which led to the emergence of ownership rights was a result of its full exploitation ("land saturation"); whereas in other regions, such as the Bete country, the monetarization of land access preceded land saturation, because of the customary control over the resource.

The fact that Djimini-Koffikro was an immigrant village facilitated the constitution of a land market on two accounts: the pioneers could manage their land patrimonies as they wanted because these had not been acquired through a customary inheritance, and the return of some planters to their native village prompted offers in the land market.

In conclusion, the land in Djimini-Koffikro is no longer an abundant free resource; it is now scarce and has a cost. The pioneers' individual private property rights over land are unquestionable (with among the Aboures). The individual rights of the buyers of a plot also are clearly established and socially recognized. The situation becomes less clear with respect to *inter vivos* donations, in that the full property right is postponed until the donor's death. The individual right of the heirs is sometimes restricted because, while *usus* and *fructus* are possible, *abusus* may require a family decision.

In short, the institution of private property in land has emerged, but it does not systematically govern all land rights in the usual atomistic way. Nowadays, a planter can exploit some land under an heir usufruct right, and other plots under an ownership right if land was obtained through the regulated access of the pioneer phase, or bought, or received as an inter vivos donation (as long as the donor is dead). The economic incidence of this duality remains limited; the type of land property right is not differentiated with regard to the management of land as a production factor. However, a new duality has emerged that differentiates those who have land ownership rights and those who do not.

The Emergence of Land Tenancy

An important new fact, since the end of the pioneer phase, is the arrival of a group of landless cultivators.[23] These landless farmers—and some land-constrained landowners—can obtain temporary access to land under several contractual arrangements which have emerged since the end of the pioneer phase. The usual one consists of renting a plot for a cropping cycle duration. Sharecropping in cassava cultivation is also common; the share does not include short term cycle food crops which may precede the cassava cultivation and which remain under the tenant's control. Several forms of labor-rent have also appeared, such as giving access to land in exchange for bush clearing, the landowner retaining half of the plot cleared and leaving the other half to the tenant for the duration of a food crop cycle; the landowner may also only authorize corn production on the entire plot. Another arrangement consists of letting the tenant cultivate one short-term cycle food crop (corn or sweet potato) in association with the owner's young oil palm tree plantation, securing in this way the upkeep of the plantation. Finally, short term loans for food crop production occur generally between kinsmen. Land rent (rent *sensu stricto*, share rent, and labor-rent) is now generated over 20% of the village territory.

Renting out land was initiated in Djimini-Koffikro in the mid-1960s, when a private company introduced pineapple cultivation under a contract farming system. The opportunity to grow pineapple led to a demand for land. Pineapple production offered two advantages in this respect. First, it was a nonperennial crop which could be grown by landless cultivators, and second, it provided the possibility of paying a rent, because of its high income per hectare. On the other hand, the supply in the land lease market came from the ageing of coffee and cocoa plantations. Since that time, since no landlord has developed a strategy of leasing land permanently, the supply of land for lease has come from the Brownian movement of landowners entering in and withdrawing from the lease market, in a process closely related to the dynamics of plantation reconversion towards new perennial crops (oil palm tree, coconut tree, hevea).

It seems that, originally, the emergence of land rent in the village was induced more by the economic nature of pineapple production ("there was money in it, so we had to take advantage of it," recalled the landowners) than by land scarcity in itself. Indeed, at first the plots intended for food crops were just lent. The monetarization of land tenure arrangements for food crops started later, when the demand increased even more with the arrival of more landless immigrants.

The emergence of land tenancy has thus been induced by a combination of factors: the impossibility of getting access to land property through regulated free access; the existence of land availability related to the progressive decline and abandonment of coffee and cocoa plantations and their reconversion; an increasing demand by landless cultivators for land to grow pineapple; the high value of pineapple production.

Conclusion

A major point of the PRS paradigm of property rights change has been verified: property rights are modified in response to the development of new opportunities or constraints which provide incentives for individuals to seek new institutional arrangements. Indeed, as land became scarcer, as land value appeared and increased in relation to population pressure and due to an increase in the land demand, a system of ownership rights was developed. An evolution in land rights toward the individualization, privatization and monetarization of land control is generally the case in the southern Ivory Coast. Also, the study of a former pioneer area has provided the opportunity to document the shift from an open access, free-for-all resource, to a socially recognized system of land property, which can be qualified as private property right without any doubt. This study also illustrated how, from a legal vacuum, people avoided the potential chaos of an open access to land, by establishing a socially acknowledged land access system.[24]

However, the PRS "consciousness argument" regarding the explanation of the absence of private property rights in land during the precolonial era ("there were no such rights because people *decided* not to develop them") has been questioned. It is not that people could not or did not want to enforce private property rights, but that they did not *even think* about establishing these rights because such rights had no meaning at that time and in those circumstances.

In both explanations, the result and the cause are the same (no private property rights in land due to no land scarcity), but I see a difference between deciding not to do something on the one hand, and not thinking of the possibility of doing it, on the other hand. The logic of economic behavior which underlies each of these statements is quite different.

Furthermore, the generalization of private property rights in land has yet to be fully carried out in southern Ivory Coast. In other words, the land rights mutation, in response to new circumstances, is not straightforward, especially regarding native communities and the relationships between native and nonnative planters. I have mentioned the nonmonetarization of land rights between native cultivators; the difficulty of delineating an indisputable boundary between use rights and private property rights, and between individual, family, or lineage rights; or, in some cases, a shift—which is not in the logic of the PRS paradigm—from individual property to family property (in the case of a pioneer land inheritance). That the institution of private property in land has emerged does not mean that it governs systematically all land rights in an atomistic way, as viewed by PRS economists. Of course, one could call up transaction costs to explain the complexity of what PRS economists would defined as a transitional stage. I am not very comfortable with this perspective for two reasons. First, because it means that the result of the transition—the establishment of private property rights—is taken for granted, and that the only unknown is the length of the transition process. Second, because it seems more promising to try to explain (using both economic and noneconomic factors) the observed results of the process of rights changes in the real, "messy" world—an explanation that remains to be fully developed—than to look to transaction costs to explain why these observed results are different from a result defined normatively *ex ante*, i.e., well-defined exclusive individual property rights.

Acknowledgments

I would like to thank Robert Hunt, Guy Pontié and Allan Schmid for their comments on a first draft of this paper. I remain responsible for its imperfections.

Notes

1. Here I cite Allan Schmid (1987: 6) in his definition of institutions as "sets of ordered relationships among people that define their rights, their exposure to the rights of others, their privileges, and their responsibilities."
2. The expression "plantation economy" often refers to a production system developed in tropical countries by foreign producers, characterized by large-scale production of tree crops for export, capital-intensive technology, and a capitalist mode of production. Although this type of system is found in the Ivory Coast, it is largely dominated, in both geographical and economic importance, by another production system, also based on export tree crops but operated by African farmers. By "peasant plantation economy" I refer to this latter agricultural and economic system.
3. For a better clarification of the concept of "common (or communal) property," it would be useful (although outside the scope of this paper) to consider the combination of at least three criteria: the conditions of *access* to the resource, the conditions of the resource *management*, and the *durability* of the common/communal right. This can be stated in a few key-questions. (1) Is the resource under open access, regulated access for the outsiders of the community, or regulated access for outsiders as well as for the members of the community (more broadly the social group)? (2) Is this access exclusive? (e.g., the possibility for animal grazing on a communal pasture for any member of the group vs an agricultural plot allowed to an household). (3) Does the group only control the access to the resource, or does it impose also resource management rules? (e.g., crop choice, such as the prohibition of perennial crops; group organization for the use of the resource; group control of its products). (4) Does the group control vanish definitively once the resource is exploited? (e.g., noncancelable exclusive use-right opening the way to an ownership right, leading to the resource's exit from the community's patrimony). Does it vanish temporarily? (e.g., individual, exclusive, but temporary use right). Or does it remain unaltered? (e.g., communal forests).
4. Regarding the Ivorian forest area, one can mention the studies of Affou Yapi (1979) on the Attie ethnic group; Bouet-Surroca (1977), Boutillier (1960), Gastellu (1978, 1980, 1982), Kindo (1975), Rougerie (1957) on the Agni; Chaléard (1979) on the Abe; Chauveau and Richard (1977, 1983) on the Gban; Dozon (1975, 1977) on the Bete; Dupire (1960) on the Abe and Agni; Köbben (1956) on the Agni and Bete; Léna (1979) on the Bakwe; Raulin (1957) on the Dida, Gouro, Gban and Bete; and Schwartz (1971, 1979) on the Guere and Bakwe.
5. Or of succumbing to what Dozon (1982) calls the "precolonial referent," an idealized model of precolonial land tenure systems. This point is also made by Bruce (1988) who underlines the multiple sources of change in African precolonial land tenure systems (innovation in agricultural

technology, changes in population densities, emergence of states, conquest, migrations).

6. Under the traditional cropping system, after clearing and burning the virgin forest (what is called locally a black forest) and a few years of food-crop cultivation, the plot was abandoned to the forest's natural regrowth (shifting cultivation) or to a long tree-fallow in order to restore soil fertility and help to prevent weed problems (cyclical cultivation).
7. See Biebuyck's (1963) and Bohannan's (1963) critiques of the oversimplifications resulting from the application of Western legal concepts to the analysis of African indigenous land-tenure systems.
8. We might also cite Bell's distinction (in this volume) between rights in persons (i.e., rights attached to the person on the basis of some intrinsic characteristics, here the right of access to land due to a group membership) and property rights; in this case he would use the concept of commons and not of common property.
9. The introduction of the tree crops proceeds from a substitution of these crops for the forest's natural regrowth or for the long fallow which previously followed the food crop cycle.
10. Very significantly, clearing the forest can be delegated to wage laborers, but planting coffee or cocoa trees is always done by the planter and his family to insure his rights to the future production and over the land (Gastellu 1980). On the relationships between trees crops and land property rights, see also Berry (1988) and Bruce (1988).
11. "When one can obtain ownership rights in a resource only by capture or use, there is a tendency to take too much too soon," writes Posner (1980: 35), too much and too soon in regard to an economic standard of productive efficiency, but not in regard to the logic of planters' aims.
12. The Ivorian Land Plan aims at clarifying the rights related to each plot and identifying their beneficiaries. This plan is implemented nowadays by the Government, partially on the request of international backers, with the explicit argument that well-defined property rights play a crucial incentive role in economic productive efficiency (Yapi Diahou 1991), a basic PRS postulate which leaves to one side the equity issue related to the question "whose right is going to prevail?" (see Schmid 1987). It will be interesting to see how the Plan handles this puzzling task.
13. A complication in the rigorous analysis of this transition comes from the scarcity of studies focused on land rights in the context of the renewal of coffee and cocoa plantations (contexts in which land rights could be more easily challenged).
14. The field-research on which this analysis is based was not just concerned with the land tenure system evolution; its purpose was to study the dynamics of a smallholder plantation economy. Two fundamentally related topics were addressed by the research: (a) the sources and features of technical and institutional changes, and their incidence on the plantation economy;

and (b) the production strategies adopted by farmers, according to their different opportunities, resource availabilities, and objectives (see Colin 1990).

15. The expression "pioneer phase" will refer to the period during which permanent access to land is possible through a kind of first occupancy right. This definition depends on the dominant form of access to land and not on the technical act of clearing the forest, which had not completely disappeared at the end of the pioneer phase.
16. This challenges Boserup's statement that "a direct passage from a situation where land is at the disposal of everybody to private property . . . never happens" (1970: 136 [translated from the French edition]).
17. In Djimini-Koffikro, besides direct observation allowed by the researcher's lengthy stay in the village, the collection of information regarding land tenure and its evolution was based on (1) an initial agricultural and demographic census; (2) the measurement and mapping of all the plots of the village territory; (3) the reconstitution of the history of property rights for each plot mapped (establishment of the pioneer's right, and then all movements which have possibly affected the plot: inheritance, donation, sale); and (4) recording the present land tenure arrangement for each plot—owner's cultivation, land rent, sharecropping, labor-rent arrangement, loan, or nonagricultural use—at the time of the study.
18. The ethnic composition of the four other villages studied differ markedly one from the other (and this has some impact on land rights, as we will see): Kongodjan is a Dioula village; Assé-Maffia is populated by the Aboures, Atties and Nzimas; Amangare is monoethnic (Aboure); and the population of Aboutou is made up of the Essoumas, Eotiles and Nzimas. These last three villages have, therefore, a "native migrant" population (on a regional scale), whereas Djimini-Koffikro and above all Kongodjan are mainly populated by migrants coming from other regions.
19. I.e., one of the first newcomers, who provided the latecomer with the possibility of settling the land, as noted in other regions of Ivory Coast.
20. The same practice has been described by Raulin (1957) regarding the west-central part of the country, and by Léna (1979) for the southwest.
21. These techniques, already described in other regions (see for example Chaléard [1979], Gastellu [1980], or Lesourd [1982]), consisted of multiplying the forest clearing epicenters in order to isolate a central area which had provisionally been preserved intact.
22. Sorcery and poisoning within families must be included under social control procedures.
23. Nowadays this represents about 44% of the 180 production units of the community. The population of the village rose from 220 inhabitants at the end of the pioneer phase (1956 census) to 1000 in 1983.
24. This case brings to mind the California gold rush (Eggertson 1990: 290).

References Cited

Affou Yapi, S.
1979 *Le Grand Planteur Villageois dans le Procès de Valorisation du Capital Social: Une Introduction à l'Organisation Socio-économique Akyé*. Abidjan: Centre ORSTOM de Petit-Bassam.

Aguilera, F.
1991 ¿La tragedia de la propriedad común o la tragedia de la malinterpretación en economía? *Agricultura y Sociedad* 61:157-81.

Alchian, A.
1987 Property rights. In J. Eatwell, M. Milgate, & N. Newman (eds.), *The New Palgrave: A Dictionary of Economics*, pp. 1031-34. London: Macmillan.

Alchian, A., & H. Demsetz
1973 The property right paradigm. *Journal of Economic History* 33(1):16-27.

Barzel, Y.
1989 *Economic Analysis of Property Rights*. Cambridge: Cambridge University Press.

Berry, S.
1988 Property rights and rural resource management: the case of tree crops in West Africa. *Cahiers des Sciences Humaines* 24(1):3-16.

Biebuyck, D.
1963 Introduction. In D. Biebuyck (ed.), *African Agrarian Systems*, pp. 1-51. Oxford: Oxford University Press.

Binswanger, H., K. Deininger, & G. Feder
1993 *Power, Distortions, Revolt, and Reform in Agricultural Land Relations*. Washington, DC: The World Bank, Working Paper WPS 1164.

Blanc, C.
1981 *Le Foncier Rural en Côte d'Ivoire*. Abidjan: Ministère du Plan et de l'Industrie, Direction du Développement Régional.

Bohannan, P.
1963 "Land," "tenure," and "land-tenure." In D. Biebuyck (ed.), *African Agrarian Systems*, pp. 101-15. Oxford: Oxford University Press.

Boserup, E.
1970 *Evolution Agraire et Pression Démographique*. Paris: Flammarion.

Bouet-Surroca, C.
1977 *Béttié et Akiekrou: Étude Comparée de Deux Terroirs en Zone Forestière Ivoirienne*. Paris: ORSTOM.

Boutillier, J.-L.
1960 *Bongouanou, Côte d'Ivoire: Étude Socio-économique d'une Subdivision*. Paris: Berger-Levreault.

Bromley, D.
1989 *Economic Interests and Institutions*. Oxford: Basil Blackwell.

Bruce, J.
1988 A perspective on indigenous land tenure systems and land concentration. In R.E. Downs & S.P. Reyna (eds.), *Land and Society in Contemporary Africa*, pp. 23-52. Hanover, NH: University Press of New England.

Chaléard, J.-L.
1979 Structures Agraires et Économie de Plantation chez les Abè (Département d'Agboville, Côte d'Ivoire). Ph.D. dissertation, UER de géographie, Université de Paris X-Nanterre.

Chauveau, J.-P.
1994 Jeu foncier, institutions d'accès à la ressource et usage de la ressource: une étude de cas dans le centre-ouest ivoirien. Paper presented at the International Symposium "Crises, ajustements et recompositions en Côte d'Ivoire: la remise en cause d'un modèle," Abidjan, Ivory Coast.

Chauveau, J.-P., & J. Richard
1977 Une périphérie rcentrée: à propos d'un système local d'économie de plantation en Côte d'Ivoire. *Cahiers d'Études Africaines* 68(18-4):485- 523.
1983 *Bodiba en Côte d'Ivoire. Du Terroir à l'État: Petite Production Paysanne et Salariat Agricole dans un Village Gban*. Paris: ORSTOM.

Colin, J.-P.
1990 *La Mutation d'une Économie de Plantation en Basse Côte d'Ivoire*. Paris: ORSTOM.

Coquery-Vidrovitch, C.
1982 Le régime foncier rural en Afrique noire. In E. Le Bris, E. Le Roy, & F. Leimdorfer (eds), *Enjeux Fonciers en Afrique Noire*, pp. 65-84. Paris: ORSTOM-Karthala.

De Alessi, L.
1983 Property rights and transaction costs: a new perspective in economic theory. *Social Science Journal* 20(3):59-70.

Demsetz, H.
1967 Toward a theory of property rights. *American Economic Review* 57:347- 59.

Dozon, J.-P.
1975 *La Problématique Rizicole dans la Région de Gagnoa*. Abidjan: Centre ORSTOM de Petit-Bassam.
1977 Économie marchande et structures sociales: le cas de Bete de Côte d'Ivoire. *Cahiers d'Etudes Africaines* 68(17-4):463-83.
1982 Epistémologie du "foncier" dans le cadre des économies de plantation ivoiriennes. In E. Le Bris, E. Le Roy, & F. Leimdorfer (eds.), *Enjeux Fonciers en Afrique Noire*, pp. 56-60. Paris: ORSTOM-Karthala.

Dupire, M.
1960 Planteurs autochtones et étrangers en basse Côte d'Ivoire, *Études Éburnéennes* 8:7-237.

Eggertsson, T.
1990 *Economic Behavior and Institutions*. Cambridge: Cambridge University Press.

Furubotn, E., & S. Pejovich
1972 Property rights and economic theory: a survey of recent literature. *Journal of Economic Literature* 10:1137-62.

Gastellu, J.-M.
1978 La course à la forêt dans le Moronou. Paper presented at the CIRES- IGT-GERDAT-ORSTOM Inter-Institute Seminar, "Le Dynamisme Foncier et l'Économie de Plantation," Abidjan, Ivory Coast.
1980 L'arbre ne cache pas la forêt, ou: usus, fructus, abusus, *Cahiers ORSTOM, Série Sciences Humaines* 18(3-4):279-82.
1982 *Fastes Agni*. Abidjan: Centre ORSTOM de Petit-Bassam.

Haeringer, P.
1982 Une approche pragmatique des situations foncières. In E. Le Bris, E. Le Roy, & F. Leimdorfer (eds.), *Enjeux Fonciers en Afrique Noire*, pp. 84-90. Paris: ORSTOM-Karthala.

Karsenty, A.
1992 Contrat et gestion patrimoniale. Paper presented at the CIRAD meeting on Institutional Economics and Agriculture, Montpellier, France.

Kindo, B.
1975 Dynamisme Économique et Organisation de l'Espace Rural chez l'Agni du N'dénéan et de Djuablin (Côte d'Ivoire). Ph.D. dissertation, UER de Géographie, Université de Paris X-Nanterre.

Köbben, A.
1956 Le planteur noir. *Études Éburnéennes* 5:7-189.

Le Roy, E.
1991 L'état, la réforme et le monopole foncier. In E. Le Bris E., E. Le Roy, & P. Mathieu (eds), *L'Appropriation de la Terre en Afrique Noire*, pp. 159-90. Paris: Karthala.

Léna, P.
1979 *Transformation de l'Espace Rural dans le Front Pionnier du Sud-Ouest Ivoirien*. Abidjan: Centre ORSTOM de Petit-Bassam.

Lesourd M.
1982 L'Émigration Baoulé vers le Sud Ouest de la Côte d'Ivoire. Ph.D. dissertation, UER de Géographie, Université de Paris X-Nanterre.

Ley, A.
1982 La logique foncière de l'état depuis la colonisation: l'expérience ivoirienne. In E. Le Bris, E. Le Roy, & F. Leimdorfer (eds.), *Enjeux Fonciers en Afrique Noire*, pp. 135-141. Paris: ORSTOM-Karthala.

Libecap, G.D.
1989 *Contracting for Property Rights*. Cambridge: Cambridge University Press.

North, D.
1990 *Institutions, Institutional Change and Economic Performance*. Cambridge: Cambridge University Press.

Pearce, D. (ed.)
1992 *The MIT Dictionary of Modern Economics*. Cambridge, MA: MIT Press.

Pejovich, S.
1990 *The Economics of Property Rights: Towards a Theory of Comparative Systems*. Dordrecht: Kluwer Academic Publishers.

Pescay M.
1994 Essai de synthèse sur les transformations des systèmes fonciers en Côte d'Ivoire. Paper presented at the International Symposium "Crises, ajustements et recompositions en Côte d'Ivoire: la remise en cause d'un modèle," Abidjan, Ivory Coast.

Posner, R.
1980 A theory of primitive society, with special reference to law. *Journal of Law and Economics* 23:1-53.

Randall, A.
1978 Property institutions and economic behavior. *Journal of Economic Issues* 12(1):1-21.

Raulin, H.
1957 *Mission d'Étude des Groupements Immigrés en Côte d'Ivoire: Problèmes Fonciers dans les Régions de Gagnoa et Daloa.* Paris: ORSTOM.

Ryan, A.
1987 Property. In J. Eatwell, M. Milgate, & N. Newman (eds.), *The New Palgrave: A Dictionary of Economics*, pp. 1029-31. London: Macmillan.

Rougerie, G.
1957 Les pays Agni du Sud-Est de la Côte d'Ivoire. *Études Éburnéennes* 6:7- 207.

Sautter, G.
1968 *Les Structures Agraires en Afrique Tropicale.* Paris: Université de la Sorbonne, Centre de Documentation Universitaire.

Schmid, A.
1987 *Property, Power, and Public Choice.* New York: Praeger.

Schwartz, A.
1971 *Tradition et Changement dans la Société Guéré.* Paris: ORSTOM.
1979 Colonisation agricole spontanée et émergence de nouveaux milieux sociaux dans le Sud-Ouest ivoirien. *Cahiers ORSTOM, Série Sciences Humaines* 16(1-2):83-101.

SEDES
1967 *Région de Sud-est: Etude Socio-économique*, Volume I: *La Démographie*, Volume II: *La Sociologie*, Volume III: *L'Agriculture.* Abidjan: Ministère du Plan.

Yapi Diahou, A.
1991 La plan foncier ivoirien. In E. Le Bris, E. Le Roy, & P. Mathieu (eds.), *L'Appropriation de la Terre en Afrique Noire*, pp. 309-13. Paris: Karthala.

Chapter Eighteen

ജ്ജ

The Erosion of Commons and the Emergence of Property: Problems for Social Analysis

Pauline E. Peters

In recent years, anthropologists have been at the center of a debate about "common property." A prime target of critiques in the literature has been Garrett Hardin's formulation of "The Tragedy of the Commons" which, since its first public airing in 1968, has captured the imagination of an entire generation of thinkers and policy-makers. The largest part of the anthropological contribution has been to provide extensive empirical grounds for rebutting Hardin's proposition of doom being inevitable in communally held resources. In addition to this rather classic role of empirical documentation of contrary cases, some anthropologists, along with others in history, political science, and agricultural economics, have challenged the theoretical and methodological premises of Hardin and other theorists addressing the problems of "common goods." Arguing against the privileging of methodological individualism, game theoretic models such as the Prisoner's Dilemma, and approaches based on utility maximization, these critiques argue that "common property systems" or "common pool resources" demand analyses privileging historical, social, and political-economic (or "institutional") dimensions.

In this paper, I wish to push these critiques a step further by problematizing the application of the concept of "property" to virtually all systems of managing land and its resources, capitalist or noncapitalist, past or present, and anywhere in the world. Many of the critiques of models premising the necessary demise of commonly held resources have focussed on showing that common property is not equivalent to open-access resources, that is, those where no rules or conventions guide use of the commons (Ciriacy-Wantrup & Bishop 1975; McCay & Acheson 1987; Feeny et al. 1990; Bromley 1992). I want to suggest here that commons systems are not equivalent to common property. Although common property is often cast as the precursor of private property of resources (and an inferior type at that), I propose that, in being defined as common "property," pre- existing commons systems become *products* of private property. It is only when there is private property in land that "common property" can exist—the latter is defined in opposition to the former. It is a mistake to conflate "common property" with pre-property or nonproperty forms of managing land since they differ in concept and practice. This proposition emerges from my attempts to understand the transformations in the "communal" range of Botswana and my comparative reading of current interpretations of the enclosure and erosion of the English commons.

I conclude from the limited comparison presented here that if, in at least these two instances, one sees an emergence of the concept and practice of "property" in land then to use the concept of property to analyze the earlier, "pre-property" systems is to risk obscuring the dynamics of social transformation. The paper proceeds by considering some directions in the history and historiography of the demise of the English commons, especially the attempts to provide sociocultural interpretations. Recent historical scholarship reconsiders the "triumphal" interpretation of enclosure as a victory for economic progress and efficiency and posits, instead, a process in which the hegemony of private property rights in land progressively displaced other rights of use. This interpretation of enclosure resembles in many ways my interpretation of changes in Botswana's communal range, which I then present, before restating the conclusion.

Changing Historiography of the English Commons

In the first half of this century, the conventional and dominant view of enclosure was that it was an inevitable response to the need for greater efficiency in production. According to this view, farmers had seen that "one sheep in an enclosure is worth two on a common" and that the overstocking of the commons was due to the lamentable fact that "that which is everyman's is no man's" (Prothero [1917] cited in Liversage 1945). Trevelyan, an influential British historian of the first half of the 20th century, was one of the popularizers of the view that the expansion of agricultural production that fuelled the industrial revolution could be seen as the result of enclosure which had "blazed a trail for the whole world" (1944: 381). This "triumphal" view (Thompson 1993) had taken form through the 18th and 19th centuries. As the struggle for ascendancy between the rights of owners of private property and the rights to the commons mounted through the 18th century, it involved legislative and administrative changes by the Whig elite and shifts in "definitions at law and in local custom" (Thompson 1976: 337). The proponents of enclosure developed an aggressive ideological attack on the commons. As enclosure proceeded, the remaining open commons were condemned as inherently stagnant ("no improvements can be made in any wastes") and defined as unregulated ("a dangerous centre of indiscipline" and "the nest and conservatory of sloth, idleness and misery").[1]

Opponents of the positive view of enclosure in the 18th and 19th centuries included David Davies who said enclosure "has beggared multitudes;" William Cobbett who indignantly stated that "those who are so eager for new inclosure seem to argue as if the wasteland in its present state produced nothing at all . . . [But, in fact i]t goes to the feeding of sheep, of cows . . . and . . . helps to rear, in health and vigor, the children of the labourers,"[2] and the poignant laments of the laborer-poet, John Clare.[3] In the early 20th century, George Sturt likened enclosure to "knocking the keystone out of an arch . . . the loss of the common . . . left the people helpless against influences which have sapped away their interests, robbed them of security and peace . . . [and] personal pride."[4] The Hammonds, probably the best known critics of the early 20th century, concluded that enclosure was "fatal to . . . the small farmer, the cottager, and the squatter."[5] Although these writers revealed the dark side of enclosure, they did not displace the dominant view. As we shall see, it was views like those of Prothero and Trevelyan that predominated overwhelmingly in colonial perspectives.

In the 1960s a new generation of historians reiterated the triumphal view. They concluded that enclosure increased the demand for labor and provided "more regular and seasonally secure employment," "it alleviated pauperism," "it did not adversely affect the small landowner and tenant farmer," "it did not cause out-migration . . . and it was conducive to rapid rural population growth" in response to the increased demand for labor (Snell 1985: 139). In turn, these assertions were challenged by researchers, including Snell, from the early 1970s on, whose conclusions I lay out in the next section.

The timing of these shifts in historiographic emphasis and interpretation is important for assessing analyses and policy applied to "commons" in Africa. In the 1930s and 1940s, the heroic perspective of Trevelyan appears to have been held by colonial officers and others, like Liversage (1945) who helped reconstruct African systems of land-holding into "communal tenure." In the 1960s and 1970s, the increased influence of methodological individualism and of neo-classical economic theory is evident not only in historians' restatement of the necessity of enclosure for a more efficient and productive economy but in theses like Garrett Hardin's "Tragedy of the Commons."[6] This influential thesis, simultaneously apocalyptic and rational, has made the "tragedy of the commons . . . part of the conventional wisdom in environmental studies, resource science and policy, economics, ecology, and political science" (Feeny et al. 1990: 2), as well as a dominant motif in livestock and range policy in Africa. It has also been challenged on theoretical and empirical grounds.[7] One can add to these critiques that Hardin's argument was inspired by W.F. Lloyd, one of the "propagandists of parliamentary enclosure" (Thompson 1993: 107). Hardin's declaration that "Freedom in a commons brings ruin to all" is premised on the same set of propositions invoked by apologists for enclosure in the 18th century, equating "commons" with "open access," to use a modernist term, and asserting the superiority of individual property rights in achieving "improvement" and progress. Such circles in assessment and prescription are essential to recognize.[8]

The Demise of the English Commons

Historians challenging the new triumphalists argue that the sole criterion used by the latter (e.g., Chambers & Mingay 1966; Yelling

1977; McCloskey 1975) for assessing the effects of enclosure was the improvement in "productivity and efficiency" of land use. Analyses going beyond the enclosed farms to assess broader social processes reveal more negative consequences of enclosure: a decline in rural employment for labourers and in real wages (Snell 1985); a sharp decrease in the number of small farmers and a parallel increase in the skewness of land distribution, and a substantial rise in the number of families who were forced to seek poor relief and/or to migrate because of the loss of access to common resources (Neeson 1989). Including these "economic considerations" as well as land productivity, concludes Snell (1985: 224), reduces the benefits and increases the costs of enclosure.

Rather than trying to assess the pros and cons of this debate, which I'm not competent to do, I wish to focus on Thompson's (1993) use of this new research in his attempt to capture the socio-cultural dynamics of the erosion of common rights. I can only sketch the complex argument here. By the 13th century, a long history documented that "common usage" based on "time-hallowed custom" had its own standing alongside that of the courts of manor or church in judging disputes (Thompson 1993: 104, citing Birrell 1987). With the rise of capitalism and the drive towards agricultural "improvement" for producing surpluses for sale, so "customary usages" and rights in the commons came to be defined as obstacles and deprived of their legal standing.

Disputes over the common resources were driven by mounting disparities in benefits to be obtained from the commons and in relative power to obtain them. The landed aristocracy was fencing in forests for their leisure pursuits in hunting and for monetary gain from selling off timber and other products. The growing urban demand for wood, turf, small game, sand, stone, and similar products of the open lands and woods produced substantial income for merchants and artisans and promoted escalating levels of exploitation and collusive agreements between "forest officers and under-keepers" and local inn-keepers, butchers, and tanners (Thompson 1993: 103). In addition, the increasingly large-scale, commercial production of corn and other crops demanded more land that was under exclusive control of the farmers. In these ways, threats to the sustainability of common use were coming as much from the big farmers, merchants, and traders as from the many small producers and collectors of common land resources.

Resistance to private appropriation of commons and to the curtailment of common rights was pervasive and constant. Records for the environs of Coventry describe "riotous resistance . . . to attempts to limit . . . rights or to enclose lands" from 1421 on, right up through the 18th century (Thompson 1993: 122-23). Less violent forms of resistance included the dramatization of old rights that were being questioned. "The regular perambulation of . . . the parish . . . to make clayme of the Lands thereto belonging and to set forth their bounds" came, by the 18th century, to entail participants' carrying implements "for the purpose of demolishing any building or fence which had been raised without permission" in the commons (cited in Thompson 1993: 119). Even more numerous were objections made through lobbying, letters, petitions, destruction of records, and other tactics, all of which served to delay some enclosures for many years and even "had some say in the terms of surrender" of the commons (Neeson 1984, in Thompson 1993: 120).

The most interesting dimension of this historiography of enclosure is less the ability of the holders of private property rights to encroach on commons because of superior political power than the hints of the cultural dynamic entailed in the displacement of the commoners and in the parallel rise of the legal, political, and ideological support for enclosure. Centrally involved was the rise of the very notion of property rights in land and the growing hegemony of property rights over common usages. The gradual erosion of common rights and the enclosure of the commons did not just displace particular uses and users of commons but displaced an entire complex of language, ideas and practices engendering legitimate and authorized rights to common usage. A central motif of this displacement was a distinction made between proper or legally upheld rights of "property" over land and "mere" usage. The shift was from recognized and authorized "coincident" use rights of various sorts to a priority given to the property rights of "owners" over "users." How did this occur?

A key dimension of the exclusion of poorer, less influential categories of commoners was a gradual narrowing in the definition of rights-holders and the scope of these rights. This appears to have picked up pace in the 18th century. Members of the gentry or other highly placed persons put new limits on what people could or could not do in the commons. Around 1720, the lord and lady of a manor in Essex informed the poor in their vicinity that, henceforth, they would be allowed to lop the trees in Waltham wood for firewood only on Mondays. The poor complained that Monday was when they sought to hire themselves out for the week to the big farmers, leaving the collection of wood to wet days when there was no work. They complained, too, that the lord was trying to reduce their use because he was felling timber for sale, using the woods to graze cattle, to plough up new land, and to set rabbit warrens (Thompson 1993: 102).

More significantly, the definition of a rightful commoner was increasingly narrowed from the mid 1600s through the 1700s. Courts found that broad descriptive categories such as "populacy," "inhabitants," "parishioners," "all within this manor" were too indefinite and limited the rights to use common resources to owners or fee-tenants of houses and lands on the grounds that "there is no limitation . . . the description of poor householder . . . or occupant . . . or inhabitant . . . is too vague and uncertain" (Thompson [1993: 132] quoting 18th century judgments). Thus, through centuries of disputes and struggles over land and its resources, users of the commons who did not have any other property rights were relegated to "vague" categories and their rights reduced to favors or custom that bordered on the illegal. Customary usages hallowed through use "from time immemorial" now became the ways of the "idle" and "disorderly." Thompson concludes that "the right of use had been transferred from the user to the house or site of an ancient messuage. It became not a use but a property" (ibid.: 135).[9]

A major rationale for the narrowing in definition was the need for "improvements" in the lands. The case of Gateward in 1607 was an influential precedent: the plaintiff's claim of common right was disallowed because he did not own the house in which he lived. In barring mere inhabitants, the court also noted that "no improvements can be made in any wastes, if such common should be allowed" (Thompson 1993: 130).[10] The rationale of making "improvements," which is akin to the call of "progress" on the lips of later modernizers, was increasingly used to justify the claims of greater rights by lords and others eager to increase their exploitation of the commons.

Precisely as many rural families became more dependent on the common resources to cobble together a living in the face of declining levels of support from a modernizing agriculture and small-scale manufacturing, so their customary rights were being redefined as "mere" custom as opposed to property rights (Neeson 1989; Snell 1985; Thompson 1993). Historians like Chambers and Mingay, who state (1966: 97) that "the occupiers of common right cottages . . . who enjoyed common right by virtue of their tenancy of the cottage, received no compensation because they were not, of course, the owners of those rights," are therefore accepting "the priority of 'the theory of the law' over usages" which was precisely the rationale of the proponents and supporters of enclosure

(Thompson 1993: 128). In summary, what was taking place was "a wholesale transformation of agrarian practices, in which rights are assigned away from users" to those whose "ancient feudal title" was translated "into capitalist property-right" (ibid.: 137).

The next phase of the hegemonic claim of property over former commons was a relative shift in emphasis from casting common usage as an obstacle to "improvement" towards presenting the commons as encouraging idleness, vagrancy, and criminality. The former commoners were recast as a class of inveterate idlers who had to be disciplined into a proper work force for the development of industry. In 1769, a writer of "Reflections on the various Advantages resulting from the Draining, Inclosing, and Allotting of Large Commons and Common Fields," referred to the users of commons as "buccaneers" who "live at large, and prey, like pikes, upon one another" (Pennington, in Thompson 1993: 163). Similarly, in 1810, a survey called for the further "appropriation of the forests" of Hampshire as "the means of producing a number of additional useful hands for agricultural employment, by gradually cutting up and annihilating that nest and conservatory of sloth, idleness, and misery, which is uniformly to be witnessed in the vicinity of all commons, waste lands, and forests" (ibid.).

Here is one reflection of the view that later was to cast the demise of the commons as due to the reckless overuse by the commoners and its reclamation due to the innovative energy of the improvers. We also see the way in which the users of the commons were being recategorized as a subordinate class of workers. In one case where the court ruled against the plaintiffs' claim to a right to glean, the judge argued not only that such a practice was "inconsistent with the nature of property, which imports exclusive enjoyment," but that to establish "such a custom as a right would be injurious to the poor themselves" since "their sustenance can only arise from the surplus of productive industry." Because their gleaning would reduce the farmer's gain, he would then have to reduce his contribution to "the rates of the parish," so, in turn, rendering their potential claim for parish relief less secure. In sum, the proper aspiration for the poor was in charity rather than common rights. As "the high tide of enclosure coincided with the political polarization of the 1790s, so arguments of property and improvement are joined to arguments of class discipline" (Thompson 1993: 163). Whereas open commons were said to encourage "habits of idleness and dissipation and a dislike to honest labour," enclosure ensured that the poor take "an honest employment, instead of losing time in idleness and waste" and produced a more "respectable class looking up to the wealthier classes for labour."[11] Precisely the same ideas were expressed in the antagonism towards the Poor Laws which had begun to provide ever more relief to the many displaced commoners. Opponents like Reverend Townsend argued in *A Dissertation on the Poor Laws* (1786) that "the poor know nothing of the motives which stimulate the higher ranks to action—pride, honour, and ambition. In general it is only hunger which can spur and goad them on to labour." For this reason, he saw "nothing . . . more disgusting than a parish pay-table" where the poor came for relief (cited in Snell 1985: 123). He concluded that hunger is the most effective guarantee of labor because it is "peaceful, silent, and continuous."[12] This is the silent partner, presumably, of the supposed invisible hand of the market (see Lubasz 1992).

From Common Use Right to Property Right

In the 17th century, "custom" was still seen to obtain "the force of a Law" where it had the four characteristics of antiquity, continuance ("being continued without interruption time out of mind"), certainty, and reason (Thompson [1993: 97], citing Carter's *Lex Custumaria* of 1696). In the many cases of competition and conflict over common resources occurring through the 18th and the 19th centuries, the common rights claimed are described as having resided in long-practiced usages. Claimants referred over and over to certain uses being carried out "as long as [they] could remember" or, in an oft-repeated phrase, "time out of mind." Some of these repeated practices were embedded in community rites and ceremonies such as the parish perambulations. Many were embedded only in succeeding generations' ideas of what was their due and in their daily and seasonal practices. Nevertheless a strong sense of belonging is revealed when, challenged in their uses, people referred to the commons as "ours."[13]

Although 17th century legal experts granted "the force of Law" to long-established customary use, in the 18th century legal decisions tended to refer to "the legal fiction that customary usages must have been founded upon some original grant, from persons unknown, lost in the mists of antiquity" (Thompson 1993: 160). The legal fiction thus cast the uses as "less of right than by grace" (ibid.). Simpson, in *A History of the Land Law*, suggests that "the tenurial system converted the villagers into tenants, and the theory of the law placed the freehold of most of the lands of the manor in the lord . . . the preeminence of the lord makes it natural to treat him as the 'owner' of the waste lands. Thus a theory of individual ownership supplants earlier more egalitarian notions" (1986: 108, cited in Thompson 1993: 127).

Thompson points out that some writers have accepted at face value the "theory of the law" outlined by Simpson and cites the opinion of Hoskins and Stamp (1963) that "contrary to widespread belief . . . all common land is private property. It belongs to someone, whether an individual or a corporation, and has done so from time immemorial." Thompson illustrates the doubt to be cast on Hoskins's claim that common land had to "belong" to someone by quoting the Russian serfs who told their lord "We are yours, but the land is ours." I'd like to link this statement with the many from the English commoners in cases cited by Thompson where they refer unequivocally to "our" commons, and to work by other historians who show the deep feelings of attachment to a locality and its commons and the profound sense of dislocation caused by enclosure and by the 1691 settlement law which, requiring "settlement" in a parish to be proved by property ownership, rent or annual labor, led many of the poor to lose their residency status (Snell 1985). What these imply is a very different sense of "belonging": not of a property belonging to someone, but of people belonging to a place. It is only when the notion of property as entailing rights to things (or places) gains priority that the older sense is turned on its head. From people belonging to a place and hence, having every right to benefit from the place's bounties, they become people who have no property which belongs to them and, hence, have no intrinsic right to the place's resources.

It is from this historical and ideological move that comes the notion that land held in common "belonged," in Sir William Blackstone's words, "generally to everybody, but particularly to nobody" (cited in Thompson 1993: 161). Blackstone, the most famous 18th century writer on law, did recognize the rights of custom but, according to Thompson, "considered [them] less as usages than as properties annexed to things" in ways that confounded, in Blackstone's own words, "that sole and despotic dominion which one man claims and exercises over the external things of the world, in total exclusion of the right of any other individual in the universe." Here, the final phase in the transformation of the concept of property to an exclusive and alienable right to a thing (including land, which is what Blackstone was addressing) is patent (Macpherson 1987).

The concept of "property," in the centuries before the rise of capitalism, had had a much broader scope. Used to refer to "the life, limbs and property of a man," it more clearly captured the sense of its origin in the Latin *proprius* and the French *propriété*, that is, something of one's own, as much to connote necessary qualities of oneself as to things outside oneself that belonged to one. Over the centuries, the concept has become progressively narrowed. Macpherson lucidly describes three degrees of narrowing: first, the earlier connotation of property as being both the right to exclude others from the use or enjoyment of something and the right not to be excluded from the use or enjoyment of something came to refer only to the first of this pair. A second narrowing came in defining property not merely as to own but as entailing the right to alienate that ownership. The third narrowing was from property as a right to the revenue from something owned to a right to the thing itself. Each phase is linked by Macpherson to stages in the development of capitalism. By the time of Adam Smith and other theorists of market economy, "property was either 'perfect' and absolute or it was meaningless."[14] As we saw above, this entailed, among other things, a displacement of coincident use-rights. "In the name of absolute individual property, the common and use rights of the 'lower orders' were eroded."[15]

In summary, the erosion of common rights and the drive to enclosure may be seen to have taken place through the erasure of rights based in customary use of belonging and their replacement by claims based on property rights. This and the narrowing in definitions of use, user, and right may be seen in the case of Botswana to which I now turn.

The Case of Botswana

Insofar as can be told from scanty archaeological and historical sources, Tswana groups have long organized themselves into small polities (*merafe*, chiefdoms or kingdoms), each centered on a *kgosi*, the political and ritual head. The people of a polity were known by the founder's name, the eponymous ancestor of the king, and a locative form of the name labelled the place (e.g., the Kgatla lived in Kgatleng). Praised with the name of *Modisa* (herder), the ruler ensured his people had the wherewithal to live, providing them not with "land," for such an unspecified resource did not exist, but with particularized fields to grow grain, bush to collect wood and other products, streams and springs for water, and pastures for grazing livestock. In the larger kingdoms, the ruler delegated authority over grazing areas to subordinates (called herders, or, *badisa*).[16] They, in turn, allocated certain pastures to their followers. Much of the political competition between and within kingdoms was over the scarce waterpoints that defined good pastures.

When the Bechuanaland Protectorate was declared by the British in 1885, there were strong kingdoms in place along the eastern edge of the country. The kings and their close relatives and advisors were, in large measure, further strengthened by the practices of indirect rule and by the impossibility of factions fissioning off to create new mini-states, as in the past. The kingdoms became Tribal Reserves and, later, Districts.

Water Development and Communal Tenure in the 1930s

As elsewhere in the African territories, the system of rights in land and water found among the Tswana was declared by the colonial administrators to be "communal tenure" (also called "tribal tenure" in the early years of the Protectorate). The analogue was private property rights: communal tenure, later to be known as common property, meant rights vested in a group, namely, a polity. As in other territories in southern Africa, Bechuanaland had some of its land carved out into "freehold areas" that were sold in lots to white ranchers, mainly from South Africa. Communal tenure was conceived in the conventional way as static, backward, and a drag on progress. The missionary-cum-administrator, John Mackenzie, working among the Ngwato of Eastern Bechuanaland in the late 19th century before the Protectorate was declared, saw this type of land-holding as merely a part of the deplorable "communistic relations of the members of a tribe." He wished for "the fresh stimulating breath of healthy individualistic competition" to be introduced (cited in Dachs 1972; cf. Comaroff & Comaroff 1991).

This view, as we saw, was well established in English thought. The same opinion but cast in a new language of enterprise is expressed by Liversage in his volume on *Land Tenure in the Colonies*, published in 1945. Invoking Prothero's views on the English commons to explain the situation in African "communal" lands (see above), Liversage states that "no regulation whatever is practised. Consequently there is no incentive on the part of any individual to restrict the number of stock turned out by him. It is the desire of every individual to amass wealth in the form of livestock. . . . No individual has any incentive to reduce his numbers: his own action will be of no avail without corresponding action by others" (1945: 13, 49). The apparent prefiguring of Hardin's Tragedy thesis reflects the common intellectual assumption that "communal" forms of organization smothered individual initiative and prevented "improvement" and "progress."

Despite such opinions, no direct attempt was made to change land tenure in the Protectorate, doubtless because it was clearly central to the chiefs' authority on which indirect rule ultimately rested. Instead, in the 1930s, one of the first examples of the colonial compilations of "customary law" was carried out by Isaac Schapera for Bechuanaland. In this, land and water tenure figured prominently. Although such "restatements" of customary law were seen at the time to be records of facts, subsequent scholarship has concluded that customary law and communal tenure were "the joint creation of colonial officials and African leaders . . . a reflection of the [then] contemporary situation" (Colson 1971: 196-97; cf. Fallers 1969; Chanock 1985; Moore 1986).

Schapera was retained by the Protectorate Administration in the early 1930s at the same time that a major water development project was initiated, in which boreholes (power-driven deep wells) were to be drilled in the grazing areas of the African reserves. Boreholes had proven themselves invaluable in ranches in neighboring South Africa and in the European freehold areas of the Protectorate. The Tswana elite, all owners of large herds of cattle, had incessantly lobbied the Administration to provide boreholes to the African areas. Most significantly, the pilot scheme for the larger project, which took place in the Kgatleng, introduced private ownership over the boreholes. Each new borehole was allocated to a syndicate of about six cattle owners who were to be the owner-managers. In a complex cultural move, the syndicate was portrayed to the Kgatla people by the chiefly elite as another type of traditional *kgotla*[17] and was described to the British government by Charles Rey, the Resident Commissioner of the Protectorate, as a "native cooperative." I have argued elsewhere that the borehole scheme and particularly the syndicates are products of the genius of the Tswana chiefs, especially Isang of the Kgatla, at negotiating their way with the Protectorate Administration (Peters 1994, 1992, 1984).

In their push to develop private rights in the communal grazing areas, the Tswana elite followed a dual strategy. In debates with the Administration in the African Advisory Council they portrayed the communal system as inhibiting "progressive" herd-owners, yet, through Schapera's compilation, they described it as flexible enough to allow for individual rights. Isang Pilane's statement in Council in 1930 that "our Reserves are communal property and nobody who is willing to progress can have freedom to use his progressive ideas" was typical of the elite's complaints and made use of the language and rationales of the colonial officials.

At the same time, these elite men—"the senior men of the tribes"—were telling Schapera that the communal system, in which land was held communally and open waters of rivers and pans were "common property," nevertheless allowed for "individual rights" (Schapera 1943: 250). Anyone putting resources into drilling a borehole, digging a dam or putting up substantial buildings was "entitled to legal protection against encroachment" (ibid.: 229) and owners of the new boreholes in the grazing areas were "entitled to the sole use of [the] water and to protection against trespass" (ibid.: 246). After pointing out that "even privately owned boreholes" were allowed by the Tribal Administration in the Kgatleng Reserve, Schapera concludes that "tribal law recognizes the validity of private rights" and the existence of such private property "strengthens the usual Native contention that there is adequate security of tenure" in customary law (ibid.: 250). Other similar statements indicate that one of Schapera's aims was to counter certain preconceptions of the Administration about the obstacles to progress in the "customary" system.

What is interesting here is that Schapera was playing the role typical of many anthropologists in providing ethnographic evidence to show how inappropriate certain official notions were. Yet, at precisely the same time, members of the Tswana elite were using these official prejudices to lobby the Administration for the development of water sources and, in particular, for the private ownership of such sources. With hindsight, one can see that the Tswana elite were playing both sides of the street in their efforts to acquire more private rights over land and water: claiming flexibility in the communal system for investment yet also complaining about the obstacles to progress in that system. The former was played out through Schapera's compilation, the latter through the debates in the African Advisory Council.

The debate about communal tenure constructed it in opposition to private property. While that opposition was more implicit than explicit in the Advisory Council debates, it was played out more clearly in the lobbying for the new boreholes to be placed under the private ownership of a new type of corporation, the borehole syndicate. To this extent, then, "common property" (or "communal tenure") was the product of the private ownership of resources rather than its precursor.

Dividing the Commons

From the 1930s through to the 1980s, most boreholes drilled in the grazing areas came under the ownership of groups of cattle-owners (syndicates) and, from the 1950s, of very wealthy individuals as sole owners. The signal consequence of the proliferation of privately owned boreholes in communal land has been the shift of claims based on property rights from the water sources to land itself. The process, in brief, has been as follows.[18]

First, the Administration's procedural rule of ensuring a minimum distance of five miles between boreholes (as protection against overgrazing) gave an official imprimatur to the owners of a borehole treating the area around it as their "own." Already in the 1930s, as we noted above, "investments" like the private ownership of boreholes had been described as giving "legal protection against encroachment" (Schapera 1943: 229). After Independence, new Land Boards replaced the chiefs as allocative authorities for land and water. The Board practices of mapping boundaries and measuring distances between new boreholes have further reinforced the notion that, in granting permission (and license) to drill a borehole, they are allocating not merely the borehole but an area of land. The significant decline in herding cattle facilitated by permanent water sources has also produced a permanent association of borehole owners with particular grazing areas.

Second, as the range has become filled with privately owned boreholes and with ever more cattle, so have people become sensitive to increasing competition over pastures. As a consequence, syndicates are beginning to become more exclusive, contrary to much of their earlier history when they tended to incorporate far more than the owners themselves.[19]

Certainly, the extension of use to the borehole water and, thence, to the surrounding land has not stopped but there is a new trend towards exclusion. There are two aspects of this trend. The syndicates have been reducing the number of hirers, people who pay a fee to use the water. And they have been narrowing the definition of relatives who can be claimed by syndicate owners as their dependents with full access, without fees, to the borehole and its pastures.

Third, the Tribal Grazing Land Policy introduced in 1975 has directly and indirectly furthered the property claims of syndicates being extended over the land. The Policy was designed to lessen overstocking on a range described as becoming degraded. In language and rationale strongly evocative of Hardin's Tragedy thesis (though not directly quoted), the Policy claimed that the core fault was "the traditional system of communal tenure." It therefore promoted the formation of limited private property in range-land in the form of leasehold ranches. These may be taken by either individual or group owners in specially demarcated commercial zones in the communal range. As a companion to the Policy (and other agricultural policies), enabling legislation for forming "Agricultural Management Associations" (AMAs) was put in place. These associations are the legal form to which borehole syndicates are supposed to convert in order to become lease-holders.

Such a legal status would form the final phase in converting owners of privately owned boreholes in a communal range into the holders of private (leasehold) property in the land itself. Conversion to AMAs and applications for ranches have not taken place in the Kgatleng not because borehole owners do not want to have legal right to the land around their boreholes but for two reasons. The small territory of the district has made it impossible politically to convince the population to accept demarcation of the range; it remains the only district in which the Tribal Grazing Land Policy has been unimplemented. And all but the very wealthiest cattle owners are highly skeptical about the utility of closed ranches in the drought-prone country, preferring to retain the open range and the partial movements still possible. As documented in other places in Africa, they wish *both* to retain an open range and hence the option of movement *and* acquire title to the land around their boreholes.

Nevertheless, the real pressures on the range with so many boreholes that cattle owners describe themselves as "boxed in" on all sides lead to pervasive competition over pastures. In the disputes brought before the Land Board and the chief's court, there are increasingly instances where borehole owners are able to sustain a stronger claim over the land around their borehole than other people who, because they do not own boreholes, are more mobile and graze their cattle temporarily in several places. In a number of instances observed during 1979-80, decisions giving greater weight to property rights over "common usage" were made (see Peters 1994).

The sense of closure among syndicates was exacerbated by a decision by district authorities in 1979. As part of their attempt to work out how a small district like the Kgatleng could follow the recommendation of the Tribal Grazing Land Policy to allow the formation of ranches, district officers decided that anyone with "traditional" or long-standing grazing rights (e.g., handed down from fathers and grandfathers) in a particular area should be accepted as co-owners by a syndicate in the same area wishing to lease a ranch. Even though very few syndicates wanted to acquire a leasehold ranch, the proposal caused a great deal of anger since it purported to force them to accept new co-owners and thus was contrary to their private property rights in the boreholes. They rejected the claim that "traditional" grazing rights held by hirers or others in an area where a borehole had been drilled was a basis for inclusion in the borehole syndicate.[20] Disputes arose when some syndicates, in a conscious attempt to preempt any claim of "longstanding" right of hirers, began to refuse to accept fee-payers. These disputes continue.

There is no space here to discuss these processes in detail nor to argue that, while they may be particularly acute in a small district like the Kgatleng, research in other areas of Botswana suggests that similar trends are occurring elsewhere as competition over land and water intensifies (see Peters 1994). For our purposes here, it is sufficient to reiterate that the gradual division of the commons in Botswana (though still in process) resembles that of England in critical ways. It entails mounting competition between categories of users and the redefinition of some users as "mere" users while others, because of private property rights, gradually acquire superior rights to the land.

The Place of "Property" in Social Analysis

Against this all too brief discussion of the English commons and the communal range of Botswana, in which we have seen "property" in land to have been an emergent set of ideas and practices in social process, I want to pose the question: should we center "property relations" in our analyses? On one side we have anthropologists like Marilyn Strathern who warns against merging Melanesian (but by extension, other people's) formulations of claims with "the Western concept of private property" which regards "singular items [to be] attached to singular owners" and which "constructs the possessor as a unitary social entity" (1988: 103). Her definition of property as "a relation between persons and things" is clearly that associated by Macpherson, Thompson, and others cited with the modern form of capitalism. Strathern's position here is a classic one for anthropologists who are rightly cautious about transferring concepts from one group to another under the guise of "neutral" analytical language but with the consequence of distorting more than one is revealing.

On the other side, David Nugent recently recommended centering analysis on the concept of "property relations" precisely because, unlike "relations of production," it is able to capture "the institutional specificity" of non-Western societies (1993). Here is the other classic anthropological position, seeking ways to compare groups and societies. Despite the over-particularizing tendencies of some postmodern approaches, it is probably correct to say that for most anthropologists the defining feature of the discipline is to occupy both positions simultaneously: comparative studies which require some language in common as well as caution over the danger that the selected language may import inappropriate meanings.

Although I favor attempts to ensure the incorporation of political economic dimensions into socio-cultural analysis and to "take into account . . . issues of power and history" (Nugent 1993: 336), I wish briefly here to suggest that "property relations" is a concept that imports more than it should into noncapitalist societies and cannot, therefore, do justice to their characteristics and internal dynamics. Nugent is very well aware of the general problem of appropriate conceptual language and explains why, though espousing a marxist approach, he avoids basing his analysis on "relations of production." He explains that, although Marx's own use of "production" was much wider than today's narrower referent of the production of material goods, he agrees with other critics that it is the latter, modern notion that dominates the concept "relations of production." He therefore has turned to property relations which he defines very broadly, following Maine, Marx, and Smith, as determining "what people are expected to do in their everyday lives, with whom and under what conditions they will do it, what they may claim of the fruit of their own labor, and what they must provide to others" (ibid.: 340).

My objections to Nugent's proposal to center analysis on property relations are as follows. First, the definition of property relations is so broad that it seems to mean all social relations: "property relations refer to *relationships* among people that are *mediated* by material and nonmaterial elements of culture" (ibid.: 341; emphasis in original). His addition that the concept of property also "seeks out the nature of the mediation in the way that social persons . . . define and redefine their relations in an unfolding history" (ibid.) would extend the concept to the entirety of society, culture, and history. Thus, one loses the utility of a concept that may be more appropriately applied to a narrower referent.

Second, although Nugent recognizes "private" property to be the defining feature of capitalist society, he cites the defining feature of "property" as its being "first and foremost a *legal* concept" (ibid.: 339). In accepting this definition from the experts he quotes—the 18th-century political-economy theorists, Adam Ferguson and Adam Smith, and a 19th- century heir, Sir Henry Maine—he surely elides, with these authors, the historical process we have just outlined in which property rights dislodged other rights inhering in common usage and in belonging to a place. Nugent is more concerned to distinguish "private property" (in which "rights to material objects are vested in . . . individuals") from "social property" (in which "persons are jurally recognized not as autonomous individuals who own private property but as members of interdependent social categories" [ibid.: 340]). Because his analysis turns on this distinction, which seems to be a replay of the commodity-gift opposition, Nugent fails to appreciate that the very notion of property, as he defines it, has the very same problem he eloquently describes for "relations of production," namely that use of this concept entails "the reification of relations specific to capitalism and their extension to all social contexts" (ibid.: 354, n. 4).

In short, I suggest that the concept of "property relations" both obscures too much and assumes too much. This is particularly unfortunate when, as Nugent so rightly suggests, the anthropologist's task is to approach "problems of social transformation . . . from the point of view of the internal potentialities of social forms rather than the unchangeable essences of timeless social structures" (ibid.: 353). I believe the cases of the English commons and the Tswana system of land rights suggest the kinds of changes in conceptions and social relations that take place as a concept of property arises. A flavor of the change is that instead of people's use rights deriving from their belonging to a place, their uses become excluded because they did not have a place that belonged to them. To avoid obscuring such fundamental differences in conception and practice, comparativist scholarship should not privilege notions of "property" and "property relations" over those of "rights." While not without problems for cross-cultural analysis, the old language of "rights" appears less freighted with particular historical (cultural, political, economic) meaning than that of "property."

Notes

1. The citations are from Thompson (1976: 339; 1993: 242) and from Rackham (1986: 297) (as cited in "Development" 1992: 133).
2. Cited in "Development" (1992: 133) from Collings (1908: 77).
3. Some illustrative lines are: "Inclosure like a Buonaparte let not a thing remain It levelled every bush and tree and levelled every hill . . . Inclosure came and trampled on the grave Of labours rights and left the poor a slave. . . . Moors . . . Where swopt the plover in its pleasure free Are vanished now with commons wild and gay . . ." (Clare 1987).
4. Both Davies and Sturt are cited by Snell (1985: 166-68).
5. J.L. Hammond and B. Hammond (1911) *The Village Labourer*; similar opinions were expressed by G. Slater (1907), *The English Peasantry and the Enclosure of Common Fields*, and W. Hasbach (1908), *The History of the English Agricultural Labourer*. All cited in Snell (1985: 139-40).
6. In Hardin's (1968) own words: "The tragedy of the commons develops in this way. Picture a pasture open to all. It is to be expected that each herdsman will try to keep as many cattle as possible. . . . As a rational being, each herdsman seeks to maximize his gain. . . . [He] concludes that the only sensible course for him to pursue is to add another animal . . . and another. . . . But this is the conclusion reached by each and every rational herdsman sharing a commons. Therein is the tragedy. Each man is locked into a system which compels him to increase his herd without limit. . . . Ruin is the destination towards which all men rush, each pursuing his own interests. . . . Freedom in a commons brings ruin to all."
7. These cannot be rehearsed here but see, among others: Godwin & Shepard 1979; Kimber 1981: Runge 1981; National Academy of Sciences 1986; McCay & Acheson 1987; Peters 1987; Berkes 1989; Feeny et al. 1990; Ostrom 1990; McKean 1992.
8. Hardin himself has responded to criticism and admitted that "the title of my 1968 paper should have been 'The tragedy of the *unmanaged* commons'" (1991: 178). Less recognized are the historical origins of analytical models.
9. There is no room here to document the fact that there were many instances in which various "commoners" (by no means all poor) were able to prevent or stall the erosion of common rights and the enclosure of common resources even in "the great age of parliamentary enclosure, between 1760 and 1820" (Thompson 1993: 110). Moreover, as Thompson points out, many of the parks and open lands found today throughout even heavily populated parts of England are there precisely because of earlier attempts by commoners to protect their rights. The point is only that, ultimately, most common rights were removed.

10. Apart from the works by historians cited in the text, see also the marvelously evocative story of the English village of Ulverton told by Adam Thorpe (1992) as a "fictional history" from 1650 to the present. The chapter on 1712 is titled "Improvements" and charts the thoughts and actions of a farmer experimenting with the new improved ways of agriculture. His diary begins: "My great-grandfather enclosed [these sixty acres] to sheep some hundred years ago but I till the greater part of it now, with no recourse to the Manor Court. Commoners are the harrow-rest to improved husbandry, is my opinion." This nicely shows the nibbling away of the commons by an inventive group of farmers that was far less visible than the grand appropriations of the Whig elite but, in total, probably as devastating to the open commons. Note, too, how "commoners" are being recast as a hindrance.
11. These are commentaries by authors writing from the end of the 18th into the mid-19th centuries, cited by Snell (1985: 170-71).
12. This last statement is cited by Polanyi (1944: 113-40) and quoted by Platteau (1991).
13. As in a 1682 report of a survey of a village in Warwickshire, where various forms of stinting are described, which says that the Lord of the manor keeps cattle but in such numbers "as to not oppress our Commons" (Thompson 1993: 134).
14. Hont & Ignatieff (1983: 25), as cited in (Thompson 1993: 162).
15. Cited by Thompson (1993: 161) from Rubin and Sugarman (1984: 23-24).
16. The English translations of such terms inevitably draw them into a different world: modisa as governor (Schapera 1943) or comptroller (Sansom 1984), king as trustee, all patriarchal images rather than the mix in Setswana—"milkpail" or "wife" as well as "herder."
17. The *kgotla* is a conventional structure of authority for Tswana. It is multireferential in Setswana, referring to the central assembly place of the chiefdom and to the constituent parts (wards, family groups), and to both the space and the group of people meeting in the space. The core meaning of kgotla is glossed as an association of people with responsibility for and legitimate stewardship over corporate resources (Peters 1984).
18. This story is told in much fuller detail for the Kgatleng District in Peters (1994), also see earlier publications (1984, 1987, 1992).
19. The members (*ditokololo*) of a syndicate are the de jure owners of the borehole. Other recognized users of the borehole are dependents, usually close relatives like children though sometimes clients, who are seen to be "under the name" of the member/owner and who do not pay separate fees; and a third category of *bahiri* or hirers who pay a fee (per unit of time or animal).
20. Moreover, few hirers have been able to continue grazing their animals in one area for many years at a time. This is precisely because the proliferation

of privately owned boreholes (as well as others owned by government or corporations like the railway) through the range has cut across the pre-borehole "traditional" patterns of allocation. Those with no secure access to permanent water necessarily move and thus, willy-nilly, loosen their association with any one area.

References Cited

Berkes, F. (ed.)
1989 *Common Property Resources: Ecology and Community-based Sustainable Development*. London: Belhaven.

Bromley, D.W. (ed.)
1992 *Making the Commons Work*. San Francisco: ICS Press.

Chambers, J.D., & G.E. Mingay
1966 *The Agricultural Revolution, 1750-1880*. New York: Schocken.

Chanock, M.
1985 *Law, Custom and Social Order: The Colonial Experience in Malawi and Zambia*. Cambridge: Cambridge University Press.

Ciriacy-Wantrup, S.V,. & R.C. Bishop
1975 Common property as a concept in natural resources policy. *Natural Resources Journal* 15(4):713-27.

Collings, J.
1908 *Land Reform*. London: Longmans, Green.

Colson, E.
1971 The impact of the colonial period on the definition of land rights. In V. Turner (ed.), *Colonialism in Africa 1870-1960* 3:193-215. Cambridge: Cambridge University Press.

Comaroff, J., & J.L. Comaroff
1991 *Of Revelation and Revolution: Christianity, Colonialism, and Consciousness in South Africa*, Volume 1. Chicago: University of Chicago Press.

Dachs, A.
1972 Missionary imperialism in the case of Bechuanaland. *Journal of African History* 13(4):647-58.

"Development"
1992 Development as enclosure: the establishment of the global economy. *The Ecologist* 22(4):131-47.

Fallers, L.A.
1969 *Law without Precedent*. Chicago: University of Chicago Press.

Feeny, D., F. Berkes, B.J. McCay, & J.M. Acheson
1990 The tragedy of the commons: twenty-two years later. *Human Ecology* 18(1):1-19.

Godwin, R.K., & W.B. Shepard

1979 Forcing squares, triangles and ellipses into a circular paradigm: the use of the commons dilemma in examining the allocation of common resources. *Western Political Quarterly* 32(3):265-77.

Hammond, J.L., & B. Hammond

1911 *The Village Labourer*. London: Longmans, Green.

Hardin, G.

1968 The tragedy of the commons. *Science* 162:1243-48.

1991 The tragedy of the *unmanaged* commons: population and the disguises of providence. In R.V. Andelson (ed.), *Commons Without Tragedy*, pp. 162-85. Savage, MD: Barnes & Noble.

Hosbach, W.

1908 *The History of English Agricultural Labourers*.

Hoskins, W.G., & L.D. Stamp

1963 *The Common Lands of England and Wales*. London: Collins.

Hont, I., & M. Ignatieff (eds.)

1983 *Wealth and Virtue: The Shaping of Political Economy in the Scottish Enlightenment*. Cambridge: Cambridge University Press.

Kimber, R.

1981 Collective action and the fallacy of the liberal fallacy. *World Politics* 1981:178-96.

Liversage, V.

1945 *Land Tenure in the Colonies*. Cambridge: University Press of Cambridge.

Lubasz, H.

1992 Adam Smith and the invisible hand—of the market? In R. Dilley (ed.), *Contesting Markets*, pp. 37-56. Edinburgh: Edinburgh University Press.

Macpherson, C.B.

1987 *The Rise and Fall of Economic Justice and Other Essays*. Oxford: Oxford University Press.

McCay, B.J., & J.M. Acheson (eds.)

1987 *The Question of the Commons: The Culture and Ecology of Communal Resources*. Tucson: University of Arizona Press.

McCloskey, D.N.

1975 The economics of enclosure: a market analysis. In E.L. Jones & W.N. Parker (eds.), *European Peasants and Their Markets*, pp. 123-60. Princeton: Princeton University Press.

McKean, M.A.

1992 Success on the commons: a comparative examination of institutions for common property resource management. *Journal of Theoretical Politics* 4(3):247-81.

Moore, S.F.
1986 *Social Facts and Fabrications: "Customary" Law on Kilimanjaro, 1880- 1980.* Cambridge: Cambridge University Press.

National Academy of Sciences
1986 *Proceedings of the Conference on Common Property Resource Management, April 21-26, 1985.* Washington, DC: National Academy Press.

Neeson, J.M.
1989 Parliamentary enclosure and the disappearance of the English peasantry, revisited. *Research in Economic History*, Supplement 5, Part A, pp. 89- 120. Greenwich, CT: JAI Press.

Nugent, D.
1993 Property relations, production relations, and inequality: anthropology, political economy, and the Blackfeet. *American Ethnologist* 20(2):336- 62.

Ostrom, E.
1990 *Governing the Commons.* Cambridge: Cambridge University Press.

Peters, P.E.
1984 Struggles over water, struggles over meaning: cattle, water, and the state in Botswana. *Africa* 54(3):29-49.
1987 Embedded systems and rooted models: the grazing lands of Botswana and the "commons" debate. In B.J. McCay & J.M. Acheson (eds.), *The Question of the Commons: The Culture and Ecology of Communal Resources*, pp. 171-194. Tucson: University of Arizona Press.
1992 Manoeuvres and debates in the interpretation of land rights in Botswana. *Africa* 62(3):413-34.
1994 *Dividing the Commons: Politics, Policy and Culture in Botswana.* Charlottesville: University Press of Virginia.

Platteau, J.-P.
1991 Traditional systems of social security and hunger insurance: past achievements and modern challenges. In E. Ahmad, J. Dreze, J. Hills, & A. Sen (eds.), *Social Security in Developing Countries*, pp. 112-70. Oxford: Clarendon.

Polanyi, K.
1944 *The Great Transformation.* New York: Farrar & Rinehart.

Prothero, R.E.
1917 *British Farming Past and Present.* London: Longmans, Green.

Rackham, O.
1986 *The History of the Countryside.* London: J.M. Dent.

Runge, C.F.
1981 Common property externalities: isolation, assurance, and resource depletion in a traditional grazing context. *American Journal of Agricultural Economics* 63:595-606.

Schapera, I.
1943 *Native Land Tenure in the Bechuanaland Protectorate*. Alice: Lovedale Press.

Simpson, A.W.B.
1986 *A History of the Land Law*. Oxford: Clarendon.

Slater, G.
1907 *The English Peasantry and the Enclosure of Common Fields*. London: A. Constable.

Snell, K.D.M.
1985 *Annals of the Labouring Poor: Social Change and Agrarian England, 1660-1900*. Cambridge: Cambridge University Press.

Strathern, M.
1988 *The Gender of the Gift*. Berkeley: University of California Press.

Thompson, E.P.
1976 The grid of inheritance: a comment. In J. Goody, J. Thirsk & E. P. Thompson (eds.), *Family and Inheritance*, pp. 328-60. Cambridge: Cambridge University Press.
1993 *Customs in Common*. New York: The New Press.

Trevelyan, G.
1944 *English Social History*. London: Longmans.

Yelling, J.A.
1977 *Common Field and Enclosure in England, 1450-1850*. London: Macmillan.

About the Contributors

DURAN BELL is a professor in the Department of Economics and the Department of Anthropology at the University of California-Irvine. Although his Ph.D. (from Berkeley) is in agricultural economics, his professional work has focussed on formal models of social processes. For the last ten years he has directed his energies toward economic anthropology, especially on models of resource allocation within groups and exchange relations associated with marriage.

CHARLES A. BISHOP is Professor of Anthropology Emeritus at the State University of New York at Oswego. His research on northern Algonquians focusses on the effects of the European fur trade on property relations and sociopolitical organization, and the implications of these for other hunter-gatherers.

PAULA BROWN is now Professor Emerita of Anthropology, State University of New York at Stony Brook. She began fieldwork among the Simbu in 1958 while a Fellow at the Australian National University and made a total of thirteen field trips between then and 1987. Her latest book, published in 1995, is *Beyond a Mountain Valley: the Simbu of Papua New Guinea*.

JEAN-PHILIPPE COLIN is an agricultural economist (his doctorate is from the University of Montpellier) and a researcher at ORSTOM (the French Scientific Research Institute for Development through Cooperation). He has conducted fieldwork in the Ivory Coast and Mexico to study problems of land tenure from an Institutional Economics perspective.

CATHY COSTIN is a lecturer in the Department of Anthropology, California State University-Northridge, where she teaches courses in archaeology, gender studies and craft production. Her research interests include the organization and technology of craft production; political economy and gender systems in ancient societies; and the origins and functions of the division of labor.

E. PAUL DURRENBERGER is Professor of Anthropology at Pennsylvania State University. Among his recent publications are *The Dynamics of Medieval Iceland* (1992), *Icelandic Essays* (1995), and *Images of Contemporary Iceland* (edited with Gisli Pálsson, 1996), as well as *It's All Politics: South Alabama's Seafood Industry* (1992) and *Gulf Coast Soundings: People and Policy in the Mississippi Shrimp Industry* (1996).

TIMOTHY K. EARLE is a professor at Northwestern University, where he is chair the Department of Anthropology, and a past president of the Archaeology Division of the American Anthropological Association. In pursuit of research interests centered on the political economy of chiefdoms, he has conducted fieldwork in Hawaii, Peru, and Denmark.

ANDREW FLEMING is Reader in Archaeology at the University of Wales-Lampeter. He has conducted fieldwork in Britain and in France on the development of ancient field systems and their significance for the history of land tenure.

ANTONIO GILMAN is a professor of anthropology at California State University-Northridge. His research interests in prehistoric political economy have been pursued through fieldwork in southeast Spain.

MICHAEL HUDSON is President of the Institute for the Study of Long-Term Economic Trends (ISLET) and co-chairman of the International Scholars' Conference on Ancient Near Eastern Economies. He is co-editor (with Baruch Levine) of *Privatization in the Ancient Near East and Classical World* (1996).

ROBERT C. HUNT is Professor of Anthropology at Brandeis University and a past president of the Society for Economic Anthropology. His research interests have centered on comparative anthropology, with a particular focus on the study of irrigation systems. He has conducted extensive fieldwork in Mexico and the western United States.

PATRICIA A. McANANY is Associate Professor of Archaeology at Boston University. She conducts archaeological fieldwork in the Maya lowlands, most recently at the Formative to Classic period site of K'Axob, in Belize, where she recently completed a study of the genesis of ancestor veneration and its links to the emergence of land tenure systems. She is the author of *Living with the Ancestors: Kinship and Kingship in Ancient Maya Society*.

WALTER C. NEALE, Professor of Economics Emeritus at the University of Tennessee-Knoxville, is the author of three books on India, where he did field research in 1955-56, 1960-61, and 1964-65. He is also the author of a cross-cultural study of money (*Monies in Societies*) and has published in *American Anthropologist*. During 1984-85 he served as president of the Society for Economic Anthropology.

PAULINE E. PETERS has held a research appointment at the Harvard Institute for International Development since 1982 and also teaches in the Department of Anthropology at Harvard University. Her fieldwork has been conducted in southern Africa, particularly Malawi and Botswana.

WILLEM WOLTERS is Professor of Economic Anthropology at the Catholic University of Nijmegen, the Netherlands. He has done fieldwork in central Luzon, the Philippines, and in west and central Java, Indonesia. His research centers on land rights and tenure, credit relationships, markets and trade, and labor relations.